Measuring Success

Measuring Success

TESTING, GRADES, AND THE FUTURE OF COLLEGE ADMISSIONS

Edited by
Jack Buckley
Lynn Letukas
Ben Wildavsky

Johns Hopkins University Press
Baltimore

Johns Hopkins University Press
2715 North Charles Street
Baltimore, Maryland 21218-4363
www.press.jhu.edu

Library of Congress Cataloging-in-Publication Data
Names: Buckley, Jack, 1965– editor.
Title: Measuring success : testing, grades, and the future of college
    admissions / edited by Jack Buckley, Lynn Letukas, Ben Wildavsky.
Description: Baltimore : Johns Hopkins University Press, 2018. | Includes
    bibliographical references and index.
Identifiers: LCCN 2017035199| ISBN 9781421424965 (alk. paper : hardcover) |
    ISBN 9781421424972 (electronic) | ISBN 1421424967 (alk. paper : hardcover) |
    ISBN 1421424975 (electronic)
Subjects: LCSH: Universities and colleges—United States—Entrance
    examinations—Validity. | BISAC: EDUCATION / Higher. | EDUCATION /
    Testing & Measurement. | STUDY AIDS / College Entrance.
Classification: LCC LB2353.2 .M43 2018 | DDC 378.1/662—dc23
LC record available at https://lccn.loc.gov/2017035199

A catalog record for this book is available from the British Library.

Contents

Eric Maguire

8   Test Scores and High School Grades as Predictors   193
William G. Bowen, Matthew M. Chingos, and Michael S. McPherson

     Comment   226
     Michael Hurwitz and Meredith Welch

     Reply   234
     Matthew M. Chingos and Michael S. McPherson

PART III. CONTEMPORARY CHALLENGES FOR COLLEGE ADMISSIONS

9   How Do Percent Plans and Other Test-Optional Admissions
     Programs Affect the Academic Performance and Diversity
     of the Entering Class?   239
     Rebecca Zwick

10   The Test-Optional Movement at America's Selective
     Liberal Arts Colleges: A Boon for Equity or Something Else?   260
     Andrew S. Belasco, Kelly O. Rosinger, and James C. Hearn

11   The Effect of Going Test-Optional on Diversity
     and Admissions: A Propensity Score Matching Analysis   288
     Kyle Sweitzer, A. Emiko Blalock, and Dhruv B. Sharma

     Conclusion: The Future of College Admissions   309
     Jack Buckley, Lynn Letukas, and Ben Wildavsky

     Contributors   313
     Index   321

Acknowledgments

This volume took shape thanks to the efforts of many colleagues, beginning with the contributors, who wrote insightful chapters and patiently responded to our many editorial queries. At the College Board, we are grateful for support from David Coleman, Stefanie Sanford, Cyndie Schmeiser, Jessica Howell, and Jennifer Merriman; for invaluable assistance from Danielle Roberts, Deb Martinelli, Ginny Heidel, and Mario Da Costa; and for the hard work of Sandra Riley, Zachary Goldberg, and Abby Jacobs on our communications team. We are also fortunate to have had the opportunity to work with the talented team at Johns Hopkins University Press and would like to thank in particular editorial director Greg Britton, managing editor Julie McCarthy, and assistant editor Catherine Goldstead.

Measuring Success

The Emergence of Standardized Testing and the Rise of Test-Optional Admissions

Jack Buckley, Lynn Letukas, and Ben Wildavsky

Near the turn of the twentieth century, on December 22, 1899, representatives of 12 universities and 3 preparatory academies met and agreed on "a plan of examination suitable as a test for admission to college," thus ushering in the era of standardized admissions testing (Maryland College Entrance Examination Board 1900). The original intent of standardized admissions testing was to offer a "practical administration of uniform entrance regulations" (Monroe 1911) or, put in contemporary terms, to make the college admissions process more transparent and fair. Within the first quarter of the twentieth century, standardized admissions testing became so widespread and ubiquitous that by 1922 a California teacher wrote to the College Board lamenting: "These examinations now actually dominate, control, and color the entire policy and practice of the classroom; they prescribe and define subject and treatment; they dictate selection and emphasis. Further, they have come, rightly or wrongly, to be at once the despot and headsman professionally of the teacher. Slight chance for continued professional service has that teacher who fails to 'get results' in the 'College Boards,' valuable and inspiring as his instruction may otherwise be" (Valentine 1987, 29).

Today, many students, teachers, parents, and policymakers share similar sentiments. Too often, they complain, middle and high school curriculum seems geared more toward students' need to "get results" on standardized tests than their own personal growth or educational development. Perhaps nowhere is this concern more acutely focused than on the ACT and SAT, the two most popular college admissions tests. Scrutiny of standardized admissions tests is understandable—and should be welcome. What, if any, biases are associated with standardized admissions tests? What value do standardized tests add to the college admissions process? What is the proper role of standardized tests in that process? Most important: What can be done to make the college admissions process more transparent and fair? Many of these questions are the same as those that the 15-member board sought to address almost 120 years ago.

This book was conceived in response to the editors' frustration with the fragmented and incomplete state of the literature around the contemporary debate on college admissions testing. Many students, teachers, parents, policymakers—frankly, nearly anyone immediately outside the testing industry and college admissions—have little understanding of how admissions tests are used. This lack of transparency has often fueled beliefs that college assessments are biased, misused, or overused. As the chapters that follow illustrate, decades of research on various aspects of testing, such as the predictive validity of assessments, makes a compelling case for their value. But all too frequently, researchers and admissions officers talk past one another instead of engaging substantively. This volume is intended as at least a partial remedy.

This collection is among the first to offer an in-depth exploration by some of the leading authors in the standardized admissions testing community and some leading authors in the test-optional community. We have sought to foster serious and robust empirical debate about the proper role of standardized admissions testing through rigorous methodological approaches. More broadly, we aim to examine the use and value of standardized tests for college admissions decisions at a time of rampant grade inflation. We hope that this research will be of great value to provosts, enrollment managers, and college admissions officers seeking to strike the proper balance between uniformity and fairness over the next decade.

Contours of Current Debate

Proponents of standardized admissions testing have long argued that tests such as the SAT and ACT are a vital tool for admissions officers at selective institutions because they most efficiently address the dual challenges of uniformity and fairness in the allocation of the scarce resource of college admission. These proponents assert that standardized admissions tests provide a neutral yardstick to assess the performance and promise of students from secondary schools whose course offerings differ widely in variety and rigor. This is a particularly salient point in an era of widespread grade inflation, where students receive higher average high school grades without corresponding increases in average standardized admissions test scores, eroding the meaning of the high school grade point average (GPA). Moreover, decades of research has independently verified the predictive validity of standardized admissions tests in future college performance, including GPA, retention, and college completion, and has found these tests provide additional information in the prediction of college outcomes beyond high school grades (Mattern and Patterson 2014; Radunzel and Mattern 2015; Radunzel and Noble 2012; Shaw 2015; Westrick et al. 2015).

Some recent research has challenged this work, noting the relationship between standardized admissions tests and socioeconomic status as well as differences in performance across racial and ethnic groups (Atkinson and Geiser 2009; Dixon-Román, Everson, and McArdle 2013; Espenshade and Chung 2012; Geiser 2015). This latter research has prompted some colleges to adopt new policies that no longer require standardized tests as a component for admission. This trend began with a few selective liberal arts institutions, including Bowdoin and Bates College, which made the ACT and SAT optional in 1969 and 1984, respectively, and now includes hundreds of colleges and universities across the United States.

The test-optional movement emerged largely in response to claims that standardized admissions tests are potentially biased and add little value beyond high school grades in measuring postsecondary readiness or in predicting postsecondary academic success. Proponents often claim that the adoption of test-optional policies have improved campus diversity, most notably by increasing the number of underrepresented minorities and low-income students, without diminishing academic standards or the quality of the institution. Research by Espenshade and Chung (2012) suggests that a college admissions process that rewards applicants with high test scores favors students with high socioeconomic status, while the adoption of test-optional policies are accompanied by an increase in geographic and ethnic and racial diversity. Others have criticized test-optional proponents and have called into question the motives of institutions that adopt these policies, suggesting they merely constitute an attempt to raise the ranking and selectivity of the institution (Diver 2006; Epstein 2009). Irrespective of the motive for changes in college admissions policies, the growth of the test-optional movement at some colleges has garnered considerable media attention and spurred discussions among admissions officers, educational researchers, policymakers, and the public about the value and continued use of standardized tests in the admissions process.

Despite widespread media coverage and public attention, proponents of test-optional policies have largely escaped empirical scrutiny. To date, the overwhelming majority of media coverage of institutions that "go test-optional" has been supported by anecdotal evidence and research of limited generalizability. Furthermore, claims that test-optional colleges become more diverse, or that those institutions significantly improve retention and achievement, are only beginning to be systematically researched, particularly when controlling for student selectivity as well as other crucial factors, such as financial aid changes adopted during the same period.

The bulk of evidence for test-optional admissions policies consists of single case studies of an institution adopting a test-optional admissions policy, but they do not all come to the same conclusions regarding the impact on student diversity and/or admissions. These studies, largely from small liberal arts colleges such as Bowdoin, Bates, Holy Cross, and Ithaca College, were conducted by internal researchers for institutional evaluation purposes, as opposed to independent empirical research conducted to examine the impact of the adoption of test-optional policies. Moreover, since their results include just one institution, their generalizability is limited in scope (e.g., Bates College 2005; McDermott 2008; Shaffner 1985).

One notable exception to this trend was a larger study by Hiss and Franks (2014), which includes data from 122,000 students enrolled at 33 test-optional institutions to determine whether college performance suffers from a test-optional policy. However, while the number of participating students and institutions is substantial and noteworthy, there are several limitations, such as the authors' use of a nonrepresentative sample of self-selecting, predominantly public institutions, and their failure to control for unobserved and possibly unrelated factors, such as institutional motivation for adopting test-optional policies. In addition, as discussed below, a more recent study by Belasco, Rosinger, and Hearn (2014) finds that on average, test-optional policies enhance the selectivity of participating institutions, rather than their racial and ethnic diversity.

Chapter Contours and Overview

In the broadest possible sense, each chapter wrestles with two large questions: To what extent should standardized tests play a role in college and university admissions? and How should an institution of higher education best assess prospective student talent in a manner that promotes fairness? As we shall see, the complete abandonment of standardized admissions tests seems unlikely, as enrollment managers would again face the same dilemma facing higher education professionals at the close of the nineteenth century: How does an institution of higher education assess talent in a uniform manner in the absence of a common examination?

To better understand these two basic questions, this volume is divided into three broad sections: Making the Case for Standardized Testing (part 1), The Rise of Test-Optional Admissions Practices (part 2), and Contemporary Challenges for College Admissions (part 3). Tracing the dominant pattern of admissions practices following World War I, part 1 offers a broad look at the role of standardized testing in college admissions, tackling such topics as misperceptions of admissions testing, predictive validity of standardized tests, high school grade inflation, and merit and scholarship aid. In part 2, the volume transitions to an in-depth exploration of test-optional admissions from the perspective of practitioners and scholars that are either currently serving at a test-optional institution or are deeply knowledgeable of the subject matter. The topics in this section raise important issues such as equity and fairness in the admissions process and increasing diversity and access to higher education. Part 3 offers a critical mass of rigorous research that systematically and critically examines current issues in test-optional admissions, including percent plans and class rank policies, other attempts to increase racial and ethnicity diversity, and issues related to college rankings and selectivity. The conclusion discusses future directions in college admissions, pointing to the enduring significance of standardized testing, the need for collaborative discussions between admissions officers, high schools, and test makers on building an opportunity-driven admissions process, and the importance of grounding college access policies in sound research.

These sections offer the reader valuable orientation for the wide range of material included in this volume. Each chapter implicitly or explicitly wrestles with the broad issues of the proper role of standardized testing in academic admissions and fairness. For example, in chapter 1, "Eight Myths about Standardized Admissions Testing," Paul R. Sackett and Nathan R. Kuncel address these themes by providing a fair look at commonly held misperceptions about standardized admissions tests related to test validity, the role of socioeconomic status, bias in test use, and "coachability." They argue that considerable research has documented the predictive power of well-designed standardized admissions tests and note that it is now well established that those tests predict student performance in college better than all other predictors, save for high school grade point average (HSGPA).

In chapter 2, "The Core Case for Testing: The State of Our Research Knowledge," Emily J. Shaw provides detailed, research-based evidence that supports the use of standardized tests in college admissions decisions. She notes that because no other criteria (e.g., HSGPA, letters of recommendation, essays), beyond admissions tests, hold a common meaning for students within and across high schools, standardized tests are among the fairest assessment tools available to the college admissions officer.

In chapter 3, "Grade Inflation and the Role of Standardized Testing," Michael Hurwitz and Jason Lee document the much-discussed grade inflation phenomenon of recent decades. This trend has occurred as other measures of academic preparation, like standardized assessment scores, have remained flat. Their chapter also reveals that high schools are increasingly withholding class rank from colleges, further detracting from the information contained in high school grades. Hurwitz and Lee conclude that standardized college admission tests offer not only the best tool for admissions officers, but also the fairest one for assessing students across diverse educational experiences.

In chapter 4, "Merit-Based Scholarships in Student Recruitment and the Role of Standardized Tests," Jonathan Jacobs, Jim Brooks, and Roger J. Thompson show how standardized tests, in conjunction with weighted high school GPA, are a valuable source of information for providing financial aid to students. The authors note that their decision to use *both* HSGPA and standardized test scores was the most fair way to allocate merit aid and additionally offered the strongest predictor of student success in college—most notably, first-year retention and graduation rates.

In chapter 5, "When High School Grade Point Average and Test Scores Disagree: Implications for Test-Optional Policies," Edgar Sanchez and Krista Mattern discuss high school GPA and test score–discrepant students, a phenomenon that occurs when students earn higher high school grades compared with what one would expect from their test scores, or when they earn higher test scores than their high school GPA would seem to predict. Although high school GPA and standardized tests scores may be discrepant, their dual use provides the fairest assessment for students, because using multiple measures of student performance provides greater prediction power for college admissions officers.

Shifting the focus in chapter 6, "Understanding the Test-Optional Movement," Jerome A. Lucido provides a qualitative, analytic description of how test-optional admissions decisions emerged. Drawing on interviews with multiple admissions practitioners, Lucido highlights the varying concerns that some college and universities have with standardized tests, including perceptions about test validity, the role of socioeconomic status, and bias in test use and prediction. Although he acknowledges that standardized admissions tests continue to be used across the higher education landscape, he argues that limiting their use may make sense at some institutions.

In chapter 7, "Going Test-Optional: A Case Study," Eric Maguire offers a detailed, firsthand account of how and why test-optional policies were introduced at two colleges (Franklin & Marshall and Ithaca College) and how (and to what extent) the policy achieved its promised goals. He argues that limiting the use of standardized admissions tests at both institutions was successful because it helped the colleges recruit and enroll a more racially diverse class.

In chapter 8, "Test Scores and High School Grades as Predictors," reprinted from *Crossing the Finish Line: Completing College at America's Public Universities*, William G. Bowen, Matthew M. Chingos, and Michael S. McPherson argue that high school GPA is a better predictor of student performance in college than standardized tests and that the SAT does not have much added value as a predictor of college performance. Bowen and colleagues conclude that there is some value in college admissions testing, but that the weighting and nature of standardized tests should vary depending on the institution and intended purpose.

In an update to this chapter, Michael Hurwitz and Meredith Welch replicate the work of Bowen and colleagues with data for students entering the same 68 colleges a decade later, in the autumn of 2009. Building on the claims from prior research on grade inflation, they find that the power of high school GPA to predict four- and six-year undergraduate completion has declined. Following this comment, Matthew Chingos and Michael McPherson revisit their original work in light of these more recent findings by Hurwitz and Welch.

The volume transitions to current and likely future debates in chapter 9, "How Do Percent Plans and Other Test-Optional Admissions Programs Affect the Academic Performance and Diversity of the Entering Class?" by Rebecca Zwick, who discusses the problems posed by several college admissions criteria, including percent plans and admissions by class rank. Zwick persuasively argues that these policies do not achieve their intended goals of promoting fairness by increasing diversity while remaining race-neutral. Zwick also finds that these plans, which largely depend on high school GPA for admissions criteria, create transparency concerns because the cutoff for enrollment varies between schools and changes over time. Absent their ability to independently deliver equity or fairness, Zwick concludes that standardized college admissions tests nonetheless offer some value and thus merit continuing significance.

In chapter 10, "The Test-Optional Movement at America's Selective Liberal Arts Colleges: A Boon for Equity or Something Else?," Andrew S. Belasco,

Kelly O. Rosinger, and James C. Hearn examine frequent claims of test-optional supporters: that test-optional policies improve campus diversity and increase the number of underrepresented minority and low-income students. Belasco and his colleagues find that on average, test-optional policies enhance the selectivity, rather than the diversity, of participating institutions. They note that the adoption of test-optional admissions policies is not an adequate solution to providing educational opportunity for low-income and minority students.

In chapter 11, "The Effect of Going Test-Optional on Diversity and Admissions: A Propensity Score Matching Analysis," Kyle Sweitzer, A. Emiko Blalock, and Dhruv B. Sharma examine whether adopting a test-optional admissions policy affects racial and ethnic diversity in freshman admissions. They find that test-requiring institutions increased student diversity to the same degree as that of test-optional institutions, which contradicts one of the often-stated claims of test-optional advocates: They find that the only real changes test-optional institutions experience is an improvement in their test score averages and selectivity. Although the improved selectivity may add value for the institution, fairness for students in the admissions process is limited. The fact that test-requiring colleges were able to increase the percentage of nonwhite incoming freshmen without implementing a test-optional policy suggests such increases may be more a matter of institutional commitment than a shift in admissions requirements.

The contributors to this volume bring with them a wealth of experience in assessment and college admissions, as academic researchers, scholars, policy experts, institutional researchers, testing experts, and enrollment managers. As we shall see in the following chapters, despite some disagreements, all are deeply committed to forging a better path forward for higher education—one that is fairer, more inclusive, and best matches students to prospective postsecondary institutions. As the debate over the role of testing in college admissions continues, we believe a continued, concerted focus on gathering high-quality research evidence will help practitioners make better use of the tools available to them, and thus provide more opportunity to students.

REFERENCES

Atkinson, R., and Geiser, S. (2009). Reflections on a century of college admissions tests. *Research and Occasional Papers Series: CSHE.4.09*. Retrieved from http://www.cshe .berkeley.edu/sites/default/files/shared/publications/docs/ROPS-AtkinsonGeiser -Tests-04-15-09.pdf.

Introduction 9

Bates College. (2005). 20-year Bates College study of optional SATs finds no differences. *Bates News.* Retrieved from http://www.bates.edu/news/2005/10/01/sat-study.

Belasco, A. S., Rosinger, K. O., and Hearn, J. C. (2014). The test-optional movement at America's selective liberal arts colleges: A boon for equity or something else? *Educational Evaluation and Policy Analysis, 37*(2), 206–223.

Diver, C. S. (2006). Skip the test, betray the cause. *New York Times*, September 18. Retrieved from http://www.nytimes.com/2006/09/18/opinion/18diver.html.

Dixon-Román, E., Everson, H., and McArdle, J. (2013). Race, poverty and SAT scores: Modeling the influences of family income on black and white high school students' SAT performance. *Teachers College Record, 115*, 1–33.

Epstein, J. (2009). Behind the SAT optional movement: Context and controversy. *Journal of College Admission*, Summer, 9–19.

Espenshade, T. J., and Chung, C. Y. (2012). Diversity outcomes of test-optional policies. In J. A. Soares (Ed.), *SAT wars: The case for test-optional admissions* (pp. 177–200). New York: Teachers College Press.

Geiser, S. (2015). The growing correlation between race and SAT scores: New findings from California. *Research and Occasion Paper Series: CSHE.10.15.* Retrieved from http://www.cshe.berkeley.edu/sites/default/files/shared/publications/docs/ROPS.CSHE_.10.15.Geiser.RaceSAT.10.26.2015.pdf.

Hiss, W. C., and Franks, V. W. (2014). *Defining promise: Optional standardized testing policies in American college and university admissions.* Retrieved from http://www.nacacnet.org/research/research-data/nacac-research/Documents/DefiningPromise.pdf.

Maryland College Entrance Examination Board. (1900). Plan of organization for the College Entrance Examination Board of the Middle States and Maryland and a statement of subjects in which examinations are proposed. Retrieved from https://archive.org/details/cu31924031758109.

Mattern, K. D., and Patterson, B. F. (2014). Synthesis of recent SAT validity findings: Trend data over time and cohorts. New York: The College Board. Retrieved from http://files.eric.ed.gov/fulltext/ED556462.pdf.

McDermott, A. (2008). Surviving without the SAT. *Chronicle of Higher Education*, September 25. Retrieved from http://chronicle.com/article/Surviving-Without-the-SAT/18874.

Monroe, P. (Ed.). (1911). *A cyclopedia of education.* Vol. 2. New York: Macmillan. Retrieved from https://babel.hathitrust.org/cgi/pt?id=uc2.ark:/13960/t6251wk11;view=1up;seq=109.

Radunzel, J., and Mattern, K. D. (2015). *Providing context for college readiness measures: College enrollment and graduation projections for the 2015 ACT-tested high school graduating class.* Iowa City: ACT.

Radunzel, J., and Noble, J. (2012). Predicting long-term college success through degree completion using ACT composite score, ACT benchmarks, and high school grade point average (*Research Report No. 2012-5*). Iowa City: ACT.

Shaffner, P. E. (1985). Competitive admission practices when the SAT is optional. *Journal of Higher Education, 56*, 55–72.

Shaw, E. J. (2015). *An SAT validity primer.* New York: The College Board.

Valentine, J. (1987). *The College Board and the school curriculum: A history of the College Board's influence on the substance and standards of American education, 1900–1980.* New York: The College Board.

Westrick, P. A., Le, H., Robbins, S. B., Radunzel, J. M., and Schmidt, F. L. (2015). College performance and retention: A meta-analysis of the predictive validities of ACT scores, high school grades, and SES. *Educational Assessment, 20*(1), 23–45. Retrieved from http://10.0.4.56/10627197.2015.997614.

PART I / Making the Case for Standardized Testing

1

Eight Myths about Standardized Admissions Testing

Paul R. Sackett and Nathan R. Kuncel

*C*ritiques *of standardized testing in college admissions take many forms—from the claim that such assessments are mired in racial, gender, and class bias; to the assertion that admissions tests are highly coachable; to the argument that they are just not a very good predictor of academic success. In this chapter, Paul R. Sackett and Nathan R. Kuncel discuss and refute these claims and others. The two professors of psychology delve into the research literature to offer a comprehensive rebuttal to what they term eight myths about testing.*

In the case of alleged bias, this chapter draws a crucial analytical distinction that is too often missing from the testing discussion. Critics frequently call admission tests biased on the basis of well-documented average score differences across race, ethnicity, and gender. Sackett and Kuncel don't dispute that these differences exist. However, they remind readers, bias in testing refers not to different score averages by group but to whether a given score predicts the same outcome for test takers regardless of their demographic group.

In fact, substantial research has shown admissions tests slightly overpredict the academic performance of black and Latino students. The opposite is true for women, whose college grade point averages (GPAs) tend to be slightly higher than their scores would predict. This doesn't occur because the tests underpredict women's true standing on the attributes the tests measure, but because women perform better than men in areas such as study habits and participation in classroom discussion.

Another oft-cited belief debunked in Sackett and Kuncel's lengthy catalog of myths is the claim that because standardized tests like the SAT are strongly correlated with socio-economic status, they amount to nothing more than what one critic called a "Student Affluence Test." The authors don't dispute the correlation, but they note that it may re-flect real skill-boosting advantages provided to children from affluent families, including encouragement of academic pursuits. Moreover, within a given income band, there is considerable score variation—and the predictive value of test scores remains high when controlling for socioeconomic status. In this case, as in others discussed in this chapter, Sackett and Kuncel conclude that the evidence points firmly toward standardized tests playing a valuable role in the admissions process, myths notwithstanding.

Public criticism of standardized testing in the context of college admissions cen-ters on a number of familiar, oft-stated claims. The purpose of this chapter is to show how such claims often don't hold up to scrutiny. One set of beliefs focuses on the predictive value of tests. Some critics maintain that admission tests just don't predict anything of value. Others assert, in variations on this theme, that (a) tests do pre-dict, but the strength of relationships is too weak to merit use, (b) tests predict in the short term only (e.g., nothing but first-year grades), (c) other measures predict better (e.g., high school grades), or (d) tests do not measure all important attributes of stu-dents, and thus should not be used. Still other test detractors argue that tests reflect nothing but, or little more than, socioeconomic status (SES), are biased against women and members of minority racial/ethnic groups, and are readily coachable.

Despite the frequency with which these positions are asserted, there is a large body of evidence that each is a myth. This chapter provides an overview of the major lines of evidence cited by testing critics in the areas mentioned above: test validity, the role of SES, bias in test use, and "coachability." Our focus is on large-scale inves-tigations of each of these issues. One can find small-sample studies that support the position of test critics on any of these topics, just as one can also find small-sample studies that support the position that tests are nearly perfect predictors. Our posi-tion is that meta-analytic syntheses of studies of a topic and large-scale represen-tative samples carry far more evidentiary value than small-sample studies. We note the tendency in journalistic treatments of any topic to treat any research as having two equally valid sides. For example, we encountered a treatment of the validity of the GRE for graduate school admissions stating, in paraphrase, "Whether the GRE predicts performance is currently under dispute. Research by Kuncel, Hezlett, and Ones (2001) says it does predict, but research by Sternberg and

Williams (1997) says it does not." However, research by Sternberg and Williams is based on a highly restricted sample of 169 students at a single university, while Kuncel's study is a meta-analysis of 1,753 samples totaling 82,659 students. We recommend caution regarding small-scale studies and place more reliance on the larger cumulative data on topics of interest.

Test Validity and Predictive Power

Standardized test scores are one piece of information that can be used by selective postsecondary institutions to make admissions decisions. When considering what to include in an admissions system, the predictive power of different pieces of information is a key consideration. That is no accident. Considerable research has demonstrated the predictive power of well-designed standardized tests. It is now well established that those tests predict student performance in college better than all other predictors save for prior high school grade point average. Here we review the usefulness of test scores across multiple academic outcomes and compare them to other pieces of information used in decision making, including personal statements, letters of recommendation, and other measures that have been the focus of recent efforts to expand admissions criteria.

Understanding predictive power requires distinguishing between two key concepts. The first is the multidimensionality of performance. Success in education is not one thing. There are multiple important dimensions of student success and multiple important outcomes. As we will see, different predictors are relatively stronger or weaker predictors of different outcomes, and this is true of all sources of information that might be used in admissions. Therefore, it is overly simplistic just to ask, Do tests predict well? The right question is, How well do tests predict outcomes on different measures?

The second key concept is one of incremental predictive power. Human behavior is notoriously difficult to forecast. It would be strange for a single predictor to be the only thing that matters. So it is also valuable to consider, whenever possible, how predictors combine in foretelling student success.

Myth 1: Tests Only Predict First-Year Grades and Don't Even Do That Well

It is certainly the case that the initial goal of most admissions tests was to predict college grades. Grades are, after all, significant measures of a student's mastery of material and are often reasonable measures of learning. Despite their imperfections, grades are related to real world outcomes, including subsequent job performance (Roth, BeVier, Switzer, and Schippmann 1996).

As a result, thousands of studies have been conducted examining the relationship between standardized admissions tests and subsequent grades at both the college and graduate school levels. Meta-analyses and large-scale studies give the clearest information and indicate that test scores are predictive of grades. On average, tests tend to be the second-best predictor of college grades (after high school GPA) and the best predictor of grades in graduate school (beating out college GPA) (Berry and Sackett 2009; Kuncel, Hezlett, and Ones 2001). The combination of the two works even better.

Sometimes the observed correlations between tests and subsequent GPA, which tend to fall around .35 for college and .24 for graduate school, are criticized for being too small to be useful. Even correlations of .20 can be extremely important (more on this later), but critics overlook two ways in which these are actually gross underestimates. The first is that these values are obtained on groups of people who are far more homogenous on scores than applicants or the overall population of test takers. This is akin to looking at height among elite basketball players and asking if height matters in basketball. Of course it does, but we won't see a huge effect for the centimeters that separate players at most positions in professional play while ignoring the half meter or greater between top players and the public at large. The same restriction of range issue holds true for test scores among students admitted to college and graduate school. We don't directly observe how students with low test scores would have performed because they were not admitted. Because the goal is to understand the relationship between test scores and performance for the full range of college applicants, we need to account for the full applicant population rather than just admitted students.

The second issue with taking the observed relationship at face value is that students in college don't all take the same classes. There is an unequal flow of talent (as measured by test scores and prior grades) into different disciplines at the start of school. In addition, disciplines do not have the same grading standards or typical course difficulty. Since students are not equally prepared or motivated, they often end up taking different sets of courses. This movement of students continues and even contributes to switching majors. The classic example is students who intend to go into medicine but then run headlong into organic chemistry and promptly choose another path. Different course taking will tend to reduce the relationship between test scores and earned grades.

If we take into account the restricted range and examine comparable curricula (by looking at individual course-level grades), we can estimate how well test scores and high school grades work without these obscuring factors. The results are a sizable increase in the predictive value of both. Figure 1.1 displays results from two studies with thousands of students and shows the predictive power of standardized tests for grades earned in college. The correlation for test scores predicting grades in a common set of college courses is one of the largest predictive relationships observed in the social sciences (Hattie 2008). Even better prediction is obtained by the combination of test scores and high school grade point average (HSGPA). In addition, tests predict grades throughout college, not just in the first year (e.g., Berry and Sackett 2009; Kuncel, Hezlett, and Ones 2001).

Even if we do not address the fact that only a subset of all students are in college, or that colleges differ considerably in difficulty and rigor, or that even within a college two students can take entirely different sets of courses, a correlation of "only" .35 is still very useful. To make it concrete, students who score in the top band

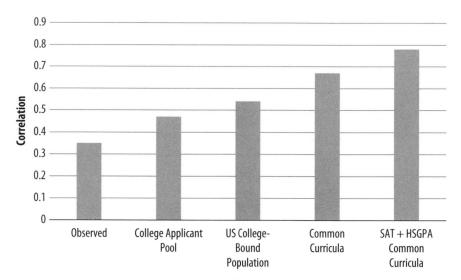

Fig. 1.1. Correlations between SAT and College GPA. *Note*: College applicant and US college-bound results are multivariate range restriction corrected estimates. Common curricula additionally addresses different course-taking patterns. SAT + high school grade point average (HSGPA) adds HSGPA to the SAT as a predictor. *Sources*: Berry and Sackett 2009; Shen et al. 2012.

of scores on the old SAT (2100–2400) are more than four times as likely to earn a B average or better compared with those in the bottom score band (600–1190).

Myth 2: Tests Only Predict Grades

Grade point averages are the most commonly studied measure of student success in admission because predicting grades is a focal outcome and also easier to study than other metrics, as grades are carefully collected and stored. Sometimes the utility of tests is dismissed on the grounds that they predict grades only. In fact, quite a few other variables have been studied.

Before entering college, test scores are associated with the academic direction students take, including the majors they are interested in and the majors they ultimately graduate in. Figure 1.2 shows how strong scores on basic verbal and reading skills are generally more strongly associated with the choice of majors such as English and journalism, while mathematic skills are generally associated with STEM (science, technology, engineering, and math) fields. At an individual level, the difference between math and verbal skills is sometimes call "tilt" and is important in understanding who will chose what major.

But after entering college, there are other outcomes that are related to test scores. We know that not every student who earns a bachelor's degree takes the same classes, and even within the same major one student can focus on lower division courses and avoid the more challenging ones. The difference can be dramatic, with one student taking numerous graduate-level courses and another taking the minimum of upper-level courses. Both test scores and prior grades are associated with taking more challenging courses. Results from a study of 61 colleges and universities and across 178,878 students are presented in figure 1.3. Stronger SAT and high school grades are associated with taking more advanced courses (Shewach et al. 2017). Multiplied by millions of college students, this link indicates a large cumulative difference in the pursuit of more in-depth and advanced knowledge.

Even within the same course level, students with stronger test scores challenge themselves by taking courses that are more difficult (Keiser et al. 2016). Within a college, high scorers are more likely to take courses that have better academically prepared students and are more harshly graded. Both sets of evidence suggest that students with strong test scores end up better educated, even at the same institution. They tend to pursue more challenging majors and take more difficult and advanced courses while earning the best grades (which are, again, related to job performance and salary). These patterns hold even when prior grades are controlled.

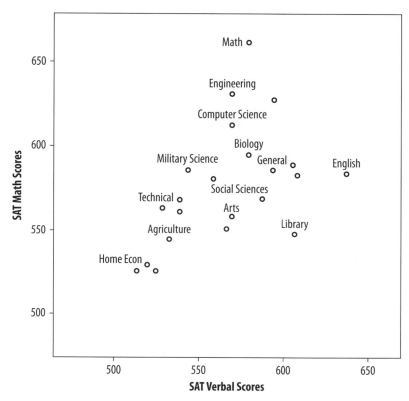

Fig. 1.2. Average SAT Math and Verbal Reasoning Scores by Intended College Major. *Note*: A representative sampling of majors is labeled.

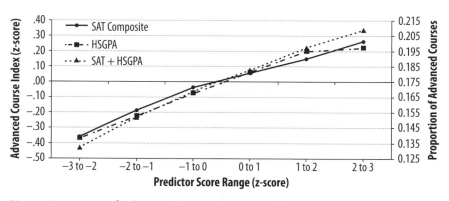

Fig. 1.3. Proportion of Advanced Courses Taken by College Students over Four Years by SAT Composite Score, High School Grade Point Average (HSGPA), and SAT + HSGPA Combined

BEYOND THE CLASSROOM

In graduate school, research has examined a wide range of outcomes beyond grades. Kuncel and Hezlett (2007) conducted meta-analyses and compiled data on thousands of studies and hundreds of thousands of graduate students for all major graduate admissions tests. Test scores were positively correlated with numerous measures of student success. For example, in addition to predicting graduate school grades, test scores are also strongly related to faculty evaluations (typically by advisers) of a student's creativity and scholarship. Scores also correlate with the research accomplishments of graduate students as well as how frequently their papers are cited by other scholars. Neither of these outcomes is easy to predict (because they occur infrequently), and test scores end up being one of the only admissions tools with substantial evidence supporting their effectiveness.

The major milestones of comprehensive or qualifying exams, which are extensive and difficult assessments of a student's ability to research and write about discipline-specific issues, are strongly predicted. Both Medical Boards and the Bar exam are well predicted by test scores, reflecting the fundamental relationship between scores and the ability to learn. Test scores even exhibit positive, although smaller, correlations with obtaining the graduate degree. Interestingly, across all outcomes, the relationships are even stronger when field-specific standardized tests (such as the GRE Subject tests) are employed, and for more motivationally determined outcomes (like degree attainment). Just as interesting is the fact that college GPA is consistently a slightly less effective predictor than standardized tests (Kuncel, Hezlett, and Ones 2001) in graduate school success, although using them together can further improve prediction.

Myth 3: Alternatives to Testing Are Superior

When evaluating predictors, it is important to compare them with alternatives. We can wish a predictor were even stronger, but if it is the best available, then it should be used. It is therefore critical to note that research on alternative measures generally finds that they typically have worse predictive power than test scores for most outcomes. For example, personal statements and student essays are often used in both college and graduate admissions, but a meta-analysis that aggregated the available literature demonstrated that they were far less correlated with grades and other outcomes than test scores (Murphy, Klieger, Borneman, and Kuncel 2009). Similarly, a meta-analysis of letters of recommendation indicated that they are generally weaker predictors of GPA outcomes in college ($r=.28$, a smaller but still useful correlation) and especially graduate school ($r=.13$). However, they do appear to provide some incremental information about a student's motivation and can contribute to predicting degree attainment, which is generally difficult to predict with anything (Kuncel, Kochevar, and Ones 2014). Some measures of study habits, attitudes, and skills come closer to tests and prior grades in their power for predicting GPA ($r=.40$), although their utility in high-stakes settings is a concern because of the potential for faking (i.e., reporting better study habits than is actually the case) (Crede and Kuncel 2008). Personality tests have similar problems with faking, although those measuring conscientiousness or grit are positively correlated with grades (albeit more modestly than tests or high school record, where the corrected correlation between grit and GPA was .18 in a meta-analysis in low-stakes settings) (Crede, Tynan, and Harms 2016).

Other efforts to develop new predictors that provide additional information about students have yielded mixed results. On the promising side, researchers examining the use of biodata (biographical experience and accomplishments) and situational judgment tests (reactions to text simulations of important and common academic experiences) reported positive prediction of grades and ratings of success in college samples (Oswald, Schmitt, Kim, Ramsay, and Gillespie 2004). Situational judgment tests have also been a useful addition to traditional measures in medical school admissions (e.g., Lievens, Buyse, and Sackett 2005), especially for predicting success at interpersonal outcomes.

However, other research on alternative admissions measures has been disappointing. For example, the Noncognitive Questionnaire (Sedlacek 2004) demonstrated near zero relationship with academic outcomes in a meta-analysis (Thomas, Kuncel, and Crede, 2007). In another case, law school simulations that felt right and had great face validity were plagued by unreliability (for a review, see Sackett 1998). The measures provided noisy and inconsistent information about people. So the score a person might obtain today would often be very different from what he or she would get tomorrow. A final example is the Rainbow Project (Sternberg et al. 2006), which produced a mixture of scales with zero criterion-related validity and some that did demonstrate useful correlations. However, the latter also tended to produce very large racial and ethnic differences, even though they were less reliable than other assessments and some claims of success were, in fact, based on trivial sample sizes (for a critique and discussion, see Hunt 2008). Overall, the literature indicates that the alternatives are not superior but that some can be very useful additions as a part of an admissions system that attempts to evaluate multiple characteristics of the applicant.

Myth 4: Tests Are Not Related to Real World Success

Of course, these are all outcomes in an academic setting, and some may reasonably wonder if tests merely measure some kind of "book smarts" that doesn't really matter for career success. To really test this, we would need a measure that was designed for academic admissions and then use it to try to predict success and performance in the world of work. Most admissions tests are not formally used for this purpose, so there is a dearth of this kind of research. There is one exception, however. The Miller Analogies Test (MAT) was developed for graduate school admissions and was later cross-marketed as a decision-making tool for professional hiring. So we have a "book smarts" test that was also studied for predicting outcomes like creativity at work or performance evaluations. The resulting meta-analyses demonstrate three things. First, the MAT was clearly related to a number of valuable academic criteria. Consistent with the results discussed above, everything from faculty ratings of a PhD student's scholarship to research productivity was positively correlated with MAT scores (fig. 1.4). So learning and academic accomplishments were predicted.

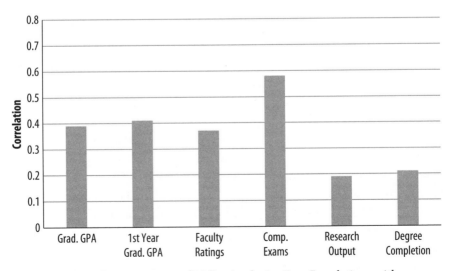

Fig. 1.4. Meta-analytic Estimates of Miller Analogies Test Correlations with Academic Outcomes. *Note*: Grad. = Graduate school; GPA = Grade point average; Comp. = Comprehensive. *Source*: Results from Kuncel, Hezlett, and Ones 2004.

Second, a number of transitionary (school to work) outcomes were also included in the meta-analysis, including performance in an internship, creativity, career potential, and even simulated samples of professional work for counselors. Overall, success and potential in these areas was positively correlated with MAT scores (fig. 1.5). Third, information about actual work success was studied, and again, test score correlated positively with evaluations of job performance and involvement in professional organizations (fig. 1.6). This pattern is consistent with enduring theories of job performance that argue that cognitive skills are invested in acquiring job-specific knowledge. In other words, people use their basic cognitive ability and foundational knowledge (e.g., reading and math) to attain job-specific knowledge and skills. Ultimately, it is their job-specific skill and expertise that are related to effective performance (see Kuncel and Beatty 2013). Tests of broad knowledge domains (e.g., math and verbal reasoning) are related to a person's quickly and effectively ramping up his or her job knowledge and skills.

The results from the MAT are a proof of concept based on a single test. If we turn to measures of verbal, quantitative, and reasoning skills that are used in making hiring decisions, we see further evidence of the importance of these foundational characteristics, whether they are measured in school or work settings. The research literature is truly vast, encompassing over 20,000 samples on over a

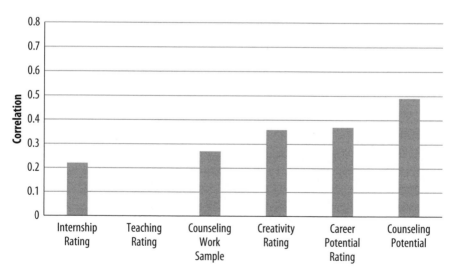

Fig. 1.5. Meta-analytic Estimates of Miller Analogies Test Correlations with Career Transition Outcomes. *Note*: The value for Teaching Rating is zero. *Source*: Results from Kuncel, Hezlett, and Ones 2004.

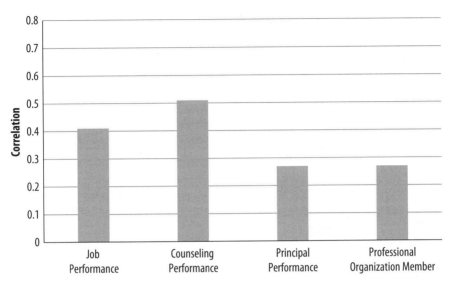

Fig. 1.6. Meta-analytic Estimates of Miller Analogies Test Correlations with Career and Work Outcomes. *Source*: Results from Kuncel, Hezlett, and Ones 2004.

million people (Ones, Viswesvaran, and Dilchert 2004). Test scores are related to job performance across all types of jobs, ranging from fairly simple occupations to highly complex ones. The importance of cognitive skills extends to creative work as well as leadership; meta-analytic reviews of team performance have found that the test scores of leaders are related to their team's performance (Judge, Colbert, and Ilies 2004). In general, the more complicated the duties, the stronger the correlation between test scores and subsequent job performance. Finally, just as is observed in the academic literature, social class does not account for the predictive power of test scores (Kuncel, Rose, Ejiogu, and Yang 2014).

Overall, even an hour of assessment provides a striking amount of information. Of course, other characteristics matter, and we are at the front of efforts to develop measures that help capture the many aspects of a person that contribute to his or her success. However, just as in medicine, where methods of diagnosis are being tested and developed, it would be a mistake to discard the tried and true blood pressure test.

Myth 5: The Good-Enough versus More-Is-Better Argument

In our experience, at about this time, some readers will say that they understand that some minimum level of verbal and math skills are important for school and work but that beyond a certain point more doesn't really matter. In fact, a number of different studies have examined this question using a variety of methods, and all have concluded that more is better. Stronger scores are associated with better grades or job performance. Some of the earliest work was in the job performance domain, where nonlinear relationships only occurred at chance levels (Coward and Sackett 1990; Hawk 1970). Recent work in the educational domain was done with three large data sets that demonstrate, if anything, the relationship between scores and GPA becomes stronger, not weaker, with top test scores (Arneson, Sackett, and Beatty 2011). The relationship between test scores and GPA was examined in a 110-college sample ($N = 150,000$), Project Talent ($N = 15,040$), and the National Education Longitudinal Study of 1988 ($N = 6,656$) with similar relationships. In each case, more is better. Finally, in a longitudinal study of exceptional talent, Lubinski (2009) demonstrated not only that SAT scores at age 13 were correlated with earning patents, publishing novels, and publishing scientific research 25 years later, but that test score differences in people *within the top 1%* of the score distribution mattered. Those in the top quartile of the top 1% were more likely to have attained these achievements than those in the bottom quartile of the top 1%. Although a bit frustrating for those of us without perfect test scores, more is better.

Tests as an External Standard

We have been conducting research on a database with over 300 colleges and universities from across the United States with over a million students. It's worth noting that the modal high school GPA is a 4.0 in this database. Grade inflation marches on at the high school (Ziomek and Svec 1995) and college levels (Kostal, Kuncel, and Sackett 2016). It would be unwise to put too much emphasis on a single piece of information in admissions decision making because it will be gamed, as is already happening for states that automatically admit a top percentage of high school students (see chapter 9).

Myth 6: Test Results Are Really a Measure of SES

A common assertion about admission is that scores are strongly linked to socioeconomic status, commonly operationalized as a composite of parental education and family income. There are variations on this theme. The first is that test scores reflect nothing but (or little more than) SES. Statements of this position include "in the interests of truth in advertising, the SAT should simply be called a wealth test" (Guinier, undated, cited in Sackett et al. 2009), "the SAT merely measures the size of student's houses" (Kohn 2001), "the only thing the SAT predicts well now is socio-economic status" (Colvin 1997), and "SAT originally stood for Student Aptitude Test. But parsing the results by income suggest that it's also a Student Affluence Test" (Zumbrun 2014).

It is indeed the case that SES is correlated with scores on admissions tests. Sackett and colleagues (2009) aggregated SAT-SES correlations across 41 colleges and universities and reported an average correlation of .22 among enrolled students and .31 among applicants to a given school. These correlations are not trivial, and if one computes and plots mean SAT scores at various SES levels, one sees a clear picture of higher mean scores at higher SES levels. Similar information is commonly presented in support of this argument, for example, in a *Washington Post* article (Goldfarb 2014) (fig. 1.7).

As drawn, the figure does not capture any information about test score variability, and it can incorrectly suggest a one-to-one correspondence between SES level and test score. Some do not fall into this trap: Zumbrun (2014), writing in the *Wall Street Journal*, does acknowledge "a final caveat: Within each income category,

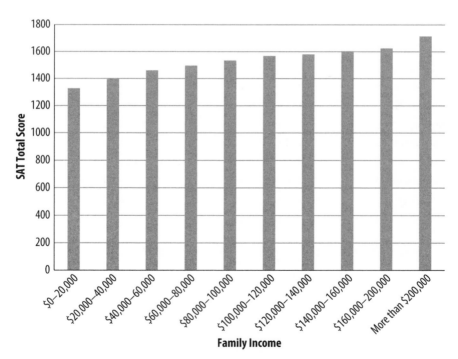

Fig. 1.7. SAT Scores by Family Income. *Source*: Goldfarb 2014.

of course, is a tremendous amount of variation. There are students from wealthy families who do very badly and students from poor families who do very well. Having wealthy parents gives a leg up. But parental income is not destiny." Kuncel, McNeal, and Sackett (2016) formalize this by reporting the degree of SAT score variability (indexed by the standard deviation) for enrolled college students at various levels of parental income (under $20,000, $21,000–40,000, etc.) in a sample of over 400,000 students. They find that the smallest amount of score variability within an SES income level band is 94% of the variability in the total sample. If the SAT measured nothing but SES, variability within each income band would be dramatically smaller than variability in the total sample. We view this is a strong refutation of the assertion that tests measure nothing but SES (see also chapter 2).

The second variation on the theme of concern about the link between test scores and SES is an assertion that the apparent validity of tests as predictors of academic performance is an artifact. The topic of SES and admissions testing first came to our attention in 2003 when two articles in the *American Psychologist* made striking claims. Crosby, Iyer, Clayton, and Downing (2003) stated that "it has now been documented with massive data sets from the University of California that SAT I scores lose any ability to predict freshman year grades if the regression analyses control for socioeconomic status." Similarly, Biernat (2003) stated that "SAT scores used for college admissions do not predict freshman year grades when socioeconomic status is controlled."

We set out to examine this issue, and have now done so in three large-scale studies (Sackett et al. 2009). The first was a meta-analysis in which we gathered all studies we could locate of test-grade, test-SES, and SES-grade relationships. Using the meta-analytic average of each relationship, we computed the partial correlation between test and grade, controlling for SES. The second investigation did the same thing using College Board SAT data on over 155,000 students. The third investigation gathered large, publically available data sets in which these same analyses could be run, including a study of Harvard admissions, two large studies of law school admissions, Project Talent, the National Longitudinal Study of 1972, and the National Educational Longitudinal Study of 1988. Table 1.1 presents the key findings: across all studies, the admissions test retains over 90% of its predictive power when SES is controlled.

These investigations focused on admissions tests alone as predictors of academic performance. As tests are commonly used in conjunction with high school grades for college admissions, Sackett et al. (2012) shifted to a regression framework in the analysis of two large College Board SAT data sets. With high school

Table 1.1. Effects of socioeconomic status on test-grade relationships

Data set	Source	Operationalization of test-grade relationship	Test-grade relationship	Test-grade, relationship, controlling for SES	% predictive power, controlling for SES
Meta-analysis (*N* = 26–60K)	Sackett et al. 2009	Observed correlations	.35	.34	0.97
College Board 1997–1999 data (*N* = 155K)	Sackett et al. 2009	Corrected correlations	.47	.44	0.94
Harvard study (*N* = 486)	Sackett et al. 2009	Observed correlations	.30	.29	0.97
LSAC (*N* = 19K)	Sackett et al. 2009	Observed correlations	.38	.38	1.00
1995Law (*N* = 3K)	Sackett et al. 2009	Observed correlations	.28	.28	1.00
Project Talent (*N* = 749)	Sackett et al. 2009	Observed correlations	.30	.29	0.97
NLS72 (*N* = 6K)	Sackett et al. 2009	Observed correlations	.35	.33	0.94
NELS88 (*N* = 6K)	Sackett et al. 2009	Observed correlations	.24	.23	0.96
College Board 2006 data (*N* = 60K)	Sackett et al. 2012	Corrected regression coefficient, school-reported HSGPA in model	.23	.21	0.91
College Board 1997–1999 data (*N* = 136K)	Sackett et al. 2012	Corrected regression coefficient, self-reported HSGPA in model	.26	.24	0.92
College Board 2006–2010 data (*N* = 415K)	Higdem et al. 2016	Corrected regression coefficient, school-reported HSGPA in model	.24	.21	0.88
Male (*N* = 185K)			.23	.20	0.87
Female (*N* = 230K)			.30	.26	0.87
Asian (*N* = 38K)			.25	.25	1.00
Black (*N* = 31K)			.19	.17	0.89
Hispanic (*N* = 26K)			.22	.19	0.86
White (*N* = 295K)			.21	.18	0.86
Univ. of California data (*N* = 78K)	Sackett et al. 2012	Corrected regression coefficient, school-reported HSGPA in model	.25	.22	0.88

Note: HSGPA = high school grade point average; SES = socioeconomic status.

grades also in the model, we examined the SAT regression coefficients with and without SES in the model. Table 1.1 contains these findings as well; again, the SAT retains the vast majority of its incremental predictive power over high school grades when SES is added to the model. Higdem et al. (2016) repeated these regression analyses in a College Board data set of over 415,000 students, reporting results separately by gender and race/ethnicity, again with similar results.

Finally, in Sackett et al. (2012), we report regression analyses for the University of California data that was the basis for the original *American Psychologist* claim that test validity disappeared when SES was controlled. However, once again, as table 1.1 shows, the SAT retains the vast majority of its predictive power. What, then, is the basis for the claim that SAT loses its predictive power once SES is controlled? We discovered that this claim is based on an elementary statistical error. The analyses of the California data by Geiser and Studley (2002) claim that the SAT coefficient is reduced dramatically when SES is added to the model. But they test a different model: they added both SES and a second admissions test, the SAT II. SAT II is highly correlated with the SAT, and either one has little incremental predictive power once the other is in the model. Thus, it is the addition of SAT II, rather than SES, that reduces the SAT coefficient. As shown in Sackett et al. (2012) and in table 1.1, proper analyses of the California data show that, like all other data sets, controlling for SES does not substantially reduce the SAT coefficient.

It is important to note that the fact that SES and test scores are correlated does not in and of itself tell us anything about the basis for the correlation. One possibility is that the correlation signals the real advantage provided to test takers by high SES parents through a variety of mechanisms, such as encouraging academic pursuits and exposure to stimulating environments. Another is that the correlation reflects a source of bias, such that high SES parents have access to mechanisms that artificially increase test scores but do not increase the actual skills and abilities tapped by the test. Note that the variance shared between test scores and SES is related to subsequent academic performance. The fact that test-grade relationships are modestly reduced when controlling for SES indicates that the shared variance was predictive of performance. If the shared variance reflected irrelevant, biasing sources of variance, then controlling for SES would increase the test-grade relationship. Thus, evidence supports the position that the high SES is linked to sources of variance that increase the skills and abilities measured by the test.

In sum, there is now extensive evidence countering both the claim that admissions tests measure nothing but SES and the claim that the apparent predictive power of admissions tests is an artifact that disappears when SES is controlled.

Myth 7: Tests Are Biased

Another oft-stated criticism of standardized admissions tests is that they are biased against women and disadvantaged racial/ethnic minority group members. Addressing this issue requires unpacking what we mean by "biased." It is indeed the case that there are mean differences, sometimes quite substantial, in mean test scores across race, ethnicity, and gender. For example, in the population of SAT test takers, black students average about 1 standard deviation lower than white students on the Critical Reading and Math subtests; Hispanic students average about .75 SD lower; and Asian students average about the same as whites on Critical Reading, and average .6 SD higher than whites on Math. Women and men average about the same on Critical Reading, while men average about .25 SD higher than women on Math (College Board 2015).

However, there is consensus within the educational and psychological fields that mean differences do not per se signal bias. Mean differences can reflect a wide range of factors. Some reflect institutional factors, such as differences in access and exposure to material. Others reflect individual factors, such as the choice of effort invested in a given domain. A more probing investigation is needed before concluding that mean differences reflect bias.

It is useful to put these mean differences in a broader context, namely, that they are not specific to admissions tests. Tests focusing on math and verbal abilities are widely used in a variety of contexts. Sackett and Shen (2009) gathered data on math and verbal tests used in elementary school, high school, college admissions, and employee selection, and found comparable magnitudes of group mean differences in each of these contexts.

Conceptually, a test is unbiased if a given score has the same meaning regardless of group membership. This is reflected in the widely used Cleary (1968) model of predictive bias. This model examines regression lines relating test scores to performance measures (e.g., grades) to determine whether a given test score predicts the same level of criterion performance for each group. If, for example, the regression equation relating scores on an admission test to college GPA shows that the mean GPA for white students with a verbal score of 500 is 2.7, one asks whether the mean GPA for black students with a score of 500 is also 2.7. If it were the case that the test was biased against black students, then their measured score of 500 would be lower than the score they would obtain on an unbiased test. Thus their score would "underpredict" their GPA; a black student with a score of 500 might subsequently earn, say, a mean GPA of 2.9 (Sackett, Borneman, and Connelly 2008).

There is extensive evidence on the question of whether admissions and other high-stakes tests under- or overpredict minority group performance. Examining race and ethnicity in educational admissions, Linn (1973) reviewed 22 studies, and Young (2001) reviewed 28 studies since Linn's review. Both concluded that the consistent finding is overprediction (the predicted GPA is higher than the actual obtained GPA), rather than underprediction, for black and Hispanic students. Findings for blacks and Hispanics in employment settings parallel those in educational admissions (Bartlett et al. 1978; Hartigan and Wigdor 1989).

In contrast, underprediction of women's academic performance is commonly found at the undergraduate level, with meta-analytic evidence from 130 studies finding that women earn GPAs about 0.24 point higher than would be predicted by admissions tests (Fischer, Schult, and Hell 2013). Most of this gender difference has been found to reflect differences in conscientiousness, in study habits, and in the course-taking patterns of men and women (Keiser, Sackett, Kuncel, and Brothen 2016; Kling, Noftle, and Robins 2013; Ramist, Lewis, and McCamley 1990; Stricker, Rock, and Burton 1993). For example, Keiser et al. examined ACT-grade relationships among several thousand students in an introductory psychology course. They administered a personality scale measuring conscientiousness to all students and found that the underprediction of women's grades disappeared when the conscientiousness measure was added to the regression equation. As a second approach, they unpacked the course grade into four separate components—exams, quizzes, ratings of participation in discussion sessions, and extra points for research participation—and examined predictive bias against each of the four components. There was no underprediction of exam or quiz scores, which are the aspects of academic performance that a test like the ACT would be expected to predict. There was underprediction of discussion ratings and research participation, which are discretionary "noncognitive" behaviors that one would not expect to predict with the ACT. In other words, underprediction is not due to bias in admissions tests, but to gender differences in these noncognitive discretionary behaviors.

The lack of underprediction for blacks and Hispanics and the substantive explanation for the underprediction of performance for females have led to a general belief that the question of predictive bias in tests for high-stakes decision making has been resolved, with little work on the topic in recent years. Aguinis, Culpepper, and Pierce (2010) challenged this conclusion with a paper explicitly aimed at reviving research on predictive bias. They argued that accepted conclusions about overprediction and underprediction were premature. Much research lacks the needed sample size to detect regression slope differences between groups, and thus the conclusion that slope differences are rare may be an artifact of research design. And intercept differences may also be artifactual: test unreliability can create the appearance of intercept differences when there are none. Aguinis, Culpepper, and Pierce showed possible effects via computer simulation, thus offering the possibility of a different pattern of findings than the conventional wisdom.

Two important responses have emerged to the challenge issued by Aguinis, Culpepper, and Pierce (2010). First, Mattern and Patterson (2013) assembled a large data base examining the relationship between SAT scores, high school GPA, and subsequent college GPA. They obtained data from the 2006–2008 entering cohorts of 177 colleges and universities. With this large data set and with sophisticated artifact corrections they did find more evidence of slope differences and smaller intercept differences than prior research. However, contrary to expectations put forth by Aguinis, Culpepper, and Pierce, these differences did not translate to differences in the substantive nature of the findings. Rather, Mattern and Patterson reaffirmed the prior substantive conclusion that the performance of black and Hispanic students was overpredicted throughout the score range, and the performance of women was underpredicted (recall the substantive explanation for the gender findings discussed earlier).

While Mattern and Patterson offered a single large data set as the basis for a response to Aguinis, Culpepper, and Smith (2010), Berry and Zhao (2015) took a different approach. They identified parameters that contribute to predictive bias equations (e.g., mean predictor group difference, mean criterion group difference, predictor-criterion correlation) and obtained meta-analytic estimates of each parameter in the context of using ability measures to predict job performance. They focused solely on black-white differences, and their findings reaffirm the conclusion that black performance is overpredicted throughout the score range. In sum, despite continuing claims that testing isn't a fair measure of current abilities or future accomplishments, the overwhelming conclusion across decades of research is that tests are not biased against women and racial/ethnic minority group members in terms of their use in predicting subsequent academic performance.

Myth 8: Coaching Often Produces Large Score Gains

A final myth is the common assertion that admissions tests are easily coached, with these assertions reinforced by providers of commercial coaching, who claim that score gains of over 100 points can be expected across sections of the SAT, for example. Pairing these claims with the argument that the high cost of commercial coaching programs makes them differentially accessible to students lower in SES makes the coachability of admissions tests a critical issue.

Coaching is a difficult issue to study. Ideally, one would conduct an experiment in which students were randomly assigned to coaching and non-coaching conditions, and then compare their subsequent admissions test performance. However, given the high-stakes nature of admissions testing, it is hard to imagine that students would agree to such conditions in the time period leading up to taking an admissions test. Students motivated to perform well would likely pursue various avenues for doing so, such as refusing assignment to a no-coaching condition or surreptitious pursuit of alternative test-preparation activities. Randomized experiments do exist, but they rely on administering coaching outside of a time frame when students would normally be motivated to prepare for a test (e.g. college freshmen) and rely on samples not representative of the population taking admissions tests (Sackett, Burris, and Ryan 1989, for a review). As a result, the best available data on coaching effectiveness comes from large-scale observational studies of students representative of the test-taking population. These studies include a pretest (e.g., a PSAT score), a post-test (e.g., an operational SAT score), a measure of intervening test-preparation activities, and a variety of control variables (e.g., demographics).

Briggs (2009) located 30 SAT coaching studies, most using very small, nonrepresentative samples. He focuses on three large-scale studies as the basis for his conclusion that coaching produces effects of about 15–20 points on SAT-Math and 8–10 points on SAT-Verbal (the studies involve data prior to the switch to the Critical Reading label).[1]

Connelly, Sackett, and Waters (2013) report a re-analysis of one of these studies (Powers and Rock 1999). We describe their study in some detail here to illustrate key issues in the examination of coaching effects. They examined 4,248 high school juniors and seniors, 515 of whom reported engaging in formal coaching between taking the PSAT and taking the SAT. Connelly et al. first examined differences between the coached and uncoached groups on a variety of variables. Those seeking coaching were more likely to have used other practice material and were from more affluent, better-educated households. Thus coached and uncoached groups were not comparable prior to coaching. The researchers then examined differences between the coached and uncoached groups on PSAT score and found that the coached group averaged 23 points higher on SAT-M and 2 points lower on SAT-V.

Connelly et al. employed a matching design in an attempt to equate the coached and uncoached groups. They made use of propensity scoring, a technique in which they developed a regression equation using 55 variables to predict whether a student would participate in coaching. The result is a propensity score for each student: the probability that each would participate in coaching. The technique then matches each coached student with an uncoached student with a comparable propensity score. In other words, it identifies pairs of student with comparable profiles, one of whom sought coaching while the other did not. The researchers documented that this method successfully equated the groups on the measured variables. For SAT-M, a coaching effect of 15 points was found when controlling for pretest scores. This effect was only modestly reduced, to 14 points, when propensity matching was used. For SAT-V, however, a 10-point coaching effect controlling for pretest scores was reduced to 4 points when propensity matching was used.

Thus, while coaching effects are found in careful, large-sample research, they are dramatically smaller than the size of effects claimed by coaching providers. The 30 studies Briggs reviewed did include some producing much larger effects, but these were from very small, nonrepresentative samples. For example, the largest effect reported (a gain of 121 points in SAT-V) is from a study comparing 23 coached students and 12 uncoached students.

Several additional observations are in order. First, the effects discussed above are mean effects. Some individual students do indeed show dramatic improvement from initial test to retest. About 15% of the students in the Powers and Rock study, coached or not, improved by 100 or more points on each SAT section. Our sense is that large-effect retest results are most commonly found for students who failed to do even the most rudimentary preparation for the initial test. Familiarizing oneself with item types and refreshing one's memory about topics once learned but not recently practiced is likely very helpful; failure to do so can result in poor initial performance. Thus coaching can be helpful for some students, but it is not clear that similar effects cannot be attained via self-study.

Second, the large-sample studies to date lump together different types of coaching programs. One response to the research findings could be "that may be the average effect across coaching programs, but our coaching program is much better than average, and produces larger effects." We acknowledge the possibility of differential effects, but note that the evidentiary burden is on those making the claim of larger effects. To date, nobody has produced high-quality research on representative populations demonstrating that coaching can create large gains on college admissions tests.

Third, it has long been acknowledged that the best response to the concern that access to coaching is differentially available to students owing to issues of cost is to make free coaching readily available to all (Zwick 2002). The College Board's partnership with the Khan Academy to develop free and personalized SAT coaching operationalizes this idea. We look forward to research that examines student use of these resources and the effect of such use on test performance.

Conclusion

We have documented that testing is the subject of numerous claims that do not hold up under scrutiny. These claims are persistent, in part because tests are not popular (who likes being tested?) and thus there is a ready audience for test criticisms. We believe that the research in support of admissions test validity is compelling. Including test information in conjunction with other valid predictors of academic achievement (e.g., high school grades) results in a clearer picture of academic preparation and improves the quality of admissions decisions.

NOTES

1. The key studies are Powers and Rock's (1999) study of a stratified random sample of SAT takers, Briggs's (2002) study of coaching activities reported by participants in the National Educational Longitudinal Study of 1988, and Briggs and Domingue's (2009) studies of coaching activities reported by participants in the Educational Longitudinal Survey of 2002.

REFERENCES

Aguinis, H., Culpepper, S. A., and Pierce, C. A. (2010). Revival of test bias research in preemployment testing. *Journal of Applied Psychology, 95,* 648–680.

Arneson, J. J., Sackett, P. R., and Beatty, A. S. (2011). Ability-performance relationships in education and employment settings: Critical tests of the more-is-better and the good-enough hypothesis. *Psychological Science, 22,* 1336–1342.

Bartlett, C. J., Bobko, P., Mosier, S. B., and Hannan, R. (1978). Testing for fairness with a moderated multiple regression strategy: An alternative to differential analysis. *Personnel Psychology, 31*(2), 233–241.

Berry, C. M., and Sackett, P. R. (2009). Individual differences in course choice result in underestimation of the validity of college admissions systems. *Psychological Science, 20,* 822–830.

Berry, C. M., and Zhao, P. (2015). Addressing criticisms of existing predictive bias research: Cognitive ability test scores still overpredict African Americans' job performance. *Journal of Applied Psychology, 100*(1), 162.

Biernat, M. (2003). Toward a broader view of social stereotyping. *American Psychologist, 58*, 1019–1027.

Briggs, D. C. (2002). SAT coaching, bias and causal inference. Dissertation Abstracts International. DAI-A 64/12, p. 4433. (UMI No. 3115515)1999.

———. (2009). Preparation for college admissions exams. Arlington, VA: National Association of College Admissions Counselors.

Briggs, D. C., and Domingue, B.W. (2009) The effect of admissions test preparation: New evidence from ELS:02. Unpublished working paper. http://www.colorado.edu/education/faculty/derekbriggs/publications.html.

Cleary, T. A. (1968). Test bias: Prediction of grades of Negro and white students in integrated colleges. *Journal of Educational Measurement, 5*, 115–124.

College Board. (2015). 2015 college-bound seniors: Total group report. New York: The College Board.

Colvin, R. L. (1997). Q & A: Should UC do away with the SAT? *Los Angeles Times*, October 1.

Connelly, B. S., Sackett, P. R., and Waters, S. D. (2013). Balancing treatment and control groups in quasi-experiments: An introduction to propensity scoring. *Personnel Psychology, 66*, 407–442.

Coward, W. M., and Sackett, P. R. (1990). Linearity in ability-performance relationships: A reconfirmation. *Journal of Applied Psychology, 75*, 297–300.

Crede, M., and Kuncel, N. R. (2008). Study habits, study skills, and study attitudes: A meta-analysis of their relationship to academic performance among college students. *Perspectives on Psychological Science, 3*, 425–453.

Crede, M., Tynan, M. C., and Harms, P. D. (2016). Much ado about grit: A meta-analytic synthesis of grit literature. *Journal of Personality and Social Psychology, 113*(3), 492–511.

Crosby, F. J., Iyer, A., Clayton, S., and Downing, R. A. (2003). Affirmative action: Psychological data and the policy debates. *American Psychologist, 58*, 93–115.

Fischer, F. T., Schult, J., and Hell, B. (2013). Sex-specific differential prediction of college admission tests: A meta-analysis. *Journal of Educational Psychology, 105*, 478–488.

Geiser, S., and Studley, R. (2002). UC and the SAT: Predictive validity and differential impact of the SAT I and SAT II at the University of California. *Educational Assessment, 8*, 1–26.

Goldfarb, Z. A. (2014). These four charts show how the SAT favors rich, educated families. *Washington Post*, March 14. Retrieved from https://www.washingtonpost.com/news/wonk/wp/2014/03/05/these-four-charts-show-how-the-sat-favors-the-rich-educated-families/?utm_term=.67d6706d61cf.

Guinier, L. (2015). Ivy league's meritocracy lie: How Harvard and Yale cook the books for the 1 percent. *Salon*, January 11. Retrieved from http://www.salon.com/2015/01/11/ivy_leagues_meritocracy_lie_how_harvard_and_yale_cook_the_books_for_the_1_percent.

Hartigan, J., and Wigdor, A. K. (1989). *Fairness in employment testing*. Washington, DC: National Academies Press.

Hattie, J. (2008). *Visible learning: A synthesis of over 800 meta-analyses related to achievement*. New York: Routledge.

Hawk, J. (1970). Linearity of criterion-GATB aptitude relationships. *Measurement and Evaluation in Guidance, 2,* 249–251.

Higdem, J. L., Kostal, J., Kuncel, N. R., Sackett, P. R. Shen, W., Beatty, A. S., and Kiger, T. (2016). The role of socioeconomic status in SAT-freshman grade relationships across gender and racial/ethnic subgroups. *Educational Measurement: Issues and Practice, 35,* 21–28.

Hunt, E. (2008). Applying the theory of successful intelligence to education: The good, the bad and the ogre. *Perspectives on Psychological Science, 3*(6), 509–515.

Judge, T. A., Colbert, A. E., and Ilies, R. (2004). Intelligence and leadership: A quantitative review and test of theoretical propositions. *Journal of Applied Psychology, 89,* 542–552.

Keiser, H. N., Sackett, P. R., Kuncel, N. R., and Brothen, T. (2016). Why women perform better in college than admission scores would predict: Exploring the roles of conscientiousness and course-taking patterns. *Journal of Applied Psychology, 101,* 569–581.

Kling, K. C., Noftle, E. E., and Robins, R. W. (2013). Why do standardized tests underpredict women's academic performance? The role of conscientiousness. *Social Psychology and Personality Science, 4,* 600–606.

Kohn, A. (2001). Two cheers for an end to the SAT. *Chronicle of Higher Education, 9,* p. B-12.

Kostal, J. W., Kuncel, N. R., and Sackett, P. R. (2016). Grade inflation marches on: Grade increases from the 1990s to 2000s. *Educational Measurement: Issues and Practice, 35,* 11–20.

Kuncel, N. R., and Beatty, A. (2013). Thinking at work: Intelligence, critical thinking, job knowledge, and reasoning. In K. Geissinger, B. A. Bracken, J. F. Carlson, J. C. Hansen, N. R. Kuncel, S. P. Reise, and M. C. Rodriguez (Eds.), *APA handbook of testing and assessment in psychology* (pp. 417–435). Washington DC: American Psychological Association.

Kuncel, N. R., and Hezlett, S. A. (2007). Standardized tests predict graduate students' success. *Science, 315,* 1080–1081.

Kuncel, N. R., Hezlett, S. A., and Ones, D. S. (2001). A comprehensive meta-analysis of the predictive validity of the graduate record examinations: Implications for graduate student selection and performance. *Psychological Bulletin, 127*(1), 162.

———. (2004). Academic performance, career potential, creativity, and job performance: Can one construct predict them all? *Journal of Personality and Social Psychology* [*Special Section, Cognitive Abilities: 100 Years after Spearman (1904)*], *86,* 148–161.

Kuncel, N. R., Kochevar, R. J., and Ones, D. S. (2014). A meta-analysis of letters of recommendation in college and graduate admissions: Reasons for hope. *International Journal of Selection and Assessment, 22,* 101–107.

Kuncel, N. R., Ones, D. S., and Sackett, P. R. (2010). Individual differences as predictors of work, educational, and broad life outcomes. *Personality and Individual Differences, 49,* 331–336.

Kuncel, N. R., Rose, M., Ejiogu, K., and Yang, Z. (2014). Cognitive ability and socioeconomic status relations with job performance. *Intelligence, 46,* 203–208.

Lievens, F., Buyse, T., and Sackett, P. R. (2005). The operational validity of a video-based situational judgment test for medical college admissions: Illustrating the importance of matching predictor and criterion construct domains. *Journal of Applied Psychology, 90,* 442–452.

Linn, R. L. (1973). Fair test use in selection. *Review of Educational Research, 43,* 139–161.

Lubinski, D. (2009). Exceptional cognitive ability: The phenotype. *Behavior Genetics, 39*(4), 350–358.

Mattern, K. D., and Patterson, B. F. (2013). Test of slope and intercept bias in college admissions: A response to Aguinis, Culpepper, and Pierce (2010). *Journal of Applied Psychology, 98,* 134–147.

Murphy, S. R., Klieger, D. M., Borneman, M., and Kuncel, N. R. (2009). The predictive power of personal statements in admissions: A meta-analysis and cautionary tale. *College and University, 84,* 83–88.

Ones, D. S., Viswesvaran, C., and Dilchert, S. (2004). Cognitive ability in selection decisions. In O. Wilhelm and R. W. Engle (Eds.), *Handbook of understanding and measuring intelligence* (pp. 431–468). Thousand Oaks, CA: Sage.

Oswald, F. L., Schmitt, N., Kim, B. H., Ramsay, L. J., Gillespie, M. A. (2004). Developing a biodata measure and situational judgment inventory as predictors of college student performance. *Journal of Applied Psychology, 89,* 187–207.

Powers, D. E., and D. A. Rock. (1999). Effects of coaching on SAT I: Reasoning test scores. *Journal of Educational Measurement, 36*(2), 93–118.

Ramist, L., Lewis, C., and McCamley, L. (1990). Implications of using freshman GPA as the criterion for the predictive validity of the SAT. In W. W. Willingham, C. Lewis, R. Morgan, and L. Ramist (Eds.), *Predicting college grades: An analysis of institutional trends over two decades* (pp. 253–288). Princeton, NJ: Educational Testing Service.

Roth, P. L., BeVier, C. A., Switzer III, F. S., and Schippmann, J. S. (1996). Meta-analyzing the relationship between grades and job performance. *Journal of Applied Psychology, 81,* 548–556.

Sackett, P. R. (1998). Performance assessment in education and professional certification: Lessons for personnel selection? In M. D. Hakel (Ed.), *Beyond multiple choice: Evaluating alternatives to traditional testing for selection.* Mahwah, NJ: Lawrence Erlbaum Associates.

Sackett, P. R., Borneman, M. J., and Connelly, B. S. (2008). High stakes testing in higher education and employment: Appraising the evidence for validity and fairness. *American Psychologist, 63*(4), 215.

Sackett, P. R., Burris, L. R., and Ryan, A. M. (1989). Coaching and practice effects in personnel selection. In C. L. Cooper and I. T. Robertson (Eds.) *International review of industrial and organizational psychology.* West Sussex, UK: John Wiley and Sons.

Sackett, P. R., Kuncel, N. R., Arneson, J. J., Cooper, S. R., and Waters, S. D. (2009). Does socioeconomic status explain the relationship between admissions tests and post-secondary academic performance? *Psychological Bulletin, 135*(1), 1–22.

Sackett, P. R., Kuncel, N. R., Beatty, A. S., Rigdon, J. L., Shen, W., and Kiger, T. B. (2012). The role of socioeconomic status in SAT-grade relationships and in college admissions decisions. *Psychological Science, 23*(9), 1000–1007.

Sackett, P. R., Laczo, R. M., and Lippe, Z. P. (2003). Differential prediction and the use of multiple predictors: The omitted variables problem. *Journal of Applied Psychology, 88,* 1046–1056.

Sackett, P. R., and Shen, W. (2009). Subgroup differences on cognitively loaded tests in contexts other than personnel selection. In J. Outtz (Ed.), *Adverse impact: Implications for organizational staffing and high stakes selection* (pp. 329–352). Mahwah, NJ: Lawrence Erlbaum Associates.

Sedlacek, W. E. (2004). *Beyond the big test: Noncognitive assessment in higher education.* San Francisco: Jossey-Bass.

Shen, W., Sackett, P. R., Kuncel, N. R., Beatty, A. S., Rigdon, J. L., and Kiger, T. B. (2012). Determinants of SAT validity variability across schools. *Applied Measurement in Education, 25*(3), 197–219.

Shewach, O., Kuncel, N. R., Sackett, P. R., and McNeal, K. (2017). Standardized test scores and high school grades predict advanced course taking in college. Unpublished manuscript. Minneapolis: University of Minnesota.

Sternberg, R. J., and Rainbow Project Collaborators. (2006). The Rainbow Project: Enhancing the SAT through assessments of analytical, practical, and creative skills. *Intelligence, 34,* 321–350.

Sternberg, R. J., and Williams, W. M. (1997). Does the Graduate Record Examination predict meaningful success in the graduate training of psychology? A case study. *American Psychologist, 52*(6), 630.

Stricker, L. J., Rock, D. A., and Burton, N. W. (1993). Sex differences in predictions of college grades from scholastic aptitude test scores. *Journal of Educational Psychology, 85,* 710–718. http://dx.doi.org/10.1037/0022-0663.85.4.710.

Thomas, L., Kuncel, N. R., and Crede, M. (2007). Noncognitive variables in college admissions: The case of the Non-Cognitive Questionnaire. *Educational and Psychological Measurement, 67,* 635–657.

Young, J. W. (1991). Gender bias in predicting college academic performance: A new approach using item response theory. *Journal of Educational Measurement, 28,* 37–47. http://dx.doi.org/10.1111/j.1745-3984.1991.tb00342.x.

———. (2001). *Differential validity, differential prediction, and college admission testing: A comprehensive review and analysis.* College Board Research Report No. 2001-6. New York: The College Board.

Ziomek, R. L., and Svec, J. C. (1995). *High school grades and achievement: Evidence of grade inflation.* ACT Research Report Series 95-3. Iowa City: American College Testing Program.

Zumbrun, J. (2014). SAT scores and income inequality: How wealthier kids rank higher. *Wall Street Journal,* October 7. Retrieved from https://blogs.wsj.com/economics/2014/10/07/sat-scores-and-income-inequality-how-wealthier-kids-rank-higher.

Zwick, R. (2002). *Fair game? The use of standardized admissions tests in higher education.* New York: RoutledgeFalmer.

2

The Core Case for Testing

The State of Our Research Knowledge

Emily J. Shaw

*A*mid continued debate about the use of standardized college entrance exams, this chapter offers a comprehensive reminder of why standardized admissions tests such as the ACT and SAT are still widely used by college admissions officers, enrollment managers, and institutions of higher education. Standardized tests are important because they offer a common benchmark against which to compare students from disparate educational backgrounds, an assessment of the skills required for success in college, and the ability to predict college and university performance.

As Shaw explains in detail, research consistently finds that standardized admissions tests are a strong predictor of postsecondary student performance. When these tests are used in conjunction with high school grade point average (HSGPA), the ability to predict student performance in college is that much stronger. Drawing on data from a national longitudinal database of hundreds of thousands of students at more than 300 four-year institutions, Shaw demonstrates that higher SAT scores are associated with better college outcomes such as college GPA, retention, and completion, and that SAT scores improve the prediction of those outcomes beyond the use of HSGPA alone

Shaw also deftly highlights often-overlooked aspects of the debate over standardized admissions tests and test-optional admissions. For example, standardized test critics frequently claim the correlations between standardized tests and first-year college GPA are not very high, and thus that standardized tests are not very useful. As Shaw notes, *these critics almost invariably report uncorrected correlations, rather than corrected correlations that account for restriction of range, which allow for a more accurate representation of the relationship between standardized admissions tests and first-year GPA. Related to this, correlations are often best understood in the context of other correlational relationships, as correlation coefficients in the social sciences are often not as high as one might expect. Similarly, critics often claim that the SAT adds little predictive power because of its purportedly low contribution to the amount of variance "explained" in a regression model. But as this chapter notes, multicollinearity—a condition whereby two or more predictors may be correlated, which can alter the interpretation of coefficients— may influence the overall amount of variance explained. Thus, when adding the SAT after HSGPA, as many researchers do, it is not surprising that this would add little value to the variance already explained by high school GPA.*

Shaw argues that the evidence that testing provides significant, incremental, predictive value beyond high grades is crucial to how we should approach admissions policy. Just as a good detective would not exclude useful evidence about a suspect, she concludes, so too should a good enrollment manager not exclude additional standardized test information about a prospective student. Not only can this additional information aid in admission and placement decision making, but it can aid in the administration of academic supports offered on campus to help all students succeed.

For generations, college and university enrollment managers have used standardized tests to inform their admission decisions. This is because tests like the SAT and ACT serve as a common metric by which to measure and understand students' college readiness. They are also powerful predictors of college success. This chapter reviews the research-based evidence that supports the use of standardized tests in college admission decisions and also evaluates some of the common claims made by advocates of test-optional admission policies. A discussion of useful ways to connect admission test validity research findings with best practices follows.

Evidence Supporting the Use of Standardized Tests in Admission Decisions

The Importance of Standardization

Colleges and universities receive many different pieces of information from students applying for admission. Among the most important, as rated by college admission professionals, are high school grades in college preparatory coursework, the rigor of the curriculum, high school grade point average (HSGPA), and admission test scores (Clinedinst, Koranteng, and Nicola 2016). Other factors often considered in admission decisions include application essays, letters of recommendation, demonstrated interest in the institution, and extracurricular activities.

With the exception of admission test scores, none of the criteria above are standardized (administered and scored or rated in a consistent and standard manner) across applicants. This lack of standardization is problematic for a number of reasons. First, there are a number of factors, such as HSGPA or the rigor of coursework in high school, that do not necessarily hold common meaning for students across, or even within, high schools (Laird 2005). For example, research has shown that there is variation in the scale and the method of calculation used for HSGPA, making it extremely difficult to make comparisons across students from different high schools. This is important because HSGPA is typically the primary criteria used for admissions decisions at colleges and universities. A high school may use a GPA scale of 0–4.00 or 60–100, for example, and may choose to recalculate and weight the HSGPA to additionally reflect the rigor of the students' coursework (Warne, Nagaishi, Slade, Hermesmeyer, and Peck 2014). These scale and calculation inconsistencies also don't account for general differences in grading standards that impact the value of an unstandardized measure. A large body of research has shown that teacher-assigned grades (such as those included in the HSGPA calculation), are highly subjective and therefore loaded with measurement error (Finkelstein 1913; Lauterbach 1928; Ruediger 1914). In addition, recent research presented by Hurwitz and Lee in chapter 3 shows that students are receiving higher average high school grades without corresponding increases in average SAT scores, indicating artificial inflation in grades that further erodes the meaning of the HSGPA.

Second, in addition to the lack of consistent meaning across unstandardized measures, there are also concerns related to the authenticity and independent authorship of application materials such as essays or information on awards, honors, or activities, which can be difficult to verify (Laird 2005). Third, the use of unstandardized measures places a substantial strain on admission offices to conduct critical, in-depth file reviews to evaluate the meaning of these measures across applicants. This process can be time-consuming and difficult to accomplish in a fair manner, particularly when an institution may receive tens of thousands of applicants (Rigol 2003; Schmitt et al. 2009). Admission reviews and ratings made by application readers are based on subjective information that is susceptible to measurement error, including the reader's level of motivation, personal values, interest, attention span, or fatigue. In addition, there is variation in the amount of training readers receive as well as differences in reader standards (Rosenthal and Rosnow 1991). While reader training exercises try to reduce these sources of human error as much as possible, one of the best approaches to alleviate some of the ambiguity that comes with the use of unstandardized measures is to also use standardized measures, such as the SAT or ACT (Shaw and Milewski 2004).

The Value of Standardized Tests above High School Grades in Understanding College Outcomes

Standardized admission tests, in addition to serving as a common yardstick by which to evaluate and compare student performance, are also strong predictors of future performance in college.[1] Decades of research has shown that the SAT and ACT are predictive of important college outcomes, including grade point average (GPA), retention, and completion, and they provide unique and additional information in the prediction of college outcomes over high school grades (Mattern and Patterson 2014; Radunzel and Mattern 2015; Radunzel and Noble 2012; Shaw 2015; Westrick et al. 2015). Research examining the relationship between test scores and their intended uses is generally referred to as validity research. The accumulation of findings from SAT and ACT validity studies provide a great deal of evidence to support the use of these tests for admission decisions.

Many studies have shown a strong, independent relationship between SAT scores and first-year college performance (Agronow and Studley 2007; Sackett et al. 2012). However, it may be more useful to focus on the added value of SAT scores above HSGPA in understanding college performance, since many institutions use both factors when examining admission and retention. Figure 2.1 shows the relationship between the SAT total score band (SAT Critical Reading + Mathematics + Writing) with mean first-year grade point average (FYGPA) at different levels of HSGPA (e.g., A, B, C or lower) (Patterson and Mattern 2013). Note that the SAT scores are from the pre–March 2016 SAT. This graph represents data from more than 200,000 students attending 149 four-year institutions. It shows that for each level of HSGPA, higher SAT score bands are associated with higher mean FYGPAs, demonstrating the added value of the SAT above HSGPA in understanding FYGPA. As an example, consider students with an HSGPA in the "A" range. Students with an SAT composite score between 600 and 1190 had an average FYGPA of 2.5. However, those same A students with an SAT score between 2100 and 2400 had an average FYGPA of 3.6. Note that similar trends are evident when narrower HSGPA levels are examined such as A+, A, A– (Shaw

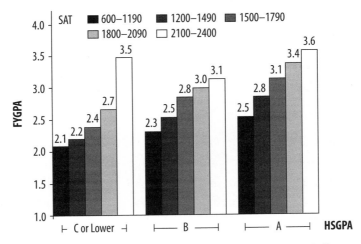

Fig. 2.1. Incremental Validity of the SAT: Mean First-Year College Grade Point Average (FYGPA) by SAT Score Band, Controlling for High School Grade Point Average (HSGPA). *Note*: SAT score bands are based on the sum of SAT-Critical Reading, SAT-Math, and SAT-Writing tests. HSGPA ranges were defined as "A" range: 4.33 (A+), 4.00 (A), and 3.67 (A−); "B" range: 3.33 (B+), 3.00 (B), and 2.67 (B−); and "C or Lower" range: 2.33 (C+) or lower. *Source*: Patterson and Mattern 2013. Figure and research materials courtesy of The College Board © 2013. Used with permission.

et al. 2016). When considering applicants with the same HSGPA, it is clear that the added information of a student's SAT score(s) can provide greater detail on how that student would be expected to perform at an institution.

The SAT remains similarly predictive of cumulative GPA throughout four years of college. Other large-scale studies and meta-analyses provide strong support for the notion that the predictive validity of test scores such as the SAT is not limited to near-term outcomes such as FYGPA but also longer-term academic and career outcomes (Sackett, Borneman, and Connelly 2008). Figure 2.2 demonstrates the added value of the SAT above HSGPA in understanding cumulative GPA through the fourth year of college (Mattern and Patterson 2011). This graph represents data from more than 55,000 students attending 55 four-year institutions. Using students with an HSGPA in the "A" range as an example, those with an SAT total score between 600 and 1190 had an average cumulative GPA of 2.8. However, those same A students with an SAT score between 2100 and 2400 had an average cumulative GPA of 3.5. The weaker pattern for students in the "C or Lower" HSGPA category is related to low sample size.

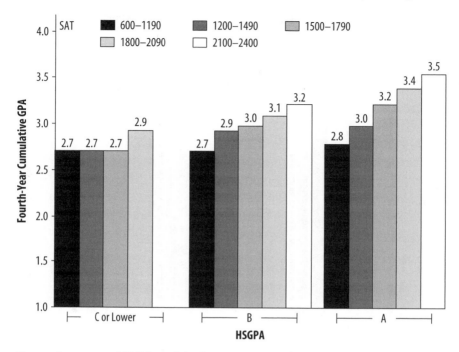

Fig. 2.2. Incremental Validity of the SAT: Mean Fourth-Year Cumulative Grade Point Average (GPA) by SAT Score Band within High School Grade Point Average (HSGPA). *Note*: SAT score bands are based on the sum of SAT-Critical Reading, SAT-Math, and SAT-Writing tests. HSGPA ranges were defined as "A" range: 4.33 (A+), 4.00 (A), and 3.67 (A–); "B" range: 3.33 (B+), 3.00 (B), and 2.67 (B–); and "C or Lower" range: 2.33 (C+) or lower. Categories with fewer than 15 students are not displayed. *Source*: Mattern and Patterson 2011. Figure and research materials courtesy of The College Board © 2011. Used with permission.

Similar evidence is available for the incremental validity of SAT scores above HSGPA in understanding student retention and completion rates in college. Figure 2.3 shows the mean second-, third-, and fourth-year retention rates *and* four-year graduation rates by SAT score band, controlling for HSGPA for the 2006 entering college cohort. The results show that higher SAT scores are associated with higher retention rates throughout each year of college, as well as with higher four-year graduation rates (Mattern and Patterson 2014). As time passed in the college experience, the percentage of students retained decreased. However, students with higher SAT scores had higher retention rates. The graph shows, for example, that students with an HSGPA in the "A" range and an SAT score of 2100 or higher had a mean four-year completion rate (from the same institution) of 76%, while those

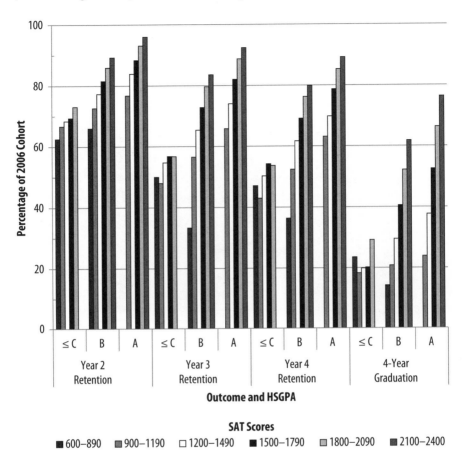

Fig. 2.3. Retention through Four-Year Graduation by SAT and High School Grade Point Average (HSGPA) (2006 Cohort). *Source:* Mattern and Patterson 2014. Figure and research materials courtesy of The College Board © 2014. Used with permission.

with an SAT score of 1200–1490 had a 38% rate of completion in four years (from the same institution). This is a clear example of how the HSGPA is useful but does not provide a truly comprehensive understanding of student performance.

In addition, a recent model-based study examined the utility of traditional admission measures in predicting college graduation within four years and found that both SAT scores and HSGPA are indeed predictive of this outcome (Mattern, Patterson, and Wyatt 2013). This study modeled the relationship of SAT scores and HSPGA with four-year graduation and confirmed that including both SAT

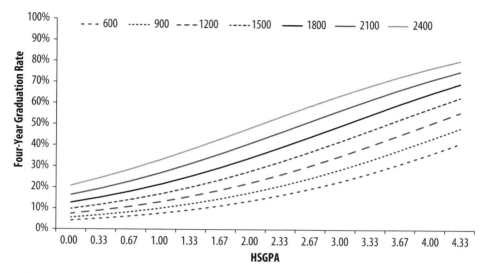

Fig. 2.4. Expected Four-Year Graduation Rates by SAT and High School Grade Point Average (HSGPA). *Source*: Mattern, Patterson, and Wyatt 2013. Figure and research materials courtesy of The College Board © 2013. Used with permission.

scores and HSGPA in the model resulted in better prediction than a model that included only SAT scores or only HSGPA. Figure 2.4 depicts the model-based, expected four-year graduation rates by different SAT scores and HSGPAs. Within HSGPA, as SAT scores increase, so too does the likelihood of graduation in four years. Note that students with an HSGPA of B (3.00) and a composite SAT score of 1200 are expected to have a 35% probability of graduating in four years, compared with a 57% probability of graduating for students with the same HSGPA but a composite SAT score of 2100.

In addition to the outcomes considered important to admission decisions noted above (e.g., GPA, retention, completion), SAT scores are also related to performance in specific college courses, providing evidence for their utility in course placement decisions (Mattern, Patterson, and Kobrin 2012). This is particularly true in instances where the content of the college course is aligned with the content tested on the SAT (e.g., the SAT writing section with English course grades and the SAT mathematics section with mathematics course grades). Figure 2.5 depicts the positive linear relationship between SAT Critical Reading and Writing scores and English course grades in the first year of college. Those students with the highest SAT Critical Reading and Writing scores (700–800 range) earned English course grades that were almost a whole letter grade higher than those of

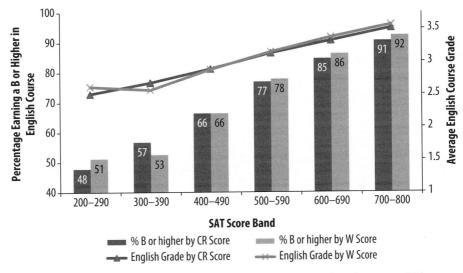

Fig. 2.5. The Relationship between SAT Critical Reading (CR) and Writing (W) Scores and First-Year College English Grades. *Source*: Mattern, Patterson, and Kobrin 2012. Figure and research materials courtesy of The College Board © 2012. Used with permission.

students with the lowest SAT scores (200–290). In addition, while only about half of the students in the lowest SAT score band in SAT Critical Reading or Writing earned a B or higher in college English, more than 90% of students in the highest SAT Critical Reading or Writing score band earned a B or higher in English.

Similar to English course grades, there is a positive relationship between SAT mathematics scores and mathematics course grades in the first year of college (Mattern et al. 2012). Figure 2.6 depicts the average mathematics course grade by SAT score band as well as the percentage of students earning a B or higher in their first-year mathematics courses by SAT score band. While students in the highest SAT Mathematics score band (700–800) earned an average mathematics course grade of a B+ (3.31) in their first year, those students in the two lowest SAT score bands (200–390) earned an average mathematics course grade below a C (1.92). Also shown in figure 2.6, 78% of those students in the highest SAT Mathematics score band earned a B or higher in their first-year mathematics courses, while only 32% of the students in the lowest SAT Mathematics score band earned a B or higher.

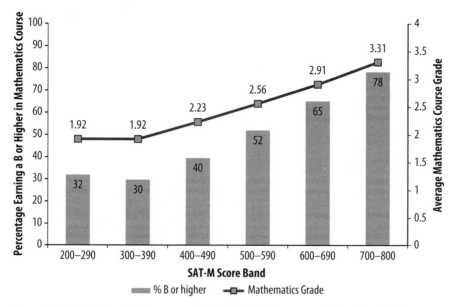

Fig. 2.6. The Relationship between SAT Math (M) Scores and First-Year College Mathematics Grades. *Source*: Mattern, Patterson, and Kobrin 2012. Figure and research materials courtesy of The College Board © 2012. Used with permission.

USING THE HSGPA AND SAT TOGETHER PROVIDES THE MOST ACCURATE PREDICTION OF COLLEGE OUTCOMES

Correlational evidence clearly shows that the SAT and HSGPA are strong predictors of FYGPA, with the multiple correlation (SAT and HSGPA → FYGPA), typically in the mid .60s (Mattern and Patterson 2014). For context, correlations of this strength represent the relationship between gender and height or the distance between the equator and daily temperature readings in the United States (Meyer et al. 2001). The SAT and HSGPA → FYGPA correlational results are consistent across multiple entering classes of first-year, first-time students (from 2006 to 2010) representing hundreds of thousands of students, providing further validity evidence in terms of the generalizability of the results. Figure 2.7 displays the correlations of SAT, HSGPA, and the combination of SAT and HSGPA with FYGPA for the 2006 through 2010 entering first-year cohorts. Both SAT scores and HSGPA are individually strong predictors of FYGPA, with correlations in the mid .50s. Combining SAT scores and HSGPA yields the highest predictive validity (i.e., the dark solid line is the highest). Using the two measures together to predict

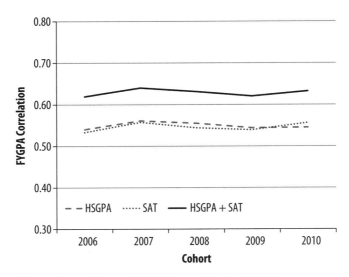

Fig. 2.7. Correlations of High School Grade Point Average (HSGPA) and SAT with First-Year College Grade Point Average (FYGPA) (2006–2010 Cohorts). *Note*: Correlations were corrected for restriction of range within institutions and pooled. *Source*: Mattern and Patterson 2014. Figure and research materials courtesy of The College Board © 2014. Used with permission.

FYGPA is more powerful than using either HSGPA or SAT scores on their own because they each measure slightly different aspects of a student's achievement (Willingham 2005).

To illustrate some of the *practical* aspects of the SAT and HSGPA validity research findings, we can review an example using actual data from a four-year institution in a pilot validity study (Shaw et al. 2016) of the new SAT (table 2.1).[2] In this scenario, Student A and Student B apply to the same institution. Both students are Hispanic and female and have an HSGPA of B, or 3.00. If the institution only used HSGPA to predict the students' FYGPA, both students would be predicted to have the same FYGPA of 3.00. However, Student A and Student B had different scores on the SAT. Student A earned a 600 and 590 on the Evidence-Based Reading and Writing and Math section of the redesigned SAT, respectively, and Student B earned a 310 and 410 on those sections. Using both HSGPA and SAT performance in the institution-specific predictive model, Student A is predicted to earn a FYGPA of 3.40 and Student B is predicted to earn a FYGPA of 2.69. Predicting FYGPA using both HSGPA and SAT performance provides more information

Table 2.1. Real-world example of improved prediction of FYGPA using the SAT with HSGPA in admission decisions

	Student A	Student B
Race/ethnicity	Hispanic	Hispanic
Gender	Female	Female
HSGPA	3.00	3.00
SAT Evidence-Based Reading and Writing score	600	310
SAT Math score	590	410
Predicted FYGPA based on HSGPA only	3.00	3.00
Predicted FYGPA based on HSGPA and SAT	3.40	2.69
Actual FYGPA earned in college	4.00	2.48

Notes: FYGPA = first-year college grade point average; HSGPA = high school grade point average. Predicted FYGPAs are based on the institution's specific models.

about each student and creates a better prediction of actual FYGPA performance. Student A ultimately earned a FYGPA of 4.00 at the institution and Student B earned a FYGPA of 2.48. Both students' actual FYGPAs were much closer to the predicted FYGPAs that were arrived at using *both* HSGPA and SAT performance rather than HSGPA alone. In other words, a clearer understanding of future student performance is arrived at by using both SAT scores and HSGPA. This will result in institutions making better decisions for the provision of additional instructional supports, interventions, or appropriate course placements for students if the institution wants to admit a student and also ensure that the student *succeeds* there.

Admission Test Misunderstandings and Clarifications

While there are thousands of institutional and national validity studies of standardized tests for use in admission decisions, the validity of these tests for use in college admission decisions remains largely misunderstood (Mattern et al. 2009; NACAC 2016). Some misunderstandings seem to be related to concerns about fairness in the construction and use of scores (Sackett, Borneman, and Connelly 2008), while others appear to be more related to the difficulty in clearly communicating the statistics or methodologies typically used in conveying admission test score validity information (Bridgeman, Burton, and Pollack 2008; Camara and Shaw 2012; Mattern et al. 2009; Sackett, Borneman, and Connelly 2008; Wainer and Robinson 2003). These test fairness and validity research misunderstandings can and often do result in flawed arguments offered for the implementation of test-optional admission policies (Dollinger 2011; Emmanuel College n.d.; Everson 2000; Schmitt et al. 2007).

FAIRNESS

It is not uncommon to hear claims that admission tests are biased against minority students, or that they serve as a barrier to admission for underrepresented students (Sackett, Borneman, and Connelly 2008).[3] While this chapter does not serve as an exhaustive review of admission test fairness research, it does present relevant information refuting such criticisms with factual and research-based information.

First, every item used in an SAT form has been previously pretested and extensively reviewed. Pretesting can serve to ensure that items are not ambiguous or confusing, to examine item responses to determine the difficulty level or the degree to which the item differentiates between more or less able students, and understand whether students from different racial/ethnic groups or gender groups respond to the item differently (also called differential item functioning). Differential item functioning (DIF) analyses compare the item performance of two groups of test takers (e.g., males versus females) who have been matched on ability. Items displaying DIF indicate that the item functions in a different way for one subgroup than it does for another. Items with sizable DIF, favoring one group over another, undergo further review to determine whether the item should be revised and re-pretested or eliminated altogether.

Many critics of tests and testing presume that the existence of mean score differences by subgroups indicates that the test or measure is biased against underrepresented minority students, that the test measures nothing more than socioeconomic status, or both. However, although attention should be paid to consistent group mean differences, these differences do not necessarily signal bias. Groups may have different experiences, opportunities, or interests in particular areas, which can impact performance on the skills or abilities being measured (Sackett, Borneman, and Connelly 2008). Many studies have found that the mean subgroup differences found on the SAT (e.g., by gender, race/ethnicity, socioeconomic status) are also found in virtually all measures of educational outcomes, including other large-scale standardized tests, high school performance and graduation, and college attendance (Aud et al. 2013; Kobrin, Sathy, and Shaw 2006).

Moreover, one would expect that if the SAT were biased against African American, American Indian, or Hispanic students, for example, it would underpredict their college performance. In other words, this accusation would presume that underrepresented minority students would perform much better in college than their SAT scores predict and that the SAT would act as a barrier in their college admission process. In reality, underrepresented minority students tend to earn slightly *lower* grades in college than predicted by their SAT scores. This finding is consistent across cohorts and in later outcomes such as second-, third-, and fourth-year cumulative GPA (Mattern and Patterson 2014).

In addition, HSGPA results in even greater overprediction of college grades than SAT scores, while the use of the two measures together results in the least amount of overprediction of college grades for underrepresented minority students (Mattern et al. 2009; Mattern and Patterson 2014). Thus, ignoring test scores in the admission process can result in the acceptance of students who will be more likely to struggle academically and to be at greater risk of leaving the institution—a proposition that presents problems for both the student and the institution (Holmes 2016). With an improved understanding of how students will likely perform at an institution, proper supports can be put in place to assist them in succeeding there.

With regard to socioeconomic status, it is important to note that almost all educational measures are *related* to measures of socioeconomic status (Camara and Schmidt 1999; Kobrin, Sathy, and Shaw 2006). However, research examining SAT scores and socioeconomic status refutes the notion that the SAT is merely a measure of a student's wealth (Sackett et al. 2012). Studies have shown that across multiple samples of college students, the relationship between SAT scores and college grades remains relatively unaffected after controlling for the influence of socioeconomic status. In other words, contrary to popular belief, scientific evidence shows that the relationship between SAT scores and college grades is largely independent of a student's socioeconomic status and not the consequence of it (Sackett et al. 2009, 2012).

Validity Research

In addition to general misunderstandings related to the fairness of admission tests, there are a number of false impressions related to the design and interpretation of test validity research. While serving as president of Reed College, Colin Diver noted that many institutions rationalize their newly initiated test-optional admission policies by stating that admission tests are flawed measures of academic ability. He offered the following observation in an opinion piece in the *New York Times*: "Standardized tests, for all their recognized imperfections, are carefully designed and tested to measure such basic intellectual skills as reading comprehension, vocabulary, critical thinking, computational ability and quantitative reasoning. Are admission officers at SAT-optional universities saying that the test scores do not provide probative evidence of the possession of these skills? Are they saying that these skills are not relevant to success in the educational programs of their colleges? Neither claim is remotely plausible" (Diver 2006, A27).

Diver's questions point up a number of misunderstandings related to conducting and consuming admission test validity research that are resulting in some misinformed claims about the utility of these tests. Many of these misapprehensions relate to the use of correlation coefficients in validity research, as well as to understanding regression models and, in particular, the concept of variance explained.

CORRELATION COEFFICIENTS

Predictive validity evidence is often reported with correlation coefficients, which can be difficult for people to interpret and for campus representatives to correctly calculate. A correlation coefficient is one way of describing the linear relationship between two measures (Anastasi and Urbina 1997). Correlations range from −1 to +1, with a perfect positive correlation (+1.00) indicating that a top-scoring person on test 1 would also be the top-scoring person on test 2, and the second-best scorer on test 1 would also be the second-best scorer on test 2, and so on, through the poorest-performing person on both tests. A correlation of zero would indicate no relationship between test 1 and test 2. Note that a correlation of .50 would *not* indicate that a test predicts well or correctly 50% of the time, thus making the correlation coefficient a somewhat difficult statistic for people to interpret and intuitively understand (Camara and Shaw 2012).

General guidelines for interpreting correlation coefficients suggest that a small correlation has an absolute value of approximately .10; a medium correlation has an absolute value of approximately .30; and a large correlation has an absolute value of approximately .50 or higher (Cohen 1988). Raw correlation coefficients in educational and psychological testing are rarely above .30 (Meyer et al. 2001). Although this value may sound low, it may be helpful to consider the correlation coefficients that represent more familiar relationships in our lives. For example, the association between a major league baseball player's batting average and his success in getting a hit in a particular instance at bat is .06; the correlation between antihistamines and reduced sneezing and runny nose is .11; and the correlation between prominent movie critics' reviews and box office success is .17 (Meyer et al. 2001).

The uncorrected, observed, or raw correlation coefficient representing the relationship between the SAT and first-year grade point average (FYGPA) tends to be in the mid .30s. When corrected for restriction of range, a concept discussed below, the correlation coefficient tends to be in the mid .50s, representing a strong relationship. Note that it is a widely accepted practice to statistically correct correlation coefficients in admission validity research for restriction of range because the raw correlation tends to underestimate the true relationship between the test score and the college outcome (American Educational Research Association, American Psychological Association, and National Council on Measurement in Education 1999; Mattern et al. 2009). Without access to information on how students who were not admitted or did not enroll would have performed at the institution, we only have a small glimpse into how the tests work for selection—for those students who were admitted and enrolled. This has the effect of restricting the variability or range in test scores available for analysis, since the test scores available tend to be the higher scores of students who were admitted (selected in part by using those scores), minimizing the test score–criterion relationship.

A college or university that is examining relationships between admission test scores and FYGPAs would most likely calculate an *uncorrected* or raw correlation coefficient. Not only is this coefficient an underestimation of the true relationship, but it may sound much lower than an SAT-FYGPA correlation coefficient shared in national validity studies, reporting on corrected correlation coefficients, averaged across hundreds of institutions (Mattern et al. 2009). This could lead to false conclusions that the relationship between test scores and college grades at an institution is much lower than the relationship reported in national research, and therefore, that the test is not useful at that particular institution.

Variance Explained

Multiple regression analysis is often used in validity research to understand how factors such as HSGPA and SAT predict outcomes such as FYGPA. An R^2 value is calculated, indicating the amount of variance in FYGPA "explained" by the model. Some critics of standardized tests have posited that with so much variance unaccounted for in the predicted outcome (e.g., FYGPA), admission tests must not be useful (Dollinger 2011). Others have argued that the additional variance in college grades that is explained by test scores above HSGPA, typically less than 10%, seems unimpressive (Bridgeman, Burton, and Pollack 2008). However, the use of R^2 as an effect size is not always the proper metric for understanding relationships between test scores and college outcomes in the real world: "It is common in education to present an R^2 as an effect size, yet there are circumstances in which the R^2 is close to 0.00 and the practical significance is considerable" (Wainer and Robinson 2003, 26). To illustrate this concept, Wainer and Robinson describe a medical study where, using random assignment, approximately 11,000 physicians were given an aspirin every other day for five years and another group of 11,000 physicians were given a placebo every other day for five years. Statistical results showed that heart attacks occurred more frequently in the control group, but the R^2 indicated that less than 1% of the variance was accounted for. The study showed that there were 189 heart attacks in the placebo group and 104 in the aspirin group, so the placebo group had almost twice the incidence of heart attacks. This seems to have more meaning than reporting an R^2 of .001 (Bridgeman, Burton, and Pollack 2008).

When a college or university examines a regression equation and cites a low percentage of variance explained in FYGPA by SAT scores, it often incorrectly dismisses the value of the SAT. However, there are more useful ways to practically examine and communicate the utility of test scores at an institution. As an example from their research, Bridgeman and his colleagues point out: "The SAT 'explaining' less than 10 percent of the variance given HSGPA may seem trivial, but the difference between a 16 percent success rate and a 73 percent success rate for students with similar high school records, but different SAT scores, appears less trivial" (Bridgeman, Burton, and Pollack 2008, 24). The College Board and ACT have adopted similar, more accessible approaches in their communication of test validity information. Specifically, they use percentages or probabilities of students that fall into different outcome categories based on test scores or grades, because they are simpler to understand and hold more intrinsic meaning than percentages of variance, which is a more complex, vague, and misconstrued concept (Mattern, Radunzel, and Westrick 2015; Shaw et al. 2016).

There is also the issue of multicollinearity in regression analysis, whereby two or more of the predictor variables are highly correlated, which alters the interpretations of coefficients and results (Mattern et al. 2009). Because SAT scores and HSGPA are at least moderately correlated, if the HSGPA is entered first into the regression model, it will account for the common variance shared between SAT and HSGPA (Shaw et al. 2016). An institution using this approach in its analyses would end up underestimating the straightforward relationship between test scores and the outcome. Thus, the institution might falsely report its results and claim, "We studied the relationship between test scores and grades at our institution, and there was essentially no relationship, while HSGPA was a strong predictor of college grades."[4] This resonates with Colin Diver's *New York Times* op-ed piece, where he noted that he could not understand how an institution could find no relationship at all between SAT scores and college grades (Diver 2006). It is more likely that institutions are misusing and misinterpreting regression results rather than truly finding no relationship.

OTHER RESEARCH-BASED MISUNDERSTANDINGS

In addition to the confusion surrounding test fairness and test validity research, there are other related misunderstandings worthy of deconstruction that shed light on public statements made in support of test-optional admission policies. One example is related to the differences in independent strength of each predictor used in an admission model, and another example is related to the notion that there should be other predictors of interest that better explain or predict student performance in college, including noncognitive factors.

First, there are instances when an institution chooses to initiate a test-optional admission policy because it claims that on its campus high school grades are more predictive of college performance than test scores. For example: "After studying national research and considering our own experiences, it is now clear that standardized test scores are not the best indicator of academic success in college. The strength of students' high school curriculum and grades are much better predictors. Based on this careful analysis and discussion with faculty, administrators, secondary school guidance counselors and students, Emmanuel College became a test-optional institution" (Emmanuel College n.d.). What is unclear from this statement is why Emmanuel College would not use the SAT, in addition to HSGPA, if it also contributes positively to the prediction. This is analogous to a detective saying she would prefer not to evaluate additional information about a suspect, even though it is known to be useful, because she already has other helpful information in the case file.

Another research-based misunderstanding that is often used to support the adoption of a test-optional policy is related to individuals or institutions mistakenly believing that because there is still a great deal more variance in college outcomes to be explained, traditional measures such as test scores and high school grades are not helpful (Dollinger 2011; Everson 2000; Schmitt et al. 2007). The more accurate reframing of this would be to say that while SAT scores and HSGPA are both strong predictors of college outcomes, it is worthwhile to explore other variables that might positively contribute to the prediction of college performance

(Dollinger 2011; Sackett, Borneman, and Connelly 2008). This is not a new concept. In the early 1980s, Willingham and Breland (1982) shared the results of a large-scale study on the role of personal qualities in college admission. They found that adding more than 20 student background variables to SAT scores and high school grades in a predictive model of FYGPA resulted in an increment of .04 to the correlation coefficient. Certainly there has been a great deal of exploration with regard to noncognitive predictors in the college admissions realm since the 1980s. However, few measures have been instituted in a broad and standardized manner because they can be susceptible to faking, with students responding in ways to gain advantage or favor (Niessen, Meijer, and Tendeiro 2017; Schmitt et al. 2007; Sedlacek 2005; Sommerfeld 2011). With that said, the exploration of new and predictive variables should not (necessarily) preclude the inclusion of other predictive, widely validated, broadly available variables like admission test scores and high school grades.

Conclusion

There is a substantial body of research that shows that admission test scores relate to the outcomes they are intended to predict (including college grades, retention, and completion) and they do so over and above high school grades. Using high school grades and admission test scores together results in the most accurate predictions of college performance. These findings are consistent across college cohorts and are based on studies that include hundreds of four-year institutions and hundreds and thousands of students. This means that tests like the SAT and ACT help college admission professionals make even better and more informed decisions about selecting applicants for their institutions. Many institutions choose to exclude standardized tests from their admission policies for reasons that don't seem to reflect sound research evidence, but rather, misunderstandings of the tests themselves or research based on the tests.

In a practical sense, when a campus is conducting and evaluating its own test validity research, it is worthwhile to consider thinking through a set of related general questions about each measure used alone and together, including the following:

1. Can I compare students and make decisions about them in a fair and consistent manner using this measure? Does it hold the same scale and meaning across students and schools? What steps have been taken to eliminate bias from the measure?

2. How does this measure relate to other measures I am currently using on campus and with the outcomes of interest? When I use this measure with all other information, am I improving my understanding of student performance?

3. If I am using correlational methods to understand the relationship between a measure and an outcome, am I accounting for the restriction of range that occurs by only studying the admitted and enrolled students? If not, I should contextualize the findings with the understanding that the correlation is typically much stronger than what I am seeing with the restricted sample.

4. Beyond examining the R^2 value or variance explained in college performance by the admission measures of interest, have I stratified the sample by different levels of the admission measure(s) and examined college performance by level(s)? What performance differences are apparent by level(s)? Will this measure provide additional information for more accurate and fairer admission, placement, advisement, and scholarship decisions?

This chapter has attempted to highlight some common misperceptions about test validity research and provide research-based evidence and clarification to the contrary, as well as identify some guidance for best practices. It is hoped that this research has informed conversation concerning the role of standardized tests in college admission and their useful contributions to difficult selection decisions.

NOTES

1. This section of the chapter is adapted from Shaw 2015.

2. The redesigned SAT launched in March 2016 and now includes two section scores: Evidence-Based Reading and Writing and Math. To learn more about the redesigned SAT, visit https://collegereadiness.collegeboard.org/sat.

3. This section of the chapter is adapted from Shaw 2015.

4. As an example, see Kalamazoo College n.d.

REFERENCES

Agronow, S., and Studley, R. (2007). Prediction of College GPA from New SAT Test Scores—A First Look. In *Annual Meeting of the California Association for Institutional Research*. Retrieved from http://www.cair.org/conferences/CAIR2007/pres /Agronow.pdf.

American Educational Research Association, American Psychological Association, and National Council on Measurement in Education. (1999). *Standards for educational and psychological testing.* Washington, DC: AERA.

Anastasi, A., and Urbina, S. (1997). *Psychological testing* (7th ed.). Upper Saddle River, NJ: Prentice Hall.

Aud, S., Wilkinson-Flicker, S., Kristapovich, P., Rathbun, A., Wang, X., Zhang, J., . . . Dziuba, A. (2013). *The condition of education 2013.* Washington, DC: NCES, US Department of Education.

Bridgeman, B., Burton, N., and Pollack, J. (2008). Predicting grades in college courses: A comparison of multiple regression and percent succeeding approaches. *Journal of College Admission, 199,* 19–25. Retrieved from https://search.ebscohost.com/login .aspx?direct=true&db=a9h&AN=31804454&site=ehost-live.

Camara, W. J., and Schmidt, A. E. (1999). *Group differences in standardized testing and social stratification: College Board report* (vol. 99). New York: The College Board.

Camara, W. J., and Shaw, E. J. (2012). The media and educational testing: In pursuit of the truth or in pursuit of a good story? *Educational Measurement: Issues and Practice, 31*(2), 33–37. Retrieved from http://10.0.4.87/j.1745-3992.2012.00233.x.

Clinedinst, M., Koranteng, A.-M., and Nicola, T. (2016). *2015 state of college admission.* Alexandria, VA: NACAC.

Cohen, J. (1988). *Statistical power analysis for the behavioral sciences* (2nd ed.). *Statistical Power Analysis for the Behavioral Sciences* (vol. 2). Hillsdale, NJ: Lawrence Erlbaum Associates.

Diver, C. S. (2006). Skip the test, betray the cause. *New York Times,* September 18. Retrieved from http://www.nytimes.com/2006/09/18/opinion/18diver.html.

Dollinger, S. J. (2011). "Standardized minds" or individuality? Admissions tests and creativity revisited. *Psychology of Aesthetics, Creativity, and the Arts, 5*(4), 329–341. https://doi.org/10.1037/a0023659.

Emmanuel College. (n.d.). Test-optional information. Retrieved from http://www .emmanuel.edu/admissions-and-aid/application-requirements-and-deadlines/test -optional-information.html.

Everson, H. T. (2000). A principled design framework for college admissions tests: An affirming research agenda. *Psychology, Public Policy, and Law, 6*(1), 112–120. https://doi.org/10.1037/1076-8971.6.1.112.

Finkelstein, I. E. (1913). *The marking system in theory and practice.* Educational Psychology Monographs (No. 10). Baltimore, MD: Warwick and York.

Holmes, J. D. (2016). *Great myths of education and learning.* Hoboken, NJ: Wiley-Blackwell.

Kalamazoo College. (n.d.). K goes test optional. Retrieved from http://www.kzoo.edu /news/test-optional.

Kobrin, J. L., Sathy, V., and Shaw, E. J. (2006). *A historical view of subgroup performance differences on the SAT.* College Board Research Report 2006-5. New York: The College Board.

Laird, R. (2005). What is it we think we are trying to fix and how should we fix it? A view from the admission office. In W. J. Camara and E. W. Kimmel (Eds.), *Choosing students: Higher education admission tools for the 21st century* (pp. 13–32). Mahwah, NJ: Lawrence Erlbaum.

Lauterbach, C. E. (1928). Some factors affecting teachers' marks. *Journal of Educational Psychology, 19*(4), 266–271.

Mattern, K. D., Kobrin, J. L., Patterson, B. F., Shaw, E. J., and Camara, W. J. (2009). Validity is in the eye of the beholder: Conveying SAT research findings to the general public. In Robert W. Lissitz (Ed.), *The concept of validity: Revisions, new directions, and applications.* (pp. 213–240). Charlotte, NC: Information Age Publishing.

Mattern, K. D., and Patterson, B. F. (2011). *The validity of the SAT for predicting fourth-year grades: 2006 SAT validity sample.* College Board Statistical Report 2011-7. New York: The College Board.

———. (2014). *Synthesis of Recent SAT Validity Findings: Trend Data over Time and Cohorts.* New York: The College Board. Retrieved from http://files.eric.ed.gov /fulltext/ED556462.pdf.

Mattern, K. D., Patterson, B. F., and Kobrin, J. L. (2012). *The validity of SAT scores in predicting first-year mathematics and English grades.* College Board Research Report 2012-1. New York: The College Board. Retrieved from http://research.collegeboard .org/taxonomy/term/37.

Mattern, K. D., Patterson, B. F., and Wyatt, J. N. (2013). *How useful are traditional admission measures in predicting graduation within four years?* New York: The College Board. Retrieved from www.collegeboard.org/research.

Mattern, K., Radunzel, J., and Westrick, P. (2015). *Development of STEM Readiness Benchmarks to Assist Educational and Career Decision Making.* ACT Research Report 2015-3. Iowa City: ACT.

Meyer, G. J., Finn, S. E., Eyde, L. D., Kay, G. G., Moreland, K. L., Dies, R. R., . . . Reed, G. M. (2001). Psychological testing and psychological assessment: A review of evidence and issues. *American Psychologist, 56*(2), 128–165.

NACAC (National Association for College Admission Counseling). (2016). *Use of predictive validity studies to inform admission practices.* Arlington, VA: NACAC.

Niessen, S., Meijer, R. R., and Tendeiro, J. N. (2017). Measuring non-cognitive predictors in high-stakes contexts: The effect of self-presentation on self-report instruments used in admission to higher education. *Personality and Individual Differences, 106,* 183–189. Retrieved from http://10.0.3.248/j.paid.2016.11.014.

Patterson, B. F., and Mattern, K. D. (2013). *Validity of the SAT for predicting first-year grades: 2011 SAT validity sample.* New York: The College Board.

Radunzel, J., and Mattern, K. D. (2015). *Providing context for college readiness measures: College enrollment and graduation projections for the 2015 ACT-tested high school graduating class.* Iowa City: ACT.

Radunzel, J., and Noble, J. (2012). *Predicting long-term college success through degree completion using ACT composite score, ACT benchmarks, and high school grade point average.* Research Report No. 2012-5. Iowa City: ACT.

Rigol, G. (2003). *Admission decision-making models: How U.S. institutions of higher education select undergraduate students.* New York: The College Board.

Rosenthal, R., and Rosnow, R. L. (1991). *Essentials of behavioral research: Methods and data analysis* (2nd ed.). New York: McGraw-Hill.

Ruediger, W. C. (1914). Communications and discussions. Standardizing grades. *Journal of Educational Psychology 1, 5*(6), 349–352.

Sackett, P. R., Borneman, M. J., and Connelly, B. S. (2008). High stakes testing in higher education and employment: Appraising the evidence for validity and fairness. *American Psychologist, 63*(4), 215–227. https://doi.org/10.1037/0003-066X.63.4.215.

Sackett, P. R., Kuncel, N. R., Arneson, J. J., Cooper, S. R., and Waters, S. D. (2009). Does socioeconomic status explain the relationship between admissions tests and post-secondary academic performance? *Psychological Bulletin, 135*(1), 1–22. Retrieved from http://10.0.4.13/a0013978.

Sackett, P. R., Kuncel, N. R., Beatty, A. S., Rigdon, J. L., Shen, W., and Kiger, T. B. (2012). The role of socioeconomic status in SAT-grade relationships and in college admissions decisions. *Psychological Science, 23*(9), 1000–1007. https://doi.org/10.1177/0956797612438732.

Schmitt, N., Keeney, J., Oswald, F. L., Pleskac, T. J., Billington, A. Q., Sinha, R., and Zorzie, M. (2009). Prediction of 4-year college student performance using cognitive and noncognitive predictors and the impact on demographic status of admitted students. *Journal of Applied Psychology, 94*(6), 1479–1497. https://doi.org/10.1037/a0016810.

Schmitt, N., Oswald, F. L., Kim, B. H., Imus, A., Merritt, S., Friede, A., and Shivpuri, S. (2007). The use of background and ability profiles to predict college student outcomes. *Journal of Applied Psychology, 92*(1), 165–179. https://doi.org/10.1037/0021-9010.92.1.165.

Sedlacek, W. E. (2005). The case for noncognitive measures. In W. J. Camara and E. W. Kimmel (Eds.), *Choosing students: Higher education admission tools for the 21st century* (pp. 177–193). Mahwah, NJ: Lawrence Erlbaum.

Shaw, E. J. (2015). *An SAT validity primer.* New York: The College Board.

Shaw, E. J., Marini, J. P., Beard, J., Shmueli, D., Young, L., and Ng, H. (2016). *The redesigned SAT pilot predictive validity study: A first look.* College Board Research Report 2016-1. New York: The College Board.

Shaw, E. J., and Milewski, G. B. (2004). *Consistency and reliability in the individualized review of college applicants.* New York: The College Board.

Sommerfeld, A. (2011). Recasting non-cognitive factors in college readiness as what they truly are: Non-academic factors. *Journal of College Admission, 213,* 18–22. Retrieved from https://search.ebscohost.com/login.aspx?direct=true&db=eue&AN=527632258&site=ehost-live.

Wainer, H., and Robinson, D. H. (2003). Shaping up the practice of null hypothesis significance testing. *Educational Researcher, 32*(7), 22–30. Retrieved from http://10.0.12.30/0013189X032007022.

Warne, R. T., Nagaishi, C., Slade, M. K., Hermesmeyer, P., and Peck, E. K. (2014). Comparing weighted and unweighted grade point averages in predicting college success of diverse and low-income college students. *NASSP Bulletin, 98*(4), 261–279. https://doi.org/10.1177/0192636514565171.

Westrick, P. A., Le, H., Robbins, S. B., Radunzel, J. M., and Schmidt, F. L. (2015). College performance and retention: A meta-analysis of the predictive validities of ACT scores, high school grades, and SES. *Educational Assessment, 20*(1), 23–45. Retrieved from http://10.0.4.56/10627197.2015.997614.

Willingham, W. W. (2005). Prospects for improving grades for use in admissions. In W. J. Camara and E. W. Kimmel (Eds.), *Choosing students: Higher education admission tools for the 21st century* (pp. 127–139). Mahwah, NJ: Lawrence Erlbaum.

Willingham, W. W., and Breland, H. M. (1982). *Personal qualities and college admissions.* New York: The College Board.

3

Grade Inflation and the Role of Standardized Testing

Michael Hurwitz and Jason Lee

*T*here are decades of research on the validity and predictive power of standardized achievement tests, particularly in the college admissions context. As we observe elsewhere in this volume, scholars, test developers, and practitioners have compared their content to various curricular standards, examined their ability to predict a wide range of postsecondary outcomes even when controlling for other factors, and have psychometrically inspected these tests item-by-item in an effort to eliminate unfairness and bias. High school grades are at least as important as standardized test scores in the admissions context—perhaps increasingly so as test-optional admissions increase in popularity—yet there is no comparable literature examining the validity, reliability, and fairness of high school grading.

In this chapter, Hurwitz and Lee take an important step in closing this gap in the literature. Through their systematic examination of high school grading, they discover some alarming trends with important implications for policymakers and admissions professionals. Echoing conventional wisdom, they present empirical evidence of pervasive high school grade inflation over at least the past 20 years. While SAT scores have declined, the high school GPAs of those SAT test-taking cohorts have steadily increased.

Why should we be concerned about this? As Hurwitz and Lee explain, as average grades inflate toward a natural "ceiling" (traditionally 4.0, although some high schools *have raised this) there is, by mathematical necessity, less variability in grades and therefore less predictive power in the admissions context. But even more important, the authors show conclusively that grade inflation is not occurring evenly in society. On average, they observe greater grade inflation among white, Asian, wealthy, and private school students than among less advantaged students and those in the public schools. In other words, the use of high school grades in admissions is fraught with equity issues and is not a panacea for concerns with standardized tests.*

In Garrison Keillor's fictionalized Minnesota town, Lake Wobegon, "all the women are strong, all the men are good looking, and all the children are above average." Statisticians of all kinds, from the armchair variety to pioneers in the discipline, are expected to smile at this description. If *all* of the children are above average, then there must be at least some disconnect between the actual average and the perceived average. Or maybe there is broader confusion in Lake Wobegon about what "average" actually means?

The characterization of Lake Wobegon as comically utopic (e.g., all the men are good looking) belies the actuality that this village is probably representative of the typical American town. Keillor doesn't elaborate on the specific qualities that make all of Lake Wobegon's youth above average. But let's assume that he is making reference to some measure of academic potential or performance. In the educational measurement sphere, academic potential/performance tends to have a bell-shaped distribution. This means that approximately half of Lake Wobegon's youth—all of whom are supposedly above average—are actually below average. One might expect that, at some point, these youth will confront the unfortunate reality that their placement into the "above average" category was a mistake.

Or will they? If the classroom assessment structure in the Lake Wobegon school system resembles that of a typical American school, lower-achieving students may mistakenly view themselves as higher-achieving. For several decades, grade inflation at high schools has taken place to a degree and extent likely unimagined when high school first became a widely shared experience for adolescents during the early part of the twentieth century (Snyder 1993). Once reserved for the top performers in a typical high school classroom, A grades are now the norm rather than the exception. The reasons for this are many, as detailed below, but the upshot is clear: It is now harder than ever to distinguish between the academic performance of different students within the same classroom or school.

Indeed, this transformation of American high schools into mini Lake Wobegons has not gone unnoticed by higher education's gatekeepers. One admissions dean from an elite private college publicly made this connection in a recent interview with the *Washington Post*, referencing a Midwestern high school (perhaps Lake Wobegon High?) where every student graduated in the top half of the class (Balingit 2015). The same article noted that some affluent high schools now graduate more than 100 valedictorians each year, as the paradigm of one valedictorian per graduating class has increasingly been replaced by an "everyone is number one" approach. Another admissions dean, also at an elite college, referred to a "traffic jam" of high grades where "standardized testing helps break that traffic jam."

Although the college admissions community has voiced its concerns about high school grade inflation, not everyone is troubled by these trends. Over the past century, there has been considerable debate about the general purpose of grades, with a fault line separating advocates of the criterion-referenced approach from advocates of the norm-referenced approach (Brookhart et al. 2016). In a world where the criterion-referenced approach dominates, grades would be assigned based on mastery of classroom material, in contrast to a norm-referenced world, where grades would be used solely to rank students. If all students demonstrate mastery, then awarding A grades to everyone would not be unreasonable. Of course, such a scenario would obviously suggest that students should be exposed to more rigorous coursework. Still, supporters of criterion-referenced grades might argue that nothing is fundamentally wrong with awarding all students high grades if they are warranted.

College admissions staff, however, rely on high school grades as a way of distinguishing applicants. Proponents of norm-referenced grading point to this as justification against a strict criterion-based approach. If all transcripts are replete with A grades, without standardized tests, admissions staff would be tasked with the impossible—using high school grade point average to predict whether the student will thrive academically. Moreover, high schools that liberally assign high grades may paradoxically disadvantage some students. Such grade inflation blurs the signal of high grades on a transcript, meaning that the students whose performance truly justifies A grades are not easily discernable from students with more modest classroom performance (Pattison, Grodsky, and Muller 2013). The end result: college admissions staff may lose faith in their ability to distinguish between students of varying academic ability based on grades, while the grade-inflating high school risks developing a reputation of awarding grades that cannot be trusted as true indicators of course performance (Ehlers and Schwager 2016).

As we show in this chapter, enormous variation exists across high schools in the assignment of grades, and these differential grading policies add another wrinkle to the already complicated process of interpreting high school grades. Rarely, if ever, can college admissions staff access transcripts of all students from a high school's graduating class. Even if a college could retrieve this information, the process of comparing transcripts side-by-side to rank-order students would be onerous. Class rank, based on high school GPA, adds important context to student grades. Achieving a "B-average" at a high school without grade inflation might prove a more impressive feat than earning all A– grades at a comparable high school with rampant grade inflation (Finder 2006).

The obscuring of important academic information about students brought on by grade inflation is compounded by a newer tactic, which we'll refer to as rank suppression. Though high schools aren't yet whiting out grades on transcripts before sending them to colleges, many are either eliminating high school class rank or withholding this rank from colleges. Some of the motives behind these decisions are noble. Class rank may create unnecessary competition as students jockey for positions in the top 5%, 10% and so on, particularly in states like Texas and California, where high class rank guarantees admission to public universities. Similarly, there are concerns that systems of class rank divert students toward less challenging curricula to minimize the risk of receiving low grades (Guskey 2014). Other possible drivers of class rank guidelines, like succumbing to parental pressures to influence school policy, are more troubling (Kohn 1998).

Grade inflation and class rank suppression are concerning not only because they complicate the jobs of college admissions staff, but because they raise issues of equity. Standardized tests like the ACT and SAT have long been the subject of equity discussions, with critics pointing toward score gaps across racial, ethnic, and socioeconomic groups as justification for the devaluation of these college entrance exams (Reeves and Halikias 2017). There exists a misguided perception that high school grades are a fairer assessment measure for underrepresented students. In this chapter, we bring to bear evidence contradicting this perception. Not only are there sharp differences in high school GPAs across socioeconomic and racial/ethnic groups, but grade inflation is disproportionately impacting white and Asian students, as well as students from higher socioeconomic backgrounds. This means that the gaps in high school GPA between these groups are growing over time. We also show evidence that the high schools enrolling these privileged students are largely driving the disappearance of class rank.

In this chapter, we carefully document the trends in grade inflation and class rank suppression over the past 15–20 years. We accomplish this by separately examining high school GPA among SAT test takers reported on the College Board's Student Data Questionnaire (SDQ) as well as administrative data from two Department of Education surveys: the Education Longitudinal Study of 2002 (ELS:02) and the High School Longitudinal Survey of 2009 (HSLS:09). Each year, colleges report the fraction of first-year students with high school class rank through the Annual Survey of Colleges. We use these data to show that high school class rank is disappearing, particularly among students enrolling at the most selective colleges.

Overall Grade Inflation

In 2004, the US Department of Education published a report, titled *The High School Transcript Study: A Decade of Change in Curricula and Achievement* (Perkins et al. 2004). On the standard 4.0 scale, the cumulative grade point average among high school graduates increased from 2.68 to 2.94 between 1990 and 2000. This surge, over just one decade, amounts to an increase equivalent to nearly one-third of a letter grade. In this chapter, we continue to track trends in grade inflation by offering a more contemporary view over the past 19 years.

We use nationally representative data sets to estimate grade inflation among all high school students, but we focus much of the following discussion on grade inflation among students who took the SAT. This emphasis is intentional. College admissions practitioners might worry less about overall high school grade inflation and instead direct their concerns to the nature of grade inflation among students aspiring to attend four-year colleges. More than 85% of undergraduates enrolled at primarily baccalaureate degree–granting public or not-for-profit colleges attend institutions where the SAT or ACT is either required or recommended for admissions.[1] By focusing on the students who took the SAT, we aim to offer insight into the magnitude of grade inflation experienced by admissions professionals.

In figure 3.1, we show high school GPA (HSGPA), as reported on the SAT's Student Data Questionnaire (SDQ), by year of high school graduation. Between the cohorts of 1998 and 2016, the average HSGPA increased from 3.27 to 3.38 on the standard 4.0 scale among SAT test takers.[2] If the average academic ability or preparation of students was increasing over time, then this increase in GPA might not actually reflect inflation. We also include average SAT scores by cohort in figure 3.1 to calibrate the shifting HSGPA. Since the SAT is designed to ensure that a given

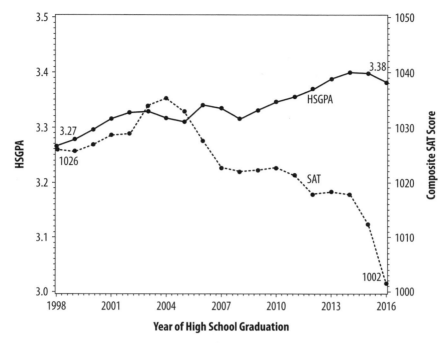

Fig. 3.1. Average High School Grade Point Average (HSGPA) and Composite SAT (Math + Verbal / Critical Reading), by High School Graduation Cohort. *Note:* For comparability over time, we remove students who last took the SAT after January of their high school senior year. In 2005, the Writing section was introduced and the name of the Verbal section was changed to Critical Reading. We do not consider Writing scores in any analyses.

score has identical meaning across test administrations, a true increase in student academic preparation over time should be accompanied by an increase in SAT scores. Looking at figure 3.1, one can see that the opposite is true. Despite the gradual increases in HSGPA since 1998, average SAT scores on the 1600 scale (math + verbal) have declined from 1026 in 1998 to 1002 in 2016.[3]

Much of this increase in average HSGPA is driven by a sharp uptick in the fraction of SAT test takers with A averages. These students indicated HSGPAs of A–, A, or A+, the numeric equivalents of which are 3.67, 4.00, and 4.33, respectively. In figure 3.2, we show the fraction of students with grades in the A, B, or C ranges.[4] Between the high school graduation cohorts of 1998 and 2016, the fraction of students with A averages increased from 38.9% to 47.0%. This increase was offset by a 4.2 percentage point decrease in the fraction of students with B averages and a 3.8 percentage point decrease in the fraction of students with C averages.

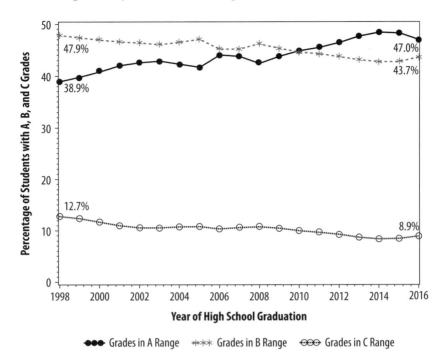

Fig. 3.2. Percentage of Students with High School Grade Point Averages in the A, B, and C Ranges. *Note:* For comparability over time, we remove students who last took the SAT after January of their high school senior year.

Increasing HSGPA despite the decline in SAT scores clearly indicates that the amount of grade inflation is larger than the HSGPA growth shown in figures 3.1 and 3.2. By fitting the student-level HSGPA and SAT data with a simple regression model, we can estimate trends in grade inflation, while accounting for the noted trends in academic ability, as measured by SAT scores. The purpose of fitting such a model is to allow for the estimation of annual differences in expected GPA for students in different cohorts with identical SAT scores. In this model, we regress a student's HSGPA on his or her SAT score and a vector of indicator variables for high school graduation cohort, as shown in equation 1.

$$HSGPA_i = \beta_0 + \beta_1 SATComposite_i + \sum_{X=1999}^{2016} \beta_x Cohort_x + \varepsilon_i \tag{1}$$

The parameter estimates, β_x, from this fitted model are shown graphically in figure 3.3. We represent the 95% confidence intervals around the point estimates with error bars. The extremely narrow range of the confidence intervals indicates that the point estimates are estimated precisely. This figure shows a fairly steady

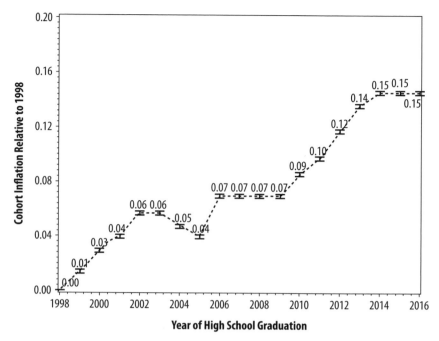

Fig. 3.3. Grade Inflation Points, Conditional on Student SAT, since 1998.
Note: For comparability over time, we remove students who last took the SAT after January of their high school senior year.

increase in high school GPA over time for students with a fixed SAT score. For example, for the cohort of students graduating from high school in 2002, an individual with an SAT score of 1000 would have a high school GPA 0.06 points higher than an identical student graduating from high school in 1998. Conditional on SAT scores, students from the 2011 cohort have HSGPAs 0.10 points higher than in the 1998 cohort. By the 2016 cohort, the magnitude of grade inflation over the 1998 cohort had increased to 0.15 points.[5]

Figure 3.3 shows the magnitude of grade inflation for the average sampled student. The story is more nuanced when students are disaggregated by SAT scores. In figure 3.4, we separately plot trends in HSGPA by student SAT scores. As shown in the previous figure, the average student has experienced grade inflation of about 0.15 GPA points. Among students with the highest SAT scores (1300+), average HSGPA increased from 3.86 to 3.90 from 1998 to 2016. Since the HSGPA ceiling is set at 4.33 on the SDQ, students achieving HSGPAs that exceed 4.33 must underreport their HSGPAs as exactly 4.33 on the SDQ. Consequently, the inflation

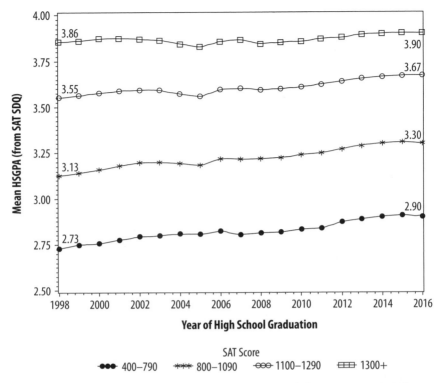

Fig. 3.4. Mean High School Grade Point Average (HSGPA), by Composite SAT Score. *Note:* SDQ = Student Data Questionnaire. For comparability over time, we remove students who last took the SAT after January of their high school senior year.

among these extremely high-achieving students may represent a lower-bound estimate on the true grade inflation over this period. For students in other SAT bands, HSGPAs have risen between 0.12 and 0.17 points since 1998.

Variation in Grade Inflation across American High Schools

An additional challenge when understanding the full scope of grade inflation is that the magnitude of inflation varies considerably across high schools. This means that recalibrating HSGPAs based on overall inflation trends and applying an adjustment factor to all students is not a viable solution. Even college admissions staff familiar with course offerings and rigor at certain high schools may be inconvenienced by the fact that an A– grade is a moving target.

To understand just how much grade inflation varies across high schools, we rank all high schools by the extent of HSGPA growth between 1998 and 2016.[6] In

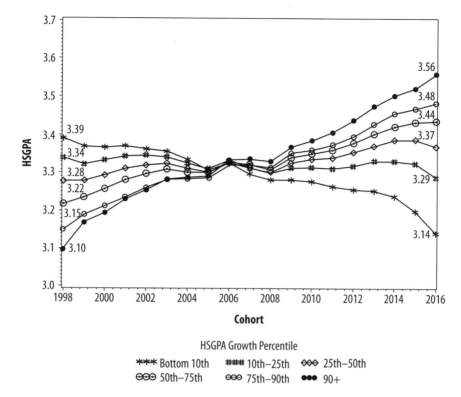

Fig. 3.5. Mean High School Grade Point Average (HSGPA), by High School Grade Inflation Percentile. *Note:* Only includes high schools with 30 or more students in the 1998 and 2016 cohorts.

figure 3.5, we show the average HSGPA, by HSGPA growth. Among high schools in the bottom tenth percentile, average HSGPA decreased from 3.39 to 3.14. In the next group—the tenth to twenty-fifth percentiles—the average HSGPA decreased slightly from 3.34 to 3.29. Schools in the remaining categories experienced positive changes in HSGPA between 1998 and 2016, with average HSGPAs soaring from 3.10 to 3.56 in the top 10% of high schools, ranked by HSGPA growth.

Variation in changing HSGPA over time across high schools might be driven by several factors. Attributing all of this growth to inflation, or in the case of some schools, deflation, implies that there are no actual changes in academic preparation over time in these high schools. It might be the case that high schools with the largest positive changes in HSGPA experienced increases in student academic ability/preparation relative to high schools with lower positive changes or negative changes. Figure 3.6 shows some evidence of this phenomenon. SAT composite scores declined by more than 100 points (from 992 to 885) at the average high school in the bottom tenth percentile of HSGPA growth. High schools in the next group (tenth through twenty-fifth percentiles) experienced a decline in composite SAT scores of more than 40 points (from 1018 to 977), despite an HSGPA that decreased only modestly—from 3.34 to 3.29. In the top 10% of high schools, HSGPA growth of 0.46 points was accompanied by a 31-point increase in SAT scores, from 1026 to 1057.

Using SAT scores as an anchoring device, we have already established that positive changes in HSGPA cannot be explained only by shifting student academic ability. For each high school, it is possible to disaggregate the changes in HSGPA attributable to grade inflation from those that might be expected based on changes

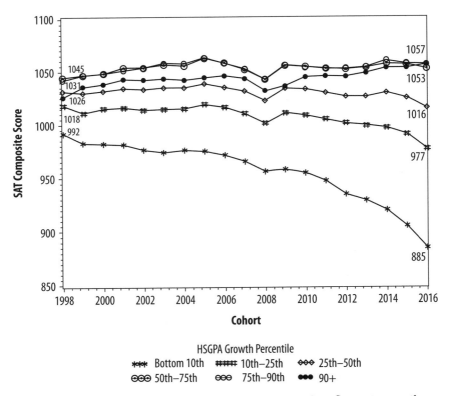

Fig. 3.6. Mean Composite SAT Score, by High School Grade Inflation Percentile. *Notes*: HSGPA = high school grade point average. Only includes high schools with 30 or more students in the 1998 and 2016 cohorts.

in SAT scores. We accomplish this by regressing the change in HSGPA between the two cohorts—1998 and 2016—on the change in average high school–level SAT scores between these two cohorts. We then group high schools based on their residual terms from this regression. Schools with the positive residuals largest in magnitude experienced the most HSGPA growth above what might be expected based on changes in SAT averages.

Next, we show the percentage of students eligible for free lunch and the percentage of black and Hispanic students against the school's HSGPA change percentile (fig. 3.7a) and the school's residual term (fig. 3.7b). These two school-level characteristics come from the US Department of Education's 2014–15 Common Core of Data (CCD) and are available for public high schools only.

The school-level poverty measures in figure 3.7a reveal that high schools with the largest increases in HSGPA over time also have the lowest shares of disadvan-

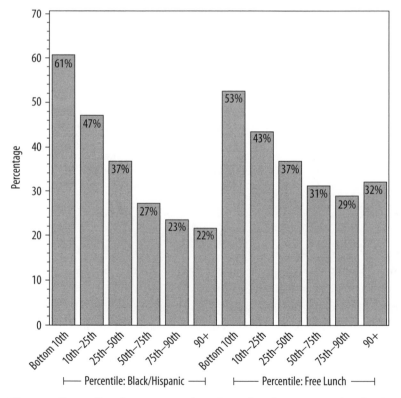

Fig. 3.7a. Share of Underrepresented Students, by Change in High School Grade Point Average Percentile

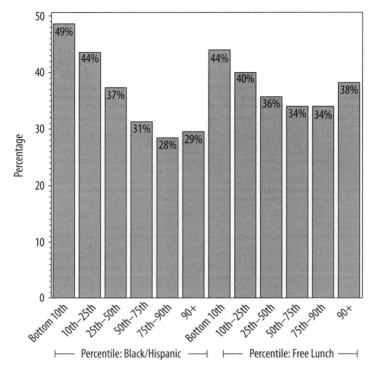

Fig. 3.7b. Share of Underrepresented Students, by Grade Inflation
Percentile. *Note*: We create bins based on the residual terms
from regressing the change in high school grade point averages
between the two cohorts—1998 and 2016—on the change in
average high school–level SAT scores between these
two cohorts.

taged students. For example, at the average high school in the top decile of
HSGPA growth, 22% of students are black or Hispanic and 32% are eligible for
free lunch. By contrast, the average high school in the bottom decile of HSGPA
growth had an underrepresented minority enrollment of 61% and more than half
of enrolled students are eligible for free lunch.

Figure 3.7b confirms that, when changes in academic ability are taken into
account, the story remains unchanged. High schools that inflated their grades the
most, conditional on changes in student SAT scores, enroll student bodies that are
only 29% black or Hispanic. At the other end of the spectrum, high schools with
the least grade inflation, after accounting for changes in academic preparation,
enroll student bodies in which nearly half (49%) of students are black or Hispanic.

The relationship between free lunch status and grade inflation, conditional on academic ability, is weaker than that shown in figure 3.7a, though, in general, the same downward-sloping pattern exists.[7]

Between 1998 and 2016, SAT participation increased in American schools, and these increases were particularly notable in schools with large shares of underrepresented minority and low-income students—the same schools that tended to experience the least grade inflation. These changes in SAT participation rates, as well as the underlying data in figure 3.7a, are shown in appendix table 3.2. SAT expansion in certain high schools may confound trends in HSGPA derived from SAT questionnaires. Controlling for SAT scores, as we did in figure 3.7b, may etch away most of the bias from shifting academic ability, but there remains the possibility that we are confusing the effects of grade inflation with the effects of SAT expansion.

It is not possible to determine the extent to which differential SAT expansion is biasing the conclusions drawn from figures 3.7a and 3.7b, or whether the relationship between grade inflation and measures of school poverty is under- or overstated as a result of such expansion. We can, however, use the other analyses in this chapter to develop empirically supported hypotheses. In a world without any grade inflation, students with an SAT score of 850 (for example) should have, on average, identical HSGPAs regardless of whether they took the SAT in 1998 or in 2016. The issue of selection into the SAT test-taking population calls into question this assertion. Perhaps the students with an 850 SAT score in 1998 were a bit more ambitious or academically prepared than students with the same SAT score in 2016, when SAT test taking was more widespread. Under this scenario, estimates of grade inflation over time at high schools with less-prepared students and rapid SAT expansion would be biased downwardly relative to high schools with flat trends in SAT test taking. If conditioning on SAT scores insufficiently addresses the possible confounding from increased SAT reach among less-prepared students, we might expect to find students with lower SAT scores to have experienced declines or more modest increases in HSGPA over time. Figure 3.4 is inconsistent with this conclusion, suggesting that figures 3.7a and 3.7b may understate the relationship between school-level poverty and grade inflation.

Because comprehensive high school–level poverty and race/ethnicity data from the CCD are only available for public schools, students from non-public high schools are omitted from figures 3.7a and 3.7b. Though no school-level wealth metrics are available for private independent and religiously affiliated high schools, it's probably a safe bet that private independent schools enroll the wealthiest students, considering that tuitions at these high schools stand at twice the amount charged by religiously affiliated schools, and except in unusual circumstances, public schools are free of charge.[8]

In figure 3.8, we show average HSGPA and SAT scores separately for students attending religiously affiliated, private independent, and public high schools. The rate of HSGPA increase among private high schools (both independent and religiously affiliated) was about three times as large as that observed in public high schools. Average HSGPAs among students attending religiously affiliated high schools and private independent high schools increased by about 0.21 and 0.26 GPA points, respectively, compared with 0.08 points at public high schools.

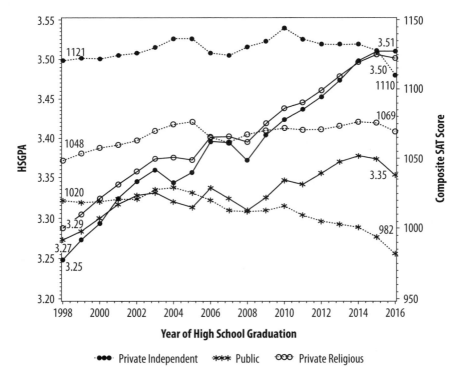

Fig. 3.8. Trends in High School Grade Point Average (HSGPA) and Composite SAT, by High School Type. *Notes:* Solid lines = HSGPA; dotted lines = SAT scores. For comparability over time, we remove students who last took the SAT after January of their high school senior year.

Though average HSGPAs increased similarly among students from both types of private high schools, it is interesting to look at this trend against the backdrop of changing average SAT scores. At religiously affiliated high schools, average SAT scores increased by nearly 21 points between 1998 and 2016, which suggests that the GPA boost among students attending these high schools at least partially reflects improved academic preparation/performance. By contrast, average SAT scores declined among students from independent private high schools by about 11 points over the same period. Taken together, these pieces of evidence point toward a pattern of heightened grade inflation at private independent high schools relative to religiously affiliated high schools.

The preceding analyses show that high schools enrolling wealthier students are inflating grades at a faster rate compared with other high schools. Although we lack access to the exact family incomes of students in our sample, the College Board prompts students to report race/ethnicity as well as parental education levels on its assessments.[9] We use both of these measures as correlates of socioeconomic status (SES).

Disaggregating trends by student race/ethnicity reveals grade inflation trends that are consistent with the previous high school–level trends. In figures 3.9a and 3.9b, we show trends in HSGPA and composite SAT scores, by student reported race/ethnicity. We incorporate all students, including those attending small public high schools and private high schools. The magnitude of HSGPA growth (0.12 points) is identical between Asian and white students; however, unlike for Asian students, the average SAT scores for white students declined slightly over this period. Among Hispanic/Latino students, the average HSGPAs increased by only 0.03 points between 2001 and 2016, compared with 0.11 points for black/African American students, despite the fact that both groups of students experienced comparable modest declines in SAT scores (approximately 15 to 20 points).

The relationship between SES and grade inflation persists when SES is approximated by parental education (fig. 3.10). Students whose parents have the lowest levels of education experienced the least grade inflation since the late 1990s. Between 1998 and 2016, HSGPAs increased by 0.15 points among students who have at least one parent with a bachelor's degree or higher. By contrast, HSGPA increased by 0.09 points among students whose parents did not complete high school. Average SAT scores over this period were relatively flat among both groups of students.

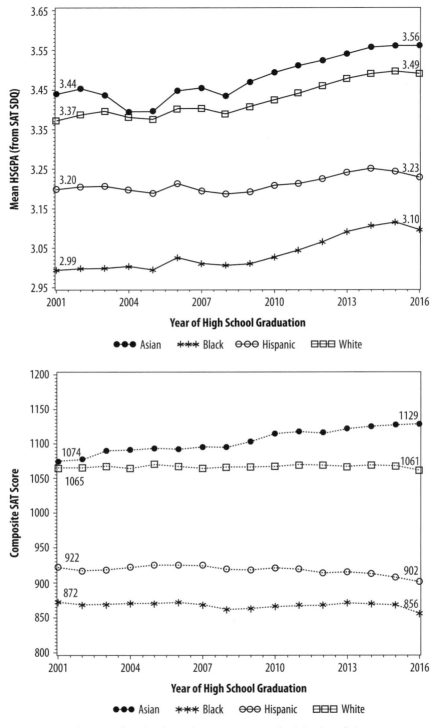

Fig. 3.9. Trends in High School Grade Point Average (HSGPA) and Composite SAT Scores, by Student Race/Ethnicity. *Notes*: SDQ = Student Data Questionnaire. For comparability over time, we remove students who last took the SAT after January of their high school senior year.

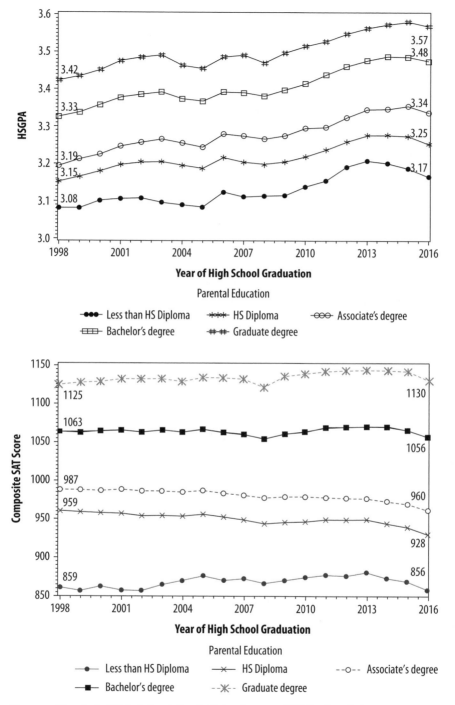

Fig. 3.10. Trends in High School Grade Point Average (HSGPA) and Composite SAT, by Parental Education. *Note*: For comparability over time, we remove students who last took the SAT after January of their high school senior year.

Grade Compression

Grade inflation, while potentially overstating student preparation for college, would not necessarily pose as much of an impediment to college admissions professionals if there were no ceiling on the grading scale. Standard grading rubrics at many high schools mean that grades higher than A+ are unobtainable, so the upward drifting must stop somewhere. The bunching of grades over time, which we refer to as grade compression, is documented in figure 3.11. Here we estimate the variance in HSGPA for each high school cohort, and we re-express this variance as a fraction of the variance in HSGPA that existed for the 1998 cohort. The thick solid line represents the overall sample and reveals that the variance in high school grades has shrunk by 10% since 1998. Disaggregating by student SAT scores reveals that this grade compression is not uniform across student SAT categories. The amount of grade compression has increased with student SAT scores. Among the most academically talented students—those with SAT scores at or above 1300—HSGPA variance decreased by 28% between 1998 and 2016.

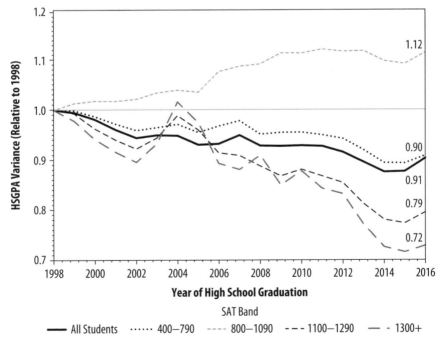

Fig. 3.11. Variance in High School Grade Point Average (HSGPA), Relative to 1998, by Composite SAT Score.

Among students with the lowest SAT scores, variation in HSGPA actually increased over time. This trend contrasts with that observed among the other students. For this group, grade inflation means that students are moving away from the grade floor. Unlike higher-achieving students who are bunching around the upper bounds of the grade scale, the lower-achieving students are drifting away from the lower-bounds of the grade scale. As a result, the variance in HSGPA for these students was 12% higher in 2016 than it was in 1998.

Rank Suppression

Class rank provides important contextual information around grades. Along with high school class size, this measure indicates the fraction of students at that school with higher grade point averages. The class rank metric therefore provides a unique lens on the school's grading policies, and whether the school doles out high grades liberally. A student with a 3.9 GPA ranked first in a class of 400 probably attends a high school with stricter grading standards compared with student with the same GPA ranked 200 out of 400.

In reality, the connection between class rank and high school GPA is more nuanced than the previous example suggests, which only reinforces the need to have some standardized measure of student ability that is comparable across high schools. If the 200 students with GPAs of 3.9 or higher in the second high school also had SAT scores above 1400, the universality of high GPAs could indicate an abundance of high-achieving students who earned their GPAs. On the other hand, if the 200 students all had below-average SAT scores, the 3.9 HSGPA probably overstates these students' preparation for college.

Though the SAT data used in previous analyses do not contain student-level data on whether class rank is relayed to colleges, the College Board collects college-level data from the Annual Survey of Colleges indicating the fraction of first-year students whose high schools provided class rank. This allows us to document the disappearance of class rank in high schools. Not only do we observe a rapid decline in high school class rank among enrolling students; we find that it is vanishing most rapidly at the nation's most competitive colleges.

In figure 3.12, we show trends in the average fraction of first-year students with high school class rank, by Barron's 2008 college guide classification. Each band of colleges is less selective than the band below it on the figure's vertical axis. Historically, more selective colleges have enrolled lower shares of first-year students with class rank, and the fanning of the lines in figure 3.12 shows that rank suppression is escalating at a faster clip among more selective colleges. For example,

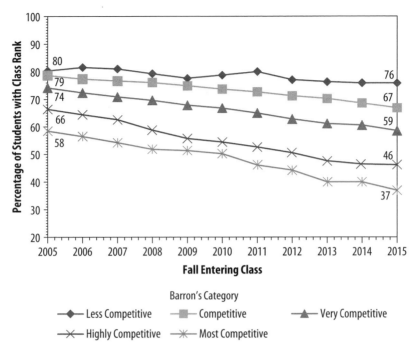

Fig. 3.12. Average Fraction of Entering College Students with Class Rank

among the "most competitive" colleges (Barron's Category 1), the fraction of first-year students with class rank declined by approximately 20 percentage points—from 58% to 37% between 2005 and 2015. On the other end of the spectrum, among "less competitive" colleges (Barron's Category 5), this fraction only declined from 80% to 76% over this time frame.[10]

Why do so many students enrolling at highly selective colleges have no high school class rank? This question is impossible to answer, because we have no data on high school policies about whether class rank is calculated and whether it is shared with colleges. However, we conjecture that pressures to suppress high school class rank among higher SES, but not necessarily lower SES high schools, may be an important driving force in these trends. If better-resourced high schools are the pipeline to the nation's most selective colleges, and these high schools are also the most likely to conceal class rank, the fanning of lines in figure 3.12 would be expected.

The College Board data allow for some insight into the plausibility of this hypothesis. Linking College Board data with student enrollment data from the

Table 3.1.   High school origins and characteristics of typical enrolling
students, by Barron's category

	% public/ charter	% private independent	% religious	% free lunch	% black/ Hispanic	Avg. high school SAT
Most competitive (Category 1)	63.9	19.5	13.8	22.7	28.4	1144
Highly competitive (Category 2)	77.1	7.7	12.7	24.5	29.2	1100
Very competitive (Category 3)	79.7	4.7	13.7	25.7	25.2	1089
Competitive (Category 4)	85.0	2.8	10.6	30.7	30.3	1045
Less competitive (Category 5)	90.8	1.5	6.4	37.1	38.0	1002

Notes: Data come from the PSAT/NMSQT, SAT, AP takers from the 2015 high school graduation cohort. College enrollment data come from the National Student Clearinghouse and reflect the first college enrolled through 2016. Barron's categorizations are taken from the Barron's *Profiles of American Colleges 2008* guide. Sample includes only the colleges that reported class rank to the Annual Survey of Colleges for first-year students entering in 2005 and 2015. Average high school SAT scores are calculated among public, charter, private independent, and Catholic high schools.

National Student Clearinghouse, we can offer a crude investigation of the high school origins among students from the high school cohort of 2015 enrolling in each of these Barron's categories (table 3.1).[11] Collectively, these data show that matriculants at the nation's most competitive colleges attend the types of wealthy, higher-achieving high schools that are more likely to suppress class rank. The differences in high school–level measures of SES across the Barron's categories are stark. Nearly one-fifth of students enrolling at colleges in the top Barron's category come from private independent high schools. This figure is 13 times higher than the corresponding estimate (1.5%) among colleges in the "less competitive" Barron's category.

The contrasts in high school sector are accentuated by differences in high school–level SES metrics among enrolling students from public high schools. In general, high schools attended by matriculants at the nation's most competitive colleges have lower shares of students eligible for free lunch and black/Hispanic students compared with matriculants at less selective institutions. The typical student who transitioned from a public high school to a Barron's Category 1 college attended a high school where 22.7% of students are eligible for free lunch and 28.4% of students are either black or Hispanic. Corresponding percentages for public high school matriculants to Barron's less competitive colleges are 37.1% and 38.0%.

Barron's categories are defined in part by the competitiveness of the admissions processes, so naturally there is a strong relationship between student achievement and Barron's classification. Table 3.1 shows that a strong relationship also exists between enrollment category and the academic preparation of the matriculant's high school classmates. The typical matriculant at a Barron's Category 1 college attends a high school where the average SAT is 1144—nearly 150 points higher than high school classmates of matriculants at Barron's Category 5 colleges.

Verification of Grade Inflation through Federal Data Sets

A possible limitation to using HSGPA from student data questionnaires is that the data are self-reported. With such self-reporting comes the temptation for students to overstate their own HSGPAs. In the context of grade inflation, the tendency of individual students to embellish HSGPAs would not be problematic unless this tendency has changed over time. In other words, if the average student from the 1998 and 2016 cohorts inflated his or her own HSGPA by 0.3 points, the actual grade inflation between these two cohorts would match exactly the self-reported grade inflation. Our trends are consistent with those calculated from federal datasets. For example, data from the National Assessment of Educational Progress (NAEP) High School Transcript Survey (HSTS) show that unadjusted high school GPA among high school graduates increased by 0.10 points between the 1998 and 2009, which is slightly larger than the 0.07 point increase over this period from SDQ data (Nord et al. 2011).

We conclude the empirical section of this chapter by estimating grade inflation from two US Department of Education student transcript data sets during the study period: the Education Longitudinal Study of 2002 (ELS:02), representing the high school cohort of 2004, and the High School Longitudinal Study of 2009 (HSLS:09), representing the high school cohort of 2013. An obvious advantage of using actual transcript data is that students' misreporting plays no role in the documented grade inflation trends. There are, however, a few drawbacks worth noting. First, as we show in figure 3.1, there are annual fluctuations in average HSGPA. Since these surveys represent only two points in time, it is possible that the overall trend is not accurately reflected. Second, though the surveys are nationally representative, the sample sizes of the college entrance examination population in the surveys are considerably smaller than those in the College Board data. It is unclear whether the college entrance examination test-taking sample in each survey year is reflective of the population of SAT test takers. Finally, and perhaps most important, estimating trends in grade inflation from the federal surveys requires applying a set of uniform rules for calculating HSGPA across high schools and over time. Policies on weighting of honors and Advanced Placement courses, as well as the inclusion of nonacademic courses in HSGPA, vary markedly across high schools. We are unable to fully account for these grading nuances in our analyses of the federal data sets.

In spite of their challenges, these data sets may provide valuable information into the mechanism behind HSGPA's upward drift. In table 3.2, we show both the weighted and unweighted HSGPAs calculated directly from student transcript data files for these two cohorts of students. Over this decade, weighted HSGPAs

Table 3.2.   Average HSGPA and standard errors from student transcripts, by SAT scores

	Weighted HSGPA (transcript-calculated)		Weighted HSGPA— academic courses		Unweighted HSGPA (transcript-calculated)	
	Avg.	SE	Avg.	SE	Avg.	SE
Panel A: Cohort of 2013 (HSLS:09)						
SAT scores						
400–790	2.44	0.033	2.28	0.038	2.40	0.031
800–1090	3.14	0.016	3.03	0.017	3.00	0.015
1100–1290	3.67	0.021	3.62	0.023	3.41	0.019
1300+	4.03	0.039	4.02	0.039	3.63	0.034
SAT takers	3.19	0.018	3.09	0.020	3.03	0.016
All students	2.76	0.020	2.65	0.020	2.65	0.018
Panel B: Cohort of 2004 (ELS:02)						
400–790	2.45	0.024	2.28	0.023	2.43	0.023
800–1090	3.03	0.014	2.91	0.015	2.97	0.014
1100–1290	3.53	0.017	3.47	0.018	3.40	0.017
1300+	3.87	0.023	3.83	0.026	3.64	0.022
SAT takers	3.11	0.014	3.00	0.015	3.03	0.013
All students	2.69	0.015	2.58	0.015	2.64	0.014

Notes: HSGPA = high school grade point average; SE = standard error. In the transcript-calculated GPA calculations, we converted letter grades to grade points in the following form: A+ = 4.33, A = 4.0, A− = 3.67 . . . D− = 0.67. All calculations are weighted to account for complex survey design. Transcript-calculated HSGPAs omit any courses for which no letter grade was assigned, and courses taken prior to ninth grade. Honors-weighted courses in which students earn higher than a failing grade receive an additional grade point. SAT scores are represented by TXEESATC from ELS (highest entrance exam composite score in terms of SAT) and X3TXSATCOMP from HSLS (college entrance exam composite score in terms of SAT). The weighted HSGPAs in academic courses are taken directly from the student-level data files in ELS and HSLS.

among the college entrance exam test-taking population increased by 0.08 points, about as large as the 0.07-point increase shown in figure 3.1. These surveys indicate that the largest increases—approximately 0.15 to 0.20 GPA points—occurred among students with SAT scores high enough (≥1100) to qualify for enrollment in four-year colleges. By contrast, unweighted HSGPA changed little between these two time points. GPA weighting is intended to account for the fact that students who elect to take more advanced courses will often earn lower grades because of increased course demands. The data in table 3.2 suggest that students taking more challenging courses are earning the same grades that they would have earned in easier courses, and that this surprising finding is contributing substantially to the upward drift in HSGPA.

Conclusion

In this chapter, we use data provided by students, colleges, and high schools to show that average high school grades are higher than ever; that more students are earning the same grades as one another, making it harder to distinguish high achievers; and that high schools are increasingly withholding important information about class rank that can be used to put grades in context. Our analysis of data from the College Board and the US Department of Education shows an upward trend in high school grades that has been in place for at least two and a half decades. On the one hand, these findings may strike readers as unremarkable. Reporters and commentators online have both exposed grade inflation in recent years and have generally treated it critically. On the other hand, our quantitative research provides rigorous evidence of the truth behind the anecdotes.

For how much longer will high school grades continue on their uphill march? As we note, despite the creative efforts of many high schools to adopt grading scales that exceed the traditional 4.0 maximum, most current grading schemes have a ceiling, and therefore averages cannot continue to increase indefinitely. Differential weighting policies across course types are redefining new heights to which GPAs can ascend.

A particularly challenging aspect of grade inflation is its inconsistency across high schools. Institutions with rampant grade inflation risk developing reputations for awarding unmerited high grades. The most academically prepared students from such high schools are indistinguishable from less-prepared students on the basis of grades and may face challenges securing admission to academically matched colleges. At the other end of the spectrum, high grades awarded to less-prepared students may misleadingly indicate to admissions staff that applicants are prepared for the rigors of college coursework. High schools resisting the temptation to inflate grades suffer too, particularly if they fail to convey their policy of upholding high standards. Average grades at these high schools might be interpreted as below average, and above-average grades might be interpreted as average. In a landscape of rampant grade inflation, high schools bucking this trend risk placing their students in danger of rejection from academically matched colleges.

Finally, we show in this chapter that, on average, high schools enrolling students from more advantaged groups are inflating grades at a faster pace than are other high schools. Some critics of standardized testing claim that score differentials on college entrance exams disadvantage lower-scoring groups during the college admissions processes, and the other chapters in this volume discuss this debate in great detail. Without evidence, these same critics suggest that high school grades are a fairer measure of performance for underrepresented students—typically defined as African Americans, Latinos, and Native American students. The implication seems to be that, unlike standardized tests, high school GPA is more equitable because differences in high school grades across different racial/ethnic groups are either smaller or nonexistent. We demonstrate conclusively that this is untrue. Not only are there differences in high school GPA by race/ethnicity and parental education; we show evidence that these gaps have widened over time.

If grade inflation continues, admissions staff may need to rely more heavily on standardized tests like the SAT or ACT to differentiate students. Given that high school grade inflation is no secret, it is surprising that some institutions continue to institute test-optional policies. The irony of test-optional admissions policies is that adopting colleges still benefit from these college entrance exams, even among students who choose not to submit them. Many high schools provide "profile sheets" that indicate important measures like average SAT and ACT scores among graduating seniors. College admissions staff can use these data to make inferences about the curricular rigor and the academic preparation of graduating students. Student grades as well as class rank can help to situate the student in his or her class, and so the admissions officer can simultaneously consider the high school's rigor and the student's own performance to draw inferences about preparation in the absence of college entrance exam results. With class rank vanishing and high school grades compressing, test-optional policies may become unsustainable.

APPENDIX

In addition to using the derived GPAs from each of the two surveys, the GPA calculations were constructed using the transcript file in HSLS and then replicated in for the ELS transcript file to ensure consistency across years. GPA calculations relied on standardized Carnegie credits provided in each of the surveys. We discarded classes where students could not earn a letter grade, as well as credits earned prior to ninth grade. One additional grade point was added to courses where students earned a non-failing grade and were flagged as honors in the HSLS and ELS transcript files. Because ELS did not have a credit-attempted variable, this variable was manually created for both surveys, using the credits earned variable for non-failing courses. The number of credits attempted for failed courses was ascertained from students who passed the same course within the same high school. In the few instances where no other student within the school

Appendix table 3.1.   Fraction of SAT test takers with missing HSGPA and average composite SAT scores of nonrespondents

Cohort	% missing GPA	Average SAT of nonrespondents
1998	10.1	1003
1999	11.0	1005
2000	13.6	1007
2001	14.8	1006
2002	18.5	1016
2003	23.1	1038
2004	16.3	1053
2005	10.4	1017
2006	8.5	974
2007	8.0	952
2008	11.9	1057
2009	6.6	996
2010	6.3	976
2011	6.8	978
2012	7.2	977
2013	9.7	995
2014	7.6	966
2015	7.6	955
2016	7.6	939

Notes: HSGPA = high school grade point average. Excludes students who last took the SAT after January of their final high school year.

Appendix table 3.2.   High school level characteristics, by HSGPA growth quartile

	Schools (N)	% free lunch (1997–1998)	% free lunch (2014–2015)	% black/Hispanic (1997–1998)
Bottom 10th	662	28.0	52.5	42.7
10th–25th	992	23.3	43.3	32.7
25th–50th	1654	18.5	36.6	24.8
50th–75th	1654	14.9	31.2	17.7
75th–90th	992	13.7	28.7	15.3
Top 10th	662	17.8	31.8	15.9

	Schools (N)	% black/Hispanic (2014–2015)	% seniors taking SAT (1997–1998)	% seniors taking SAT (2014–2015)
Bottom 10th	662	60.5	36.1	50.9
10th–25th	992	46.8	41.3	47.8
25th–50th	1654	36.6	48.1	51.6
50th–75th	1654	27.1	52.9	53.5
75th–90th	992	23.5	55.3	54.6
Top 10th	662	21.8	52.8	51.3

Notes: HSGPA = high school grade point average. Only includes high schools with 30 or more SAT test takers in the 1998 and 2016 cohorts. The unit of analysis in all calculations is the high school.

passed/attempted that course, we used the modal number of credits earned for all survey participants to determine the number of credits attempted.

The following tables present supporting data for information provided in note 4 and in figure 3.7a.

NOTES

1. We calculated this statistic from the Integrated Postsecondary Education Data System (IPEDS) 2014 survey.

2. Students also have the option of indicating that they have an A+ grade point average, which is represented by a 4.33 GPA. In March 2016, the College Board began administering a revised SAT. From the cohort of students graduating from high school in 2016, we omit these "late" SAT test takers. To maintain comparability across cohorts, we remove all students who last took the SAT after January of their high school senior year.

3. In 2005, the Verbal section of the SAT was renamed as Critical Reading, and the Writing section was introduced. The total maximum score went from 1600 to 2400. For consistency over time, we do not include Writing scores in these analyses.

4. Less than 1% of students report grades below the C range, so we omit these students from figure 3.2. Reporting HSGPA on the SDQ is optional, and each year some students fail to report this metric. Appendix table 3.1 presents the fraction of sampled students who do not comply with the request to provide HSGPA. Over time, there have been fluctuations in the fraction of students reporting GPA as well as the mean SAT scores of students withholding HSGPAs.

5. An additional assumption here is that the composition of courses students take in high school has not shifted during this period such that students have become more likely to take "easier" courses, where earning high grades requires less effort.

6. We only consider high schools with 30 or more test takers between 1998 and 2016 in order to minimize noise from small sample sizes.

7. Figure 3.7 is constructed from public high schools only, also with the restriction that high schools had 30 or more SAT test takers in the 1998 and 2016 cohorts. The intercept term in this regression is 0.17, indicating that the typical sampled high school experienced a jump in HSGPA of 0.17 points between 1998 and 2016, which is similar to the student-level estimate of 0.15 in figure 3.3. The tenth, twenty-fifth, fiftieth, seventy-fifth, and ninetieth percentiles of residuals are −0.24, −0.12, 0.00, 0.12, and 0.23 HSGPA points.

8. Digest of Education Statistics, 2015 Tables, National Center for Education Statistics, table 205.50, https://nces.ed.gov/programs/digest/d15/tables/dt15_205.50.asp?current=yes.

9. The College Board also asks students about family income, but many students do not respond to this question or incorrectly estimate income.

10. We partitioned colleges identically to Hurwitz and Kumar 2015, focusing on Barron's-ranked colleges providing complete data through the College Board's Annual Survey of Colleges. Estimates represent the unweighted averages with Barron's categories.

11. These analyses are imperfect because enrollment data are restricted to College Board students who took either the AP, SAT, or PSAT/NMSQT, which results in varied coverage, depending on selectivity, university location, and test-optional policies.

REFERENCES

Balingit, M. (2015). The new trend in validating top students: Make them all valedictorians. *Washington Post*, July 13. Retrieved from https://www.washingtonpost.com /news/grade-point/wp/2015/07/13/high-schools-are-doing-away-with-class-rank-what -does-that-mean-for-college-admissions.

Brookhart, S. M., Guskey, T. R., Bowers, A. J., McMillan, J. H., Smith, J. K., Smith, L. F., Stevens, M. T., and Welsh, M. E. (2016). A century of grading research: Meaning and value in the most common educational measure. *Review of Educational Research, 86,* 1–46.

Ehlers, T., and Schwager, R. (2016). Honest grading, grade inflation, and reputation. *CESifo Economic Studies, 62*(3), 506–521.

Finder, A. (2006). Schools avoid class rankings, vexing colleges. *New York Times,* March 5. Retrieved from http://www.nytimes.com/2006/03/05/education/05rank .html.

Guskey, T. R. (2014). Class rank weighs down true learning. *Phi Delta Kappan, 95*(6), 15–19.

Hurwitz, M., and Kumar, A. (2015). Supply and demand in the higher education market: College admission and college choice. New York: The College Board. Retrieved from https://research.collegeboard.org/sites/default/files/publications/2015/8/college-board -research-brief-supply-demand-college-admission-college-choice.pdf.

Kohn, A. (1998). Only for my kid: How privileged parents undermine school reform. *Phi Delta Kappan, 79*(8), 568–577.

Nord, C., Roey, S., Perkins, R., Lyons, M., Lemanski, N., Brown, J., and Schuknecht, J. (2011). The Nation's Report Card: America's High School Graduates (NCES 2011-462). U.S. Department of Education, National Center for Education Statistics. Washington, DC: U.S. Government Printing Office.

Pattison, E., Grodsky, E., and Muller, C. (2013). Is the sky falling? Grade inflation and the signaling power of grades. *Educational Researcher, 42*, 259–265.

Perkins, R., Kleiner, B., Roey, S., and Brown, J. (2004). The high school transcript study: A decade of change in curricula and achievement, 1990–2000. Washington, DC: National Center for Education Statistics. Retrieved from https://nces.ed.gov /pubsearch/pubsinfo.asp?pubid=2004455.

Reeves, R. V., and Halikias, D. (2017). Race gaps in SAT scores highlight inequality and hinder upward mobility. Washington, DC: Brookings Institution. Retrieved from https://www.brookings.edu/research/race-gaps-in-sat-scores-highlight-inequality-and -hinder-upward-mobility.

Snyder, T. (1993). 120 years of American education: A statistical portrait. Washington, DC: National Center for Education Statistics. Retrieved from https://nces.ed.gov /pubs93/93442.pdf.

4

Merit-Based Scholarships in Student Recruitment and the Role of Standardized Tests

Jonathan Jacobs, Jim Brooks, and Roger J. Thompson

*C*ollege and university enrollment managers use a variety of recruitment strate-gies to encourage highly qualified students to apply and enroll at their institu-tions. As the net price of tuition has increased in recent years, these strategies often take the form of merit- and need-based financial aid. Financial aid is important because it enables institutions to increase access to postsecondary education for disadvan-taged students who might otherwise struggle or be unable to attend college. Through strategic allocation of financial aid, colleges are often able to establish and main-tain a competitive advantage in attracting highly qualified applicants over peer institutions.

This chapter offers a rare glimpse into how one highly selective public institution, the University of Oregon, restructured its 15-year-old merit aid program and attracted a highly qualified and more diverse incoming class while providing more transparency in the award process. Jacobs, Brooks, and Thompson provide extensive details on their strategic planning process, the selection criteria used for financial aid metrics, and their decision to use weighted high school GPA (HSGPA) and standardized test scores (SAT/ACT) as key selection criteria. The authors note that their decision to use both HSGPA and standardized test scores was based on their interest in using measures that were strong predictors of student success in college, most notably, first-year retention and graduation rates.

The chapter also examines the impact of financial aid on student enrollment deci-sions. The authors fully discuss how they simulated several hypothetical aid package scenarios in order to understand enrollment yields at different scholarship amounts. Successful restructuring of the University of Oregon's scholarship program meant cre-ating a program that not only increased the academic profile of the incoming class, but also accurately anticipated yield and fit within the institution's budget. Despite declining state appropriations and rising expenditures, the authors effectively implemented a data-driven approach that enabled the university to lower the net cost of attendance for highly qualified residents, compared with previous cohorts who received aid.

In the fall of 2013, the University of Oregon restructured its largest merit scholar-ship program for students with the highest levels of academic preparation. For the first time in university history, our flagship merit-based aid program introduced a standardized test score component as part of the eligibility criteria. This program was expected to disburse more than $20 million to more than 3,500 students in the 2016–2017 academic year. The scholarship restructuring was successful, with entering classes achieving record-setting high school GPA (HSGPA) and SAT/ACT scores in the years following its implementation. In addition, retention rates in-creased and the cohorts are on track to achieve record four- and six-year gradua-tion rates. Despite continued moderate tuition increases each year, we were also able to reduce the net cost of attendance for residents who receive aid following the restructuring. The 2013 and 2014 resident freshmen had a net cost after schol-arships below that of the 2011 and 2012 classes.

This chapter discusses the importance of financial aid as a recruiting tool as well as the impact financial aid has on student enrollment decisions. First, we explore the use of standardized test scores and HSGPA in financial aid program creation and then highlight the thought process and data analysis that went into restructuring the financial aid program and how we predicted the change would impact student enrollment decisions. Finally, we look at the changes to enrollment yield as a result of the new award structure.

This conversation is relevant to high schools, as it sheds light on how public institutions think about financial aid awards in a recruitment environment. Our analysis also highlights the relevance of HSGPA and standardized test scores for university outcomes and the scholarship potential of high school students. Higher education institutions may find relevance in our analysis of the impact aid has on the decision to enroll as they seek to restructure their own merit-based financial aid programs.

Identifying the Problem

Between 2007 and 2012, in the face of the global recession, the University of Oregon was rapidly changing; enrollment increased by 21% (from 20,376 to 24,591), and at the same time, resident tuition and fees increased by about 9% each year (from $6,168 to $9,310) because of a decline in state support. Scarce public resources and funding were not uncommon during this time for our peer institutions, as well as universities nationwide.

This changing funding structure emphasized the importance of providing financial aid to students who were considering the University of Oregon (UO), with that scholarship aid positively impacting their enrollment decision. The existing scholarship program, known as the Dean's Scholarship, had remained virtually unchanged for an estimated 15 to 20 years. In addition, there had been no examination of its effectiveness in recruiting the highest-achieving high school students. The primary metric for awarding aid was HSGPA, but students had no way of knowing what minimum GPA was required to be eligible for the award. Even the award amounts were uncertain and not keeping pace with the new financial environment. Thus, it was clear that the current scholarship program was not serving as an effective recruiting tool, and a complete restructuring would be required.

Creating an Improvement Plan

The scholarship review project was launched in early 2012 with a goal of restructuring the program for new students who would enroll in fall 2013. Our goal was to determine what criteria would be used to award aid and how different aid packages would impact a student's decision to enroll.

There are many reasons why a university offers scholarships to students. Aid helps increase access to postsecondary education for students with lower incomes who might otherwise struggle to afford college (Scott-Clayton 2015). Aid also allows students to focus more on academics and less on next year's tuition bill and has been shown to have a positive effect on graduation rates for low-income students (Franke 2014). Scholarships are used as recruiting tools because they impact the decision making of academically prepared students as they narrow their college choices. Enrolling greater numbers of highly prepared students generally increases the academic profile of an institution, which in turn makes it more attractive to future classes of high-achieving students. The primary intent of the UO merit aid restructuring was clear: increase the attractiveness of the university to academically prepared students and enroll a better-prepared freshman class.

We planned to evaluate the impact of the restructured program by targeting increases in average HSGPA and standardized test scores as key indicators of a better-prepared class. In order to maximize the ability to recruit prospective students, it was also important for the restructured program to be transparent; parents and students needed a clear understanding of the award eligibility criteria.

The Restructured Summit and Apex Awards

The restructured awards replaced the existing merit-based Dean's Scholarship, the award amounts of which varied based on students' HSGPA. In fall 2012, awards ranged from four-year awards of $1,000 to $2,000 for residents with a 3.70 HSGPA and above. Nonresidents received $4,000 to $7,000 with a 3.60 high school GPA or better. These awards were not automatic, and not all students with eligible HSGPA received the award, owing to funding limitations. Moreover, students did not find out what award they received until an award letter arrived; the formula by which aid was determined was not publicly available.

Since improving academic quality was a central goal, we wanted the restructured merit-based scholarships to reward students for reaching the peak of high school achievement. Thus, the new Summit Scholarship awards top scholars in-state $24,000 over four years. Because of differences in tuition, out-of-state top scholars receive $36,000 over four years. The Apex Scholarship awards Oregon residents $12,000 in total, and out-of-state students receive $16,000 over four years. For the first time in university history, the flagship, merit-based financial aid awards include a standardized test score eligibility component. Scholarships are awarded to incoming freshmen based on the criteria set forth in table 4.1.

These awards are automatic and do not require students to do anything other than be admitted to the university and meet the minimum requirements of the program. A Free Application for Federal Student Aid (FAFSA) is not required and there is no supplemental financial aid application for this award, though we strongly recommended that students with financial need complete the FAFSA to be eligible for other scholarship and grant programs. With this new structure,

Table 4.1.   Summit and Apex scholarship criteria

Summit	Apex
3.80 high school GPA on a 4.00 scale	3.60 high school GPA on a 4.00 scale
1190 old SAT, 1260 new SAT, or 26 ACT	1150 old SAT, 1220 new SAT, or 25 ACT
(Math and Critical Reading only)	(Math and Critical Reading only)

scholarship criteria became clear and easy for admissions and financial aid office staff to communicate to prospective students.

Choosing Financial Aid Criteria

Using high school GPA as a component in defining who received a financial aid award was an obvious consideration, but selecting which high school GPA was not so obvious. As it turned out, this was one of the most difficult decisions connected with scholarship restructuring. We considered three choices for high school GPA:

1. Weighted high school GPA: This was the GPA on most students' high school transcripts and reflected what they believed was their GPA from their high school. Certain courses such as honors or AP classes (through which students can earn college credit, advanced placement, or both, for qualifying AP Exam scores) might give additional GPA weight to strong grades. For example, an A in an AP course might be counted as a 5.00 while a standard A in a college preparatory course might only be counted as a 4.00.

2. Unweighted high school GPA: This was the GPA of students when calculated with every A counting as a 4.0 and every B as a 3.00 regardless of any characteristics of intensity or rigor. In other words, AP and college preparatory courses are treated equally.

3. Core course high school GPA: This was the GPA for only the core curriculum, typically the 15 college preparatory courses we required for admission at the University of Oregon. This would have excluded any consideration of grades in high school elective courses, where student grades tended to be stronger. If we chose to use the core courses, we would also have needed to make a decision on whether we would have unweighted the high school GPA of the core courses.

Consider our dilemma: Did we want scholarship consideration for an A grade in college preparatory writing to mean the same as an A grade in AP English? If we chose an unweighted high school GPA, we would have standardized each letter grade, but we still would not have controlled for the rigor of the coursework. Alternatively, if we chose to use weighted grades, there would have been inconsistency in how high schools computed their weights. One high school might have transcribed an A in an AP English course as a 6.00, and a high school that did not weight grades might have transcribed an A in the same AP English course as a 4.00. This inconsistency would have disadvantaged students from schools that did not offer the same increased weighting on transcripts. Policies on how to weight grades differed at both the school and state levels, making this conversation especially difficult.

Besides the issues of weighting and using core courses, we ultimately considered one other question: what HSGPA did the student *expect* to be used when calculating the scholarship award? This is important because weighted GPAs tend to increase the GPA of a student relative to unweighted GPA and core coursework GPA. If a student worked hard over the course of his or her high school career to achieve a weighted 3.81 GPA, he or she would be very proud of that accomplishment and could point to it on the application for admission. With the right standardized test score, the student would expect to receive a Summit-level award. If we recalculated the high school GPA to be unweighted, we might have found ourselves in the position of telling the student, "Sorry, despite what your transcript says, you only have a 3.78 high school GPA." This would reduce the scholarship to an Apex-level award. A nonresident applicant would receive $20,000 *less* over four years than what would be expected with a Summit-level award.

Expectations are a powerful thing, even for students who are overwhelmingly likely to come to the University of Oregon. Making the mistake of mismanaging expectations, especially on something as important as a financial aid award, can have a strong negative impact on a student's impression of the college and their desire to enroll, and there are many admitted students who do not qualify for scholarships that we still hope to enroll.

In the end, after considering the strengths and weaknesses of each type of high school GPA, the University of Oregon chose to use weighted high school GPA for consideration of scholarships. This GPA has the closest alignment with students' expectations and aligned with our recruitment goals. This is a conversation that continues to come up when we speak with our high school administrators, especially at schools that do not weight high school GPA. Understandably, those schools feel that using the weighted GPA disadvantages students from their high school. We expect to have continued conversations with our advisory board of high school principals and counselors to make sure the high school GPA we are using considers all perspectives.

Considering Test Scores in Scholarships

Previously, we discussed how using weighted high school GPA for merit scholarships could lead to inequity across students from different high schools owing to different GPA weighting strategies. The fact that these pitfalls existed was a good starting point for discussing why the consideration of standardized test scores

(SAT/ACT) in merit scholarships was helpful. The university requires a test score for admission, which makes considering test scores in determining scholarship eligibility very practical.

A student's test score tells us something very different about the student from his or her high school GPA. While a high school GPA is an average portfolio measure of a student's performance in four years of secondary school, a standardized test score is a measure of a student's knowledge as assessed during a test on a single day. The fact that it is standardized is valuable as a complement to high school GPA, where there can be great difference in the reliability of the measure between high schools using different weights. Not only that, teachers' grading practices are a subjective process that lacks standardization across states, schools, teachers, and even individuals within a class (see chapter 3 on grade inflation).

Another benefit of the standardized test score, especially in Math, is that a higher score is associated with more content knowledge. A strong high school GPA can be obtained from courses with great variation in the level of math content. For example, a student who averages B grades in the high school three-course sequence Algebra 1, Geometry, and Algebra 2 will have the same GPA, but a lower expected standardized test outcome, than a student who averages B grades in the four-course sequence Geometry, Algebra 2, Pre-Calculus, and Calculus.

Standardized tests are not completely free of concerns about what they measure. Studies show test scores have a strong correlation with gender, socioeconomic status, race/ethnicity, and other groupings (Zwick 2004). For example, students from traditionally underrepresented races and lower socioeconomic status perform lower on average on standardized tests. While the College Board, ACT, and others have produced research showing how subgroup differences relate to differences in academic preparation for college (Kobrin, Sathy, and Shaw 2006), there is still a perception of test score bias in the high school community (see chapter 1 on myths about standardized tests). Awareness of these biases, or at least the perception of these biases, is important as the University of Oregon makes scholarship decisions based in part on standardized test scores.

Do High School GPA and Test Scores Predict Academic Success?

The previous section discussed some of the validity concerns and practical considerations of high school GPA and SAT/ACT. It was also important to examine the empirical outcomes for our students and determine whether high school GPA or test score were strong predictors of college success. To do that, we examined the relationship between high school GPA, standardized test score, and the outcome metrics of the first-year university GPA and graduation in six years. We provide data in table 4.2 on the correlation between high school GPA and standardized test score at the University of Oregon. A correlation of 1.00 would be a perfect fit that would allow us to perfectly predict one measure by looking at another, while a 0.00 would mean no relationship at all. Looking at the Pearson correlation co-efficients we saw that high school GPA had the stronger correlation with first-year university GPA, with a correlation of .47. The correlation between standardized test score and first-year university GPA was .40, which was very strong as well. To better understand how each variable related to first-year university GPA independent of the other, we used a partial correlation analysis (table 4.3), which showed both high school GPA and standardized test score each retained a strong correlation—.35 and .25, respectively—even after controlling for the other.

We note that the correlation between high school GPA and six-year graduation rates was .14, and the correlation between standardized test score and six-year graduation rates was .09. Part of the reason the correlation was low is because graduation rate is a binary metric, which makes correlation more troublesome. Descriptive data in the following tercile analysis was in many ways a better way

Table 4.2.   Pearson correlation between HSGPA, test score, and FYGPA of new entering domestic freshmen, and graduation in six years (fall 2015 cohort)

	HSGPA	SAT/ACT	FYGPA	Graduation in six years
HSGPA	1.00	.43	.47	.14
SAT/ACT		1.00	.40	.09
FYGPA			1.00	.37
Graduation in six years				1.00

Notes: HSGPA = high school grade point average; FYGPA = first-year college grade point average. Fall 2015 N = 3,688 students. Six-year graduation rate correlations use fall 2009 cohort because of the delay between starting college and graduating. Pearson correlation is not corrected for restriction of range.

Table 4.3.   Pearson partial correlation between HSGPA, test score, and FYGPA, new entering domestic freshmen, fall 2015

	HSGPA removing the effect of SAT/ACT	SAT/ACT removing the effect of HSGPA
FYGPA	.35	.25

Notes: HSGPA = high school grade point average; FYGPA = first-year college grade point average. N = 3,649.

to describe the relationship between high school GPA, test score, and six-year graduation rate as they applied to this analysis.

Correlations are important tests but are not an effective way to descriptively show university performance of first-year students based on their high school GPA and test scores. To demonstrate the outcomes of our first-year students, we divided the student population into terciles by academic preparation to show how outcome metrics differed between students with high, average, and low levels of academic preparation.

Tables 4.4 and 4.5 show the fall 2015 population based on the terciles used for analysis. The populations do not split evenly into thirds in this sample, because the original tercile definitions were created from an older population. This descriptive report showed the expected correlations: students with more preparation in either high school GPA or stronger test scores tended to perform better on university outcome metrics.

These tables only examine high school GPA or SAT/ACT in isolation. They do not consider both metrics together. Our question here is: What is the added value of considering both high school GPA and test score? Also, what about the cases in which a student has a strong high school GPA and weak SAT/ACT, or vice versa (see chapter 5 on discrepant performance)?

Table 4.4. Outcomes by HSGPA tercile, fall 2015 first-time, full-time freshmen

HSGPA—Low tercile 3.45 or lower	HSGPA—Mid tercile 3.46 to 3.76	HSGPA—High tercile 3.77 or higher
Percentage of total: 33%	Percentage of total: 30%	Percentage of total: 36%
Retention rate: 82%	Retention rate: 86%	Retention rate: 90%
FYGPA (average): 2.81	FYGPA (average): 3.06	FYGPA (average): 3.47

Notes: HSGPA = high school grade point average; FYGPA = first-year college grade point average. $N = 3,593$.

Table 4.5. Outcomes by SAT/ACT tercile, fall 2015 first-time, full-time freshmen

SAT/ACT—Low tercile 1060 or lower	SAT/ACT—Mid tercile 1070 to 1190	SAT/ACT—High tercile 1200 or higher
Percentage of total: 31%	Percentage of total: 34%	Percentage of total: 35%
Retention rate: 81%	Retention rate: 87%	Retention rate: 90%
FYGPA (average): 2.83	FYGPA (average): 3.11	FYGPA (average): 3.40

Notes: FYGPA = first-year college grade point average. $N = 3,593$. SAT analysis uses the old 1600 scale for SAT Critical Reading and Math. The ACT Composite score uses concordance tables to convert the score to an SAT score. If a student took both an ACT and an SAT test, the highest score on the SAT scale is used.

By accounting for both high school GPA and test score tercile (table 4.6) we achieved a more nuanced understanding of the academic preparation of these students. While the largest groupings of students were those with high performance or low performance in both metrics, we still saw significant portions of the population in which the student performed well in high school GPA and poorly in test score or vice versa. We observed from this table that if students had either a low high school GPA or a low test score, regardless of their performance in the other, they were less likely to succeed. Students who were at least in the middle tercile of both populations had on average a stronger university GPA and a stronger retention rate. To illustrate this, we found that the nearly 49% of the population who had either a low tercile high school GPA *or* a low tercile test score (shaded on the table) had an average high school GPA of 2.86 and a retention rate of 82%. This was only marginally higher than the 33% of students with a low high school GPA (2.81 and 82%), or the 31% of students with a low SAT/ACT (2.83 and 81%) individually. In other words, by looking for either low SAT/ACT or low high school GPA, our ability to descriptively identify who did not perform as strongly in the university setting increased.

We see a pattern in graduation rates (table 4.7) that we expected overall: whether a student has higher test scores or higher GPA, the graduation rate improves. There is an exception among the high–test score but low–high school GPA students, where we saw a graduation rate of 64%, five points lower than the mid–test score low–high school GPA group graduation rate of 69%. This is a smaller, nontraditional group, but we did replicate the outcomes pattern in the earlier 2008

Table 4.6.   Outcomes by HSGPA and SAT/ACT terciles, fall 2015 first-time, full-time freshmen

	HSGPA—Low tercile 3.45 or lower	HSGPA—Mid tercile 3.46 to 3.76	HSGPA—High tercile 3.77 or higher
SAT/ACT—High Tercile 1200 or higher	Percentage of total: 6% Retention rate: 86% FYGPA (average): 2.97	Percentage of total: 7% Retention rate: 88% FYGPA (average): 3.22	Percentage of total: 21% Retention rate: 92% FYGPA (average): 3.58
SAT/ACT—Mid Tercile 1070 to 1190	Percentage of total: 11% Retention rate: 83% FYGPA (average): 2.88	Percentage of total: 12% Retention rate: 90% FYGPA (average): 3.11	Percentage of total: 10% Retention rate: 90% FYGPA (average): 3.34
SAT/ACT—Low Tercile 1060 or lower	Percentage of total: 16% Retention rate: 80% FYGPA (average): 2.69	Percentage of total: 10% Retention rate: 82% FYGPA (average): 2.87	Percentage of total: 5% Retention rate: 81% FYGPA (average): 3.20

Notes: HSGPA = high school grade point average; FYGPA = first-year college grade point average. *N* = 3,593. SAT analysis uses the old 1600 scale for SAT Critical Reading and Math.

Table 4.7.   Six-year graduation rates by HSGPA and SAT/ACT terciles,
fall 2009 first-time, full-time freshmen

	HSGPA—Low tercile 3.45 or lower	HSGPA—Mid tercile 3.46 to 3.76	HSGPA—High tercile 3.77 or higher
SAT/ACT—High tercile 1200 or higher	64%	77%	83%
SAT/ACT—Mid tercile 1070 to 1190	69%	71%	77%
SAT/ACT—Low tercile 1060 or lower	64%	68%	75%

Notes: HSGPA = high school grade point average; FYGPA = first-year college grade point average. N = 3,763. SAT analysis uses the old 1600 scale for SAT Critical Reading and Math.

cohort. Further analysis was not conducted, as this group fell outside the group we were targeting for scholarship consideration.

The most important question for us was the relationship between test scores and graduation rates for the students who might receive financial aid. For the majority of tercile groups, we saw a pattern of increasing graduation rates with increases in either test score tercile or high school GPA tercile. For the non-shaded groups in the middle- and high-terciles this pattern was especially apparent. As these are the groups we would consider for scholarships, this reinforced using both of these metrics in a merit-based scholarship award.

We combined the knowledge we gained from these correlation and tercile analyses with the earlier discussions on what high school GPA and standardized test scores actually measured. This combination of professional judgment and empirical clarity led us to the strategic decision to use both test scores and high school GPA in our restructured Summit and Apex Scholarship awards.

Modeling Changes to the Scholarship Programs

Our analysis thus far has focused on the correlation and relationship of high school GPA and test scores with university outcomes. Next, we examined the impact of financial aid on students' enrollment decisions. Our team explored two core questions as we engaged in the restructuring:

1. What effect does additional merit aid have on the probability of enrollment?
2. How do we model the effect of restructured aid on an entering class?

In order to better isolate the effect of a change in the financial aid package, it was important to account for the effect of other factors on enrollment decisions, such as university reputation and the success of students after graduation. To better understand these issues, we examined a freshman survey that was administered in summer 2016. Among entering freshmen, 65% responded to questions about the importance of both cost and financial assistance in their decision to come to UO.

As shown in figure 4.1, cost and financial aid were very important factors for two out of every five of our freshmen, and somewhat important to at least three out of five. This alone suggested that cost and aid were important considerations in selecting a college. There were other generally more important factors that students were considering in their choice of a college. The academic and social reputation of the University of Oregon were the most important reasons students cited in their decision to come to the school, significantly more important than financial aid and cost. This is in a way a calculation of return on investment; students desire to pick the college that is right for them, and perceived reputation is a very important part of that.

As shown in figure 4.2, cost and financial assistance were on average much more important for resident students than nonresident students. This gap in the importance of cost and aid exists by residency even when controlling for family income. In some ways, this reinforced the reality that even wealthy residents

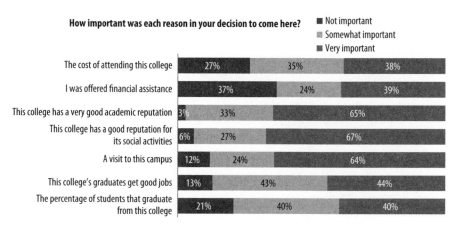

Fig. 4.1. Factors That Affect the Decision to Enroll at the University of Oregon ($N = 2{,}549$). *Source*: University of Oregon Freshman Survey.

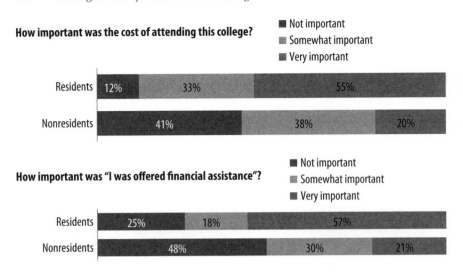

Fig. 4.2. Importance of Cost and Aid in Choosing to Attend the University of Oregon (*N* = 2,537). *Source*: University of Oregon Freshman Survey.

benefit from resident tuition, which is only one-third of what a nonresident student will pay. Wealthy residents may have the ability to pay for out-of-state schools, but the lower cost of the University of Oregon is a good deal at any income level. The reverse was true for out-of-state students. Despite the potential to be admitted and enroll at a subsidized public institution in the state where they reside, out-of-state students chose the University of Oregon—presumably because of all the other factors in their decision making. From the reputation of the college to the outcomes of graduates, these factors ended up being more important than cost and financial aid. Knowing the relative difference in prospective students' minds between reputation and cost is important.

It is important to note limitations of these analyses. First, this survey only included students who were expected to enroll at the university and excluded what could be very different perspectives of those who chose another institution. Contrary to our findings, we would expect that students who reside in Oregon but selected an out-of-state school would prioritize perceived value and outcomes above college cost and aid. Second, cost and financial aid were still at least somewhat important for more than half of nonresidents, so it was still a very important part of recruitment.

While a portion of the population will make their decision regardless of cost and aid, the majority of students in most groups cited cost and aid as important. As access is an important part of our mission as a public university, we would not be achieving our goals if we did not effectively recruit the populations that depend on aid when making their decision. What this analysis reveals is the larger picture that cost and financial aid are two considerations among many when students are choosing which college is right for them. This reinforces the need to create an aid program that emphasizes the academic and social benefits of the university.

Our next step was to better understand the impact of merit aid on a student's decision to enroll. To do this, we built a statistical model for freshman enrollment using the independent variables: total institution scholarship aid (minus federal/state), categorical income from FAFSA, SAT or converted ACT, admission to honor's college, residency, early action submission, first generation, underrepresented race/ethnicity, and significant interactions (see table 4.8 for model fit). As the decision to enroll is a yes or no decision, we used a logistic regression to determine the impact of aid, controlling for other variables that are significant in the decision to enroll. Variable selection in logistic regressions is a complicated process with the goal of selecting all known independent variables that brought additional information to the target result, in our case whether the student would enroll at the University of Oregon. A full summary of the coefficients from the model are available in the appendix. Please note that since the final model was built for prediction and not explanation, there are multiple interactions that may make interpreting each coefficient difficult.

The end goal was to determine the impact of grants and scholarships on the decision to enroll. We excluded federal and state aid from the financial aid variable we used in the model. In our judgment, federal and state aid does not impact a student's decision to enroll. Federal aid would be received by students wherever they chose to enroll and did not give a competitive advantage that would influence them to choose the University of Oregon. State aid was similar in that students would get the award at any in-state college or university, whether it was public or private, two-year or four-year.

This model revealed the unique effect our scholarship awards had on the decision to enroll after controlling for the other variables. Once we finalized the model from the original data, we then used these results for the next steps of our analysis.

Table 4.8. Logistic regression fit indices for predicting a freshman student's decision to enroll

C-statistic	.76 (0.5 = coin flip; 1.0 = perfect fit)
Max-rescaled pseudo R^2	.24
Hosmer and Lemeshow goodness-of-fit test	.33 (target > .05)

A logistic regression model is essentially a complex algebraic formula that explains the impact of each independent variable on a probability—in our case the chance that a student would enroll. If we believed the model was built correctly to accurately predict the impact of aid, then we could feed into the logistic model each student's data and modify only one characteristic—the amount of aid they received. This allowed us to determine, according to the model, the probability of enrollment for all students individually, not only at the original aid amount that we actually provided, but also the estimated impact on their decisions if we changed their scholarship amounts. It is important to note that we were not changing the regression model when we did this; we were merely looking at potential alternative probabilities of enrollment if we had offered each student different amounts of aid.

Model Restructured Aid on an Entering Class

The important strategic question was not the impact aid had on an individual but the impact an entire aid program had on an entering class of students. The objectives of the restructuring were to identify which admitted students should be offered aid packages, how much aid they should be awarded, what increases to enrollment yield we would expect, the overall impact on the budget, and how the change would impact the characteristics of the entering class.

In any given year, the University of Oregon admits 16,000 freshman for the fall term, and from this group, we expect to enroll approximately 4,000 new freshmen. To determine the impact of aid on an entire class, we took all 16,000 admits and ran them through the logistic model to determine their probability of enrollment as defined by the model. We modeled the changing probability of enrollment for each student if we gave them no aid, a $1,000 grant, a $2,000 grant, a $3,000 grant, all the way up to a $20,000 grant. This allowed us to say hypothetically what would happen to each student if we were to award more or less aid compared with the original amount they were actually awarded.

Table 4.9.   Probability of enrollment for three hypothetical students at different levels of aid (in percentages)

	Original award	$0	$1K	$2K	$3K	$4K	$5K	$6K	$7K	$8K	$9K
Resident 1	57	53	55	57	59	61	63	65	67	69	70
Resident 2	56	56	58	60	62	64	65	67	69	71	72
Nonresident 3	8	6	6	7	7	8	9	9	10	11	12

Table 4.9 shows a simulation of different hypothetical aid packaging scenarios. It took seconds to rule out the possibility of giving everyone large amounts of aid, as it showed the unsustainable final cost. This allowed us to pinpoint different populations by high school GPA and SAT/ACT cut points, and the model predicted yield at different scholarship amounts. Although the number of potential scenarios to test is very large, by having predicted yields for all students at all potential levels of aid, we could explore any scenario. Through a process of examining empirical data on screen and heartfelt discussion about what most benefited students, the group had the tools to understand what would happen, according to the model, with whatever plan was put in place.

At a very high level, we modeled the impact on an entire class if all students were given different amounts of aid. Figure 4.3 shows that difference illustrated for two populations: all Oregon residents and all nonresident students. This showed how a hypothetical scenario with all admitted students receiving equal levels of aid would result in a corresponding increase in enrollment yield. Our finding was that, in general, a resident student who was more likely to enroll in the first place, would have approximately 2% higher likelihood of enrolling per $1,000 in additional aid. The actual impact to yield varied greatly depending on the individual student's characteristics that we controlled for in the model. Nonresident students had a lower yield in general, and a smaller impact of on average a 1% increase to the modeled likelihood of enrollment per $1,000 in additional aid, again with great variability depending on student characteristics.

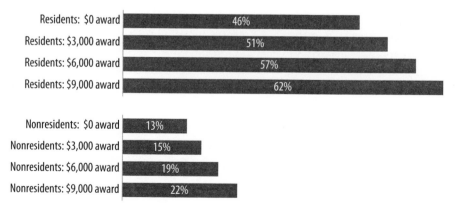

Fig. 4.3. Predicted (Modeled) Enrollment Yield at Different Scholarship Amounts

Selecting Scholarship Cut-Offs

Successfully restructuring a scholarship program meant creating a program that increased the academic profile of the class, accurately anticipated yield, and fit within a budget. It was initially unclear whether increasing the academic profile of the class was best done by awarding a large amount of aid to a small population or by awarding smaller amounts of aid to a large population. Based on professional judgment and the earlier empirical analysis of the impact of both high school GPA and standardized test score, we made the decision to use both metrics as eligibility criteria in a new scholarship award. This did not answer the question of the manner in which we would set the criteria. Was it better to set a lower GPA and a higher test score? Or was it better to set a higher GPA and a lower test score? What was the best distribution of aid?

We considered two important things. The correlation analysis established that high school GPA was the better independent predictor of college success for University of Oregon freshmen, despite the reliability issues connected with weighting. Also, high school GPA is a culmination of an individual's work over time. That said, test score was a valuable academic preparation metric to consider and offset many of the weaknesses of high school GPA. A combination of the two best predicted who was most prepared to succeed at the UO academically. After considerable modeling based on predicted yields with increased awards, and multiple meetings with decision makers to discuss which approach best served our students, would be easy to communicate, and fit within our budget, we arrived at a final decision:

The Summit Award was set to a 3.80 high school GPA and either 1190 SAT or 26 ACT. Based on expected increases to yield with the larger aid package, we knew about 20% of the entering class would receive the award. If we had instead used high school GPA as the only academic measure, we would have been forced to set the high school GPA to 3.93 to yield the same size scholarship class. If we awarded purely by test score, we would have required an SAT of 1270 or ACT of 28. Selecting students by a demonstrated academic quality in both measures allowed us to set the scores at significantly lower rates and ask students to meet both criteria to be eligible. The Apex Award was initially set to a 3.65 high school GPA and 1150 SAT or 25 ACT, which was expected to result in about 10% of the entering class with the award. The high school GPA cut was later lowered to 3.60 to slightly expand the scholarship.

When finalizing these scholarship criteria, we were aware that the approach could result in some financial risk if a higher-than-anticipated number of students met these cut points. For example, an unexpected increase in fall Summit-level applicants by 10% might throw a wrench into the program budget. It was ultimately decided that having "too many" academically strong students would be a good problem. Since these were four-year awards, any entering class would represent only about one-quarter of the program budget, and the program could potentially be changed for future classes before funding became unsustainable.

The benefits of a more transparent approach outweighed the potential financial risk. We found that parents and students have greatly appreciated the new approach because it was readily apparent what automatic scholarships were available, and students had aspirational high school GPAs and test scores that they could work to achieve. The decision to make scholarship requirements transparent came from a conversation with our high school advisory board, a group of high school principals and counselors who advise the University of Oregon on changes to policy. They also appreciated the greater clarity and reduction in student anxiety that came with the increased transparency.

The tiered system, having both a Summit and an Apex Award, allowed us to reward students below a Summit level and not have a sudden cliff from a large aid package to nothing. For students who met the Apex or Summit high school GPA, but had a test score below the Apex level, we had a third, unadvertised tier, which was a smaller one-year scholarship. The scholarships unfortunately are not as generous as the Summit or Apex program and are subject to restructuring each year. They did, however, allow us to recognize students who did not qualify for Summit

Table 4.10.   Summit, Apex, and university scholarships by grade point average and SAT/ACT criteria

	3.80+ HSGPA	3.60+ HSGPA
1190 SAT or 26 ACT or better	**SUMMIT** **Four-year award** $6,000/yr residents $9,000/yr nonresidents	
1150 SAT or 25 ACT or better		**APEX** **Four-year award** $3,000/yr residents $4,000/yr nonresidents
1050 SAT or 23 ACT or better		**University scholarships** $2,000 single-year award

Note: HSGPA = high school grade point average.

and Apex with smaller awards. Students were proud of their GPA and test performance at all levels, and we did our best to recognize that through the addition of this smaller scholarship. Table 4.10 summarizes our final program and the high school GPA and SAT/ACT scores students must receive to be eligible for these programs. These criteria were simple enough to allow for fast and easy communication to students and families.

Impact to Yield Resulting from the Restructured Aid Program

We spent a lot of time modeling the potential structure, yield, and budget impact of the new Summit and Apex Awards. Of course, one of the complications of modeling yield on an entering class is that the environment is not standing still. Our recruitment operations are changing at the same time as our competitors'. It was important to evaluate the actual impact of the aid after the program was restructured. Did students respond to the aid as the models predicted?

We increased the average resident award for our best and brightest students from about $2,000 per year to a $5,000 per year Summit Award in the first year of the program. Our original model anticipated that we would increase the enrollment yield of this population from a predicted 37% at the original awards levels to 45% at the revised aid package levels. As shown in figure 4.4, we met the yield expectations of the revised packages in two of the three years where data are available. There was one year, the fall 2014 cohort, where the Summit Award did not yield as many students as expected. In fact, the yield matched the 2011 level we used as the baseline for modeling, a time when students were only receiving a $2,000 scholarship. This decline was largely attributed to negative publicity within the state at the time students were making their enrollment decisions.

Apex Awards for in-state students increased in average amount from about $1,500 to $3,000 per year. This is for the students below the Summit criteria of 3.8/1190, but above a 3.60 high school GPA and 1150 SAT/ACT. We anticipated an

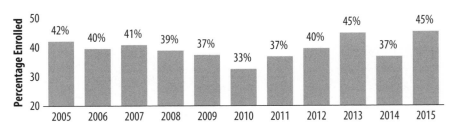

Fig. 4.4. Enrollment Yield of Resident Summit-Level Students before and after Introduction of the Award (2013)

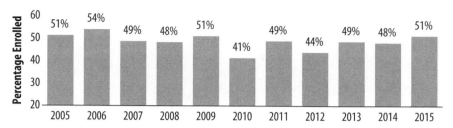

Fig. 4.5. Enrollment Yield of Resident Apex-Level Students before and after Introduction of the Award (2013)

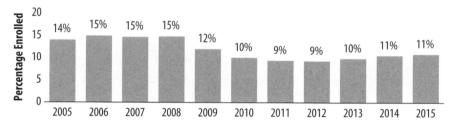

Fig. 4.6. Enrollment Yield of Nonresident Summit-Level Students before and after Introduction of the Award (2013)

approximate increase in yield of about 3%. As shown in figure 4.5, the three-year average yield before the award (fall 2010 through fall 2012) was 45%, and in the first three years of the new award, the average yield was 49%. This 4 percentage point increase to yield for this population was just slightly higher than the modeled value.

Nonresident yield declined significantly between 2008 and 2010 as the university significantly increased its marketing and recruitment reach to out-of-state markets. This helped us capture many more applications from out-of-state students than ever before, and nonresident enrollment grew significantly during this time. A by-product of capturing so many additional students in the nonresident funnel was that yield suffered, as new incremental applicants were less likely to enroll at the University of Oregon. The question, however, was what would happen in the future? Without changing our recruitment strategy, would the additional aid for nonresident Summit scholarships increase yield in the 2013 class? We predicted an increase in the model from 8.6% to 11.1%, a 2.5 percentage point increase to yield. In reality, as figure 4.6 shows, we increased from a 2010 to 2012 average yield of 9.5% to a 2013 to 2015 average yield of 10.4%, which is only a 0.9 percentage point gain.

The model did not seem to accurately predict nonresident yield. In an attempt to explain why the model did not work effectively, we explored what changed

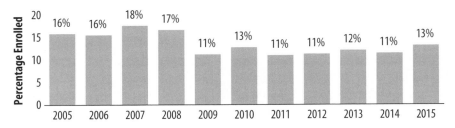

Fig. 4.7. Enrollment Yield of Nonresident Apex-Level Students before and after Introduction of the Award (2013)

between the time the original model was created (based on 2011 admitted students) and the 2013 freshman cohort. In general, the award to nonresidents was increasing by $2,000, from $6,000 to $8,000. Between 2011 and 2013, however, the total cost of attendance for nonresidents increased from $40,600 to $44,000. The buying power of the scholarships decreased faster than the nominal value of the scholarships themselves increased.

The Apex Award to nonresidents was interesting. We decreased the average award to students at this indication of academic preparation from $5,000 under the Dean's Scholarship to $4,000 with the Apex Award. With a decrease in awards, the model unsurprisingly predicted a decrease in yield of less than 1%. As shown in figure 4.7, in the three years before the new award (between 2010 and 2012), students yielded at 11.6%. After the new reduced award was introduced between 2013 and 2015, students yielded on average at 12.3%, a 0.7 percentage point increase.

Does this mean the model is wrong? What we likely experienced is that other factors were at play with this population, which drove them to the University of Oregon at higher rates. Factors like positive news coverage, positive perceptions of the university, increases in the quality of our recruitment events, better campus visits, or other influences may have played a part in those results. In the end, a slight expected decrease versus a slight increase was in reality about a 1 percentage point yield more than expected, which was strikingly similar to the higher-than-expected increase in resident Apex yields.

Conclusion

Restructuring an aid program is a complicated process, and we feel fortunate that the changes we have made to include Summit and Apex Awards has assisted with increasing the academic profile of the University of Oregon as well as increasing access for students with need. More than anything else, it is the increased transparency and clear eligibility that have created a program that is easy for students to understand and for our team to share with future students.

As we seek to clearly communicate with and reward the best and brightest prospective freshmen, selecting the right metrics and clearly communicating the awards are important strategic imperatives. In the context of this book, the most important lesson concerns the use of both high school GPA and standardized test scores as criteria for our restructured merit-based aid program. Empirical analysis showed that both metrics were correlated with academic success at the university. Indeed, the two metrics are measured in such different ways that they tell us very different things about a student's academic preparation before college. By using both criteria in our financial aid programs we were able to mediate the flaws present in either metric individually.

There is one final thing we cannot lose sight of in any conversation about metrics, scholarship criteria, and access to financial aid. As stewards of the financial aid programs, we are making decisions that change the lives of individual students. That impact is best expressed in the words of one of our students: "The willingness of the University of Oregon to partner with me in this way will always be remembered. I will not forget this kindness, nor will I forget the message that it sends to me and the belief in me that you all have shown. I absolutely love my life." We worked hard to design a more transparent aid award program. With sustained effort we hope our scholarship efforts and strategic goals will continue to inspire future Ducks in similar ways.

APPENDIX: LOGISTIC REGRESSION MODEL

Population: Fall 2016 admitted students
Model: Binary Logit, Fisher's Scoring
Number of observations used: 15,820
Response profile: 12,157 = 0 (did not enroll), 3,663 = 1 (enrolled)
Max-rescaled R^2: .2444
C-statistic: .764
Hosmer and Lemeshow Goodness-of-Fit Test, Pr > ChiSq: 0.33
Notes about parameter estimates: Institution scholarship support is per $1,000.
    SAT or converted ACT is per 10 points on the SAT CR+M scale (400–1600).
    Income category reference is Income of $0–$60K. Residency reference is
    Oregon Resident.

Appendix table 4.1.   Logistic Model for Predicting Freshman Enrollment
at the University of Oregon

Parameter		Estimate	Standard error	Wald chi-square	Pr > chi-square
Intercept		−1.9655	2.2464	0.7655	0.3816
Institution scholarship support		0.2478	0.0402	38.0237	< .0001
Income category	FAFSA not filed	−0.5575	0.1377	16.3855	< .0001
Income category	Income 140K+	−0.4587	0.1222	14.0794	0.0002
Income category	Income 60K–139K	−0.3463	0.1174	8.7020	0.0032
High school GPA		0.9006	0.6492	1.9243	0.1654
SAT or converted ACT		0.6120	0.2002	9.3462	0.0022
Honors college admit		2.4694	1.1574	4.5518	0.0329
Residency	Nonresident	−0.0543	0.3709	0.0214	0.8836
Applied by early deadline		0.3513	0.1096	10.2718	0.0014
First generation		−2.4025	0.5712	17.6910	< .0001
Underrepresented race		−0.1929	0.0971	3.9495	0.0469
Institution scholarship support * SAT or converted ACT		−0.0129	0.00336	14.8436	0.0001
High school GPA * SAT or converted ACT		−0.2050	0.0576	12.6669	0.0004
SAT or converted ACT * Honors college admit		−0.1732	0.0880	3.8730	0.0491
Institution scholarship support * Residency	Nonresident	−0.0456	0.00837	29.6347	< .0001
Income category * Residency	FAFSA not filed * Nonresident	0.4935	0.1415	12.1609	0.0005
Income category * Residency	Income 140K+ * Nonresident	0.5150	0.1302	15.6437	< .0001
Income category * Residency	Income 60K–139K * Nonresident	0.3041	0.1274	5.6990	0.0170
SAT or converted ACT * Residency	Nonresident	−0.1424	0.0349	16.6396	< .0001
Applied by early deadline * Income category	FAFSA not filed	−0.1916	0.1329	2.0803	0.1492
Applied by early deadline * Income category	Income 140K+	0.3250	0.1263	6.6238	0.0101

Parameter		Estimate	Standard error	Wald chi-square	Pr > chi-square
Applied by early deadline * Income category	Income 60K–139K	0.0974	0.1329	0.5374	0.4635
Applied by early deadline * Residency	Nonresident	−0.2165	0.0926	5.4697	0.0193
First generation * Income category	FAFSA not filed	−0.3537	0.1723	4.2137	0.0401
First generation * Income category	Income 140K+	0.2200	0.1550	2.0145	0.1558
First generation * Income category	Income 60K–139K	0.1036	0.1319	0.6174	0.4320
High school GPA * First generation		0.4019	0.1647	5.9564	0.0147
SAT or converted ACT * First generation		0.0803	0.0351	5.2242	0.0223
Underrepresented race * Income category	FAFSA not filed	−0.4195	0.1731	5.8744	0.0154
Underrepresented race * Income category	Income 140K+	0.1708	0.1377	1.5385	0.2148
Underrepresented race * Income category	Income 60K–139K	−0.1353	0.1385	0.9540	0.3287

Note: An asterisk indicates an interaction between the two metrics—essentially an indication that the impact of one of the variables differs depending on the level of the other variable.

REFERENCES

Franke, Ray. (2014). Toward the education nation? Revisiting the impact of financial aid, college experience, and institutional context on baccalaureate degree attainment for low-income students. Lecture prepared for presentation at the annual meeting of the American Education Research Association (AERA).

Kobrin, J. L., Sathy, V., and Shaw, E. J. (2006). *A historical view of subgroup performance differences on the SAT.* College Board Research Report 2006-5. New York: The College Board.

Scott-Clayton, J. (2015). The role of financial aid in promoting college access and success: Research evidence and proposals for reform. *Journal of Student Financial Aid, 45*(3), article 3. Retrieved from http://publications.nasfaa.org/jsfa/vol45/iss3/3.

Zwick, R. (2004). *Rethinking the SAT: The future of standardized testing in university admissions.* New York: RoutledgeFalmer.

5

When High School Grade Point Average and Test Scores Disagree

Implications for Test-Optional Policies

Edgar Sanchez and Krista Mattern

A *lmost everyone—parent, educator, administrator—has known a student whose* *standardized test scores and grades just don't seem to match. "They just don't test well," or, "those tests don't capture their learning style," are the sorts of phrases one hears when describing these students with such "discrepant" performance. In this chapter, Sanchez and Mattern investigate the potential causes and consequences of this potential mismatch between grades and scores. How common is this phenomenon? Are there types of students more likely to have discrepant achievement? And what does discrepant achievement mean for validity and fairness in college admissions?*

One of the biggest challenges to understanding discrepant performance is defining it, and the authors illustrate several competing methods, each yielding somewhat different estimates of the prevalence of this phenomenon. No matter what measure is chosen, however, it is clear that somewhere between about a quarter and a third of tested students exhibit some degree of mismatch between their grades and their test scores. Moreover, certain student characteristics are associated with discrepancy: girls and students who are from disadvantaged minority groups or low-income families are somewhat more likely to have higher high school GPAs than might be expected from their test scores. Interestingly, as the authors discuss, there is some evidence of differential prediction of college success depending on the type of discrepancy. For example, students with ACT scores higher than their high school grade point average (HSGPA) have a lower proba-

bility of persisting to bachelor's degree completion compared to students with consistent grades and scores and students with higher grades than test scores.

Sanchez and Mattern conclude that discrepant performance may have important implications for admissions. Test scores and grades are not perfectly correlated, and observed discrepancies may be signaling important information about students' preparation and likelihood of postsecondary success. Ignoring one piece of information or the other will increase errors in prediction.

In support of the goal of advancing scientific knowledge about test-optional policies, this chapter examines empirical evidence to counter claims that test scores are poor predictors of student success and that using high school grade point average (HSGPA) as the sole achievement indicator is the best predictor of student success. In particular, it focuses on a phenomenon known as "discrepant" HSGPA and test performance. Discrepant performance is of particular relevance to test-optional policies because under such policies, students are given the choice of whether to submit their test scores.

In this chapter, we review existing research on discrepant performance as well as present new analyses on the topic. We use this knowledge as the basis for understanding the behavior and outcomes of students who are likely to withhold their test scores from their college applications when test-optional policies are in place. The demographic characteristics of students with discrepant performance is an important factor to consider, as this can impact the types of students attracted to institutions with test-optional policies. We also examine how discrepant performance is related to high school course-taking patterns that can result in differential academic preparation for college. We further highlight the differences observed in college outcomes such as enrollment, persistence, first-year GPA, and degree completion between students with and without discrepant performance. Collectively, the empirical evidence synthesized in this chapter underscores the value of considering as much information about prospective students as possible rather than electing to omit useful information.

One may assume that students who appear more academically qualified if they withhold their test scores—that is, students with higher HSGPAs than expected from looking at their test scores alone—are the students who are most likely to take advantage of test-optional policies. Indeed, test-optional practices were designed to assist these very students, under the assumption that their low test scores are not representative of their true academic achievement and that their high HSGPA is a better indicator of their college success.

To begin our analysis, we need to know whether these initial assumptions are correct. Are students with lower test scores more likely to withhold their test scores? Moreover, for students who do not submit scores, are test scores actually a poor indicator of how they will perform in college? Research by Howard Wainer (2011) provides some insights into these questions. In his book *Uneducated Guesses: Using Evidence to Uncover Misguided Education Policies,* he presents an analysis of students at Bowdoin College who were admitted under a test-optional policy. Wainer found that students who elected not to submit their SAT scores had considerably lower scores than students who had submitted their test scores. In fact, non-submitters had SAT scores about 120 points lower, a difference of about one standard deviation. Moreover, non-submitters earned lower grades in their first year of college compared with submitters, as would be predicted by their lower test scores. This research suggests that (1) under conditions where students are not required to submit their test scores, students with lower scores are less likely to submit, confirming the first assumption; and (2) test scores for non-submitters are predictive of future college success and thus reflective of their true academic standing, disconfirming the second assumption.

Given that research indicates that test scores are valid for submitters and non-submitters, knowing what percentage of students display discrepant performance, and in what direction, would be useful information to better understand the impact of discrepant performance on test-optional admission decisions. Additionally, it is important to examine whether discrepant students have different post-secondary trajectories. For example, are discrepant students more, less, or as likely to enroll, persist, and succeed in higher education as compared with students who display consistent performance? This chapter reviews literature on discrepant HSGPA and test score performance, highlighting implications as they relate to test-optional policies and practices. It is subdivided into five sections and summarizes pertinent research on the following questions: How common is discrepant performance? Which types of students are more likely to display discrepant performance? Do discrepant students perform similarly in college to their consistent performance peers? What factors are related to discrepant performance? And, perhaps most important, what are the implications of students with discrepantly lower test scores suppressing their test scores for the validity and fairness of admission decisions?

The distinction drawn here between students with consistent and discrepant achievement has important consequences for the interpretation of the vast majority of existing validity research on test scores and HSGPA. As will be demonstrated, consistent achievement students make up the vast majority of all tested students. Therefore, they drive the statistical conclusions that are drawn from an analysis that is based on the entire population. As the following studies point out, however, there are important distinctions to be made.

When Test Scores and HSGPA Disagree: Research on Discrepant Performance

Evidence of the predictive validity of college admission measures is clear: both HSGPA and admissions test scores, such as the ACT and SAT, are positively correlated with a variety of college outcomes, such as enrollment, first-year grade point average (FYGPA), persistence to the sophomore year, degree completion, and on-time degree completion (Allen 2013; Cambiano, Denny, and DeVore 2000; Godfrey and Matos-Elefonte 2010; Kobrin et al. 2008; Lichtenberger and Dietrich 2012; Mattern, Patterson, and Wyatt 2013; McNeish, Radunzel, and Sanchez 2015; Patterson and Mattern 2012; Radunzel and Noble 2012; Sawyer 2010; see also chapter 2). Furthermore, holding constant HSGPA, increases in test scores result in increases in probabilities of postsecondary success; and vice versa (Radunzel and Noble 2013; Sanchez 2013; Sawyer 2008). In short, each measure provides incremental validity. Moreover, research has shown that these relationships tend to hold across race/ethnicity, income, gender, and course-taking patterns (Patterson and Mattern 2011; Radunzel and Noble 2013; Sanchez 2013; Sawyer 2008; Zwick and Sklar 2005).

Despite the fact that each measure provides incremental validity, admission test scores and high school grades often send consistent messages about student academic achievement. That is, students with good high school grades tend to earn high test scores, whereas students with poor high school grades tend to earn low test scores. There are times, however, when this is not the case and a student might perform better on either a standardized test or high school course assignments. There are three scenarios of test score–HSGPA performance combinations. First, there are students who do roughly equally well on the two academic measures; these students can be called "consistent achievement" students. Second, there are also students who earn higher high school grades compared with what one would expect from their test scores; these students can be called "HSGPA discrepant" students. Finally, there are students who earn higher test scores in comparison with their HSGPA. These students can be referred to as "test score discrepant," for example, SAT Total score discrepant or ACT Composite score discrepant.[1]

Readers may be wondering why these discrepancies occur. For example, why would a student earn a higher test score than what would be expected given her HSGPA? One scenario that could lead to being classified as test score discrepant is when a student takes rigorous coursework, such as AP courses, that academically prepares her for college, but results in a lower HSGPA because of the rigor of the course load. This student, who has been challenged in high school, may score well on an admissions test, perhaps owing to her exposure to this advanced coursework. Yet her superior test performance may be viewed as merely "good test taking."

Alternatively, imagine a student who has good high school grades, but low test scores. The lower test score may be a result of test anxiety or a lack of academic preparation. Again, popular, nonacademic opinion might assume that for this "poor tester," the student's HSGPA is the more accurate indicator of achievement while the test score *must* be a poor indication of achievement. In reality, it is also plausible that the low test score is a more accurate indicator of academic preparation. This would make sense for students who take less rigorous courses and are able to maintain a high HSGPA while simultaneously not taking the requisite courses to prepare for college or if their high school teachers routinely "inflate" grades (see chapter 3). Given this tripartite classification of discrepant performance, the next section discusses the prevalence of such test score–HSGPA performance combinations.

How Common Is Discrepant Performance?

To identify how common it is for students to have discrepant performance between test scores and HSGPA, it is important to first define discrepancy. Research on the discrepancy between test scores and HSGPA has traditionally used standardized scores to create three groups (Edmunds 2010; Edmunds and Sanchez 2014; Kobrin, Camara, and Milewski 2002; Mattern, Shaw, and Kobrin 2010; Ramist, Lewis, and Jenkins 1997; Sanchez and Edmunds 2015). Test scores and HSGPA are first converted to z-scores, and the standardized scores are directly compared.[2] The comparison between z-scores allows a direct distributional comparison of a student's performance relative to his peers. Often students whose standardized test score and HSGPA fall within a single standard deviation are considered to have consistent achievement. Students with test scores greater than one standard deviation above their HSGPA are considered test score discrepant. Finally, students with HSGPAs greater than one standard deviation above their test score are considered HSGPA discrepant.

To illustrate this at a national level, table 5.1 uses the one standard deviation rule and the mean and standard deviation of the ACT-tested graduating class of 2016 to show the combinations of ACT Composite and HSGPA categorized into three discrepancy groups. This table contains all possible combinations of ACT Composite and HSGPA. For example, a student with an ACT Composite score of 21 and an HSGPA between 2.7 and 3.8 would be categorized as having consistent performance. If that same student had an HSGPA between 3.9 and 4.0, he or she would be classified as HSGPA discrepant, with relatively higher grades than test scores. In the ACT-tested graduating class of 2016, about 14% of students are classified as test score discrepant, 11% are classified as HSGPA discrepant, and 75% of students are classified as consistent achievers.

Table 5.1 contains all possible categorizations of discrepancy and consistent achievement, including many combinations that rarely occur. To get a sense for how frequently combinations of scores occur, a distribution displaying the frequency of any two scores occurring is provided in figure 5.1. It shows that

Table 5.1.   Unique combination of ACT Composite and HSGPA scores by discrepancy group based on statistics from the ACT-tested graduating class of 2016

ACT Composite	ACTC discrepant	Consistent	HSGPA discrepant	ACT Composite	ACTC discrepant	Consistent	HSGPA discrepant
1	0.0–0.3	0.4–1.5	1.6–4.0	19	0.0–2.3	2.4–3.6	3.7–4.0
2	0.0–0.4	0.5–1.7	1.8–4.0	20	0.0–2.4	2.5–3.7	3.8–4.0
3	0.0–0.5	0.6–1.8	1.9–4.0	21	0.0–2.6	2.7–3.8	3.9–4.0
4	0.0–0.6	0.7–1.9	2.0–4.0	22	0.0–2.7	2.8–4.0	
5	0.0–0.7	0.8–2.0	2.1–4.0	23	0.0–2.8	2.9–4.0	
6	0.0–0.8	0.9–2.1	2.2–4.0	24	0.0–2.9	3.0–4.0	
7	0.0–0.9	1.0–2.2	2.3–4.0	25	0.0–3.0	3.1–4.0	
8	0.0–1.1	1.2–2.3	2.4–4.0	26	0.0–3.1	3.2–4.0	
9	0.0–1.2	1.3–2.5	2.6–4.0	27	0.0–3.2	3.3–4.0	
10	0.0–1.3	1.4–2.6	2.7–4.0	28	0.0–3.4	3.5–4.0	
11	0.0–1.4	1.5–2.7	2.8–4.0	29	0.0–3.5	3.6–4.0	
12	0.0–1.5	1.6–2.8	2.9–4.0	30	0.0–3.6	3.7–4.0	
13	0.0–1.6	1.7–2.9	3.0–4.0	31	0.0–3.7	3.8–4.0	
14	0.0–1.7	1.8–3.0	3.1–4.0	32	0.0–3.8	3.9–4.0	
15	0.0–1.9	2.0–3.2	3.3–4.0	33	0.0–3.9	4.0–4.0	
16	0.0–2.0	2.1–3.3	3.4–4.0	34	0.0–4.0		
17	0.0–2.1	2.2–3.4	3.5–4.0	35	0.0–4.0		
18	0.0–2.2	2.3–3.5	3.6–4.0	36	0.0–4.0		

Note: ACTC = ACT Composite score; HSGPA = high school grade point average.

while students with an ACT Composite score of 36 and an HSGPA of 3.0 would be considered ACT Composite score discrepant, this combination of scores did not occur in the 2016 ACT-tested cohort. Also evident from figure 5.1 is that there were many students with an ACT Composite score of 27 and an HSGPA of 4.0. The data displayed underscore the fact that ACT Composite score and HSGPA do not align perfectly. In fact, a student's HSGPA could be associated with a wide range of possible ACT Composite scores, particularly for students with high HSGPAs.

To further illustrate this, figure 5.2 shows the distribution of ACT Composite scores for students in the graduating class of 2016 who reported an HSGPA of 4.0. Under a test-optional admission policy, these students would appear to be

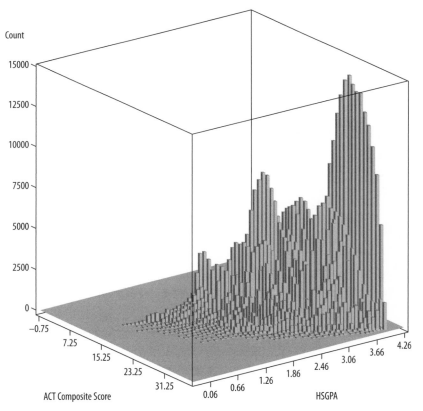

Fig. 5.1. Distribution for ACT Composite Score and High School Grade Point Average (HSGPA) for the ACT-Tested Graduating Class of 2016 ($N = 1{,}709{,}659$)

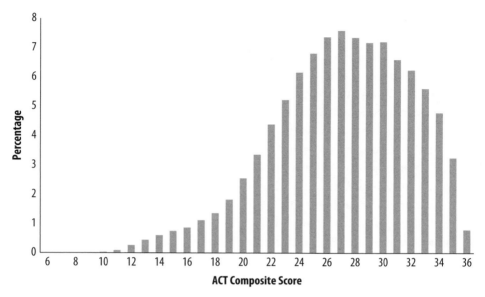

Fig. 5.2. Histogram of ACT Composite Scores Associated with a High School Grade Point Average of 4.0 for the ACT-Tested Graduating Class of 2016 (*N* = 191,304)

well prepared to enter college, despite the fact some students have quite low ACT scores.

One limitation of this analysis is the reliance on self-reported high school grades rather than transcript grades, although research has demonstrated that a student's self-reported high school GPA, based on information provided at registration for the ACT, is a reliable estimator for a student's transcript GPA (Sanchez and Buddin 2016). This study found a moderately strong median correlation (0.66) between self-reported and transcript course-specific grades. Furthermore, the correlation between overall transcript and self-reported HSGPA, as used in the present discussion, was high (0.83). Other research on self-reported HSGPA also finds high correlations between overall self-reported and transcript HSGPA (Kuncel, Credé, and Thomas 2005; Shaw and Mattern 2009).

The one standard deviation rule has been used by many studies that have examined the phenomenon of discrepant performance. Each of these studies has examined discrepancy between high school GPA and either SAT Total or ACT Composite scores. The frequency of discrepant performance based on SAT Total results are generally similar to, but slightly higher than, the ACT results reported above.

A second approach to defining discrepancy uses a different distributional approach that is based on percentiles to examine whether scores are high, moderate, or low in their respective distributions. For example, Edmunds (2010) used quartiles to create an alternative set of discrepancy groups to that traditionally seen with the one standard deviation rule. Based on data from Belmont University, students were classified into four groups: (1) neither low; (2) both low; (3) HSGPA low; and (4) test score low. Using this definition, about 32% of students were identified as having discrepant performance. In the "neither low" group, neither their HSGPA nor test score were at or below the twenty-fifth percentile of their respective distribution. In the "both low" group, both their HSGPA and test score were at or below the twenty-fifth percentile of their respective distribution. In the HSGPA and test score low groups, achievement in the respective scores was in the bottom 25 percent of their respective distributions but achievement for the other measure was above the twenty-fifth percentile.

Another study that used a variant of this percentile approach used quartiles to construct discrepancy groupings. Sanchez and Lin (2017) used standardized ACT Composite and HSGPA scores to define nine distinct discrepancy groups to capture both direction and magnitude of discrepancy (as shown in table 5.2). This categorization scheme is based on classifying students into discrepant groups depending on whether their test scores and HSGPA are in the top 25%, middle 50%, or bottom 25% of scores in a distribution. The nine discrepancy groups can be classified into three larger groups: students whose ACT Composite (ACTC) score and HSGPA are consistent (Consistent achievement groups: Consistent_H, Consistent_M, and Consistent_L); students whose ACT Composite score is higher than their HSGPA (ACTC discrepancy groups: $\text{ACTC}_H\text{-HSGPA}_L$, $\text{ACTC}_H\text{-HSGPA}_M$, and $\text{ACTC}_M\text{-HSGPA}_L$); and students whose HSGPA is higher than their ACT Composite score (HSGPA discrepancy groups: $\text{HSGPA}_H\text{-ACTC}_L$, $\text{HSGPA}_H\text{-ACTC}_M$, and $\text{HSGPA}_M\text{-ACTC}_L$). Based on this approach, 42% of students were classified as having discrepant performance, with 18% being HSGPA discrepant and 24% being test score discrepant.

A third approach to defining discrepancy also uses a distributional methodology but is not contingent on traditional groupings. This methodology uses the difference between two standardized scores to quantify the magnitude of discrepant performance (e.g., $\text{ACTC}_Z - \text{HSGPA}_Z$; Mattern, Shaw, and Kobrin 2011; Sanchez and Edmunds 2015). Whereas the traditional approach is limited by the somewhat arbitrary definition of discrepancy (> 1 SD), in that students with nearly iden-

Table 5.2.   Definition of the nine achievement groups, based on
ACT Composite scores and HSGPA

ACT Composite group	HSGPA group	Discrepancy group (%)	Definition of groups	Direction of discrepancy	Magnitude of discrepancy
High	High	Consistent$_H$ (15%)	Both ACTC and HSGPA scores in top 25%	Consistent	N/A
Moderate	Moderate	Consistent$_M$ (31%)	Both ACTC and HSGPA scores in the middle 50%	Consistent	N/A
Low	Low	Consistent$_L$ (12%)	Both ACTC and HSGPA scores in the bottom 25%	Consistent	N/A
High	Moderate	ACTC$_H$-HSGPA$_M$ (11%)	ACTC score in the top 25% and HSGPA in the middle 50%	ACT Composite discrepant	Small
High	Low	ACTC$_H$-HSGPA$_L$ (1%)	ACTC score in the top 25% and HSGPA in the bottom 25%	ACT Composite discrepant	Large
Moderate	Low	ACTC$_M$-HSGPA$_L$ (12%)	ACTC score in the middle 50% and HSGPA in the bottom 25%	ACT Composite discrepant	Small
Moderate	High	HSGPA$_H$-ACTC$_M$ (9%)	ACTC score in the middle 50% and HSGPA in the top 25%	HSGPA discrepant	Small
Low	High	HSGPA$_H$-ACTC$_L$ (1%)	ACTC score in the bottom 25% and HSGPA in the top 25%	HSGPA discrepant	Large
Low	Moderate	HSGPA$_M$-ACTC$_L$ (8%)	ACTC score in the bottom 25% and HSGPA in the middle 50%	HSGPA discrepant	Small

Note: ACTC = ACT Composite score; HSGPA = high school grade point average.

tical discrepancy scores (0.99 versus 1.01) will be classified into different discrepancy groups, this approach allows the examination of discrepant performance along the continuum and is not constrained by prescribed definitions. On the other hand, this approach may present problems in determining how many students display discrepant performance and which students are most likely to display discrepant performance because classification is no longer categorical in nature, but one of degree.

Differences in methodology used to define discrepant performance, coupled with differences in the content assessed and populations served by the ACT versus the SAT, have produced slight variations in the percentages of students that are classified as having discrepant performance. Studies of SAT scores tend to identify about 30% of the population as having discrepant performance, while studies of ACT Composite scores show that about 25% of the population tends to be identified as having discrepant performance (Edmunds and Sanchez 2014; Kobrin, Camara, and Milewski 2002; Mattern, Shaw, and Kobrin 2010; Ramist, Lewis, and Jenkins 1997; Sanchez and Edmunds 2015). The exceptions to this were found in Edmunds (2010) and Sanchez and Lin (2017) where 35 to 42% of students were classified as having discrepant performance.

Across studies, usually between 60 and 70% of samples had consistent performance between HSGPA and test scores. In terms of the direction of discrepant performance, between 11 and 18% of the samples included students with an HSGPA that was higher than their test score, and between 12 and 24% of the samples had students with a test score that was higher than their HSGPA. Thus, despite the fact that the majority of students have consistent performance, a nontrivial percentage display discrepant performance. With millions of students taking the ACT and SAT each year, this translates to hundreds of thousands who have test scores and HSGPA that are not consistent. Clearly, for these students, each measure is not interchangeable, as each provides a unique perspective about students' abilities and academic experiences and preparation, underscoring the importance of having both pieces of information for decision making.

Which Types of Students Are Mostly Likely to Display Discrepant Performance?

Despite the various methods that have been used to define discrepancy, there has been remarkable consistency in identifying which students are most likely to display discrepancy between their test scores and HSGPA. Studies have found that students who have higher HSGPAs than test scores tend to be female, minority, and low-income students (Edmunds and Sanchez 2014; Kobrin, Camara, and Milewski 2002; Mattern, Shaw, and Kobrin 2011; Ramist, Lewis, and Jenkins 1997; Sanchez and Edmunds 2015; Sanchez and Lin 2017). For example, Sanchez and Lin (2017) found that the gender distribution of students who had a high HSGPA but a moderate or low ACT Composite score to be more heavily represented by females (66% and 62%, respectively). Additionally, for students with a moderate HSGPA and low ACT Composite score, only 60% of students were female. More than 50% of students with a high HSGPA and low ACT Composite score or moderate HSGPA and low ACT Composite score were minority and low-income students. On the other hand, only a small percentage of minority and low-income students constituted the high HSGPA and high ACT Composite score group (8.77% of minorities; 9.63% of low-income students) as well as the high ACT Composite score and moderate HSGPA group (12.78% of minorities; 12.57% of low-income students).

There are also several noteworthy findings about the differences between these groups. HSGPA discrepant students are more likely to have lower socio-economic status backgrounds (e.g., household income, parental education level) than either the SAT discrepant or consistent achievement groups (Mattern, Shaw, and Kobrin 2011; Ramist, Lewis, and Jenkins 1997). HSGPA discrepant students also tend to speak languages other than English at home (Kobrin, Camara, and Milewski 2002). Furthermore, an examination of subgroup differences reveal that while the average discrepancy for the student subgroups of gender, race/ethnicity, and family income can be considered consistent (difference in standardized achievement between −1 and 1), this average discrepancy was often nonzero (Sanchez and Edmunds 2015). African American and Hispanic, female, and low-income students, for example, tended to have slightly higher standardized HSGPAs than ACT Composite scores. Conversely, white, male, and middle- and higher-income students tended to have a slightly higher standardized ACT Composite score than HSGPA.

Do Discrepant Students Perform Similarly in College to Their Consistent Performance Peers?

The following section examines research on postsecondary outcomes for students with discrepant performance and highlights unique outcomes for this population in terms of enrollment in college, persistence to the second year of college, first-year GPA, and degree completion.

Enrollment in College

About 75% of ACT Composite discrepant and consistent achievement students enrolled at a four-year institution (as compared with only 65% of the HSGPA discrepant group), and a greater percentage of HSGPA discrepant students enrolled at a two-year institution as compared with the other two discrepancy groups (Edmunds and Sanchez 2014). This is an interesting point, given that institutions where test-optional policies are being considered are four-year institutions (two-year institutions tend to have open-enrollment policies and do not require test scores). Thus, HSGPA discrepant students who may have previously been targeting two-year institutions may now consider applying to four-year institutions, and in particular, test-optional institutions.

Edmunds and Sanchez (2014) found that when enrollment rates are modeled for the total sample, the results indicate very different probabilities of enrollment for discrepant achievement students than if the three groups are considered separately. For example, in figure 5.3, for students with a median HSGPA of 3.31, HSGPA discrepant students with an ACT Composite score between 14 and 16 have a greater than 50% chance of college enrollment. However, based on the total analyses (dashed line), those same students have a predicted enrollment rate of above 70%. Students in either the consistent or ACT Composite discrepant achievement groups had a greater than 75% chance of enrolling in college based on both the overall analyses and the analyses conducted separately by discrepancy group. These findings underscore the fact that the likelihood of enrolling in college for HSGPA discrepant students at the median HSGPA of 3.31 will be fairly dramatically overestimated. With similar trends found at other HSGPA values, the results suggest that ignoring discrepancy will result in considerable overestimation

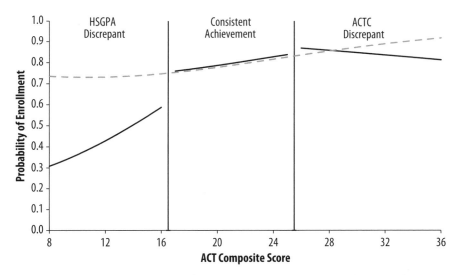

Fig. 5.3. Probability of Enrollment for Students with a 3.31 High School Grade Point Average (HSGPA), by Discrepancy Group, in the ACT-Tested Graduating Class of 2012 (*N* = 953,887). *Notes*: ACTC = ACT Composite score. Dashed line = total analyses; solid lines = separate analyses.

Table 5.3.   Average probabilities of enrollment and persistence for the ACT-tested graduating class of 2014 ($N = 1,719,039$)

	Consistent$_H$	Consistent$_M$	Consistent$_L$
Enrollment	0.896	0.820	0.513
Persistence	0.813	0.691	0.566

	ACTC$_H$-HSGPA$_M$	ACTC$_H$-HSGPA$_L$	ACTC$_M$-HSGPA$_L$	HSGPA$_H$-ACTC$_M$	HSGPA$_H$-ACTC$_L$	HSGPA$_M$-ACTC$_L$
Enrollment	0.874	0.769	0.686	0.878	0.688	0.669
Persistence	0.733	0.597	0.598	0.76	0.672	0.646

Source: Sanchez and Lin 2017.
Note: ACTC = ACT Composite score; HSGPA = high school grade point average. Subscripts: H = high, M = moderate, L = low.

of college enrollment rates at either a two- or four-year institution for students with a higher HSGPA than test score.

Another study found that while students with consistently high ACT Composite and HSGPA scores had the highest probability of enrollment, students with either a high ACT Composite or HSGPA and its counter achievement indicator in the middle 50% of its distribution had similarly high probabilities of enrollment (Sanchez and Lin 2017). This suggests that as long as one of the achievement indicators is high and there is a small discrepancy in the two scores, there is not a large associated drop in likelihood of enrollment.

There is, however, a considerable drop in the probability of enrollment for students who had large discrepancies between their ACT Composite and HSGPA, that is, ACTC$_H$-HSGPA$_L$ and HSGPA$_H$-ACTC$_L$ students. This effect is even more pronounced for students with a moderate ACT Composite or HSGPA and low HSGPA or ACT Composite score, respectively. As shown in table 5.3, students who have a high HSGPA but a low ACT Composite score are less likely to enroll in a postsecondary institution than students with consistently high or moderate achievement. Moreover, while the magnitude of the discrepancy had an impact on the probability of enrollment, having either a low ACT Composite or HSGPA was associated with much lower probabilities of enrollment.

Persistence to the Sophomore Year

Research by Edmunds (2010) found that while test score discrepant students tended to be less likely to persist to their second year of college relative to consistent achievement students, HSGPA discrepant students had a similar likelihood of persistence as students with consistent achievement. This study also found that students who had an ACT Composite score in the bottom 25% (with an HSGPA not in the bottom quartile) had a higher persistence rate than students who had a low HSGPA or both a low HSGPA and ACT Composite score. Furthermore, having either or both achievement indicator in the bottom 25% of their distribution was associated with lower rates of persistence than that shown by students who did not have either achievement indicator in the bottom 25% of their distribution.

When interpreting these findings, it is important to consider the data used for this analysis. This study was based on admitted and enrolled students at a private liberal arts college. As such, there are two possible factors at play with this sample. Statistically, the models are likely affected by a restriction of range resulting from the selection process. Second, the admissions process utilizes a larger holistic methodology for making admissions decisions. This means that the students in this study were admitted because it was believed that they had a good chance of succeeding in college and meeting institutional goals. The lack of inclusion of students not viewed as likely to have successful outcomes is an important factor to consider.

Edmunds's (2010) persistence findings were consistent with later findings by Sanchez and Edmunds (2015). This study focused on the mitigating effect of students' noncognitive variables on postsecondary success. As seen in figure 5.4, HSGPA discrepant and consistent achievement students have very similar probabilities of persistence to the second year. For ACT Composite discrepant students, however, the probability of persistence was lower. While, on average, HSGPA discrepant and consistent achievement students had a 0.77 probability of persistence to the second year, ACT Composite discrepant students had a 0.70 probability of persistence.

Edmunds and Sanchez (2014), however, found that HSGPA discrepant students had a lower rate of persistence and a higher dropout rate when compared with test score discrepant or consistent performance students. This study showed that students whose ACT Composite score and HSGPA were consistent tend to have the highest probabilities of persistence as well as the lowest probabilities of not reenrolling for their sophomore year. The differences in results may be due to the differences in the samples used. While Edmunds (2010) used a sample based on admitted and enrolled students at a single private liberal arts college, Edmunds and Sanchez (2014) used a sample of high school graduates that attended over 2,500 different two- and four-year postsecondary institutions. This national perspective provided a different view into discrepant performance.

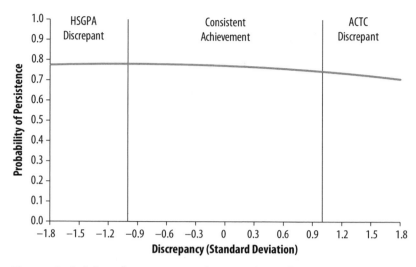

Fig. 5.4. Probability of Persistence to the Second Year for Students in the ACT-Tested Graduating Classes of 2006–2013 ($N = 953,887$). *Notes:* ACTC = ACT Composite score; HSGPA = high school grade point average. The mean is 0.17 and the standard deviation is 1.02.

The finding from Edmunds and Sanchez (2014) held across student demographic subgroups. This suggests that students who have a discrepant achievement may require additional supports to mitigate negative postsecondary outcomes, in particular for HSGPA discrepant students. Again this is particularly relevant for institutions with test-optional policies that will likely attract students with high HSGPAs and low test scores—scores they may elect not to share. These findings raise an interesting question as to whether the genesis of their risk arises from academic difficulties or from nonacademic factors like perceived self-efficacy. To explore this question, it would be beneficial to examine the noncognitive characteristics of students with discrepant achievement students (more on this below).

Sanchez and Lin (2017) found that students with consistently high scores on both ACT Composite and HSGPA had the highest probabilities of persistence. Students who had either a high ACT Composite or a high HSGPA had the second-highest persistence rate (see table 5.3). This included students with a high HSGPA and a moderate or low ACT Composite score or students with a high ACT Composite score and a moderate or low HSGPA. Students with consistently moderate scores had the next highest probabilities of persistence; this group of students outperformed other students with discrepant achievement (i.e., moderate ACT

Composite score and low HSGPA; low ACT Composite score and moderate HSGPA), while students with consistently low scores had the lowest likelihood of persisting. Finally, students with a higher HSGPA than ACT Composite score and a moderate or large discrepancy between ACT Composite score and HSGPA had a lower likelihood of persisting to the second year of college than students with consistently high or moderate ACT Composite score and HSGPA.

First-Year GPA

One study examined the differences in first-year GPA outcomes for students who have discrepant performance and found that holding constant HSGPA, SAT discrepant students had a higher FYGPA than students with consistent achievement and students with a higher HSGPA than test score (Mattern, Shaw, and Kobrin 2010). Conversely, holding constant SAT, HSGPA discrepant students had higher FYGPA than students with consistent achievement and students with higher test scores than HSGPA. These results highlight the compensatory nature of the two measures and the unique contribution each provides as it relates to future college success.

Degree Completion

Edmunds (2010) also found that students with HSGPA discrepancy had a similar likelihood of degree completion as consistent performance students. On the other hand, ACT Composite discrepant students tended to be less likely to complete a bachelor's degree than consistent performance students. Students who had a low ACT Composite score also had higher degree completion rates than students with a low HSGPA or both a low HSGPA and ACT Composite score. Having low scores on either or both ACT Composite or HSGPA was associated with lower rates of degree completion than that of students who did not have low scores in either achievement indicator. This study also found that while both test score and HSGPA were predictive of graduation for students who did not have a low ACT Composite score or HSGPA, HSGPA was found to predict graduation among students with a low HSGPA, and neither HSGPA nor test score was predictive of graduation for students with a low ACT Composite. Edmunds (2010) is the only study, to our knowledge, that has examined the impact of discrepant performance on college graduation. Recall, however, that her sample was based on a single liberal arts institution; future research should examine whether these results replicate with other samples, preferably a large, national representative sample.

Summary

The results summarized above clearly indicate that discrepant performance—both the magnitude and direction—is related to important college outcomes, highlighting the usefulness of having information on both students' grades and test scores when making high stakes admissions decisions. In particular, the results suggest that HSGPA discrepant students are less likely to enroll in college than students with consistent performance or discrepantly higher test scores. On the other hand, the findings generally suggest that HSGPA discrepant students are more likely to persist to the sophomore year than consistent or test score discrepant students; one study found this to not be the case, however. There is also evidence that HSGPA discrepant students have lower FYGPAs relative to consistent achievement and test score discrepant students, holding constant HSGPA. Finally, HSGPA discrepant students appear to have a similar probability of degree completion as consistent achievement students, at least in a limited sample.

Overall, the impact of discrepant performance on college outcomes is mixed. These mixed and nuanced findings across outcomes make an even stronger case for considering both pieces of information when considering an applicant's likelihood of future success. Knowing both pieces of information provides a more accurate picture of whether or not a student will be successful across a multitude of dimensions of college outcomes. Likewise, more precise diagnoses of a student's level of college readiness are useful not only for admissions but also for providing tailored interventions for at-risk students, thus making the case for the collection of test score data from applicants and/or enrolled students.

What Factors Are Related to Discrepant Performance?

Given the important differences that research has found in successful postsecondary outcomes by discrepancy group, it is worth seeking to determine what factors are related to discrepant performance. There is evidence that in high school, HSGPA discrepant students were less interested in pursuing a graduate or professional degree and less likely to take advanced coursework in mathematics and science (Edmunds and Sanchez 2014). Additionally, test score discrepant students were found to take more math, science, and advanced courses in other disciplines during their freshman year of college than HSGPA discrepant or consistent achievement students (Ramist, Lewis, and Jenkins 1997). On the other hand, HSGPA discrepant students took more social science and language courses. This study also found that test score discrepant students took fewer remedial courses relative to other groups while HSGPA discrepant students took the largest proportion of remedial courses. These finding have strong implications for admissions decisions. They suggests that HSGPA discrepant students may be entering into college less academically prepared and less likely to take courses that are more rigorous in nature. This finding is consistent with a more recent SAT study on discrepant performance (Mattern, Shaw, and Kobrin 2011). Colleges and universities must decide if it's their institutional goal to simply admit students who are likely to earn high grades or to admit students who are likely to complete rigorous programs of study *and* earn high grades in those programs. Test score discrepant students may be more likely to fulfill the latter goal.

Researchers have also examined whether students' motivational and noncognitive factors vary by discrepancy group. Sanchez and Edmunds (2015) examined the effect of accounting for psychosocial factors on persistence to the sophomore year for students with discrepant achievement. This study found that the ACT Engage motivational scales of academic discipline, general determination, commitment to college, and study skills, as well as the social engagement domains of social connection and social activity (as defined in table 5.4), were predictive of sophomore year persistence. It also demonstrated that noncognitive psychosocial factors slightly moderated the effect of HSGPA discrepancy on college persistence—by the same amount that these factors affected consistent performance students (table 5.5).

Table 5.4.   ACT Engage scales

Academic discipline	Amount of effort a student puts into schoolwork and the degree to which a student sees himself/herself as hardworking and conscientious
General determination	The extent to which one strives to follow through on commitments and obligations
Commitment to college	One's commitment to stay in college and get a degree
Study skills	The extent to which students believe they know how to assess an academic problem, organize a solution, and successfully complete academic assignments
Social connection	One's feelings of connection and involvement with the school community
Social activity	One's comfort in meeting and interacting with other people

Source: ACT Engage User Guide, https://www.act.org/content/dam/act/unsecured/documents /ACT-Engage-user-guide.pdf.

Table 5.5.   Average probability of students' persistence to the sophomore year prior to and after controlling for noncognitive psychosocial factors ($N = 27{,}131$)

	Without noncognitives	With noncognitives
Consistent	0.78	0.77
High school grade point average discrepant	0.77	0.76
ACT Composite score discrepant	0.72	0.72

Source: Sanchez and Edmunds 2015.

Table 5.6.   Average Engage scale scores ($N = 27{,}131$)

	Academic discipline	General determination	Commitment to college	Study skills	Social connection	Social activity
Consistent	65.20	64.17	64.14	60.62	60.44	54.67
High school grade point average discrepant	72.96	69.25	66.48	67.59	60.99	52.26
ACT Composite score discrepant	50.64	53.16	59.03	53.58	56.13	51.70

Source: Sanchez and Edmunds 2015.

This is confirmed by the average ACT Engage scale scores by discrepancy group reported in table 5.6. Notably, the ACT Composite score discrepant group scored considerably lower than the HSGPA discrepant group on academic discipline—the ACT Engage scale that consistently shows the strongest relationship with educational outcome among all the ACT Engage scales. This reinforces the argument that ignoring the differences associated with discrepancy may not be prudent.

Implications of Students' Suppression of Discrepantly Lower Test Scores on the Validity and Fairness of Admission Decisions

Based on the findings reviewed above, it is clear that discrepant performance may have implications for the fairness and validity of test-optional policies. More specifically, Kobrin, Camara, and Milewski (2002) examined the over- and underprediction of FYGPA between the three achievement groups. This was calculated as the difference between the predicted and observed FYGPA for students in each discrepancy group. While this study did not find large observed differences in FYGPA, the authors found greater overprediction for minority students (African American, Hispanic, and American Indian) as compared with white students among HSGPA discrepant students than among other student groups examined. This suggests that for students with a high HSGPA but low test score (the typical scenario under test-optional policies), the estimated FYGPA will be an overestimate of their true performance once admitted into an institution.

Furthermore, Edmunds (2010) found that while HSGPA was predictive of persistence and degree completion for consistent achievement students, the ACT Composite score was not predictive of persistence for consistent achievement students. This finding, however, may have been influenced by the use of accepted and enrolled students who had been selected based on their incoming achievement, including their ACT score, thereby potentially reducing its ability to discriminate. In this study, the average ACT Composite score was 25.6, which is well above the national average; based on the 2016 ACT-tested graduating high school cohort, this score would be roughly at the eighty-third percentile.

Mattern, Shaw, and Kobrin (2011) conducted additional analyses that demonstrated that using both test scores and HSGPA jointly provides a more optimal prediction of performance than using either in isolation. Using both SAT and HSGPA jointly resulted in minimal over- or underprediction of FYGPA for the three achievement groups. When prediction of FYGPA was based on a model that included only HSGPA, however, as is the case for students who do not submit test scores at test-optional institutions, estimates of FYGPA were notably overestimated for HSGPA discrepant students and underestimated for SAT discrepant students. Similarly, if HSGPA is omitted from prediction models of FYGPA, there is notable overprediction of FYGPA for SAT discrepant students and underprediction for HSGPA discrepant students. Consistent achievement students had only minimal prediction error when either SAT scores or HSGPA were ignored. These are particularly important findings relative to test-optional policies where HSGPA is used as the sole achievement indicator for success.

While demonstrating that there are negative effects associated with having discrepant achievement between ACT Composite score and HSGPA, Sanchez and Lin (2017) also show the compensatory nature of ACT Composite scores and HSGPA. That is, higher grades can offset lower test scores, and vice versa, in terms of future college outcomes. There are many possible reasons for this relationship, such as an explanation offered by Willingham (2005). He noted that high school grades encompass students' noncognitive factors, such as scholastic engagement, self-regulation, discipline, or habits of inquiry, *in addition* to providing information on cognitive skills. Despite capturing noncognitive factors, HSGPA fails to provide a standard measure of academic achievement or cognitive skills given variability in course-taking across students and course content across courses and high schools. Standardized tests, on the other hand, provide a more narrow assessment that focus on cognitive skills but in a standardized manner. Differences in constructs and measurement methods result in both sources providing unique information about the student. It is this compensatory relationship that is lost when institutions elect to institute test-optional policies. This is in agreement with the previous findings reported above that looked at the relationship between ACT Engage scores and discrepant performance.

In closing, empirical evidence of the validity of test scores for use in college admissions underscores the value of multiple measures. By taking multiple pieces of information into consideration, a clearer picture of students' strengths and weaknesses and their likelihood of future success emerges. This is particularly true when the various pieces of information are inconsistent, as demonstrated by our research on students with discrepant performance. Interestingly, these are the very students who are mostly likely to be attracted to test-optional institutions. While test-optional policies promote discarding useful information, we stand behind the belief that more information is better than less information.

NOTES

1. For each of the discrepancy scenarios, we define discrepancy as occurring only when observed differences are larger than would be expected from measurement error.

2. A z-score is computed by subtracting the population mean from an individual raw score and then dividing the difference by the population standard deviation. The properties of the transformed variable are a mean of zero and standard deviation of one. Because HSGPA and test scores are on different scales, converting both to z-scores allows one to compare performance on each measure on the same scale.

REFERENCES

Allen, J. (2013). *Updating the ACT college readiness benchmarks.* ACT Research Report Series 2013 (6). Iowa City: ACT.

Cambiano, R., Denny, G., and DeVore, J. (2000). College student retention at a midwestern university: A six-year study. *Journal of College Admission, 166,* 22–29.

Edmunds, A. O. (2010). *An examination of the likelihood of persistence of students with discrepant high school grades and standardized test scores* (doctoral dissertation). University of Alabama, Tuscaloosa, Alabama. Retrieved from http://gradworks.umi .com/34/23/3423016.html.

Edmunds, A., and Sanchez, E. I. (2014). *Examining the likelihood of admission and persistence of students with discrepant high school grades and standardized test scores.* Presentation at the annual convention of the Southern Association for College Admissions Counseling, Myrtle Beach, SC.

Godfrey, K. E., and Matos-Elefonte, H. (2010). *Key indicators of college success: Predicting college enrollment, persistence, and graduation.* Retrieved from https://research .collegeboard.org/sites/default/files/publications/2012/7/presentation-2010-8-key -indicators-college-success.pdf.

Kobrin, J. L., Camara, W. J., and Milewski, G. B. (2002). *Students with discrepant high school GPA and SAT I scores.* Research notes. RN-15. New York: The College Board.

Kobrin, J. L., Patterson, B. F., Shaw, E. J., Mattern, K. D., and Barbuti, S. M. (2008). *Validity of the SAT for predicting first-year college grade point average.* Research Report no. 2008 (5). New York: The College Board.

Kuncel, N. R., Credé, M., and Thomas, L. L. (2005). The validity of self-reported grade point averages, class ranks, and test scores: A meta-analysis and review of the literature. *Review of Educational Research.* 75(1), 63–82.

Lichtenberger, E. J., and Dietrich, C. (2012). *College readiness and the postsecondary outcomes of Illinois high school students.* Policy Research: IERC 2012-1. Edwardsville: Illinois Education Research Council at Southern Illinois University.

Mattern, K., and Allen, J. (2016). *More information, more informed decisions: Why test-optional policies do not benefit institutions or students.* Retrieved from http://www .act.org/content/dam/act/unsecured/documents/MS487_More-Information-More -Informed-Decisions_Web.pdf.

Mattern, K. D., Patterson, B. F., and Wyatt, J. N. (2013). *How useful are traditional admission measures in predicting graduation within four years?* Research Report no. 2013 (1). New York: The College Board.

Mattern, K. D., Shaw, E. J., and Kobrin, J. L. (2010). *A case for not going SAT-optional: Students with discrepant SAT and HSGPA performance.* Retrieved from http://files.eric .ed.gov/fulltext/ED563419.pdf.

———. (2011). An alternative presentation of incremental validity discrepant SAT and HSGPA performance. *Educational and Psychological Measurement,* 71(4), 638–662.

McNeish, D. M., Radunzel, J., and Sanchez, E. (2015). *A multidimensional perspective of college readiness: Relating student and school characteristics to performance on the ACT.* ACT Research Report Series, 2015 (6). Iowa City: ACT.

Patterson, B. F., and Mattern, K. (2011). *Validity of the SAT for predicting first-year grades: 2008 SAT validity sample.* Statistical Report no. 2011 (5). New York: The College Board.

———. (2012). *Validity of the SAT for predicting first-year grades: 2009 SAT validity sample.* Statistical Report no. 2012 (2). New York: The College Board.

Radunzel, J., and Noble, J. (2012). *Predicting long-term college success through degree completion using ACT [R] composite score, ACT benchmarks, and high school grade point average.* ACT Research Report Series, 2012 (5). Iowa City: ACT.

———. (2013). *Differential effects on student demographic groups of using ACT College Readiness Assessment composite score, ACT benchmarks, and high school grade point average for predicting long-term college success through degree completion*. ACT Research Report Series, 2013 (5). Iowa City: ACT.

Ramist, L., Lewis, C., and Jenkins, L. M. (1997). *Students with discrepant high school GPA and SAT scores*. Research in Review, 1997 (1). New York: The College Board.

Sanchez, E. I. (2013). *Differential effects of using ACT college readiness assessment scores and high school GPA to predict first-year college GPA among racial/ethnic, gender, and income groups*. ACT Research Report Series, 2013 (4). Iowa City: ACT.

Sanchez, E., and Buddin, R. (2016). *How accurate are self-reported high school courses, course grades, and grade point average?* ACT Research Report Series 2016 (3). Iowa City: ACT.

Sanchez, E. I., and Edmunds, A. (2015). *How discrepant high school GPAs, test scores, and engagement impact persistence*. Presentation at the annual convention of the Association for Institutional Research, Denver, CO.

Sanchez, E. I., and Lin, S. (2017). *Effects of discrepant ACT and high school GPA on enrollment and persistence*. Unpublished manuscript, ACT, Iowa City.

Sawyer, R. (2008). *Benefits of additional high school course work and improved course performance in preparing students for college*. ACT Research Report Series, 2008 (1). Iowa City: ACT.

———. (2010). *Usefulness of high school average and ACT scores in making college admission decisions*. ACT Research Report Series 2010 (2). Iowa City: ACT.

Shaw, E., and Mattern, K. (2009). *Examining the accuracy of self-reported high school grade point average*. Research Report no. 2009 (5). New York: The College Board.

Wainer, H. (2011). *Uneducated guesses: Using evidence to uncover misguided education policies*. Princeton, NJ: Princeton University Press.

Willingham, W. W. (2005). Prospects for improving grades for use in admissions. In W. J. Camara and E. W. Kimmel (Eds.), *Choosing students: Higher education admission tools for the 21st century* (pp. 127–139). Mahwah, NJ: Lawrence Erlbaum Associates.

Zwick, R., and Sklar, J. C. (2005). Predicting college grades and degree completion using high school grades and SAT scores: The role of student ethnicity and first language. *American Educational Research Journal, 42*(3), 439–464.

PART II / The Rise of Test-Optional Admissions

6

Understanding the Test-Optional Movement

Jerome A. Lucido

W*hy do college admissions leaders make the decisions they do? How much does research on standardized admissions testing inform enrollment practice? In this chapter, veteran admissions director Jerome Lucido, who now heads the University of Southern California's Center for Enrollment Research, Policy, and Practice, draws on interviews with chief enrollment officers at public and private test-optional institutions to provide insight into their reasons for adopting this type of admissions policy.*

In the interviews, Lucido finds little blanket opposition to the use of standardized testing for admissions decisions. However, respondents voiced considerable concern about what they viewed as misuse of standardized tests, including a narrow focus on testing at some institutions as a heuristic for students' overall level of preparation. In other instances, interviewees fretted that some students may not apply to colleges where they may be qualified, but have the perception that SAT and ACT scores are heavily weighted. In the same vein, some said they are sympathetic to test-optional admissions because they believe it makes the process more welcoming to underrepresented minorities.

There are other motivations behind the test-optional movement, of course. Lucido notes that test-optional policies are attractive to enrollment managers: they can boost the number of applicants to a college and increase selectivity while raising average SAT scores, because lower-scoring students are less likely to submit scores. Dropping testing requirements can also generate positive publicity. Yet the students who are the intended beneficiaries of test-optional policies may suffer, Lucido suggests; on some campuses they are admitted at lower rates by admissions officers who have less information on which to base their decisions.

Lucido concludes that standardized testing is too useful to go away—as a sorting device, as a predictor of future academic achievement, and as a common benchmark against which to measure students from disparate educational backgrounds. Nevertheless, he contends that test-optional policies may serve as a useful bridge between different camps in the testing wars. By moving admissions offices away from rigid use of testing, test-optional policies allow them to match their actual use of assessments to their public statements. Going test-optional, Lucido argues, can lay the groundwork for future practices that put tests into better perspective.

The charge of this chapter is to provide an analysis of test-optional admissions policies from the vantage point of a practitioner, which I have been for some three and a half decades, and a scholar, to which I claim only a decade's experience and expertise. The chapter offers an opportunity to examine the long-standing policy debate between test providers and test detractors, and to ask the question: Does the test-optional movement offer some common ground that serves the interest of students?

To pursue these aims, this chapter examines the origins, stated purposes, and claims of test-optional policies and practices; it considers the research on the matter; and, it offers commentary on the way forward for those who wish to consider policy options, examine their results, and draw upon the latest thinking in this realm. Additionally, the chapter places test-optional practices within the evolution of the admission and enrollment management profession by examining the role of testing and test-optional policies in promoting college access. Finally, it considers the potential of both to further influence thinking and practice.

To animate the analysis with the lived experience of those who are managing test-optional programs, structured interviews were conducted in February 2017 with chief enrollment officers representing nine test-optional institutions. In many cases, these men and women also introduced the test-optional policy change to their institutions. The institutions represented in the interviews varied by location, private or public control, selectivity, size, and the length of time that the test-optional program was or has been in place. The observations of the respondents are embedded within the text, and brief institutional descriptors accompany their remarks.

For a full appreciation of the findings and analyses within this chapter, it is important to note from the start that although the world of research and the world of professional practice in higher education may overlap, they do not form concentric circles. Some practices are well steeped in research, and some are not. Indeed, researchers may well argue with the policy decisions of the leaders interviewed here. The purpose of this chapter is not to prove whether test-optional policies are right or wrong. Instead, it is to illuminate why they came into being and to consider their place in the future of college admissions. The chapter draws heavily on research, but the enrollment leaders interviewed for the chapter adopted their policies for a variety of reasons. Some of those were supported by research, some were geared to seeking market effectiveness, others emerged from their professional experience, and still others were grounded in personal educational values. What is represented is a faithful rendition of some reasons practitioners adopted test-optional policies and why these rationales will likely persist.

A Brief History of the Emergence of Test-Optional Admission Policies

In 1969, Bowdoin College eliminated the requirement of the SAT for admission as newly inaugurated president Roger Howell Jr. cited his desire to focus admission to Bowdoin "on the human quality of its students" (Belasco and Bergman 2016, 98). Bowdoin's move was a sign of the times, coming near the conclusion of the turbulent 1960s, and Howell was also credited with providing the first access to Bowdoin for women and for the introduction of the Afro-American Studies Program, now the Africana Studies program. It was not until Bates College also eliminated its testing requirement in 1984 that a peer institution joined Bowdoin. At that time, the faculty at Bates College voted to stop requiring high school seniors to submit SAT scores as part of the admissions process. The *New York Times* reported the College's reasoning: "Thomas H. Reynolds, president of the liberal arts college, said the decision, which takes effect immediately, reflected a 'deep concern with the effectiveness' of the widely used admissions test, including fears that it discourages applications from minority and economically disadvantaged students" (Fiske 1984).

Later in the 1990s, often in response to falling applications, reduced selectivity rates, and dropping indicators of student preparation, other well-known institutions added test-optional policies. As reported by the *Washington Post*, "A slew of other small schools eventually joined them, including Smith, Bryn Mawr, and College of the Holy Cross" (Anderson 2015). Supporting this observation, one interview respondent (moderately selective East Coast liberal arts university) noted that the phenomenon occurred at "institutions in the 1990s that were highly competitive but not most competitive. . . . As their applications declined with demographic change, they reasoned that applications would increase if they eliminated test scores. There was an open conversation about this as a strategy to increase apps."

Test-optional policies began to take stronger hold when University of California President Richard Atkinson spoke at the eighty-third annual meeting of the American Council on Education in February 2001. There, he argued that over-reliance on the SAT was "distorting educational priorities and practices" (Atkinson 2001). Bolstering Atkinson's position was work begun in early 2001 by the Board of Admissions and Relations with Schools (BOARS) of the Academic Senate of the University of California. In a discussion paper, it noted,

> The primary conclusions of the BOARS' research on the usefulness of admissions test scores in identifying successful students include the following:
> 1. Overall, high school GPA is the best predictor of freshman grades at the University of California.
> 2. Test scores do contribute a statistically significant increment of prediction when added to a regression analysis combining grades and test scores.
> 3. The SAT II appears overall to be a better predictor of freshman grades at UC than the SAT I. (Board of Admissions and Relations with Schools 2002)

Beyond Atkinson's speech and the research done by the faculty at the University of California, the notion of conducting college admissions without standardized tests gained popularity as a result of research contending that test scores have low predictive validity and pointing to the high correlation of test scores to socioeconomic status (Belasco et al. 2014; Geiser and Santelices 2007; Hiss and Franks 2014). In response, the College Board engaged in a redesign of the SAT, which included dropping controversial aspects of the exam, including verbal analogies, and adding an optional writing assessment (Lawrence et al. 2003).

Although the University of California presented research that cast doubt on the efficacy of the examination, there is a large, competing literature that embraces the predictive validity of the SAT. More recently, for example, Sackett and his colleagues examined an extensive data set that spanned two versions of the SAT and found that both the SAT and high school grades contributed to the prediction of academic performance in college. Moreover, they reported that family income and parental education had little effect on the predictive ability of the examination (Sackett et al. 2012). Further, both the College Board and ACT have published reports that include company-sponsored and independent research that demonstrates the examinations add to the prediction of first-year college grade point average when used in tandem with high school grades (Mattern and Allen 2016; Shaw 2015). Nonetheless, some institutions remained unconvinced that these studies and changes to the SAT were convincing enough to address previous flaws, and they found differential average test results among ethnic groups, along with the strong correlations between test scores and family income, troubling (Morgan 2016).

Among the pivotal moments was a presentation at the National Association of College Admission Counseling annual meeting in 2004 by William Hiss, who led the Bates admissions office as dean or vice president from 1978 to 2000 and who was vice president for external relations at the time. He presented a study of the Bates College test-optional program across its 20-year history, noting that its results "raise a national policy issue: Does standardized testing narrow access to higher education, significantly reducing the pool of students who would succeed if admitted?" The study's findings include the following:

1. The difference in Bates graduation rates between submitters and non-submitters over the term of the policy was 0.1% (one-tenth of 1%).

2. The difference in overall GPAs at Bates was .05 (five-hundredths of a GPA point), 3.06 for non-submitters and 3.11 for submitters.

3. Bates almost doubled its applicant pool during the period; about a third of each class entered Bates without submitting testing in the admissions process.

4. Testing was not necessary for predicting good performance; the academic ratings assigned by Bates admissions staff were highly accurate for both submitters and non-submitters in predicting GPA.

5. Bates increased its enrollment of students of color and international students. But white students using the policy outnumber students of color by five-to-one.

6. The policy drew sharply increased application rates from all the subgroups who commonly worry about standardized testing, including

women, US citizens of color, international students, low-income or blue-collar students, rural students, students with learning disabilities, and students with rated talents in athletics, the arts, or debate. (Hiss and Neupane 2004)

The *Report of the Commission on the Use of Standardized Tests in Undergraduate Admission* published by the National Association for College Admission Counseling (NACAC) in 2008 became another focal point for institutions considering test-optional admission policies. As documented in a short history of the test-optional movement published by DePaul University, "The report challenges universities to 'consider dropping the [standardized] admission test requirements if it is determined that the predictive utility of the test . . . support[s] that decision [to go test-optional] and if the institution believes that standardized test results would not be necessary for other reasons such as course placement, advising or research'" (Why a Test-Optional Program at DePaul? 2017).

In 2014, Hiss and Franks followed-up the 2004 Bates College study with large-scale longitudinal research covering 33 test-optional institutions using 122,916 student and alumni records across a maximum of eight cohort years. Included in their sample were 20 private colleges and universities, 6 public state universities, 5 minority-serving institutions, and 2 arts institutions. Their data demonstrated no significant difference in graduation rates among admitted and enrolled students who submitted test scores versus those who did not (Hiss and Franks 2014; Why a Test-Optional Program at DePaul? 2017) The methodology of the study has been challenged, partly because a significant portion (56%) of the sample was composed of public university students who were admitted based on grade point average and coursework thresholds, and partly because not all participating institutions provided data over the eight-year period. Still, the comprehensiveness of their work and the consistency of their results with earlier research marked another important boost to the test-optional movement (Mattern and Allen 2016).

In sum, test-optional policies arose at, and were dominated by, small liberal arts colleges in the introductory years, but the current list of institutions with such policies is much more varied. FairTest: The National Center for Fair and Open Testing, an advocacy organization with a self-described charge to "place special emphasis on eliminating the racial, class, gender, and cultural barriers to equal opportunity posed by standardized tests," publishes a widely cited list of colleges and universities that have test-optional or test-alternative admission policies

(National Center for Fair and Open Testing n.d.). Examination of this list reveals that the ranks of test-optional institutions now also include medium- to large-size private institutions; public colleges and universities with coursework patterns, grade point averages, and class rank requirements; art institutes; and proprietary schools (National Center for Fair and Open Testing n.d.; Why a Test-Optional Program at DePaul? 2017). The FairTest list is referenced here because it is widely cited and demonstrates the diversity of campuses that have adopted test-optional policies. On the other hand, it should be noted that FairTest is an organization that advocates for test-optional programs. Some institutions listed are not strictly test-optional, and others, such as art institutes and proprietary schools, would not likely require standardized testing as a matter of course.

Purposes and Objectives; Stated and Unstated

The reasons underlying the adoption of test-optional admission policies are numerous. Prominent among them, as evidenced by the name of the policies themselves, are concerns about standardized admission testing. These include issues inherent in the tests and those that are the by-products of testing. The latter include misuse of test results in admission offices; narrow application of results in admission decisions; the test-preparation industry, which favors those who can afford to avail themselves of such services; and student stress related to high-stakes examinations. Beyond testing, though, the reasons for adopting test-optional policies and practices are tightly bound to institutional objectives.

The research of Belasco et al. (2014) points to the complexity involved. They report that institutional adopters of test-optional policies seek a reduced reliance on standardized tests, which they challenge in terms of validity and bias, and a desire to enhance the ethnic and economic diversity of the campus without compromising the quality and performance of the student body. Interview respondents capture this dynamic:

> I always felt testing was not the be-all end-all. With new leadership on our campus we began a focus on good solid academic students who can be successful and to increase diversity. (Private mid-Atlantic university)

> When I was first in admissions, I was at places that always required testing. I realized the dependency that grows around the scores, including accountability with trustees—scores cannot go down. I'm in favor of choices. The current higher education system is outdated. It should be more flexible. (Highly selective East Coast liberal arts college)

We serve a large population of first-generation students. We wanted to promote [the policy] for students that had high test anxiety. We also have a large population of . . . students . . . with learning disabilities. (Western public flagship university)

The institution was not among the most selective—not the highest—and we thought that if we eliminated test scores as a barrier to application, our applications would increase. Then, too, with African American and Latino students performing below their white counterparts, we would reduce that barrier. (Eastern liberal arts college)

There is a lot of stress for students around testing, a lot of great students who get shut out. . . . There are multiple intelligences to gauge talent—we can't base it on single score. Tests are useful—we use every bit of information that we can get. I can't foresee a time where we'll have no testing . . . also because rankings have taken hold. (Private mid-Atlantic university)

Observers and consultants suggest that institutional motivations are often less altruistic than those that are publicly stated. Ehrenberg (2005) notes that manipulating institutional rankings is a strong incentive for test-optional policies:

First, it provides an incentive for them to make the reporting of test scores optional. Doing so should lead more applicants to apply to a school (making the institution look more selective) because low-scoring students with otherwise acceptable records will now be more likely to apply. It should also increase the average test scores of students who report their scores, because it will be students with lower test scores who will be the non-reporters. Whether on balance students admitted without submitting their test scores will do as well at the institution as students who submit test scores is an open question. (32)

In addition, a 2006 *Inside Higher Ed* article notes the commentary of a prominent consultant who echoes these themes: "Richard A. Hesel of Art and Science Group, which advises colleges on admissions and enrollment strategies, said he is currently evaluating the possible impact of dropping an SAT requirement for a client he couldn't name except to say that it was a top liberal arts college. Hesel said that he expected more colleges to make testing optional as they see the benefits of having more applicants and higher average SAT scores" (Jaschik 2006).

The article further illuminates the nuances of the test-optional policy decision, documenting the case in which an enrollment dean argues that it is not inconsistent to require test scores and do a good holistic admission review:

> One institution—Lafayette College—went test-optional in the 1990s, only to resume a testing requirement. Barry McCarty, dean of enrollment services at Lafayette, said he too thinks that colleges are motivated by strategy more than anything else. "There are a lot of motivations here, and the one that the media is not very often addressing is the attractiveness of eliminating many of the lowest SAT performers in calculating the mean of a college's class," he said. McCarty said that he didn't like the implication from many of those abandoning SAT requirements that places like Lafayette can't conduct sensitive reviews of applicants. He said that the college places more or less weight on the SAT score based on a variety of factors in a student's background and credentials. "I believe that we are looking at students holistically," he said. (Jaschik 2006)

That test-optional policies are adopted for a variety of reasons is also echoed in research. Morgan (2016) notes a number of motives for the decision to go test-optional, depending on the institution:

1. A marketing decision to increase publicity.
2. A way to increase an institution's appearance of selectivity, prestige, and value by encouraging students to submit higher scores and those with lower scores to not submit.
3. For public colleges and universities, a reflection of the view that high school performance was a better way of predicting college success, and a way to increase diversity given affirmative action restrictions.
4. For private selective colleges and universities, a way to attract a more diverse applicant pool (with some citing their mission).

Yuko Mulugetta, director of enrollment planning at Ithaca College, by contrast, is more singular in focus. Drawing from her research on the impacts of Ithaca's test-optional policy, she cites a direct connection between the adoption of test-optional policies and the nature and usage of standardized tests. In particular, she asserts that the SAT is culturally biased against some groups, including racial minorities, females, first-generation, and low-income students, and therefore acts to "structurally maintain—or worse augment—the already existing gap between advantaged and disadvantaged applicants" (Mulugetta 2013, 2).

How Do Test-Optional Policies Play Out in Practice?

Studies examining the outcomes of test-optional policies show results that mimic the various motivations for the policies themselves. Belasco and colleagues sampled 180 selective liberal arts colleges in the United States from 1992 to 2010, of which 32 were test-optional, to find that:

1. On average, test-optional policies did not increase the diversity (racial/ethnic or economic) of students.
2. Test-optional institutions received approximately 220 more applications on average annually than non-test-optional institutions, although this was not statistically significant.
3. On average, test-optional institutions saw an increase of 26 points on reported SAT scores, enhancing appearance of selectivity.

The study concluded that test-optional policies were not an "adequate solution to providing educational opportunity for low-income and minority students" (Belasco et al. 2014, 13). Moreover, the researchers suggested that such policies may contribute to existing stratification by giving greater importance to factors like strength of curriculum or involvement outside of the classroom, which may not be as accessible to high school students from low socioeconomic backgrounds. Indeed, the authors make a pointed argument that selective institutions should be more transparent about the "extent to which they can accommodate disadvantaged populations" and ask, "Would an Amherst or Pomona, for example, if faced with a flood of academically qualified but needy students, admit more needy students or would they make competition fiercer among needy students for the same number of slots?" (Belasco et al. 2014, 14).

On balance, the findings in the Belasco et al. (2014) study were reported in the aggregate. Therefore, we do not know to what extent those schools among the 32 liberal arts colleges with test-optional policies realized increases or decreases in ethnic or economic diversity, nor do we find reasons why they may or may not have done so. Such reasons may include the level of endowment or the lack of financial aid policies to support non-submitters (merit aid, for example, is still most often determined using test scores). Ultimately, test-optional policies in this large study appear to be ineffectual. At the same time, it uncovers no negative outcomes in terms of ethnic or socioeconomic diversity, which holds steady with no significant difference detected. With no apparent negative impact, alongside substantial institutional gain in the number of applications (and thus selectivity), and higher test scores (and thus the perception of selectivity), one implication is that test-optional policies have potential benefits, albeit not always those that are cited at adoption.

In contrast to the Belasco et al. (2014) study and as noted earlier, Hiss and Franks (2014) examined a large-scale sample of institutional data collected over an eight-year period and reported the following results for test-optional campuses:

1. Among all students in the sample, 30% of were non-submitters for admission consideration.
2. There were no significant academic, either cumulative GPA or graduation rate, differences in non-submitters from submitters.
3. Cumulative GPA was highly correlated with high school grade point average (HSGPA). They also reported that students with strong HSGPAs and weak test scores performed equally well in college, and noted that students admitted under the test-optional policy with weak HSGPAs, despite high test scores, earn lower cumulative GPAs and graduate at lower rates.
4. The authors also note that non-submitters were more likely to be first-generation college students, minorities, women, Pell Grant recipients, and have learning differences.
5. Finally, they uncover a bimodal income distribution among non-submitters. Both students with financial need, including first-generation, underrepresented, and Pell Grant recipients, and students from high socioeconomic backgrounds were prominent among those students who exercised their option not to submit test scores for their admission determinations.

Other studies show more mixed results. In a recent examination of the test-optional policy at Smith College, McLaughlin (2014) reports a short-term rise in applicants (first year of implementation), but the effect wore off by year three, with applicants dropping to slightly below year one of the new policy for Smith. Additionally,

1. On average for the three years during the test-optional admission policy, white women were disproportionately more likely to apply as a result of the new policy, with black women less likely to apply to Smith.
2. Women from high-income schools (less than 33% free and reduced lunch) were significantly more likely to apply to Smith during the test-optional

years, and there was no difference in response from female applicants from lower-income schools.

3. Black, Latina, and women from low-income schools were not more likely to apply as a result of the test-optional policy but were much more likely to withhold their test scores. White, Asian, and women from high-income schools were less likely to withhold their test scores.

At Smith the test-optional policy did not lead to greater economic or cultural diversity, though it seems to have been successful in broadening the application pool by encouraging new applicants who may not have considered a private, selective liberal arts institution prior to the test-optional policy. Moreover, the study found that unique applicants to Smith (those women who applied only to Smith) were much more likely to withhold their test scores.

More recently, a study by Morgan considered 14,000 applicants at small, test-optional, liberal arts colleges in the East during the years 2008–2011. The study examined the interaction of financial aid with test-optional practices. The findings included the following:

1. Non-test submitters were more likely to have enrolled than test submitters.
2. FAFSA filers responded positively to merit-based and need-based aid. The more money awarded, the more likely they were to enroll.
3. Non-submitters responded more strongly to a $1,000 increase in institutional aid than submitters. In the words of the author, "the impact of an additional $1,000 of institutional merit or institutional need based money to a FAFSA filing student who withholds standardized test scores, relative to a comparable peer that submits scores, does more to influence the probability of enrollment than nearly two campus visits." (Morgan 2016, 94)

Generally, these findings comport with other literature showing that non-submitters tend to have greater enrollment rates than submitters (Mulugetta 2015; Robinson and Monks 2005).

Test-Optional Policies Do Not Act in a Vacuum

The significance of the Morgan (2016) study, in part, is in its insight that test-optional policies do not act in a vacuum. Results may vary based on other initiatives and actions on the campus, in this case, student financial aid policy. Mulugetta's work at Ithaca College similarly reports that the adoption of a test-optional policy there included integrative marketing and a strategic increase in financial aid while raising tuition at slower pace (2013, 2015). Interview respondents support this assertion:

> Prior to my arrival, we had a test-optional policy here that failed. Enrollment decreased. But it was not the test-optional policy that led to the enrollment drop earlier—there were price issues, reduced staff positions in admissions and aid, and the institution went to a gapping policy that had a negative impact on yield. [Gapping occurs when an institution does not or cannot provide financial assistance to meet all applicants' full demonstrated financial need.] Currently, we have a stronger market position with 15% more apps and increased diversity with an eight-point gain in students of color. (Moderately selective East Coast liberal arts university)

> Yes, we have risen, but this is not tied to test-optional but how we make decisions. We use big data to predict well who will enroll, and we have much better funding decisions. So we can admit less and predict enrollment better. (Private mid-Atlantic university)

> We overhauled more than test-optional. We went to the Board and reinstated an essay. We stated that might reduce apps—and we actually had 20% fewer apps—but yield rose from 22 to 31% in one year. Faculty really opposed it first, but then became really happy about students enrolled. (Highly selective East Coast liberal arts college)

Given the complexity of policy introduction, alongside other enrollment strategies, interview respondents nonetheless reported satisfaction with their implementation of the policy:

> We were able to admit and to fund more multicultural students. We stopped gapping and created real opportunity. (Private mid-Atlantic university)

> Part of it is to enroll more students who otherwise would not have the opportunity to go to an institution like ours. On the other side to increase apps so we can be more selective, and that is working as well. Look at the Coalition, which was something done to serve those schools who felt poorly served by the Common App, and they then fell back on the notion of access as a selling point.

We can do things for institutional reasons that can have a positive impact on realizing our mission. (Moderately selective East Coast liberal arts university)

This all started with small liberal arts colleges. But using data and analytics, you not only meet goals but can get stronger. (Large, private, highly selective mid-Atlantic university)

I worked with IR [institutional research] and the school of education to determine how students might perform. I was also interested in learning what impact it would have on the pool in general. In our pilot, we got our highest number of multicultural students in early decision ever. So we knew we were discouraging in the past. (Private mid-Atlantic university)

The academic profile was slipping, and there were a lot of reasons for that, but the change wouldn't have been so fast. When I introduced them to the research, I showed national studies. People think your standards will go down . . . concern for *US News.* I showed good predictability, how institutions thrived; then I took our peer group and their movement in *US News* since their policy was created. For the majority of those institutions, they went up. (Highly selective East Coast liberal arts college)

We are now bringing students through the door that would've never even considered us . . . with the highest number of diversity and first-generation college students in college's history. Our faculty sent a letter to Board of Trustees about how pleased they were with class of 2020. That was a strong sign that things are working. (Highly selective East Coast liberal arts college)

One of the benefits we've seen is that there is a higher conversion rate on the test-optional students. For them [our school] really is the dream. It puts the student's dream school in reach. (Private mid-Atlantic university)

Our STEM [science, technology, engineering, and math] faculty were very concerned about not having students that could do well in classes and less students overall. Actually they had more students. (Highly selective East Coast liberal arts college)

A view of the test-optional adopter as pragmatic idealist emerges from this commentary. With these leaders at once institutional agents, advocates for the underserved, and savvy enrollment managers, multiple motivations are at play, and a wide variety of outcomes are acceptable.

Does Test-Optional Amount to a Movement in College Admissions Today?

As noted above, FairTest publishes a widely cited list of colleges and universities that have test-optional or test-alternative admission policies. A close examination of the list is warranted. Of the 965 colleges and schools on the FairTest site, only 265 are considered in the top tier in their respective *US News* categories. Many on the list are proprietary institutions, most are noncompetitive, and some require some alternative form of testing, a practice known as "test-flexible." If the adoption of test-optional admission policies is a movement, then the movement is not one of sweeping change (National Center for Fair and Open Testing n.d.).

Nonetheless, the trajectory of test-optional policies demonstrates an upward trend as the number of colleges and universities that have adopted them grows, as their efficacy is examined and demonstrated, and as institutions grapple with an increasingly diverse and economically stratified college-bound population (Bransberger and Michelau 2016). Indeed, as demonstrated by the commentary of test-optional adopters, the rise of these policies has roots in and is contributing to a changing profession, one that has progressed beyond gatekeeping to a complex calculus of who shall be recruited and admitted, who shall receive student aid and how much, and for what institutional purposes. Hossler and Bontrager (2014) point out that enrollment leaders sit at the nexus of institutional prestige, net revenue, and access and diversity. Serving multiple masters institutionally, while at the same time serving a more diverse population of students nationally, is one of the most vexing problems in higher education today. Increasingly, enrollment leaders seek policy levers, tools, and strategies to meet these demands.

Recent research sponsored by the College Board demonstrates that nonacademic factors, those aspects of a student's moral and performance character, are widely utilized in decision making across the spectrum of college admission offices (Hossler, Lucido, and Chung 2017). Moreover, tools are being developed by the College Board and elsewhere to aid institutions in systematically identifying educational disadvantage (Ballinger and Perfetto 2017). Tying these together is the research of Bastedo, who identifies heuristics and biases among admission readers and who cites how their decisions change when presented with well-documented contextual information about applicants (Bastedo and Bowman 2017; Bastedo, Howard, and Flaster 2016).

To this mix add the role of the courts, gubernatorial executive action, and citizen referenda related to the use of race as a factor in college admissions, and we find that institutions increasingly seek race-neutral means to identify talent and potential in order to diversify their student body and to meet their societal missions (Broder 1998; *Fisher v. University of Texas at Austin* 2013; Totenberg 2014; Traub 1999; Tucker 2016).

What Do Test-Optional Policies Bring to the Table? Identifying Barriers and Contributions

Test-optional policies provide a way to address many of the complex issues noted above. Specifically, the research noted and the interview responses gathered for this chapter contain a body of evidence that test-optional policies can aid in the reduction of real and perceived barriers to opportunity and admission. Moreover, they can contribute to improved practice in the office of admissions. After reading the literature, coding interview results, and viewing both through the lens of my experience as a practitioner, I can identify a number of barriers and opportunities that test-optional policies offer one way to address. As they are discussed, interview responses are incorporated to illustrate how improved practice may be facilitated with well-considered test-optional practices.

The barriers identified here are not problems inherent within standardized tests. Rather, they are problems with how the results are used and perceived. Finally, it is important to note that these barriers occur on both ends of the spectrum of predominant stakeholders in the admission decision: students and their families and institutions of higher education.

Self-Limiting Application Decisions

Some students restrict their applications to colleges and universities based primarily on the institutions' reported test score averages. These decisions are driven by the perceptions of students and families that the SAT and the ACT play a more prominent role in admission decisions than they actually do. This is a self-selection phenomenon that finds support in a growing literature that qualified students, often of low-income backgrounds, under-match in their application behavior (College Board 2013; Hoxby 2004; Hoxby and Turner 2015). According to interview respondents:

> We hoped students would take us at our word. We always said we value hard work over testing. We had students telling us, "I can't apply here. . . . I don't have those scores." And we would have taken her. We'd hope to diversify our students, and we've seen that change. (Private mid-Atlantic university)

[We are] bringing students through the door that would've never even considered us. (West Coast liberal arts college)

This is anecdotal, but students have told me, "I was told I was out of your range, and now I can apply." (Highly selective East Coast liberal arts college)

[Test-optional] allows students to win both ways. "Smart" kids want to be in the same club when they see average SAT scores. It allows students that are below "average" to submit an app. (Selective East Coast liberal arts college)

Addressing these misperceptions, whether with the introduction of test-optional admission policies or otherwise, frees students from self-limiting application behavior. A strong institutional message that test scores will not make or break an application is an important step in doing so.

Hasty Heuristics

Some admission decision makers use standardized test scores as a heuristic for the overall quality of a student's preparation to the extent that a student's testing unduly influences an admission decision. Dropping testing requirements can make admission choices less mechanical.

[Our test-optional policy] is testing us to do what we have always said to students that we would do. That is one of the biggest changes. It forces us to really understand the student in their context without the easy on/off switch. . . . [It addresses] our own misuse. (Private mid-Atlantic university)

[Test-optional] is better admission practice because it forces us to not take shorthand . . . look at whole application. . . . What we tell applicants and what we do are sometimes two different things. The standard line is standardized testing is just one factor, but for highly selective schools it is an incredibly critical factor. To the extent a staff buys-in to test-optional, it helps make the rhetoric and practice align. It puts testing in its proper light. (Moderately selective East Coast liberal arts university)

Reducing the use of tests as a heuristic brings rhetoric and policy and practice into alignment.

Overreliance on Institutional Profile

When institutional accountability and reporting is based on standardized testing averages, the result can be to restrict access by narrowing admission decisions to a small band of applicants within a college's usual testing norms. This represents an unwarranted restriction of scope in admission decision making, one that limits access in service to "looking good" in the eyes of presidents, trustees, and public perceptions of prestige.

> [Before test-optional] we wouldn't really look at scores of 1400 or less. We might relax this for women or disadvantaged students, but required testing served to exclude students without a lot of analysis. Even though testing is useful, it can be abused. (Large, private, highly selective mid-Atlantic university)

> I realized the dependency that grows around the scores, including accountability with trustees—scores cannot go down. (Eastern liberal arts college)

> Institutions turn away students who are amazing in favor of students who may not be as good to improve the profile. (Selective East Coast liberal arts college)

> From the enrollment management perspective, to be in a space where no one asks about SAT averages is amazing. The quality has gone up based upon our internal academic rating rather than scores. (Highly selective East Coast liberal arts college)

Addressing overreliance on institutional profile permits a wider range of decision making in admission decisions and a wider range of metrics to describe institutional quality. Merit can and should be defined in many ways. The application for admission provides multiple opportunities for students to demonstrate their abilities and proclivities and for admission decision makers to recognize them.

Discouraging Minority Applicants

This barrier occurs in the admission process when real and perceived issues with standardized admission tests discourage promising and otherwise qualified underrepresented students from submitting applications. This is similar to the self-selection barrier described above, yet it is distinct as it represents a cultural, rather than strictly quantitative, phenomenon.

> When I was doing dissertation research, we looked at students' decisions before they took the tests. More so for students of color, particularly African American females had lowered aspirations for college after taking the tests. And these were good students with a 3.7 or more. If it tempers the aspirations of those students, what does it do to those with only a 3.0? (Southern liberal arts college)

Test-optional is part of a solution. The entire idea of tests as a gateway is part of the culture. The more schools that go to test-optional, the more the culture can change. (Southern liberal arts college)

This year we went to several schools to attract more students of Latino/a backgrounds, and we didn't even talk about scores. We wanted to avoid even the notion that tests mattered for them because counselors would steer them away from even test-optional because of concern that we would not take these students. We were super-successful. (Southern liberal arts college)

I did it for better choices and freedom for students and the institution. Testing is inhibiting for students of color and others. (Highly selective East Coast liberal arts college)

We could not have anticipated how well people would respond, especially multicultural students. (Moderately selective East Coast liberal arts university)

Addressing how testing requirements may inadvertently discourage some minority applicants facilitates student choice and provides students with encouragement to pursue their educational goals. Moreover, it encourages admission representatives to seek the information they need to understand the contexts in which student achievement occurs.

The Intimidation Factor

At times the high stakes associated with admission testing acts as an inhibitor to student application behavior. Not fully distinct from self-limiting application decisions or discouraging minority students, the presence of testing requirements in the admissions process can lead students to self-select, or self-select-out, where, in the latter case, some students opt out of the college application process entirely. The intimidation and stress associated with college admissions is not related only to testing, of course, but interview respondents pointed to their test-optional policies as a way to help reduce stress and send a message of ease of access.

[There is] a lot of stress for students around testing. Probably shuts out good students who don't do well on tests. . . . There are multiple intelligences to gauge talent—can't base it on single score. (Private mid-Atlantic university)

We wanted to promote the idea that they didn't need to have high anxiety. They do pretty well here, so we didn't need to have to worry about it . . . more toward answering the question of access . . . that students could show their ability without test scores . . . an opportunity to enroll without the pressure of a test-score. (Western public flagship university)

Makes the process more humane, reduces stress. The NACAC survey shows that the number one factor is GPA, and this allows us to demonstrate that. It is student-friendly. We do so many things that are not student-friendly that this is one thing we can do . . . [provide] student choice in the application process. (Private mid-Atlantic university)

Addressing the potentially intimidating nature of testing provides better alignment of public statements with admission practice, is a signal of accessibility, and allows students to take into account a broader set of factors when considering their educational options.

On Balance: Neither Panacea nor the Only Way

Test-optional policies are neither a panacea nor the only way that the complexities of college admissions and the mandates of enrollment managers can be addressed. Indeed, not all test-optional campuses realize greater student diversity. Moreover, holistic review processes apply their own brand of pressure on students. Fundamentally, there is no substitute for expertise across all of the vectors of admission decision making, including the predictive validity of testing, understanding the concepts being assessed in testing, understanding student performance more broadly, including the context in which it occurs, and conducting local studies of the factors under consideration. To illustrate, given the particular focus of this chapter, test-optional policies are often championed to encourage campus diversity, yet one virtue of standardized testing is to identify talent that otherwise may not have been revealed. The two notions are not as oppositional as they appear. Otherwise stated, while it is true that misuse, rote reliance, and the limitations of test scores may reduce opportunity for many, it is also true that the talent and capacity of other students is uncovered with better-than-expected testing results. In fact, expanding access was one of the original purposes for the creation of the SAT (Lemann 2000).

Moreover, test-optional policies can act to exacerbate rather than resolve the inherent advantages that well-to-do families have over lower socioeconomic status families. This may occur by virtue of the differential access to savvy admission counselors and application strategies that these families enjoy. More than one study noted here found that the ranks of students who did not submit test scores were swelled with well-heeled applicants. McLaughlin (2014), for example, posits that better college guidance may explain why white and high-income school applicants were more likely to apply, as awareness of the test-optional policy may have been higher with greater access to college counseling resources that are more readily available to white and high-income schools. Hiss and Franks (2014) also noted the strong presence of students not qualifying for or requesting financial aid within their large sample of "non-submitters."

Further, there is a sense that all students get a better shake when test-optional policies are implemented. That is not necessarily true. Among some institutions in the interview sample, students who chose the test-optional route were admitted at lower rates, which is a rational outcome given reduced information for admission decision making. In other cases, those choosing the "test submitter" option may be disadvantaged. As one respondent noted, "At a highly selective, a student who brings low testing and exercises (the test submission) option will be disadvantaged. A bit of a double standard is applied there" (Large, private, highly selective mid-Atlantic university).

Standardized testing will not soon go away. It simply has too much usefulness, for better or for worse. It provides fundamental and comparable information on particular academic strengths and weaknesses of applicants. It adds, albeit variously, predictive validity to admission decisions. It finds usefulness, efficiency, and efficacy as a sorting device, and it is a standard measure across states and systems with wide variations in educational quality and grading standards. Regretfully, it also has a deep foothold in the rankings industry and in the minds and hearts of trustees and institutional leaders who seek prestige as a leading institutional outcome. Narrow definitions of quality and the challenges noted above, including overemphasis on institutional score averages, and on testing as an admissions heuristic, occur in part when one eye of decision makers is always on the rankings.

While test-optional, whether a movement or a slow evolution of good practice, seeks to mitigate the negative impacts of testing and test misuse, the need for sound information in the admission decision remains. Test results, in the hands of thoughtful practitioners, add value to admission decisions. Can wise decisions be made without them? Years of test-optional practice now suggest that they can. What seems intriguing is that the test-optional "movement" may hold the seeds of better, more highly informed practice. Such practice would include mitigating the negative impact of test shortcomings and misuse while enlightening admission decision makers with information that illuminates academic strengths and weaknesses, information that can lead to better admission decisions, better academic advising, and better results for students.

Enlightened Practice Is Informed Practice

What does enlightened practice mean? For one thing, it goes beyond cursory usage of testing. In practice, a reader and/or an admission committee does not evaluate a student who submits a test score and concludes, "I like this score because I can predict this student's success a little bit better." Indeed, as Hiss and Franks (2014) remind us, "The reliance on FYGPA [first year grade point average] seems a systemic weakness of much validity research, as by definition it ignores the core mission of our colleges and universities: to graduate students who have learned how to succeed, often in the face of obstacles. Much of that learning, and the visible success that follows from it, occurs over the longer course of a college education" (12). Instead, the reviewer and the admission committee often discuss how the student fits within the testing profile. What is too often not discussed, either in admission committees or in testing company research and validity studies, is what learning constructs the tests reveal and for whom. As a result, discussion revolves around testing as a proxy, testing as a rationing device, testing as static score, testing as adding to the margin of prediction, and testing as a shortcut to thoughtful review.

In point of fact, the interview respondents for this chapter, all of whom operated test-optional policies, were not "anti-testing." Instead, they expressed concern about how tests were misused, how tests were imperfect, about how much stress testing placed on students, and how potentially promising students were discouraged from making application based on reported test score ranges. Further, they fretted openly about gaps between the rhetoric of their offices about the relative importance of testing in their admission decisions and the reality of what they do in practice. They spoke of test-optional as a way to bring their practice into alignment with their public statements. This can only be interpreted as a positive step toward better understanding between students and the admission office. With some cooperation and good research, it can also build a bridge between test "opponents" and test "advocates." In the words of one respondent, "[Implementing our policy] is liberating because it has reduced emphasis on average SAT scores, and we now have latitude to admit students that may have lower scores but who are stellar in all other ways. For those that have grown up in the testing world and identify with test scores—taking that option away also wouldn't be fair. They have worked really hard and should get credit for it if that's the way they choose to tell their story" (Highly selective East Coast liberal arts college).

Still, these policies require local research to be done well. One respondent observed wryly, "People who have joined this movement have done it for good reasons. There are easier ways to move up [the rankings]. . . . This takes too much blood, sweat, and tears" (West Coast liberal arts college). The "easier ways" left silent in this response might include pandering to rankings by creating class sizes of 19 or less, adopting partial "fast-apps" and counting them as completed applications, congealing faculty resources to inflate institutional financial commitment to undergraduate education, and outright misrepresentation of selectivity percentages and testing results.

When President Atkinson of the University of California grappled with the role of testing in 2001, he too struggled with its rightful place in decision making: "When faced with large numbers of students applying for relatively few spots, admissions officers, unless they are very careful, will give undue weight to the SAT. All UC campuses have tried to ensure that SAT scores are used properly in the admissions process. However, because California's college-age population will grow by 50 percent over the next decade and become even more diverse than it is today, additional steps must be taken now to ensure that test scores are kept in proper perspective."

The stakes are no less daunting or important today. Thoughtful and knowledgeable practitioners, bolstered by research that is national in scope and locally relevant, can craft thoughtful polices that advance wise and socially beneficial decision making in college admissions. Testing is one element, but research needs to done across the spectrum of factors to continue the evolution of the profession that test-optional policies and practices likely represent.

REFERENCES

Anderson, Nick. (2015). George Washington University applicants no longer need to take admissions tests. *Washington Post*, July 27. Retrieved from https://www.washington post.com/news/grade-point/wp/2015/07/27/george-washington-university-applicants -no-longer-need-to-take-admissions-tests/?utm_term=.962c6551048f.

Atkinson, Richard C. (2001). *Standardized tests and access to American universities*. UC and the SAT, February 18. Retrieved from http://www.ucop.edu/news/sat/speech .html.

Ballinger, Philip, and Perfetto, Greg. (2017). *The systematic identification of disadvantage in educational opportunity*. Presented at the USC CERPP 2017 Conference: Student Selection: Art, Science and Emerging Trends, January. Retrieved from https://cerpp .usc.edu/conferences/2017con/2017-conference-blog-monday-january-23.

Bastedo, M. N., and Bowman, N. A. (2017). Improving admission of low-SES students at selective colleges: Results from an experimental simulation. *Educational Researcher, 46*(2), 67–77. https://doi.org/10.3102/0013189X17699373.

Bastedo, M. N., Howard, J. E., and Flaster, A. (2016). Holistic admissions after affirmative action: Does "maximizing" the high school curriculum matter? *Educational Evaluation and Policy Analysis, 38*(2), 389–409. https://doi.org/10.3102/0162373716642407.

Belasco, A., and Bergman, D. (2016). *The enlightened college applicant: A new approach to the search and admissions process.* Lanham, MD: Rowman and Littlefield. Retrieved from https://rowman.com/ISBN/9781475826920/The-Enlightened-College-Applicant-A-New-Approach-to-the-Search-and-Admissions-Process.

Belasco, Andrew S., Rosinger, Kelly O., and Hearn, James C. (2014). The test-optional movement at America's selective liberal arts colleges: A boon for equity or something else? *Educational Evaluation and Policy Analysis, 37*(2), 206–223.

Board of Admissions and Relations with Schools (BOARS). (2002). *The use of admissions tests by the University of California.* Retrieved from http://senate.universityofcalifornia.edu/_files/committees/boars/admissionstests.pdf.

Bransberger, Peace, and Michelau, Demarée. (2016). *Knocking at the college door.* Projections of High School Graduates. Western Interstate Commission for Higher Education (WICHE). Retrieved from https://static1.squarespace.com/static/57f269e19de4bb8a69b470ae/t/583f0ab6440243e9ace54c41/1480526524984/Knocking2016FINALFORWEB.pdf.

Broder, David. (1998). Affirmative action gets key test in Wash. *Washington Post,* October 24. Retrieved from http://www.washingtonpost.com/wp-srv/politics/campaigns/keyraces98/stories/ballot102498.htm.

College Board. (2013). *The college keys compact: 2013 catalog of effective practices.* New York: College Board. Retrieved from http://media.collegeboard.com/digitalServices/pdf/advocacy/policycenter/collegekeys-compact-2013-catalog-effective-practices-130115.pdf.

Ehrenberg, Ronald G. (2005). Method or madness? Inside the *U.S. News & World Report* college rankings. *Journal of College Admission, 189,* 29–35.

Fisher v. University of Texas at Austin. (2013). No. 11-345. Retrieved from https://www.supremecourt.gov/opinions/12pdf/11-345_l5gm.pdf.

Fiske, E. B. (1984). Some colleges question usefulness of S.A.T.'s. *New York Times,* October 9. Retrieved from http://www.nytimes.com/1984/10/09/science/education-some-colleges-question-usefulness-of-sat-s.html.

Geiser, S., and Santelices, M. V. (2007). Validity of high-school grades in predicting student success beyond the freshman year: High-school record vs. standardized tests as indicators of four-year college outcomes. Center for Studies in Higher Education. Retrieved from http://files.eric.ed.gov/fulltext/ED502858.pdf.

Hiss, William C., and Franks, Valerie W. (2014). *Defining promise: Optional standardized testing policies in American college and university admissions.* Arlington, VA: National Association for College Admission Counseling (NACAC). Retrieved from https://www.luminafoundation.org/files/resources/definingpromise.pdf.

Hiss, William C., and Neupane, Prem R. (2004). *20 years of optional SATs*. Presented at the 60th annual meeting of the National Association for College Admissions Counseling. Retrieved from http://www.bates.edu/news/2004/10/01/sats-at-bates.

Hossler, Don, and Bontrager, Bob. (2014). Summing up: The present and future tense for SEM. In *Handbook of Strategic Enrollment Management* (pp. 585–590). San Francisco: Jossey-Bass. Retrieved from http://www.wiley.com/WileyCDA/WileyTitle /productCd-1118819489.html.

Hossler, Don, Lucido, Jerry, and Chung, Emily. (2017). *The past, present, and future use of non-academic factors in admission decisions.* Presented at the USC CERPP 2017 Conference, Student Selection: Art, Science and Emerging Trends, January. Retrieved from https://cerpp.usc.edu/conferences/2017con/2017-conference-blog -monday-january-23.

Hoxby, Caroline M. (Ed.). (2004). *College choices: The economics of where to go, when to go, and how to pay for it.* Chicago: University of Chicago Press. Retrieved from http://www.press.uchicago.edu/ucp/books/book/chicago/C/bo3643231.html.

Hoxby, C. M., and Turner, S. (2015). What high-achieving low-income students know about college. *American Economic Review, 105*(5), 514–517. https://doi.org/10.1257 /aer.p20151027.

Jaschik, Scott. (2006). Momentum for going SAT-optional. *Inside Higher Ed*, May 26. Retrieved from https://www.insidehighered.com/news/2006/05/26/sat.

Lawrence, I. M., Rigol, G. W., Essen, T. V., and Jackson, C. A. (2003). *A historical perspective on the content of the SAT.* ETS Research Report Series, 2003(1). https://doi.org/10.1002/j.2333-8504.2003.tb01902.x.

Lemann, N. (2000). *The big test: The secret history of the American meritocracy.* New York: Macmillan.

Mattern, Krista, and Allen, Jeff. (2016). *More information, more informed decisions: Why test-optional policies do NOT benefit institutions or students.* Retrieved from http:// www.act.org/content/dam/act/unsecured/documents/MS487_More-Information -More-Informed-Decisions_Web.pdf.

McLaughlin, John T. (2014). *The effect of test-optional policy on application choice* (doctoral dissertation). Harvard University, Cambridge, MA. Retrieved from https://search.proquest.com/docview/1645337001?pq-origsite=gscholar.

Morgan, Hillary. (2016). *Estimating matriculation with a focus on financial aid and test optional policies: Data from a liberal arts institution in the Northeast* (doctoral disserta- tion). Seton Hall University, South Orange, NJ. Retrieved from http://scholarship .shu.edu/dissertations/2164.

Mulugetta, Yuko. (2013). Going test optional: Gathering evidence and making the decision at Ithaca College. Presented at the 40th NEAIR (North East Association for Institutional Research) annual conference, Newport, RI. Retrieved from https://offices.depaul.edu/enrollment-management-marketing/test-optional /Documents/Mulugetta-GoingTestOptionalIthacaCollege.pdf.

———. (2015). *Understanding the impacts of the test optional admission policy.* Presented at the 42nd NEAIR (North East Association for Institutional Research) annual conference, Burlington, VT. Retrieved from https://offices.depaul.edu/enrollment

-management-marketing/test-optional/Documents/Mulugetta-GoingTestOptional
  IthacaCollege.pdf.

National Center for Fair and Open Testing. (n.d.). About FairTest. Retrieved from
  http://fairtest.org/about.

Robinson, Michael, and Monks, James. (2005). Making SAT scores optional in selective
  college admissions: A case study. *Economics of Education Review, 24*(4), 393–405.

Sackett, P. R., Kuncel, N. R., Beatty, A. S., Rigdon, J. L., Shen, W., and Kiger, T. B.
  (2012). The role of socioeconomic status in SAT-grade relationships and in college
  admissions decisions. *Psychological Science, 23*(9), 1000–1007. https://doi.org/10
  .1177/0956797612438732.

Shaw, Emily J. (2015). *An SAT validity primer.* New York: The College Board. Retrieved
  from http://research.collegeboard.org/sites/default/files/publications/2015/2/research
  -report-sat-validity-primer.pdf.

Totenberg, Nina. (2014). High court upholds Michigan's affirmative action ban. *NPR,*
  April 22. Retrieved from http://www.npr.org/2014/04/22/305960143/high-court
  -upholds-michigans-affirmative-action-ban.

Traub, J. (1999). The class of Prop. 209. *New York Times,* May 2. Retrieved from
  http://www.nytimes.com/1999/05/02/magazine/the-class-of-prop-209.html.

Tucker, Neely. (2016). Jeb Bush got his way on affirmative action in Florida: Then he got
  a mess. *Washington Post,* January 7. Retrieved from http://www.washingtonpost.com
  /sf/national/2016/01/07/decidersbush/?utm_term=.092fa3526ab9.

Why a Test-Optional Program at DePaul? (2017). [Blog post, March 24]. Retrieved from
  https://offices.depaul.edu/enrollment-management-marketing/test-optional/Pages
  /why-test-optional.aspx.

7

Going Test-Optional

A Case Study

Eric Maguire

*T*he growth of the test-optional movement has garnered considerable media attention and spurred discussions among admissions officers, educational researchers, policy-makers, and the public about the value and continued use of standardized tests in the ad-mission process. This chapter offers case studies from two institutions that implemented test-optional admissions policies: Ithaca College and Franklin & Marshall College. Eric Maguire offers comparisons between each institution and how each came to adopt a test-optional policy from his unique perspective of having served as a chief enrollment officer at both colleges. Maguire notes that the decision to implement a test-optional policy re-sulted from an interest in (1) attracting a larger proportion of underrepresented racial and ethnic minority students at both colleges; and (2) at Ithaca College, expanding the col-lege's applicant pool beyond college-bound high school graduates in the Northeast. But each college approached the decision differently.*

Ithaca College engaged in months of strategic planning, goal setting, and research prior to adopting a test-optional policy. At the same time, the institution revamped its brand and marketing strategies, adopted an early action admission policy, and in-vested additional resources in financial aid to attract a larger applicant pool and more diverse students. While Franklin & Marshall had a long-standing test-optional policy for students that met certain criteria, the college recently allowed all students to apply under that policy and increased financial aid resources. Maguire notes that following these changes, both colleges saw an increase in applications, including an increase among underrepresented minorities.

The chapter concludes with a discussion about the future of college admissions. Maguire encourages colleges and universities to conduct incremental validity studies to better understand the impact of standardized admissions testing on the prediction of student success at their institutions. While Maguire accepts that standardized tests are predictive of student success, he suggests that there is a beneficial trade-off in increasing racial and economic diversity through adopting test-optional policies in exchange for what he calls a modest decline in GPA among test-optional students. He expresses hope that the current debate about college and university admissions will lead to new and broader metrics that improve our understanding of student retention and success.

The use of standardized testing for college admission traces its beginning to 1900, when presidents from a dozen universities created the College Entrance Examination Board (or College Board). Their intent was an entrance exam that would standardize college admission and encourage high school curricular cohesion around specific academic areas found in the test (PBS n.d.). In June 1901, the College Board administered its first entrance exams to 973 test takers from New York, New Jersey, and Pennsylvania.

The test grew in popularity over the next several decades, aided by Harvard President James Conant, who championed it as an opportunity to identify underserved students outside of the more familiar New England prep schools. By the 1950s, the newly formed Educational Testing Service (ETS) served more than half a million annual test takers and was joined by rival American College Testing (ACT). Today, more than 3.5 million students take the SAT or ACT (FairTest 2016), and standardized testing has become a cornerstone of the college admissions process.

While the majority of postsecondary institutions in the United States use the SAT and ACT as a component of their admissions criteria, a number of colleges and universities have begun to question the tests' value. Specifically, these institutions seek to understand whether standardized tests are good predictors of student success and to what extent that predictive value remains useful relative to concerns of equity and access. Beginning with Bowdoin College in 1969, some institutions researched and ultimately changed their admissions policies by removing the standardized test requirement. In the decades since, a growing number of colleges and universities have reached the same conclusion, sparking much debate and discussion regarding the trade-offs associated with standardized testing.

Proponents of test-optional admission argue that standardized testing offers little value to the admission process and may in fact be detrimental to college and university goals of greater access and diversity. Meanwhile, testing proponents have defended the use of standardized tests as a valid and reliable predictor of student success, whose uniformity and bell-shaped distribution are welcome attributes in an environment of high school disparity and escalating grade inflation. This group suggests that the predictive value of standardized tests outweighs the potential biases and troubling correlations that accompany the tests.

The purpose of this chapter is to lend my perspective to this debate, having served two test-optional institutions as chief enrollment officer. From 2009 to 2015, I served Ithaca College as vice president for enrollment and communication. During my tenure, the college considered, and ultimately adopted, a test-optional admissions policy in 2012. In addition, I served Franklin & Marshall College (F&M) on two separate occasions (2000–2009 and 2015–present) and in several different roles, most recently as vice president and dean of admission and financial aid. F&M adopted a test-optional admission policy in 1992, decades before Ithaca College's recent policy change.

In this chapter, I share from my experiences at both institutions. I describe the catalyst for the adoption of a test-optional policy at both institutions and discuss the development of primary institutional research, policy implementation, and outcomes since adopting test-optional admission. In addition, the chapter explores the extent to which the transition to test-optional admission at both institutions achieved the originally stated goals. My concluding remarks offer some suggestions to professional colleagues who are considering adopting a test-optional policy on their own college campuses. Finally, I lend my thoughts on the test-optional admission debate and suggest ways we might advance the conversation. Before I discuss case studies of Ithaca College and F&M, I will first consider why this debate is so important.

Our Current Practice

American higher education is an engine of academic and economic opportunity. As enrollment leaders, particularly at the most selective and sought-after institutions, we must be thoughtful and deliberate to ensure that criteria for admission are as valid, reliable, and as free from bias as possible. It is in the best interest of our institutions and the students we serve to focus on admission criteria that are predictive of student success and align with institutional goals and values. Enrolling students who fit these criteria should lead to academic success in the classroom and a strong learning environment for all.

In some ways, higher education has been successful in this endeavor, as our current slate of admission criteria lead to positive outcomes. We can predict in fairly meaningful ways the students who are most likely to succeed on our college and university campuses. At the most selective of institutions (which, correspondingly, have the greatest ability to shape their classes in the admission process), it is not uncommon to see first-year retention rates above 90% and graduation rates over 80%. Clearly, these institutions are selecting students who can handle the rigors of college academics and demonstrate success throughout their educational experiences. However, in other ways, our current slate of admission criteria is failing entire categories of students.

This underrepresentation often occurs along racial, ethnic, and socioeconomic lines. For example, in the 2004 book *America's Untapped Resource: Low-Income Students in Higher Education*, Carnevale and Rose demonstrate that students from the lowest quartile of family income are 25 times less likely than their wealthy peers to attend the country's most selective colleges and universities.

Higher education's challenge to improve class and race diversity is not news to those inside the profession or the professorate. Many schools are exploring ways to expand access for underrepresented students. This chapter and the examples from Ithaca College and Franklin & Marshall College present one possible approach to achieving those goals.

Ithaca College

Ithaca College is a comprehensive institution located in the Finger Lakes region of central New York. It is home to 6,400 undergraduate students distributed among five schools: Business, Communications, Health Science and Human Performance, Humanities and Sciences, and Music. When I joined the college, it drew roughly 13,000 applications and admitted about two-thirds of those students to enroll an incoming first-year class of approximately 1,600. In the summer of 2009, Ithaca College had just enrolled its largest class on record, but senior leadership remained concerned about the impact of the recent economic recession and the college's reliance on students from a declining Northeast population.

Incoming students at Ithaca College are an impressive group who achieve strong high school grade point averages, enjoy above-average standardized test scores, and excel athletically and artistically. In addition, Ithaca enrolls students from diverse socioeconomic backgrounds, with Pell Grant percentages that hover above 20%. However, the college has historically struggled to attract students from underrepresented racial and ethnic backgrounds. The incoming class of 2009 was no exception, as the collective percentage of African American, Latino, Asian, and Native American students was 15%.

Given these concerns, and under the leadership of a relatively new president, Tom Rochon, the college embarked on a strategic planning process, which over the course of several months resulted in two important recruitment- and enrollment-related objectives (among several others). First, the school had long valued diversity in its campus community and wanted to more formally underscore its aspiration to increase the enrollment of traditionally underrepresented students. More specifically, Ithaca College sought to increase the proportion of ALANA (African American, Latino, Asian, and Native American) students it enrolled from approximately 15% to at least 20% of the incoming class by the year 2020.

Second, the college recognized a correlation between the number of college-bound high school graduates in the Northeast and its own applicant pool. As high school graduate numbers in the Northeast grew throughout the 2000s, so did applications to Ithaca. Unfortunately, the opposite was also true, and with forecasts predicting a notable decline in the Northeast college-bound population, the college needed to take action. Ithaca articulated a goal of increasing its "market share" of college applicants to offset this predicted demographic decline.

The college explored a number of strategic ideas in support of these goals. In order to attract a greater number of applications from the Northeast and beyond, it consolidated disparate marketing messages into a well-researched brand identity, invested in digital advertising, and explored an early action round for admission. The school also began investing additional resources into financial aid, recognizing that as a limitation to greater ALANA enrollment. Simultaneously, and in support of both strategic objectives, the college began to consider a test-optional policy for admission. Our experience led us to believe that such a policy would help us increase our applicant pool by attracting candidates who were strong students in their daily classwork, but less successful standardized test takers. When coupled with requisite financial aid resources, we also believed a test-optional approach would help enhance the diversity of our incoming class and achieve our stated goals.

It is important to pause for a moment to point out that Ithaca's path to test-optional admission began with institutional goal setting and problem solving. We did not lead with an ideological endpoint in mind or a predetermined interest in transitioning the institution to a test-optional approach. Our goals and objectives served as a catalyst for policy exploration. Standardized testing had been a requirement for admission at Ithaca College since 1960. Presumably, the test held some ability to predict student success and was therefore a necessary criteria to consider, but it had been quite some time since we had researched and tested that assumption. As we examined the topic, our curiosities were distilled into a more formal research question: To what extent do standardized tests contribute to our understanding of a student's likelihood for success on our campus?

In order to explore this question, we compiled and reviewed a collection of approximately two dozen case studies from colleges and universities, articles in prominent journals, and literature from the College Board and ACT. While some of these studies questioned the predictive value of standardized tests, the majority drew some connection between SAT scores and collegiate GPA. For example, a 2008 College Board report showed a correlation of .35 between a student's SAT score and first-year collegiate GPA (Kobrin et al. 2008). Such a correlation is certainly significant and would justify the continued use of standardized testing in the admission process.

Our inquiry might have ended with this review if it were not for three reactions that our enrollment leadership team had to the literature. Our first response was a sobering recognition of the troubling correlation between standardized test scores and student demographic information, such as race/ethnicity, family income, and parental educational attainment. These correlations did not come as a surprise, as we had long known of the connection, but our literature review served as a stark reminder of the challenges that particularly plague standardized tests. Table 7.1 details the correlation between total SAT score (combined Critical Reading, Math, and Writing sections) with reported family income, which is troubling for both its magnitude and near linearity (College Board 2013). While SAT score is not necessarily a proxy for family income (as there is a large standard deviation of scores within each income category), it is important to note that admission factors such as high school GPA are not nearly as correlated with family income (Geiser 2015; Sackett et al. 2009).

Our second response to the literature review was a subtle, yet important, criticism of the research methodology employed by many of the studies. Much of what we read explored the relationship between standardized tests and first-year GPA. Perhaps this should not come as a surprise, as the SAT was originally designed to predict academic achievement, and first-year GPA is the most immediate

Table 7.1.   Total SAT score by reported family income bands

Family income band	Average total SAT score (CR+M+W)
$0–20,000	1326
$20,000–40,000	1402
$40,000–60,000	1461
$60,000–80,000	1497
$80,000–100,000	1535
$100,000–120,000	1569
$120,000–140,000	1581
$140,000–160,000	1604
$160,000–200,000	1625
More than $200,000	1714

Source: College Board 2013.

and readily available metric. Our group decided that first-year GPA was not the ideal dependent variable. As an enrollment manager, I am much less interested in predicting which students can best navigate the transition to college academics in their first year. I am more interested in discovering which students are most likely to persist and demonstrate academic success throughout their four-year college experience. In order to reduce the impact of first-year transitional transcript anomalies and recognize the importance of long-term student success, we believed it was important to look beyond the first year and correlate standardized tests with success metrics later in a student's academic career.

Our final criticism of previous research was the often isolated way in which some researchers explored the relationship between standardized tests and student success. If you were to read some of these studies, you would gain the impression that standardized test scores were the only criteria used to consider students for admission. In reality, most selective colleges and universities employ some form of holistic review that considers an entire portfolio of application information. To view standardized tests in a vacuum outside of this context removes them from their typical environment. We wondered whether this contextual information was important to understanding the relationship between standardized test scores and student success on our campus. Our research question shifted the focus from exploring the validity of standardized tests (to what extent are SAT scores correlated with student success?) to exploring the *incremental* validity of standardized tests (to what extent are SAT scores correlated with student success once you control or account for important contextual information that is part of the application review process?).

At the conclusion of our literature review, we recognized the important relationship that research had established between standardized test scores and student success, but we remained concerned about the connection to student demographic variables and believed that some of the existing research was limited in its methodology. As such, we crafted our own study to explore the impact of standardized testing on our college campus. Our research effort was led by Dr. Yuko Mulugetta, director of enrollment planning. Joining her were contributors from the Office of Admission and the Office of Institutional Research. I mention this multidepartmental structure because it was an asset to our research. It invited critical questions from various viewpoints, provided an important checks-and-balances structure, and avoided any appearance of unwanted data manipulation.

The data team began by addressing some of the methodological shortcomings that we believed to be present in some of the earlier research. Instead of correlating standardized test scores with first-year GPA, we correlated test scores with sixth-semester GPA, recognizing that a student's cumulative GPA varies relatively little after the sixth semester of academic work. We also structured our study to control for information that is often available in a student's application. In doing so, we explored the incremental validity of standardized testing at Ithaca College, or the amount of predictive power the standardized tests contributed beyond our knowledge of other admission factors.

After establishing our random sample data set across all academic areas, we examined the relationship between demographic factors (gender, ethnicity, and first-generation status) and a student's sixth-semester GPA. The results showed that the three demographic variables combined to account for 8.5% of the variance in sixth-semester GPA. This is not a huge correlation, but an important baseline to establish nonetheless. From there we explored the impact of adding three transcript-related variables to our model; cumulative high school GPA, AP credit hours, and our subjective ranking of a student's strength of high school curriculum (on a 10-point scale). Once that information was incorporated into our model, our correlations rose significantly. Transcript-based information added 35.3% to our understanding of GPA variance, taking our total correlation (of demographic plus transcript variables) to .437.

Now that we understood the impact of these variables in our prediction of student success, we wanted to discover what additional validity standardized tests would contribute. As a final step, we converted a small number of ACT submissions to their SAT equivalents and added SAT Critical Reading, SAT Math, and

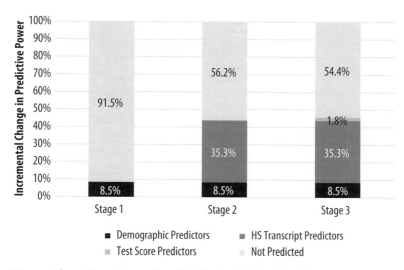

Fig. 7.1. Three-Stage Approach to Predicting Students' Sixth-Semester Grade Point Average. *Note*: "HS Transcript Predictors" includes high school GPA, AP credit hours, and strength of the student's high school curriculum.

SAT Writing scores to our model. Standardized tests added a small, yet statistically significant, 1.8% to our understanding of GPA variance. These statistics provided the college with a more precise understanding of the role of standardized testing in our ability to predict student success. Figure 7.1 summarizes the research findings that Dr. Mulugetta presented to the National Association of College Admission Counseling in 2016.

While illuminating, our results posed a serious question. Was the relatively minimal predictive power of standardized tests at Ithaca College worth the more troubling characteristics and associations of such tests? Members of our team expressed opinions in both directions. Advocates for standardized testing suggested that any amount of predictive power was justification for their continued requirement, while proponents of change argued that the opportunity to increase the applicant pool, decrease the importance of family income in our admission process, and further diversify the campus outweighed the tests' minimal predictive contributions. In the end, the latter of these perspectives emerged as our preferred stance, and we decided to take a test-optional policy recommendation to the campus community.

Before taking our research findings and policy recommendation to the appropriate governing bodies, we brainstormed and addressed some of the common criticisms typically lobbied against test-optional admission policies: Is this a dilution of admission standards? Are you doing this just to boost applications, SAT averages, and rankings? If SAT scores don't matter, why accept them for any applicant? We knew from our experience (and confirmed in our literature review) that adopting a test-optional policy would likely increase applications to the college (much less information was available for the impact on actual enrollment). This, of course, was in alignment with the goals we had established in our strategic planning process. Based on our review of literature, we estimated a potential policy change would increase applications by approximately 10% to 15%, a by-product that we would absolutely recognize and welcome.

We also knew there would be critics who would label this potential policy change as a decline of admission standards and accuse us of trying to boost rankings through SAT average and selectivity gains. We believe our research adequately addressed the standard-lowering allegations by demonstrating the relatively inconsequential incremental validity of standardized tests in our admission process. To those claiming our test-optional policy recommendation was inspired by third-party rankings, we point to two important facts. First, the biggest name in college rankings, *U.S. News & World Report*, penalizes institutions that report a significant percentage of entering students who do not submit standardized test scores as part of their applications. The threshold and size of the penalty have changed in the past and are subject to future changes from the *U.S. News* editors, so I will not list them here. But it is fair to suggest that this penalty offsets the boost that test-optional schools typically experience in average SAT score (as lower-performing students tend to employ the option). Second, Ithaca College has been identified as a top 10 Northeast regional university throughout most of the *U.S. News and World Report* ranking history. Given that placement and consistency, the college would have little to gain from any boost in rankings. It cannot be reclassified as a national college or university, and it cannot do much better than top 10 in its current category.

Finally, we recognized that a certain portion of our audience would be encouraged by our research results and would likely suggest that standardized testing be removed altogether from the admission process. If we believe that standardized testing is more hindrance than help in the college admission process, why accept the results from any applicant? While the thought process is logical, I was not convinced that such a policy held up to marketplace realities. The fact remains that even at test-optional institutions, a majority of applicants continue to submit standardized test scores. Many students are proud of their scores and believe their results represent them well in the admission process. We did not want to risk alienating these students, who have many colleges and universities to potentially choose from, by discouraging or prohibiting them from submitting standardized test scores as part of their application portfolio. While it was neither the most data-driven or ideological approach, we believed that choice represented the best practical policy.

With this information in hand, we took our policy proposal to the college's president, board of trustees, and faculty. I wrote a white paper outlining our literature review, institutional history of standardized testing, research findings, and associated policy recommendations to President Tom Rochon and Bill Schwab, chairman of the board of trustees. The paper was convincing enough to warrant additional conversations, such as faculty forums and additional trustee discussions.

I presented the policy recommendation and supporting research findings during several well-attended faculty forums. After my presentations, faculty responded with a number of thoughtful questions seeking clarity. Very few faculty offered comments in opposition to the proposed policy change. During one of the sessions, a faculty member who once served as an admission representative at a test-optional school discussed the positive experience she had in a test-optional environment. After another session, a faculty member approached me and said that he had attended with the expressed purpose of opposing the policy change on the grounds that it lowered admission standards, but he remained silent during the forum and reversed his opinion given the strength of our data. Thus, with relatively little debate and disagreement, our faculty supported the policy recommendation.

The confidentiality that envelops board of trustee conversations prohibits me from articulating the details of that discussion, so I will simply mention that after some clarifying questions and thoughtful discussion, the board joined the faculty in support of the policy change. Based on this support, President Rochon approved the test-optional policy and asked my team to prepare a public statement and accompanying message to key constituents.

The test-optional policy was announced in the spring of 2012 and took effect for students applying for the fall 2013 entry term. Our version of test-optional admission allowed any non-home-schooled student to withhold standardized test scores as part of his or her application portfolio. Test-optional students would also remain eligible for merit-based scholarships, which isn't always the case at test-optional schools. In addition to citing our research, our public announcement of the policy change referenced the growing cohort of selective schools that were adopting test-optional policies, recognized the policy's fit with our holistic application review, and expressed an interest in expanding and further diversifying our applicant pool.

Public reaction to the policy announcement was largely positive. Prospective students and their parents generally appreciated the opportunity to present themselves in the strongest light possible. Guidance counselors applauded the policy change, as it helped reduce the stress and anxiety associated with standardized testing. The policy also provided counselors with another college to recommend to students who were strong in their daily classroom activity but did not have corresponding standardized test scores. Even our alumni were largely supportive of the policy change, recognizing the opportunity to improve access and further diversify the student body.

As previously mentioned, the implementation of test-optional admission did not occur in isolation; a wave of enrollment initiatives was announced at roughly the same time. The college had launched a new branding and advertising campaign, increased its commitment to financial aid, and added an early action round of admission. These initiatives make it difficult to completely disentangle and pinpoint the exact impact of our transition to test-optional admission, but hindsight has been illuminating.

Like many colleges that make the transition to test-optional admission, we noticed an increase in applications. In fact, our multipronged effort to increase applications achieved results that surpassed our wildest expectations. Our 13,810 applications for the fall 2012 cohort (a record prior to test-optional admission) jumped to 18,206 for the fall 2014 incoming class, a 31.8% increase in just two years. Among applicants, roughly 25–33% chose to withhold standardized test scores from their application portfolios.

While applications from all subgroups and categories increased during this period, more dramatic gains were observed among underrepresented student populations. Perhaps most notably, applications from ALANA (African, Latino, Asian, and Native American) students increased by 66% during this two-year span, while applications from non-ALANA students increased by a less dramatic 21%. With additional and intentional investment in financial aid resources, the college was able to translate these application gains to a more diverse student body. In the four years preceding test-optional admission (2009–2012), the full-time ALANA population averaged 16.5% of the incoming fall class. In the four years after test-optional admission was introduced (2013–2016), ALANA enrollment jumped 32% to an average of 21.7%.

While I cannot claim causation, I find the evidence fairly convincing that test-optional admission has helped Ithaca College with its aspiration to expand its applicant pool beyond demographic destiny and further diversify its student body. Despite contributing to those strategic achievements, it is important to note that test-optional admission is still in its relative infancy at the college. More can and will be learned about test-optional admission at Ithaca, helping it reach its fullest impact and potential. For example, for all of its successes in improving ALANA recruitment and enrollment, the policy has done little to increase the enrollment of first-generation or Pell-eligible students, the proportions of which hover in the teens and low 20s, respectively. This is surprising and requires more detailed analysis to understand.

In addition, Ithaca College is just now beginning to graduate students who were first enrolled under the test-optional admission policy. As such, the college can begin to assess how non-submitters have fared relative to their test-submitting counterparts in success metrics such as retention and GPA. This research will be a helpful next step as test-optional admission continues to mature and evolve at the college.

Franklin & Marshall College

Franklin & Marshall College (F&M) is a classic and historic liberal arts institution of 2,400 undergraduate students located in the heart of Lancaster, Pennsylvania. In recent years, the college has received nearly 7,000 applications annually and admitted just over one-third of those students to enroll an incoming class of approximately 600. Incoming students boast strong high school grades and AP classes, with average SAT (CR+M) scores above 1300 (for those who choose to submit). Franklin & Marshall has always been known as an academically focused institution, with discussion-based classes, abundant opportunities for student research, and a 9:1 student-to-faculty ratio. While the academic rigor of the institution has never been in question, the college believed it could do more to enrich the intellectual environment by further investing in its student body. Doing so would bring new perspectives to the school, deepening and elevating the classroom environment for all.

Under President Dan Porterfield's leadership and strategic plan, the college sought to enroll a highly talented and more diverse student body. As a result, it invested in need-based financial aid, while retiring and reallocating its former merit-based scholarship program. This investment allowed F&M to enroll talented students from a broader array of socioeconomic, racial/ethnic, and geographic backgrounds. The college was supported in this effort by a long-standing test-optional policy, which was first adopted in 1992. According to Peter Van Buskirk, former dean of admission, a test-optional policy was carefully considered and relatively easily embraced by faculty. The catalyst for the test-optional policy, according to Van Buskirk, was an institutional interest in increasing diversity and freeing the admission process from the "tyranny of numbers." Leadership at the college also consulted with test-optional pioneer Bill Hiss, at Bates College, for insight into this process. Under this new policy, the admission team felt it could admit students who were academically strong and came from remarkable backgrounds, but who lacked the standardized test scores that would make them competitive candidates for admission. According to Van Buskirk, the school was initially and modestly successful in those goals, but progress slowed in subsequent years, owing to a lack of broader support structures for a more diverse student population.

The original test-optional policy at Franklin & Marshall College was somewhat complicated. To qualify for test-optional admission, a student needed to be ranked in the top 10% of his or her high school graduating class. If a student's high school chose not to provide an official rank, a student would qualify for test-optional admission with a cumulative, unweighted GPA of 3.6. Instead of simply withholding standardized test scores from admission consideration, test-optional students were required to submit two graded writing samples from either their junior or senior year. These writing samples allowed admission counselors to assess students' work firsthand and gauge their writing ability.

This policy existed for nearly 20 years and was generally regarded as a success, but it was revised in 2007 in an effort to expand its reach. Admission staff at the time believed the existing parameters were confusing to many families and discouraged admission of deserving students who fell just outside those GPA or class-rank restrictions. Starting with the incoming fall 2007 cohort, class rank and GPA qualifiers were dropped, allowing any student to be admitted to the institution under a test-optional policy. Students who chose this option would still be required to submit two graded writing samples in lieu of the SAT or ACT.

F&M's rich history of test-optional admission allows us to delve a bit deeper into the data to understand the academic performance of test-optional students relative to their test-submitting classmates. I was supported in this effort by my colleague in institutional research, Christine Alexander, who examined first-year GPA information for the incoming cohorts enrolled from 2010 to 2015. Over that six-year period, 1,055 test-optional students enrolled at the college and earned an average GPA of 2.93 during their first year. In contrast, the 2,061 test-submitting students who enrolled during those same years earned an average first-year GPA of 3.13. The average GPA difference of .2 is statistically significant, indicating that test-submitters tended to perform 7% better, on average, than non-submitters during their first year of college academics. This statistically significant GPA difference remained intact in a follow-up linear regression analysis, which controlled for gender, race/ethnicity, and institutional financial aid (as a proxy for family income).

We also wanted to look beyond the first year to uncover any variances in performance over the sum of a student's academic career. To do that, we examined final GPA information for seniors in the graduating classes of 2014, 2015, and 2016. The 468 students admitted under the test-optional policy who graduated over those three years had an average cumulative GPA of 3.08, compared with their 874 peers who submitted standardized tests and had an average cumulative GPA of 3.28. On average, the statistically significant .2 difference in GPA remained intact throughout a student's academic career. Follow-up linear regression analysis, which controlled for gender, race/ethnicity, and institutional financial aid, showed similar results.

Overall, findings showed that students who submitted standardized test scores performed, on average, 7% better than their peers who were admitted under a test-optional policy. This difference was observed in the students' first year and persisted throughout their educational experiences, even when factors such as gender, race/ethnicity, and institutional financial aid were taken into account. From a practitioner's perspective, a 7% performance margin is not an overwhelming difference, but it does support the use of standardized test scores as a requirement of the admission process in the absence of other considerations.

When faced with this information, we were curious to find out if this performance differential had any impact on student retention at the college. Were test submitters, who were performing slightly better, more likely to persist? After again controlling for gender, race/ethnicity, and institutional financial aid, we explored both first- to second-year retention and graduation rates for both groups. We found no statistically significant difference between test-optional students and standardized test submitters.

When considering the impact of test-optional admission at Franklin & Marshall, we see that it "costs" the college a small performance differential, but we believe the benefits outweigh these costs. Our exploration of benefits was not expansive (we only explored one variable), but it was profound. We wanted to

Table 7.2.   Pell Grant representation among Franklin & Marshall
test-optional and test-submitting groups

	Applications	Enrollment
Fall 2015		
Test-optional	42.9%	28.0%
Test submitters	23.4%	17.8%
Fall 2016		
Test-optional	45.9%	32.8%
Test submitters	24.7%	14.6%

understand if our test-optional policy helped promote access in a way that we anec-dotally assumed. To examine this impact, we explored Pell representation among test submitters and test-optional students. In this instance, Pell eligibility serves as a proxy for socioeconomic status, as federal Pell Grants generally support families in the bottom 40% of family income distribution.

Table 7.2 shows the incoming classes of 2015 and 2016 separated as test-optional and standardized test submitters. The far right column shows the percentage of Pell-eligible students who enrolled at the college from each group. Test-optional students are nearly twice as likely to be Pell-eligible as their test-submitting counterparts.

When averaging these two years, Pell representation is 83% higher among test-optional applicants and 88% higher among test-optional enrollees relative to their test-submitting peers. Stated another way, our country's most financially needy and underrepresented group is nearly twice as likely to apply for admissions under a test-optional policy, if offered the opportunity. Perhaps the magnitude of this difference should not come as a shock given some of the aforementioned cor-relations between standardized test score and family income. As a practitioner, I find this to be clear and compelling evidence that test-optional admission can be a helpful tool for increasing access and economic diversity on campus.

I'd like to pause and provide two important notes on the data above. First, all of the Franklin & Marshall data focus exclusively on domestic applicants and en-rollees. International students are an important and sizable (15% overall) portion of the Franklin & Marshall student body, but they are not eligible for federal Pell Grants and have had inconsistent assess to our test-optional policy. As such, they were excluded from our analyses. Second, and perhaps most important, I do not suggest that a test-optional policy, adopted in isolation, will automatically increase access and diversity. Recall that Franklin & Marshall College adopted a test-

Table 7.3.   Franklin & Marshall Pell
Grant–eligible student enrollment, 2006–2016

Cohort	Percentage eligible for Pell Grants
Fall 2006	7.8
Fall 2007	6.7
Fall 2008	5.3
Fall 2009	13.2
Fall 2010	12.8
Fall 2011	16.8
Fall 2012	16.7
Fall 2013	17.1
Fall 2014	21.1
Fall 2015	19.0
Fall 2016	17.7

optional policy in the early 1990s. Immediately afterward, the school did not notice significant increases in underserved populations. As table 7.3 indicates, our institutional Pell percentage was in the single digits as late as 2008. It was only after we paired our test-optional policy with increased financial aid resources that we were able to more markedly increase our Pell-eligible enrollment. Beginning with the incoming 2009 cohort, the college began increasing its financial aid budget and reallocating existing dollars from merit-based scholarships to need-based financial aid (F&M no longer offers merit-based aid).

Franklin & Marshall College conducts periodic examination of its test-optional admission policy. Never has the college uncovered concerns that cast the policy, and its continuation, in doubt. In that regard, F&M is like many of its peers that have benefited from the policy and intend to keep it in place. Of the top 50 national liberals arts colleges identified in the 2017 *U.S. News & World Report* rankings, 17 are test-optional, and 4 others are "test flexible" (FairTest 2017). To my knowledge, only one top-50 national liberal arts college has ever adopted and later eliminated a test-optional policy.

One might assume that after 25 years of test-optional admission there is little else for Franklin & Marshall College to learn, but that is not the case. As mentioned earlier, F&M's test-optional policy requires applicants to submit two graded writing samples in lieu of standardized test scores. The goal of these writing samples is to provide a snapshot of a student's writing ability, creativity, and ability to develop a thesis and defend an argument. These samples also speak to a student's high school context, revealing the relative rigor of the coursework and identifying potential grade inflation. We have always appreciated these samples in our evaluative process, but we have never taken the time to critically examine how they contribute to our prediction of student success. Are evaluations of graded writing samples correlated to important success metrics? If so, is this predictive power similar to other application information, or does it lend its own incremental validity? And if incrementally valid, are the writing samples free from unintended bias? We are currently conducting research to shed light on these very questions. Perhaps we will find that graded writing samples have little predictive power, or even worse, negative correlations with student success. In that case, we would revisit our policy and likely eliminate the requirement of graded writing samples. However, we may find that graded writing samples offer important insights about an applicant and contribute in meaningful ways to our prediction of student success. We also might find that graded writing samples bear little correlation to demographic information such as race/ethnicity or socioeconomic status. In that case, we would not only want to continue our graded writing sample tradition—we might encourage the expansion of its use at other colleges and universities.

Our test-optional admission policy has also encouraged us to consider new ways to evaluate applicants for admission. Inspired by Angela Duckworth's groundbreaking work, *Grit: The Power of Passion and Perseverance*, we are attempting to better assess metacognitive qualities in our incoming students. For the past several years, we have evaluated our new enrollees via a double-blind review process on five characteristics: resilience, leadership, intrinsic motivation, self-advocacy, and social responsibility.

To be clear, admission decisions are not currently influenced by these evaluations. In fact, we don't conduct this review until after we have identified our enrolled class. Once identified, we review each application for evidence of each of these five characteristics. If both reviewers agree that a student exemplifies one or more of these characteristics, we code the student as such. After a few years of conducting this evaluation and allowing students to flow through our educational pipeline, we will have the ability to research these assessments and correlate their presence with student success metrics. If we are successful, we will have developed a new lens through which we can predict student success. With further testing, we can understand if these correlations are repetitive of current admission criteria or offer new insights. We also might learn if these new metrics suffer from any bias that would limit their continued use. It is a high bar to achieve (and in fact more likely to fail), but if these metrics offer new and meaningful insights about student success—and if they are relatively free from bias—we will have identified a meaningful new tool in the admission process; a tool that we would want to fully incorporate at F&M and share with the broader higher education community.

Conclusion

I would never suggest that my experience at two institutions is representative or directly transferable to the broad mosaic of American higher education, nor do I claim to be a subject matter expert on the topic of test-optional admission. That said, my readings, research, and experience in this space have allowed me to form certain observations.

First, it appears that standardized test scores do contribute to our understanding and prediction of student success. Our research on testing has unearthed small, yet statistically significant differences in both predicted and realized student GPA. These differences were observed in the first year and continued through graduation. Second, and quite important, this relatively small difference in student performance did not translate to differences in student retention. Test-optional students were just as likely as test submitters to persist and take advantage of the engine of opportunity that is higher education. Third, given the correlation between standardized test scores and race/ethnicity, family income, and parental educational attainment, it is not surprising to see that Ithaca College experienced immediate gains in ALANA enrollment upon implementing a test-optional policy. Similarly, it makes sense that Pell representation is nearly twice as high in test-optional applicants as it is in test-submitting peers at Franklin & Marshall College. When aligned with requisite financial aid and support structures, test-optional admission can be a useful tool in creating a more diverse learning environment and improving the current access discrepancies.

To my colleagues in the enrollment profession, I would suggest that the test-optional debate is about trade-offs and alignment with institutional mission and values. If my experiences at Ithaca and F&M are at all generalizable to your campus, you may find that requiring standardized tests is smart policy if your institution prioritizes maximizing students' GPAs. If, on the other hand, your institution is willing to sacrifice a small amount of GPA performance for greater diversity and socioeconomic access, then you might consider a test-optional approach. Research conducted from your college's data sets can more fully inform you of the likely trade-offs and help align policy with institutional mission and values.

I would be remiss if I did not call upon my colleagues at top research universities and ask for your particular attention. As previously mentioned, 17 of the top 50 national liberal arts colleges (as identified by *U.S. News & World Report*) currently offer test-optional admission, and another 4 offer test-flexible policies. In contrast, only 2 of the top 50 *U.S. News & World Report* national research universities offer test-optional admission, and another 2 offer test-flexible policies (FairTest 2017). Given their sizeable resources and interest in greater access and diversity, I am surprised by the relative underrepresentation of test-optional policies among this cohort. This discrepancy is all the more surprising because my experience at Franklin & Marshall and Ithaca suggests that the cost to student GPA is relatively small, does not extend to retention, and pales in comparison with potential gains in diversity and inclusion.

Regardless of institutional type, I would encourage all colleges and universities to conduct incremental validity studies to better understand and quantify the impact of standardized testing on the prediction of student success. Coupling those results with strategic discussions of institutional goals can reveal the potential costs and benefits of a test-optional policy. Should a college or university decide that test-optional admission may be a potential option, I recommend that the institution should establish goals in advance for what it hopes to achieve and pair those objectives with the requisite support structures and institutional resources.

Finally, for my colleagues who are deeply engaged, and perhaps entrenched, on the topic of test-optional admission, let me suggest that the current debate is somewhat of a fool's errand. We find ourselves arguing a false dichotomy—and do so with unfortunate consequences. Test-optional proponents have focused their energy on condemning standardized tests and the organizations that produce them. At times, their arguments have drifted into the anti-testing camp, suggesting that it is impossible to develop a test or set of measures capable of predicting student success. I find that perspective to be problematic and defeatist. Such a position does not allow for the likelihood that it is possible to develop a test that proves to be an increasingly valid, reliable, and bias-free instrument to predict student success—a test that would benefit both college-bound students and institutions of higher education.

Meanwhile, testing organizations and their allies have diligently and predictably defended the use of standardized testing in college admission. In doing so, testing organizations and their allies are missing an opportunity to markedly improve their tests. It could be argued that the SAT remains anchored to its past and that the only changes the SAT has undergone in the past 20 years were the result of political and competitive pressures (in the form of pressure for change from the University of California system and the competitive threat from the ACT, respectively), not a genuine interest in rethinking standardized testing. Perhaps a newly researched, rethought, and reconstructed test would be an admission that previous testing was not nearly as valuable as presented, but I would argue that is exactly what is needed.

By limiting our discussion to a debate about current admission criteria (in this case standardized tests), we fail to acknowledge and explore a broader range of possibilities and new metrics that could improve our understanding of student success and do so in ways that are increasingly free from bias. The test-optional debate does not need to result in the declaration of a winner. The debate needs to be rendered irrelevant in light of new analytical measures that are identified through new partnerships and collaborations.

I envision the College Board, ACT, or perhaps a new and emerging disruptor in this space partnering with institutions to explore new opportunities. Combining the thoughtful leadership, financial resources, and analytical horsepower of these testing organizations with the creativity and data sets of institutional partners would form a developmental foundation that has never reached such scale and sophistication. I envision a Menlo Park model, where a testing organization collaborates with countless institutional partners to conduct experiments and test new hypotheses. In many of these instances, the tests might fail to identify meaningful correlations, but I am convinced this model of innovation would identify new insights and analytical tools that would prove even more powerful than the current slate of possibilities. Only then will we move past the current debate and truly identify criteria that are increasingly predictive and that more fully recognize student potential.

REFERENCES

Carnevale, A. P., and Rose, S. J. (2004). Socioeconomic status, race/ethnicity, and selective college admission. In R. D. Kahlenberg (Ed.), *America's untapped resource: Low-income students in higher education* (pp. 101–156). New York: Century Foundation.

College Board. (2013). *2013 college-bound seniors: Total group profile report.* New York: College Board. Retrieved from http://media.collegeboard.com/digitalServices/pdf/research/2013/TotalGroup-2013.pdf.

Duckworth, A. (2016). *Grit: The power of passion and perseverance.* New York: Scribner.

FairTest. (2016). University admissions test takers 1986–2016. National Center for Fair and Open Testing. Retrieved from http://www.fairtest.org/sites/default/files/ACT-SAT-Annual-Test-Takers-Chart.pdf.

———. (2017). *275+ "Top tier" schools that deemphasize the ACT/SAT in admissions decisions per U.S. News & World Report "Best Colleges" Guide (2017 edition).* National

Center for Fair and Open Testing. Retrieved from http://www.fairtest.org/sites
/default/files/Optional-Schools-in-U.S.News-Top-Tiers.pdf.

Geiser, S. (2015). *The growing correlation between race and SAT scores: New findings from
California.* Research and Occasional Paper Series: CSHE.10.15. Berkeley: University
of California–Berkeley Center for Studies in Higher Education. Retrieved from
http://www.cshe.berkeley.edu/sites/default/files/shared/publications/docs/ROPS
.CSHE_.10.15.Geiser.RaceSAT.10.26.2015.pdf.

Kobrin, J. L., Patterson, B. F., Shaw, E. J., Mattern, K. D., and Barbuti, S. M. (2008).
Validity of the SAT for predicting first-year college grade point average. New York: The
College Board. Retrieved from https://research.collegeboard.org/sites/default/files
/publications/2012/7/researchreport-2008-5-validity-sat-predicting-first-year-college
-grade-point-average.pdf.

PBS. (n.d.). *The 1901 College Board.* Retrieved from http://www.pbs.org/wgbh/pages
/frontline/shows/sats/where/1901.html.

Sackett, P. R., Kuncel, N. R., Arneson, J. J., Cooper, S. R., and Waters, S. D. (2009).
*Socioeconomic status and the relationship between the SAT and freshman GPA: An analysis
of data from 41 colleges and universities.* College Board Research Report No. 2009-1)
New York: College Board. Retrieved from https://research.collegeboard.org/sites
/default/files/publications/2012/9/researchreport-2009-1-socioeconomic-status-sat
-freshman-gpa-analysis-data.pdf.

8

Test Scores and High School Grades as Predictors

William G. Bowen, Matthew M. Chingos, and Michael S. McPherson

*A*dvocates *of test-optional admissions often claim that standardized tests add little value beyond high school grades in predicting success in college. They frequently cite the chapter that follows, reprinted from* Crossing the Finish Line, *an influential 2009 volume on college graduation by the late economist William G. Bowen and coauthors Matthew M. Chingos and Michael S. McPherson. Using records from nearly 150,000 undergraduates at 68 public colleges and universities who entered college as first-time, full-time students in 1999, the authors found that high school grades are a much better predictor than SAT/ACT scores of both four- and six-year college graduation rates.*

Bowen, Chingos, and McPherson acknowledge that tests like the SAT are designed primarily to measure the academic skills needed in college, not to predict graduation rates, and perhaps not surprisingly find the tests more useful for the former. At the same time, their analysis shows that high school grades are "extremely strong" predictors of college graduation rates regardless of the academic strength of the high school attended. Bowen, Chingos, and McPherson argue that the predictive power of high school

Note: The appendix tables referred to in this chapter are available online only, via the Princeton University Press website (http://press.princeton.edu/chapters/appendix_8971 .pdf). We have retained their original numbering (which is to chapter 6 in the original publication) for the reader's convenience.

grades lies not only in what they show about students' content mastery, but also qualities like perseverance, motivation, and consistency, which say a lot about a student's likelihood of graduating from college.

To be sure, the authors stress they are not against the use of standardized testing but want to ensure that the right tests are used in the right ways in the appropriate setting. They generally advocate using a combination of high school grades and SAT or ACT scores for college admission, but argue that the weighting and nature of tests given should vary—which echoes the recommendations of the test publishers themselves. Given their finding that SAT/ACT scores have more incremental power to predict college grades than graduation rates, for example, they suggest those tests are most useful to highly selective colleges that seek top scholars and are confident their students will graduate. A typical state university seeking to ensure higher graduation rates, by contrast, would find grades and subject achievements tests more useful for predicting whether an applicant will graduate.

In a short response following this chapter, Michael Hurwitz and Meredith Welch of the College Board update the Bowen, Chingos, and McPherson analysis using data from a more recent cohort of students who attended the same colleges, but enrolled in 1999. They find that although the power of high school grades to predict both four- and six-year graduation rates remains strong, it has declined since the first study. Conversely, SAT scores now have higher predictive value than they did before, particularly for students with the highest grades in high school. Hurwitz and Welch attribute the change to widespread grade inflation; while a low grade point average (GPA) may continue to be a valuable signal of academic risk, a high GPA isn't a reliable indicator of strong preparation for college.

In a brief reply, Chingos and McPherson write that grade inflation is a plausible but incomplete explanation for the improved ability of tests to predict college graduation rates since their original study. They note that Hurwitz and Welch's analysis differs from theirs in two ways: it includes only SAT takers, not both ACT takers and SAT takers, and it relies on self-reported rather than actual GPA. These differences, they suggest, may bias upward the predictive power of test scores in the Hurwitz/Welch analysis and bias downward the predictive power of high school grades.

This chapter, more than any other, has its roots in the past, with branches that extend in many directions. Since at least the 1930s, back to the time of James Conant at Harvard and his close relationship with Henry Chauncey, the first director of the Educational Testing Service (ETS), there has been an ongoing debate over standardized testing and its proper role in "matching" students to suitable educational programs. Important books, including Nicholas Lemann's *The Big Test: The Secret History of the American Meritocracy*, have been written on this subject. Richard C. Atkinson, president emeritus of the University of California, has stimulated debate over how various standardized tests should be used. Eminent deans of admissions, such as William R. Fitzsimmons at Harvard, have tried to move beyond ideology by encouraging rigorous assessments of the claims of various admissions criteria in different settings.[1] Recent studies of high schools, such as the work of the Chicago Consortium, have produced valuable new evidence on the significance of high school grades. Organizations such as the College Board and ACT have had an entirely understandable interest in how the work of their organizations is received. There is an extraordinary degree of public interest in testing, a veritable industry of entities and individuals eager to help students improve their test-taking skills, and no lack of advocacy organizations opposed to testing (such as the National Center for Fair and Open Testing).

Our role is not to revisit this vast territory but rather to contribute what we regard as important new evidence based on the college records of nearly 150,000 first-time, full-time members of the 1999 entering cohorts at flagship public universities spread across the country and in four state systems. It would be wrong to fail to connect our findings to the major themes that have emerged in this ongoing debate, and we will intersperse references where they seem especially appropriate; but we must inevitably fail to do justice to this part of our task if we are to keep the length of this chapter under some semblance of control.

Our main interest is in how test scores and high school grades relate to the outcomes of most interest to us—especially graduation rates—and in how they affect disparities in outcomes that are related to socioeconomic status (SES) and to race. To anticipate one of our principal conclusions, different tests and other sources of evidence that can be used to predict academic potential and academic outcomes, such as high school grades, measure different things. A particular piece of evidence may be of great value for one purpose and of little or none for another. For example, an instrument that is useful in predicting college grades may have negligible value in predicting graduation rates. Moreover, which measures are most useful may vary depending on what population is under study; tests and other indicators that differentiate well among applicants to the most selective universities may differ from those that work best at less selective ones.

The issues discussed in this chapter can be highly contentious, and it may be helpful if we provide some context. To minimize the risk of misunderstandings, we wish to emphasize at the outset that standardized tests can be used for many purposes and that neither the SAT nor the ACT was designed to predict gradua-tion rates. The results of the ACT, for example, "can be used to help guide stu-dents into the appropriate remedial or standard-level college courses . . . and can also help campuses identify students most in need of academic support programs" (Sidhu 2009, 15).[2] Our work is limited to studying the power of these tests to predict graduation rates, time-to-degree, and college grades; we have no way of assessing their (perhaps considerable) value for placement and other purposes. It is useful for our purposes to convert ACT scores to the SAT scale so that we can work with a sin-gle measure of test results regardless of which test a student took. Later in the chapter we present data showing that for the universe of students and institutions that we are studying, the two tests generate nearly identical predictions of graduation rates.[3] But of course the two tests are by no means the same, and readers interested in understanding the differences between the tests should consult the websites of the College Board and ACT.

The Main Story Line: High School Grades Are a Much Better Incremental Predictor of Graduation Rates Than Are SAT/ACT Test Scores

In this chapter, the single outcome of greatest interest is graduation rates. At the same time, we recognize that other measures of success in college are also important, and near the end of this chapter we consider college grades, fields of study, and time-to-degree.

In light of our focus on graduation rates, the main story line is straightforward. High school grades are a far better predictor of both four-year and six-year gradu-ation rates than are SAT/ACT test scores—a central finding that holds within each of the six sets of public universities that we study.[4] As we will say again later in the chapter, it generally makes sense to use a combination of high school grades and test scores in predicting outcomes of all kinds, but how much weight to assign to the different predictors in various settings remains a most important question— a question to which our evidence speaks directly. The most convenient way to summarize the mass of data that underlies our conclusion concerning the pri-mary role of high school grades is by presenting coefficients from regressions used to predict graduation rates (see appendix tables 6.1 and 6.2).[5]

The basic results obtained from this analysis for six-year graduation rates are summarized in figure 8.1. We show pairs of regression coefficients, one for test scores and one for high school GPA, that predict six-year graduation rates within each of the six sets of universities in our study. Each of these coefficients shows the "net" (or "incremental") effect of the variable in question after allowing for the effects of the other predictor as well as the effects of any control variables included in the regression.[6] These coefficients are all standardized, with each unit representing a difference of one standard deviation in the measure—a convention that allows us to make direct comparisons of the sizes of coefficients for test scores and high school grades.

The findings are dramatic. As can be seen from the light gray bars in figure 8.1, the coefficients for SAT/ACT scores are always less than 0.02, which means that an increase in test scores of one standard deviation is associated with an increase of less than 2 percentage points in six-year graduation rates; this relationship is even negative at the historically black colleges and universities (HBCUs). In sharp contrast, an increase of one standard deviation in high school GPAs is associated with increases of more than 10 percentage points in graduation rates at the less selective sets of universities (an impact that is five times greater than the impact of a comparable difference in test scores) and with differences of more than 6 percentage points at the selectivity cluster (SEL) II flagships and the SEL A state system schools. Even at the most selective public institutions (the SEL I flagships), a difference of one standard deviation in GPA has more than twice as large a net impact as a difference of one standard deviation in test scores. Results for four-year graduation rates are very similar. The main difference between the two sets of results is that both test scores and high school grades are stronger predictors of four-year graduation rates than of six-year graduation rates. The far greater relative predictive power of high school grades is again evident. (See bottom panel of appendix table 6.1.)

To check on the broad applicability of this key finding concerning the net effects of high school grades and SAT/ACT scores as predictors of graduation rates, we ran separate regressions for each of the 52 individual universities for which we had enough data. The consistency of the results is extraordinary. *In all but one of these more than 50 public universities, high school GPA remains a highly significant predictor of six-year graduation rates after taking account of the effects of test scores.* The standardized coefficients for high school grades cluster tightly around the values shown in figure 8.1 and, as the figure implies, tend to be larger at the less selective universities. In the SEL III and SEL B universities, as well as in the HBCUs, the standardized GPA coefficients are regularly in the range 0.9–0.12 and occasionally reach 0.16–0.17, which implies that an increase of one standard deviation in high school grades is associated with increases in graduation rates of 10–20 percentage points.[7]

Test scores, on the other hand, routinely fail to pass standard tests of statistical significance when included with high school GPA in regressions predicting

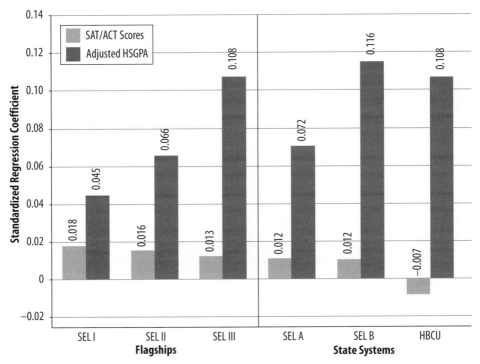

Fig. 8.1. SAT/ACT Scores and HSGPA as Predictors of Six-Year Graduation Rates, Standardized Regression Coefficients, 1999 Entering Cohort. *Note*: HSGPA = high school grade point average; SEL = selectivity cluster; HBCU = historically black colleges and universities. *Source*: Appendix tables 6.1 and 6.2.

graduation rates—especially once we leave the realm of the most highly selective public universities (where, as we saw in appendix tables 6.1 and 6.2, there is a modestly significant relationship). In the larger set of less selective public universities, there is rarely any significant relationship between SAT/ACT scores and graduation rates (the modal "net" coefficient is in the range 0.00–0.01), and in the half dozen institutions where there is a mildly significant relationship, it is as likely to be negative as positive. These institution-specific data underscore the exceedingly modest added value of test scores as predictors of graduation rates, especially when seen alongside the added value of high school grades. And, as we will see later in the chapter (see fig. 8.5), the remaining incremental predictive power of the SAT/ACT scores disappears entirely when we add controls for high school attended, whereas the predictive power of high school GPA increases.[8]

Finally, we looked separately at the predictive power of the SAT and the ACT to be sure that our decision to consolidate the two test scores into a single measure was not a mistake. Looking first at the 24,000 students in the flagships who took both tests in 1999, we find that the incremental effects of an increase in scores of one standard deviation are nearly identical for the SAT and the ACT. For six-year graduation rates, the coefficients on the SAT and ACT scores are, respectively, 0.011 and 0.014. The corresponding coefficient on high school GPA is 0.07—about five or six times larger. The results for four-year graduation rates and for students in the SEL B Ohio universities who took both tests are qualitatively similar (see appendix table 6.3). In short, there is no difference of consequence between the SAT and the ACT when used as predictors of graduation rates—and both are dominated by the predictive power of high school grades.[9]

Looking inside the Regression "Black Box"

One convenient way to provide more texture and a more intuitive sense of these results is to look at a "portfolio" of grids that show six-year graduation-rate outcomes in relation to both high school grades and SAT/ACT scores (see appendix tables 6.4–6.8).[10] To make it easier to recognize patterns in these data, we have highlighted selected "slices" of these tables.[11] In effect, we first hold grades constant and look at differences in graduation rates related to test scores *with a defined GPA range* (the vertical slices in the tables); then we hold SAT/ACT scores constant and look at differences in outcomes related to grades *within a defined SAT/ACT range* (the horizontal slices). In forming these slices, we have chosen the SAT/ACT and GPA ranges that include the largest number of students at each set of universities.

These grids are, we hope, easy to read, and we will comment only on the most distinctive finds. As we saw in figure 8.1, the relative importance of test scores versus high school grades varies markedly by institutional selectivity. But even in the case of the SEL I flagships, we see from appendix table 6.4 that the relationship between SAT/ACT scores and graduation rates, holding GPA constant at 3.67–3.99, is quite "flat." Specifically, the graduation rate rises 6 percentage points (from 84% to 90%) as the SAT/ACT score increases from the 1000–1090 range to 1300 and above. The slope of the relationship between high school GPA and graduation rates is much steeper. When we hold the SAT/ACT score constant at 1300 and above, the graduation rate rises by 12 points (from 81% to 93%) as GPA increases from the 3.33–3.66 range to 4.2 and above. The findings are similar at the SEL II flagships (appendix table 6.5), but it is worth noting that the relationship between SAT/ACT scores and graduation rates is even flatter here than it was in the case of the SEL Is.

The differences in slopes are even more pronounced at the less selective universities, and here we use figures to make it even easier to visualize the findings (figs. 8.2–8.4). Again we look at "slices" that first hold GPA constant (top panels) and then hold SAT/ACT constant (bottom panels). In the case of the SEL IIIs, the least selective of the flagship universities, what is striking is how much graduation rates rise when GPA increases from 3.0 to 4.0 and above—from 52% to 87% (fig. 8.2 and appendix table 6.6). The state system SEL Bs are in many ways the most interesting of all in that SAT/ACT scores had almost no power to predict graduation rates for the more than 41,000 students who attended these mid-level universities. In the "slice" of data shown in figure 8.3 and in appendix table 6.7, the six-year graduation rate increases only erratically as SAT/ACT scores rise from below 900 to 1100 and above (and is actually slightly lower in the top SAT/ACT range than in the 900–990 and 1000–1090 ranges). High school GPA, on the other hand, is an extremely strong predictor of graduation rates at these universities; the six-year

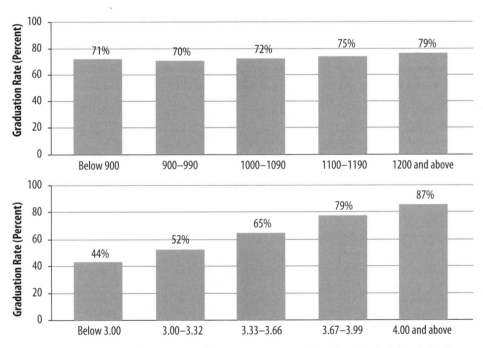

Fig. 8.2. Six-Year Graduation Rates by SAT/ACT Scores (Holding High School Grade Point Average Constant at 3.67–3.99) and by High School Grade Point Average (Holding SAT/ACT Scores Constant at 1200 and above), 1999 Entering Cohort, Selectivity Cluster III Flagships. *Source*: Appendix table 6.6.

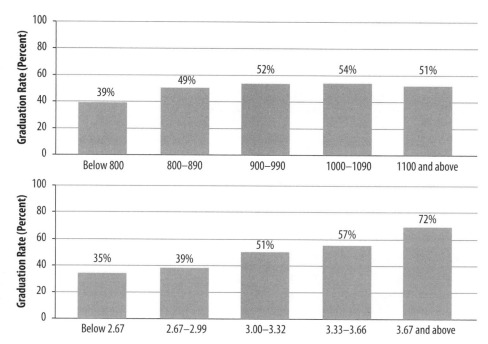

Fig. 8.3. Six-Year Graduation Rates by SAT/ACT Scores (Holding High School Grade Point Average Constant at 3.00–3.32) and by High School Grade Point Average (Holding SAT/ACT Scores Constant at 1100 and above), 1999 Entering Cohort, State System Selectivity Cluster Bs. *Source*: Appendix table 6.7.

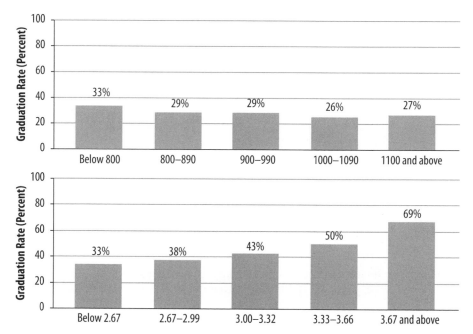

Fig. 8.4. Six-Year Graduation Rates by SAT/ACT Scores (Holding High School Grade Point Average Constant at below 2.67) and by High School Grade Point Average (Holding SAT/ACT Scores Constant at below 800), 1999 Entering Cohort, State System Historically Black Colleges and Universities. *Source*: Appendix table 6.8.

graduation rate increases dramatically, from 39% to 72%, as GPAs rise from below 3.0 to 3.67 and above. Finally, at the HBCUs (fig. 8.4 and appendix table 6.8), the graduation rate rises steadily and sharply with high school GPA and not at all with SAT/ACT scores.

Does the High School Attended (and Its Grading Standards) Matter When Assessing the Predictive Power of High School Grades and SAT/ACT Scores?

Suspicions about the reliability of high school grades are deep-rooted and grow in part out of the decentralized nature of American secondary education. Following his election as president of Harvard in 1933, James Conant was determined, in the words of Nicholas Lemann, "to depose the existing, undemocratic American elite and replace it with a new one made up of brainy, elaborately trained, public-spirited people drawn from every section and every background." In considering how to set up a new scholarship program that would enroll students of academic excellence, initially from the Midwest, Conant and his young colleague, Henry Chauncey, had to answer the following question (again using Lemann's formulation): "How could you tell which high school seniors, in all the vastness of public education in the United States which was under the purview of 15,000 local school boards each free to set its own standards, were the most likely to perform brilliantly at Harvard?" (Lemann 1999, 5, 28).[12] Concerns about varying and even erratic grading standards are of course entirely understandable, and admissions officers constantly wrestle with the question of how much weight to give to an excellent academic record earned at what they regard as a poor high school.

Thanks to the huge set of nationwide data available to us, we are able to offer a new perspective on this perennial issue. The findings already presented in this chapter certainly suggest that high school grades matter—indeed, that they matter a lot—but these initial findings do not tell us what the relationship between high school GPA and graduation rates would look like if we also controlled for the characteristics of the high school attended. The most straightforward approach is to add dummy variables identifying the student's high school to the regression equations used to predict six-year graduation rates—an approach that permits us, as it were, to "hold the high school constant" and compare the effects of high school grades on graduation rates at particular high schools on an "other-things-equal basis" (fig. 8.5 and appendix tables 6.9a and 6.9b).[13]

Two findings stand out. The first one, which concerns the "net" predictive power of SAT/ACT scores, initially surprised us. Adding the high school dummies

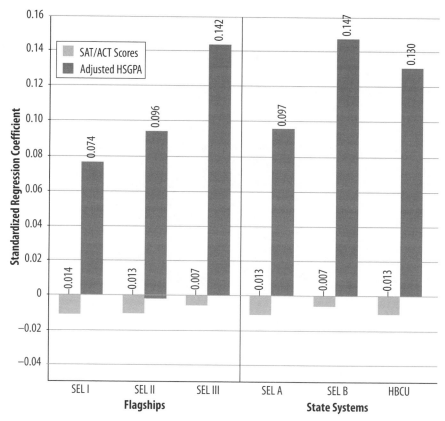

Fig. 8.5. SAT/ACT Scores and HSGPA as Predictors of Six-Year Graduation Rates with High School Dummies Included, Standardized Regression Coefficients, 1999 Entering Cohort. *Note*: HSGPA = high school grade point average; SEL = selectivity cluster; HBCU = historically black colleges and universities. *Source*: Appendix tables 6.9a and 6.9b.

deprives SAT/ACT scores of any significant incremental impact on graduation rates; indeed, the adjusted coefficients for SAT/ACT scores used to predict six-year graduation rates become slightly *negative* within all six sets of universities.

We interpret this at first surprising reversal of the apparent direction of impact as indicating that in the previous regressions SAT/ACT scores were serving as a proxy for high school effects ("better" high schools had both higher SAT/ACT scores and students who ended up with slightly above-average college graduation rates).[14] This finding demonstrates that, where it is not possible to include high school fixed effects in the analysis, SAT/ACT scores may function as a means of adjusting at least crudely for differences in high school quality. This is an argument for using both high school grades and SAT/ACT scores in assessing the qualifications of a student, especially in the absence of reliable information about the high school attended.

The second and even more consequential finding is that, as we had expected, adding high school dummies consistently increases the sizes of the GPA coefficients—by between 2.3 and 3.1 percentage points within all six sets of universities when predicting six-year graduation rates. We believe these increases in the sizes of the GPA coefficients reflect the fact that—as Conant understood— some high schools have tougher grading standards than others. Secondary school grades, which we saw are highly consequential independent of knowledge of the high schools attended, are even stronger predictors of graduation rates when we take account of the characteristics of particular high schools. The adjusted coefficients suggest that, other things equal, an increase of one standard deviation in high school GPA is associated with an increase in the six-year graduation rate of 7.4 percentage points at the SEL Is, 9.6 points at the SEL IIs, 14.2 points at the SEL IIIs, 9.7 points at the state system SEL As, 14.7 points at the state system SEL Bs, and 13.0 points at the HBCUs. These are *very* big coefficients by any reckoning— especially when we recognize that the overall six-year graduation rate at the state system SEL Bs, for example, is just 51%.

We were also able to examine the relationships among high school grades, the academic standing of the high school attended, and college graduation rates in an even more fine-grained way using the North Carolina data. Because we know so much about particular high schools in that state, we can compare outcomes for students within specified high school GPA ranges who attended high schools classified as Level I, Level, II, and Level III. Put crudely, the questions of most interest to us can be stated as follows: Does, say, a high school GPA in the range 3.5–4.0 have the same predictive power in terms of college graduation rates if a student attended a Level I, Level II, or Level III high school? Should admissions officers take seriously a high GPA earned by a student who attended a relatively weak (Level III) high school? Conversely, should admissions officers overlook a low GPA earned by a student who attended a high school with a strong academic profile (a Level I school)?

Simple tabulations (appendix table 6.10) reveal, first, that across both SEL As and SEL Bs in North Carolina, six-year graduation rates *within specified GPA ranges* tend to be only modestly higher for students from Level I high schools than for students from Level II and Level III high schools. The differences by level of high school are clearest among students with high school GPAs above 4.0 who attended the most selective universities; there are only small differences at SEL Bs and none at HBCUs. More generally, most of the differences between Level II and Level III high schools are very small.

The parallel, and even more revealing, finding is that high school GPA is very positively and very consistently associated with six-year graduation rates *whatever the level of the high school that the student attended.* From the perspective of our interest in predicting the probability that a student will earn a bachelor's degree, the conclusion is straightforward: with modest qualifications, "a grade is a grade is a grade."[15] Students with very good high school grades who attended not-very-strong high schools nonetheless graduated in large numbers from whatever university they attended. On the other hand, students with relatively weak academic records in high school have much lower graduation rates than their higher-achieving high school classmates—again, whatever the academic level of the high school that they attended.

This is not to say that the academic level of the high school makes no difference when it comes to interpreting the meaning of high school grades. It does—as we saw clearly in the national data when we added high school dummies to the regressions predicting graduation rates, and as we see again in the North Carolina data.[16] There are also a number of other studies that indicate that both peer effects and grading standards in high schools affect success in college (e.g., Bassiri and Schulz 2003; Woodruff and Ziomek 2004).

Still, the central point to take away from this analysis is that grades earned by students in high school are extremely strong predictors of graduation rates even when we cannot (or do not) take account of the characteristics of the high school that the student attended. From our perspective, what is most striking about the high school GPA coefficients reported in appendix tables 6.9a and 6.9b is how large they are *before adding dummies that identify the high school attended.* It is these only-partially-adjusted coefficients (which are based on regressions that include standard controls but do not take account of high school attended) that speak most directly to the importance of a student's performance at whatever high school the student attended.

One other piece of evidence from North Carolina reinforces all of these conclusions. The richness of the North Carolina data allows us to study the power of the SAT and high school GPA to predict bachelor's degree attainment (including graduation from colleges and universities into which students transferred) for all '99 seniors who took the SAT, wherever they went to college. (This discussion pertains only to the SAT, because the ACT is not widely used in North Carolina.) We thought that this even larger data set, and this even broader investigation, might increase the predictive power of the SAT because bachelor's degree attainment reflects *both* enrollment rates and graduation rates—and SAT scores clearly influence admission decisions and enrollment patterns. But this is not what we have found (appendix table 6.11). Using "partial controls" (i.e., controlling for all of the standard variables but *not* controlling for high school fixed effects or university attended), the standardized regression coefficients for SAT scores and high school GPA are, respectively, 0.044 and 0.155—that is, the high school GPA coefficient is almost four times larger. When we add high school fixed effects, this difference becomes even more pronounced: the SAT coefficient falls from 0.044 to 0.017 while the high school GPA coefficient rises from 0.155 to 0.185. In short, this analysis reinforces the point that high school grades measure a student's ability to "get it done" in a more powerful way than do SAT scores—a conclusion that holds, we wish to emphasize, regardless of the high school attended but that is even stronger when we take account of high school characteristics.[17]

Our interpretation of this entire set of findings is a simple one. High school grades are such a powerful predictor of graduation rates *in part* because they reveal mastery of course content. But the "in part" formulation is critically important. In our view, high school grades reveal much more than mastery of content. They reveal qualities of motivation and perseverance—as well as the presence of good study habits and time management skills—that tell us a great deal about the chances that a student will complete a college program. They are one measure of coping skills and whether a student is likely to "stay the course." They often reflect qualities such as the ability to accept criticism and benefit from it and the capacity to take a reasonably good piece of one's work and reject it as not good enough. Getting good grades in high school, however demanding (or not) the high school, is evidence that a student consistently met a certain standard of performance. It is hardly surprising that doing well on a single standardized test is less likely to predict the myriad qualities a student needs to "cross the finish line" and graduate from college.[18]

Evidence from Chicago

Many other studies, including some conducted in California by Saul Geiser and his colleagues and a number carried out by the College Board and the ACT, have also shown that high school grades, seen alone and looked at in conjunction with various test score results, are powerful predictors of college outcomes.[19] Research carried out by the Chicago Consortium on School Research is yet another strong indicator that the findings we report, and our interpretations of them, are consistent with other evidence.

The results for students in Chicago mirror those reported here very closely. A recurring theme is that high school grades are a much stronger predictor of both college enrollment and college graduation than either test scores or the rigor of the high school curriculum. The Chicago Consortium study finds: "Students who graduated from high school with a GPA less than 3.0 were very unlikely to graduate from college. . . . On the other hand, more than 60% of students who graduated from high school with an A average (a 3.6 or higher) completed a 4-year college degree within six years. . . . To put it simply, students who were not successful in their high school courses were unlikely to succeed in college" (Roderick et al. 2006, 68).[20]

Interestingly, the data for the SEL III flagships and the SEL B state system universities in our study also show that there is a real break in the probability of graduating between students with high school GPAs above and below 3.0. At SEL IIIs, only 47% of students with high school GPAs below 3.0 graduated compared with 58% of those with high school GPAs between 3.0 and 3.3; at state system SEL Bs, only about 37% of matriculants with high school GPAs below 3.0 graduated compared with 51% of those with high school GPAs between 3.0 and 3.3 (refer back to appendix tables 6.6 and 6.7).[21]

The Chicago study also debunks the idea that differences in grading standards make high school grades in a city like Chicago of dubious value as predictors:

> There is a popular and compelling folktale of the urban high school student who gets straight A's, graduates at the top of her class and then, on entry to college, finds that she is not adequately prepared. There is a common perception that grades are vastly inflated in lower-performing high schools, and that students are given higher grades for doing more basic and poorer quality work than they would receive in selective enrollment or suburban high schools. . . . Data on the GPAs of CPS [Chicago Public Schools] graduates suggest that few fit the characterization of the urban folktale. In fact, many struggle throughout high school and graduate with GPAs that reflect mediocre performance in their coursework. . . . Low GPAs do not resolve the question of whether grades are inflated, [but] it appears that CPS teachers are not reluctant to give students D's or F's in core classes. (Roderick et al. 2006, 41)

The report is unequivocal in stating: "The [highly positive] GPA-graduation relationship was consistent regardless of the high school that the students attended" (84). The authors' explanation for these findings also resonates with our interpretation of the reasons that high school grades have such strong predictive value. They write, "Grades are . . . a measure of whether students have mastered the material in their classes, and *they indicate to colleges a different kind of college readiness— whether students have demonstrated the work effort and the study skills needed to meet the demands of a college environment*" (37, our emphasis).

Race and SES

Another important question posed at the start of this chapter is, Do the same relationships among SAT/ACT scores, high school GPAs, and graduation rates hold for subgroups of students defined by race/ethnicity, gender, and SES—or are there substantial differences in the predictive power of these measures across these subgroups? The answer is easy: there are few, if any, differences of consequence when we look at these subgroups separately (appendix tables 6.12–6.14). In general, the relationships are so consistent, and so much like those that we have already reported for all students, that there is little more to be said. High school GPAs are invariably stronger incremental predictors of six-year graduation rates than are SAT/ACT scores, across all categories of race/ethnicity, gender, and SES. Nor are the sizes of the coefficients among the subgroups sufficiently different to merit extensive comment.[22] These highly consistent results are, we believe, both important in their own right and further grounds for trusting the overall findings reported in the previous sections of this chapter.

Race and SES interact with SAT scores in another, quite different, way that raises questions about the "equity" effects of relying heavily on these scores in the admissions process. The equity issue is hardly a new concern. In *The Big Test*, Lemann reports that during World War II, Henry Chauncey had been disturbed to learn that aptitude test results sternly reflect social inequalities: "During the War, Chauncey had himself been quietly shocked and mystified when he saw, as the public and the test-takers had not, that overall statistics on the Army-Navy College Qualification Test showed far below average scores for southerners, Negroes, and [the] poorly-educated" (Lemann 1999, 66–67). In the summer of 1948, two well-known educators, Davis and Havighurst, published an article in *Scientific Monthly* in which they argued that, in Lemann's words: "Intelligence tests were a fraud, a way of wrapping the fortunate children of the middle and upper-middle classes in a mantle of scientifically-demonstrated superiority. The tests, they said, measured only 'a very narrow range of mental activities,' and carried a 'strong cultural handicap for pupils of the lower socio-economic groups'" (Lemann 1999).[23]

Our data for all '99 high school seniors taking the SAT in North Carolina are consistent with the findings of other research in showing that race and SES are more highly correlated with SAT scores than with high school grades (appendix table 6.15).[24] In fact, race/ethnicity is quite a strong predictor of SAT scores. Other things equal—including family circumstances and high school attended—both black male and black female test takers had SAT scores that were almost one standard deviation lower than the SAT score for a comparable white man (and just over half a standard deviation lower than the score for a comparable white woman). Hispanic females had predicted SATs that were about one-half of a standard deviation lower than the SAT scores for white males, and Hispanic males and predicted SATs that were one-third of a standard deviation lower. The coefficients for high school GPAs are all smaller (i.e., closer to zero), and, except for black males, much smaller.

Our two measures of SES (parental education and family income) also prove to be statistically significant predictors of SAT scores on an "other-things-equal" basis. Parental education is an especially consequential predictor of SAT scores and high school GPA, even after controlling for differences in family income. This important finding demonstrates again that highly educated parents have a major impact on the skills that their children take to high school, to college, and then on into life. Looking across all high schools, family income is also a stronger predictor of SAT scores than of high school GPA, but this difference largely vanishes when we look within high schools. In any case, the central point is clear: SES and race predict both high school GPA and SAT scores, but, in general, the impact on SAT scores is somewhat greater.[25]

The policy implications of these relationships between various predictors and race and SES need to be considered thoughtfully. On the one hand, it is clear that the association between SES and test scores is not spurious or an artifact but rather reflects a real "learning" advantage enjoyed by the children of high-SES families. Our own data and other studies show that, although test scores are correlated with SES, controlling for SES does not have much impact on the estimated predictive validity of the SAT/ACT.[26] However, it is also true that when test scores do not provide much additional information about likely outcomes, putting heavy weight on them has the (no doubt unintended) effect of giving an admissions boost to children from high-SES families with little commensurate gain in expected educational attainment. High school GPA is also correlated with SES, as we have seen, but less strongly. In its report on testing, the National Association for College Admission Counseling's commission devotes a long section to "test score differences" and warns against allowing an overemphasis on SAT/ACT scores to "exacerbate existing disparities among under-represented students."[27]

Predicting College Grades

Thus far in this chapter, when reporting statistical results, we have focused on predictions of graduation rates because our principal interest is in understanding factors that affect "finishing." The College Board, on the other hand, has focused on predicting first-year college grades (FYGPA) since its earliest days—in part, presumably, because Conant was interested from the first in finding tests that would identify high school students from the Midwest who not only would graduate (that was assumed) but would "perform brilliantly" at Harvard.[28] This emphasis on the ability of tests to predict FYGPA (which is how "validity" is defined) continues to this day, as can be seen by perusing the College Board's research reports.[29] Similarly, the ACT has also focused on predicting first-year college grades, as the materials at its website indicate.

Our data can be used to study the power of the SAT/ACT and high school GPA to predict first-year college grades, but we prefer, in most of our work, to predict cumulative GPA (or, often, rank-in-class) "on exit"—that is, when a student leaves the college or university first attended, whether by graduating, transferring, or dropping out. Rank-in-class on exit is a fuller measure of academic performance than is FYGPA, but we also make some use of FYGPA.

Our results are easily summarized. We find that SAT/ACT scores have a greater incremental power to predict college grades than to predict graduation rates. (Compare figure 8.6 with figure 8.1, and compare appendix tables 6.16 and 6.17 with appendix tables 6.1 and 6.2.) SAT/ACT scores clearly add "value" as predictors of college grades (as the research reports of the College Board and ACT correctly emphasize).[30] Still, here again, high school GPA is an even more powerful incremental predictor than is the SAT/ACT. This general conclusion holds for students at all six sets of universities that we study.

However, there are differences in findings depending on institutional selectivity. SAT/ACT scores are stronger predictors at the more selective universities than elsewhere (especially at the SEL Is, where they are nearly as strong as high school GPA). At the less selective flagships and state system SEL Bs, as well as at the HBCUs, a difference of one standard deviation in high school GPA has roughly double the incremental impact on predicted rank-in-class of a difference of one standard

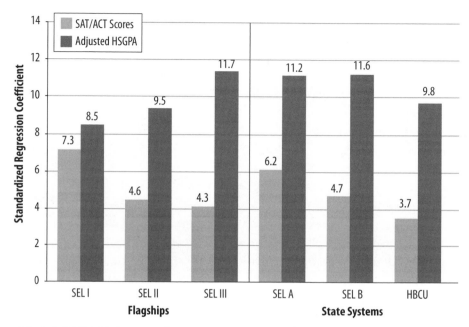

Fig. 8.6. SAT/ACT Scores and HSGPA as Predictors of Rank-in-Class at Exit, Standardized Regression Coefficients, 1999 Entering Cohort. *Note*: HSGPA = high school grade point average; SEL = selectivity cluster; HBCU = historically black colleges and universities. *Source*: Appendix tables 6.16 and 6.17.

deviation in the SAT/ACT score. At both the SEL III flagships and the state system SEL Bs, a difference of one standard deviation in high school GPA predicts a difference of 12 percentile points in rank-in-class, whereas a difference of one standard deviation in the SAT/ACT score predicts a difference of roughly 5 percentile points in rank-in-class.

Because our data all pertain to the '99 entering cohort of students, we have no evidence concerning the predictive power of the "new" SAT and the writing test that is part of it.[31] The College Board, however, has published the results of its assessment of the validity of the new SAT. Its report is based on results for a large sample of students who entered 110 four-year colleges and universities in the fall of 2006 and completed their first year of college in May or June 2007. In brief, the College Board found: "The changes made to the SAT did not substantially change how predictive the test is of first-year college performance. Across all institutions, the recently added writing section is the most highly predictive of the three individual SAT sections. As expected, the best combination of predictors of FYGPA is high school GPA and SAT scores" (Kobrin et al. 2008, 6). Three economists at the University of Georgia studied the predictive power of the new SAT for 4,300 University of Georgia first-time freshmen in the 2006 freshman class. The authors found that the SAT Writing test (SATW) is a better predictor of FYGPA than SAT-Verbal or SAT-Math and that the effect of the new SATW largely subsumes the effect of the SAT-Verbal. Another key finding is: "At the margin, high school GPA is a stronger predictor of first-year GPA than any individual SAT score" (Cornwell, Mustard, and Van Parys 2008, 11).[32]

Achievement Tests, "Signaling" Effects, and General Conclusions about Testing

We had not expected to find that SAT/ACT scores are such relatively weak incremental predictors of college outcomes—as compared with high school grades—but now that the new evidence is in, we want to warn against misinterpreting its implications. We do not conclude that testing in general is to be deplored. The right way to frame this entire set of questions is not, we believe, by asking whether tests are good or bad but rather by asking in what settings different kinds of tests are particularly useful as complements to a careful examination of a student's high school record.

SAT II Tests ("Subject Tests") and Advanced Placement Test Scores

Right now, an especially trenchant aspect of this discussion focuses on tests of "achievement" versus tests of "general reasoning." The SAT, certainly as it existed at the time it was taken by the '99 seniors in our study, was widely regarded primarily as a test of ability to learn rather than as a test of mastery of content (achievement). ACT has always argued that its exam is more a test of achievement, but the fact that the scores on the two tests are so highly correlated and generate such similar predictions of graduation rates and grades makes it hard to assess this difference; Atkinson and Geiser (2009) argue that the two tests have tended to converge over time. Both SAT II subject tests and Advanced Placement (AP) tests, on the other hand, unquestionably measure a student's knowledge of the content of specific subjects, such as math and history.

These two sets of achievement tests have been administered by the College Board for many years, and we have data showing the scores on the SAT IIs of about 14,000 students in the '99 entering cohorts at SEL I flagships and of 11,000 at state system SEL As (appendix table 6.18). When we add a measure of SAT II scores to regressions predicting six-year graduation rates that already include both regular SAT/ACT scores and high school GPA, we find that the coefficient for SAT II scores is small but statistically significant at the SEL Is and that including this variable drives the value of the coefficient for the regular SAT variable to zero (while leaving the coefficient for high school GPA essentially unchanged). But in the state system SEL As, the SAT II coefficient is itself zero.[33] However, the average SAT II scores are very strongly correlated with SAT/ACT scores (0.80 at both the SEL Is and the SEL As), so coefficients from regressions that include both variables should be interpreted with caution.

Fortunately, we have AP scores for many more students across a wider range of universities—indeed, we have scores for almost 60,000 students spread more or less evenly over SEL I and SEL II flagships and state system SEL As and SEL Bs.[34] (But here too there were insufficient data to allow us to present results for students at Flagship SEL IIIs and at HBCUs.) The average AP score is a significant predictor of six-year graduation rates at three of these four sets of universities (see appendix table 6.19a); only at the state system SEL Bs do we fail to find a statistically significant relationship.[35] The standardized coefficients are in the 2- to 3-point range, which means that an increase of one standard deviation in average AP scores was associated with an increase of 2 to 3 percentage points in graduation rates (after controlling for associated differences in regular SAT/ACT scores, high school GPAs, and university attended). This achievement test score was a far better incremental predictor of graduation rates than were scores on the regular SAT/ACT and, as in the case of SAT IIs, including this achievement-test variable in the regression equation entirely removed any positive relationship between the regular SAT/ACT scores and graduation rates. High school GPA, in contrast, continued to be an even stronger incremental predictor of graduation rates than was the AP score when all three measures were included in the same regression—especially in the SEL IIs and the state system SEL As and SEL Bs.[36]

We conclude that scores on achievement tests of various kinds, especially AP tests, are very useful additions to the bank of information used to select and place students—particularly high-achieving students who are applying to highly selective universities. It is also important to emphasize that scores on achievement tests are better predictors of outcomes than SAT scores for all students, including minority students and students from low-SES backgrounds. It is ironic that in the 1930s President Conant opposed achievement tests because he thought that "they favored rich boys whose parents could buy them top-flight high school instruction" (Lemann 1999, 38).[37] Contrary to what Conant believed in an earlier day (and he later expressed a different viewpoint), a judicious combination of cumulative high school grades and content-based achievement tests (including tests of writing ability) seems to be both the most rigorous and the fairest way to judge applicants. If AP scores of large numbers of students are not available, standard SAT/ACT tests also have a role to play, particularly as calibrators of high school quality and high school grading standards.

We think careful consideration should be given to the possibility, over time, of making much more extensive use of the results of the AP examinations. These tests are especially good predictors of four-year graduation rates (appendix table 6.19b), and we agree with Gaston Caperton, president of the College Board, that timely completion of bachelor's degree programs is especially important when financial pressures on individual students and institutions are so pronounced. At present, however, the general usefulness of AP test scores is reduced somewhat because—in spite of recent progress—African American students are still much less likely to take AP tests than are other students.[38]

If there is a movement toward wider use of content-based achievement tests, as we hope there will be, one consequence could be at least some push toward development of a national curriculum—again, in our view, a potentially desirable (though also surely controversial) development. The value of content-based achievement tests clearly depends on how well such tests are aligned with curricula. It is revealing to note that where there is a close match, as in the case of the Graduate Record Examination subject tests at the graduate level, the predictive power of achievement tests is very strong (see Kuncel and Hezlett 2007).

SIGNALING EFFECTS

Among the many participants in the long debate over the respective merits of test scores and high school grades, Richard Atkinson, president emeritus of the University of California (and a distinguished psychologist), has been unusually persistent and thoughtful. In his "personal perspective" on these issues, presented as an invited lecture to the American Educational Research Association in 2004 and then published in 2005, President Atkinson called attention to the "signaling" effects of different kinds of tests. Atkinson recalled that when he visited his granddaughter, then in the sixth grade, he found her "already diligently preparing for the SAT by testing herself on long lists of verbal analogies" (Atkinson 2005). He continued: "She had a corpus of quite obscure words to memorize, and then she proceeded to construct analogies using the words. I was amazed at the amount of time and effort involved, all in anticipation of the SAT. Was this how I wanted my granddaughter to spend her study time?"[39] At the end of his talk, Atkinson observed: "One of the clear lessons of history is that colleges and universities, through their admissions requirements, strongly influence what is taught in the schools. From my viewpoint, the most important reason for changing the SAT [as it has now been changed] is to send a clear message to K–12 students, their teachers and parents, that learning to write and mastering a solid background in mathematics is of critical importance" (Atkinson 2004). Even though the predictive value of the "new" SAT is about the same as the predictive value of the old SAT, it can be regarded as a definite improvement over its predecessor precisely because of the clear signals it sends about the importance of writing and mathematics (Atkinson and Geiser 2008).[40]

Curriculum-based achievement tests, especially AP tests, would seem to have even stronger signaling effects. As Geiser has suggested, these signaling effects may be a better argument in their favor than modest statistical differences in their predictive power. They reinforce teaching and learning of a rigorous academic curriculum, and they also serve a diagnostic function: "Achievement-test scores provide feedback on the specific areas of the curriculum where students are strongest and weakest" (Geiser 2009).

Signaling effects can of course be negative as well as positive. If greater emphasis were to be given to both high school grades and achievement tests, it would be important to be alert to the possible presence of "general equilibrium" effects. One person has suggested that such a move might trigger the establishment of an "AP-exam-coaching" industry, much as the emphasis on the SAT has stimulated Kaplan and others to help students prepare to take these tests. Putting more weight on high school grades might also increase incentives to "game" such grades as well—for example, families might be more inclined to choose high schools with easier grading policies, and high schools might find themselves under more pressure to ease up on grading standards. We believe that putting more emphasis on content-based tests of various kinds can serve as some protection against "grade inflation" at the high school level—at the same time that the achievement tests provide valuable diagnostic information in their own right. In general, it is a judicious combination of high school grades and achievement tests (especially AP tests, including the writing component) that we regard as especially promising.[41] In many settings (especially in the case of highly selective institutions, and especially in the absence of AP scores for many applicants), standard SAT/ACT tests also have definite value—in part because of their usefulness in predicting grades and in part as a check on any tendency to "game" high school GPA measures.

In concluding this discussion, we want to return to the theme that the right question is not "To test or not to test?" Rather, the basic question is this: What set of tests and other measures is most useful in a particular setting? What makes sense for the small number of Harvards of this world may make little if any sense for the typical university in a state system. The case for continued use of standard SAT/ACT tests is, as we have said, strongest at the most selective colleges and universities. It is easy to understand why President Conant was interested in the creation of a test that would predict "academic brilliance." He did not have to worry about Harvard's graduation rate. But most universities do have to be concerned about how many of their entering students finish, and the evidence is compelling that high school grades and scores on achievement tests are the best predictors of whether a student will graduate.

From a national standpoint, it is unfortunate, in our view, that so much emphasis has been placed on predicting first-year grades. It is easy to understand the appeal of this metric because evidence can be obtained so early in a student's academic career and so soon after the test was administered—and predicting grades is a valuable thing to do. But it would be better, we believe, to exercise more patience. Testing organizations need to continue working to devise tests that complement high school grades, including both content-based achievement tests and tests of noncognitive skills, in order to help students, parents, high schools, and colleges make the best possible educational matches—bearing in mind the importance of "finishing" and not just getting off to a good start. It is also important that we continue to devise tests that will not further disadvantage students who are already disadvantaged—tests that will not discourage worthy students from modest backgrounds from even applying to an appropriate college. Finally, tests should send the right signals to all parties about the need for students to master content and not just be good at test taking, which is of course a means to an end, not an end in and of itself.

NOTES

1. In September 2008, the National Association for College Admission Counseling (NACAC) released a report by a commission chaired by Dean Fitzsimmons proposing that colleges and universities give less emphasis to the SAT and ACT and that the entire standardized testing process, including the uses of tests, be reformed (along with the tests themselves) (Fitzsimmons 2008). Overall, the conclusions of the Fitzsimmons Commission closely mirror the broad thrust of the arguments presented in this chapter.

2. See also the extensive materials at the ACT website, including "Issues in College Success: What We Know about College Success: Using ACT Data to Inform Educational

Issues," http://www.act.org/content/dam/act/unsecured/documents/what_we_know.pdf. The College Board has of course also been concerned with placement issues and with efforts to improve the high school curriculum. Reports on their work can be found at the College Board's website.

3. We have converted ACT scores to the SAT scale (using the concordance tables published by the College Board) rather than the other way around because our data sets contain roughly two and a half times more SAT scores than ACT scores. (We write "SAT/ACT" rather than "ACT/SAT" for the same reason.) Rescaling ACT scores to the SAT scale introduces no significant measurement error; the conversion preserves the rank ordering of students, and the correlation between ACT scores and ACT-converted-to-SAT scores is 0.999. The use of a single measure of test score results works for our purposes because of the high correlation between the scores earned by students on these tests (see Coyle and Pillow 2008; Dorans 1999). Within our more limited universe, we have found similarly high correlations. Although our data sets contain many more SAT scores that ACT scores, we have both scores for more than 30,000 students, and it is this sub-universe of overlapping test takers that we use to compare the coefficients of the two tests in regressions used to predict graduation rates.

4. Some of our universities rely mainly on SAT scores, some mainly on ACT scores, and some on a mix of SAT and ACT scores. For an informative history of the ACT and how it was created to challenge the Educational Testing Service (ETS) and the SAT, see Lemann 1999, 95, 102–104. The National Association for College Admission Counseling's commission report (NACAC 2008) and studies cited in it also discuss the evolution of selective admission and testing (pp. 16ff). See also Atkinson and Geiser 2009.

5. In these regressions, we first use only university dummies as controls; then we include additional controls for state residency status, race/ethnicity, gender, family income, and parental education (when the availability of data permits). Adding these controls has only a negligible effect, however, on our estimates of how graduation rates vary with test scores and high school grades. Our data also show that limiting the set of universities studied to those for which we have data on parental education has a minimal effect on the results. Thus, we are able to adopt the simple approach of focusing on the regressions containing only SAT/ACT scores, high school grades, and institutional dummies as independent variables. We should also note that in these regressions we use "adjusted high school grades," which is a measure of high school performance we are able to calculate on a consistent basis across groups of students and groups of universities. Our calculation begins with self-reported grades and takes into account other self-reported data, including the number of years every subject was studied, the number of honors courses taken, and the number of AP courses taken. This measure is slightly less precise than the grades that can be obtained from institutional data, but institutions do not always use the same scales, and thus it is hard to compare grades across institutions. Fortunately, the adjusted GPAs turn out to have a predictive value that is very similar to the predictive value of the institutionally reported data when the two measures can be compared (see appendix table 6.9c). Finally, although we show results for both six-year and four-year graduation rates in most appendix tables, the patterns are quite similar, and we generally focus on six-year graduation rates in the text for ease of exposition.

6. As the "grid" data shown later in this chapter (in appendix tables 6.4–6.8) indicate, there are positive "raw" or "bivariate" relationships between graduation rates and both SAT/ACT scores and high school GPA, and these grids also illustrate the simple correlation between test scores and high school GPA. But it is the "incremental" or "net" effects of different predictors that are most relevant to our analysis (and to admissions offices choosing among candidates). A key question, which the coefficients shown here answer, is how much *additional* information is provided by both test scores and high school GPA after taking account of the information provided by the other variable. We are indebted to Professor Paul Sackett at the University of Minnesota for emphasizing the importance of distinguishing between incremental ("net") effects and bivariate relationships.

7. Promises of institutional confidentiality preclude our showing the actual results for individual institutions, but we can report that the GPA coefficients are somewhat larger, both in absolute terms and in relation to their standard errors, when we use students' actual high school grades as recorded by the universities (which we can do when working with the data for individual universities) rather than the adjusted measure of grades that we use to achieve consistency across universities.

8. An op-ed column in the *New York Times* by Peter D. Salins illustrates how easy it is to confuse discussions of the predictive power of test scores versus grades by conducting the "wrong experiment"—or, more generally, by failing to invoke normal standards of evidence (Salins 2008). Salins reports that State University of New York campuses that raised SAT admission standards while leaving high school GPA the same observed higher graduation rates than did campuses that left both measures alone. This "finding" is hardly surprising, because *any* increase in selectivity is going to raise graduation rates. Salins fails to ask this key question: What would have happened to graduation rates had campuses raised the high school GPA standard and left SAT scores alone? Based on the massive amount of evidence assembled for this study, it is highly likely that graduation rates would have risen even more. As a number of letters to the editor (e.g., "Just Name, Rank and SAT Number" 2008) point out, naive interpretations of the kinds of comparisons Salins uses can lead to serious confusion about effects of admissions policies.

9. Regressions that control for (in addition to university attended) race/ethnicity, gender, state residency status, and family income quartile (appendix table 6.3) yield very similar results.

10. Before discussing the tabular data presented next, we wish to make four general comments about the regression analysis: First, these regressions predict graduation rates at the institution initially attended and do not give institutions "credit" for students who transfer and then earn a degree elsewhere. But we have determined that treating transfer-out students as nongraduates has no effect on the conclusions pertaining to the predictive power of test scores and GPAs. Second, a commentator on an early draft of this chapter warned that multicollinearity between SAT/ACT scores and high school GPAs might make it hard to interpret the regression results. We know that SAT/ACT scores and high school GPAs are correlated and that failing to take account of such correlations can obscure the real relationships. However, the simple correlations between SAT/ACT scores and high school GPAs in these data are not as strong as one might have expected them to be. They are 0.40 at SEL Is, 0.39 at SEL IIs, 0.49 at SEL IIIs, 0.42 at state system SEL As, 0.42 at state system SEL Bs, and 0.35 at HBCUs. Moreover, the tabular comparisons of

graduation rates by both SAT/ACT scores and high school GPAs discussed next in the text and reported in appendix tables 6.4–6.8 convincingly demonstrate that the regression results mirror the underlying data. Third, another commentator thought that we might have misspecified our regression equations by failing to recognize that the relationships between SAT/ACT scores and graduation rates, and between high school GPAs and graduation rates, may be nonlinear. This is an important question, and we performed an extensive analysis of it (using local polynomials) that shows very little evidence of nonlinearity over the relevant ranges. Fourth, it is true that we are looking at students who matriculated when what we would really like to know is predictive power among applicants. There is some evidence, however, that this is not likely to be a significant problem. As we understand the concern, as expressed by another commentator, it is that if colleges are putting more weight on test scores than on high school GPA in the admissions process, the range of test scores among the admitted students will be smaller than among the applicants (and to a greater extent than the same is true for high school GPA). As a result, the predictive power of test scores among the enrolled students will be smaller than the predictive power would have been among all applicants (and the test score versus high school GPA comparison will be biased). However, the admissions data we have for two public universities in our 1999 data (Chapel Hill and NC State) and three public universities in our 1995 data (Penn State, UCLA, and UVa) indicate that the opposite pattern prevails—more weight was put on high school GPA in the admissions process than was put on SAT scores. At all of these universities, the standard deviation of both test scores and high school GPA is, as one would expect, smaller among admits than among all applicants, but this is true to a much greater extent for high school GPA than for test scores. In other words, if this pattern holds more generally, our results likely *understate* the predictive power of high school GPA relative to test scores because of the greater selection on high school GPA than on test scores in the admissions process.

11. The bottom panels of these appendix tables show results for four-year graduation rates, which again mirror closely the results for six-year rates and thus require no separate discussion.

12. This splendid book contains a full account of the evolution of the SAT (and other standardized tests, including especially the ACT) over the years and documents the ways in which reality often overtook the idealistic aspirations of people like Conant.

13. The notes to these tables specify the other control variables, which include family income quartile, race/ethnicity, gender, and university dummies. The data set is restricted to students with non-missing data on all the control variables and to students from high schools that sent at least two students to the universities in the study and whose students did not all either graduate or fail to graduate.

14. This finding is qualitatively the same as the finding of Jesse Rothstein in his work with data from California. In studying the power of SAT scores to predict first-year GPA in college, he found that when he added high school fixed effects, "the SAT coefficient falls by nearly half." As the bottom panels of appendix tables 6.9a and 6.9b show, the SAT/ACT net regression coefficients are essentially zero when we include high school fixed effects and predict four-year graduation rates. One commentator raised the question of whether using high school fixed effects deprives test scores of their "rightful" predictive power, given the correlation between SAT/ACT scores and high school attended. This could be

true to some degree, but note that including the high school dummies simply drives what are already exceedingly small test-score coefficients (refer back to appendix tables 6.1 and 6.2) to zero. Also, and more fundamentally, it seems relevant to ask what information is added by the SAT scores on top of that provided by high school GPA and the characteristics of the high school attended.

15. One commentator reminded us that we adjust raw self-reported grades to take account of aspects of coursework, and therefore it is a mild exaggeration to say that "a grade is a grade is a grade." But the adjusting process makes very little difference. We get essentially the same results when we use actual university-reported high school GPAs, which also take rigor into account to some degree by weighting honors courses more heavily (see appendix table 6.9c); in fact, the actual high school GPA results presented in this appendix table show even stronger effects of grades per se on graduation rates, presumably because the adjusted high school GPAs are measured with error.

16. A more rigorous way of answering the same basic question is (using the North Carolina data) to take account of interactions between high school grades and the academic level of the high school when predicting graduation rates. For both SEL As and SEL Bs in North Carolina, this approach yields results that are essentially the same as those shown by the more intuitive tabulations reported in appendix table 6.10 and described in the text. At the more selective SEL As, the slope of the relationship between high school grades and graduation rates is steeper for students from Level I high schools than for students from Level III high schools. This is not true, however, in the case of SEL Bs, where the slope is steeper among students from Level III high schools.

17. Although the North Carolina data cover a broader population than just those students who attended the universities in our study, they do not include all high school seniors in the state, because not all seniors take the SAT. An important question is whether we would obtain the same results if we looked at an unselected population of students. The state of Illinois requires that all high school graduates take the ACT, and Jesse Rothstein and his colleagues have rigorously looked at selection bias using these data. They find that there is indeed, as one would expect, positive selection bias in test participation both within and across schools. Despite this, they conclude that "school-level averages of observed scores are extremely highly correlated with average latent scores. . . . As a result, in most contexts the use of observed school mean test scores in place of latent means understates the degree of between-school variation in achievement but is otherwise unlikely to lead to misleading conclusions" (Clark, Rothstein, and Schanzenbach, 2008). Also reassuring is the fact that results based on data we have for four entire state systems are basically the same as the results we obtain for more limited populations.

18. A study by Allen and associates of the importance of "academic self-discipline" as a determinant of academic success comes to the same conclusion that we do; that study is based on a detailed study of students' personal behaviors (Allen et al. 2008, 647–664). We are indebted to Ranjit Sidhu of NCCEP for directing us to this highly relevant piece of research, as well as to other studies conducted by ACT itself.

19. Recent work in California has attracted a great deal of attention and has provoked a spirited debate over both methods and findings (see Agronow and Studley 2007; Geiser 2009; Geiser and Studley 2001). For discussions about the relationship between the SAT and SES in this context, see Sackett et al. 2009; Zwick and Green 2007. Tempting as it is

to plunge into this important discussion, we have made no independent investigation of the California data and do not know enough about the particular features of the California educational system to permit us to assess conflicting claims. Perusal of the references we have given should allow interested readers to come to their own conclusions. For a summary of relevant studies by the College Board, see Kobrin et al. 2008; Mattern et al. 2008. For studies about using the ACT to predict readiness for college, see Allen and Sconing 2005.

20. Much of the "raw" relationship between graduation rates and both course rigor and test scores disappears after controlling for high school GPA. High school GPA, on the other hand, remains a powerful predictor of graduation rates after controlling for course rigor and test scores (Roderick et al. 2006, 69, fig. 3.3).

21. We cannot present similar comparisons for the more selective universities because they admit very few students with high school GPAs below 3.0.

22. The high school GPA coefficients for black men in appendix table 6.12 are especially interesting in that they are very much the same no matter which set of universities we look at. If black men with relatively low high school GPAs were doing particularly poorly at the most selective universities (where the competition is keener and there is, presumably, more risk of "mis-match"), we would expect to find larger high school GPA coefficients for them at, say, the SEL Is; in fact, the high school GPA coefficient for black men at the SEL It is actually slightly lower than the high school GPA coefficients for black men at the less selective universities. One other interesting difference is that the high school GPA coefficients for students from the top quartile of the family income distribution are modestly larger at the less selective universities, which is consistent with our general impression that students from these families attending the less selective universities have surprisingly low graduation rates unless they have quite high high school GPAs (appendix table 6.13). The reason for including appendix table 6.14, for all flagships taken together, is to give us enough observations for Hispanics to allow us to see if the coefficients for this important demographic group are noticeably different from those for black students. They are not.

23. The key statistician at ETS who worked on the Coleman Report (published in 1966), Albert Beaton, was confident that northeastern Negroes would score higher than southern whites on the basic ETS tests. This did not happen. According to Beaton, "The magnitude of the black/white difference and the uniformity over the country was mind-boggling. I can say it was a total surprise to me" (quoted in Lemann 1999, 160). Lemann observes: "Because of how they had grown up, where they lived, and so on, Negroes as a group were in a uniquely bad position to perform well on tests designed to measure school-bred skills such as reading and vocabulary and mathematics." As Lemann points out, there was an inherent tension between the emerging meritocratic system and the cause of Negro advancement (156).

24. We rely here on our North Carolina data because they are available for a large fraction of all high school seniors, regardless of where (or whether) they went to college. The students at our flagships, in particular, are too select a group to permit a proper assessment of these relationships.

25. Data from California also demonstrate that race and ethnicity are highly correlated with SAT scores in that state. Geiser (2009) reports: "When UC applicants were rank-ordered by SAT scores, roughly half as many Latino, African American and American

Indian students appeared in the top third of the applicant pool than when the same students were ranked by high-school grades." The original study that produced these (and other) results is reported in Geiser and Santelices 2007. Working with data for all California residents who applied to any of the University of California campuses for admission as regular freshmen for the 1993–94 academic year and seeking to predict first-year college GPA, Jesse Rothstein found that school-average SATs had considerable predictive power but that a substantial portion of the predictive power of this measure derived from its association with the racial composition of high schools. He then observed: "One might conclude from [the findings] that colleges should give preferences to students from high-scoring schools." But, he added, "the predicted-performance-maximizing admissions rule amounts to affirmative action for socioeconomically advantaged students" (Rothstein 2005, esp. 20–21). Along these same lines, there was an earlier report by Allan Nairn of ETS, published in 1980, in which, Lemann notes, "Nairn's central premise was that ETS, under a veneer of science, functioned as the opposite of a meritocratic force in American society. It provided an official way for people with money to pass on their status to their children" (Lemann 1999, 227). In a chapter of his book on ETS, Nairn referred to "class in the guise of merit" (Nairn and Nader 1980; cited in Lemann 1999, 271).

26. See appendix tables 6.1 and 6.2. See also Sackett et al. 2009.

27. Fitzsimmons 2008, 39. This report also contains a long discussion of "uneven preparation for tests" ("coaching") and how it can give an advantage to students from families sufficiently affluent to afford test preparation. The report recommends further study of the extent to which coaching alters test scores (24ff.).

28. Lemann 1999, 39. In fact, 8 of the first 10 students chosen under Conant's new scholarship program, in part on the basis of test scores, were elected to Phi Beta Kappa. The Nobel laureate James Tobin was chosen two years later.

29. See, for example, Kobrin et al. 2008; Mattern et al. 2008. The title of the former makes entirely clear the purpose to be served by this research program: "Validity of the SAT for Predicting First-Year College Grade Point Average." These two reports provide a careful explanation of the methodology used by the research scientists at the College Board, along with extended summaries of their findings. Other relevant work includes Burton and Ramist 2001; Camara 2008; Camara and Echternacht 2000.

30. We ran separate regressions for the overlapping set of students who took both the SAT and the ACT to see if there is any noticeable difference in the power of these two tests to predict rank-in-class. As in the case of graduation rates, the respective regression coefficients are strikingly similar.

31. In March 2005, the College Board introduced a revised ("new") SAT. The most notable change was the addition of a Writing section (the SATW) that measures basic writing skills and includes a student-produced essay. The Verbal section of the test was renamed the Critical Reading section; analogies were removed and replaced by questions on reading passages. The Math section was changed to include items from more advanced mathematics courses such as second-year algebra (see Kobrin et al. 2008, 1).

32. The authors go on to say: "For example, one standard deviation in high school GPA corresponds to a 0.27-point higher first-year GPA, whereas a one standard deviation increase in the SATW score corresponds to a 0.05-point higher first-year GPA." The regres-

sions used in this study include the same controls that we use: race/ethnicity, gender, parental education, and high school fixed effects.

33. In constructing our measure of SAT II test scores, we simply averaged the scores on all tests taken by students who took at least one SAT II test (64% of students at the SEL Is and 49% at the SEL As). Too few students at the other flagships and at the state system SEL Bs and the HBCUs took these tests to permit us to carry out this analysis for students at these schools. Similarly, we averaged the AP test scores. This analysis of achievement test results includes all of the flagships except Rutgers and three of the four state systems with which we have worked. (The Ohio system, but not Ohio State, had to be excluded because of a lack of SAT II and AP scores.)

34. Additionally, AP scores are much less strongly correlated with SAT/ACT scores than are SAT II scores. The correlations between SAT/ACT scores and average AP scores are 0.58 at SEL Is, 0.53 at SEL IIs, 0.57 at SEL As, and 0.24 at SEL Bs.

35. An important caveat: it is scores earned on AP exams, not participation in AP courses, that predicts outcomes. Enrollment in AP courses per se is a poor predictor.

36. There has been a lively debate about the predictive power of SAT II scores versus regular SAT scores in California, which is the only state, to the best of our knowledge, that has required the SAT II for a long time. Geiser (2009) has argued in favor of the SAT II. Other scholars have criticized Geiser's work and, on the basis of a re-analysis of the same California data, have argued that the SAT I and the SAT II are very similar in predictive power (Zwick, Brown, and Sklar 2004). We should add that Geiser agrees with our conclusion that AP results are the best predictors of all of these tests.

37. In his memoirs, Conant also wrote, "Subject-matter examinations were of slight value. The aptitude, not the schooling, was what counted" (Conant 1970, 424; quoted in Hoover 2008).

38. Hispanic students, on the other hand, appear to make up about as high a percentage of AP test takers as do high school students in general. (See Bushong 2009 for a discussion of trends in AP test taking. See also Lewin 2009 for comments by Gaston Caperton on the benefits of the AP tests in promoting speedy completion of degrees.) We applaud the determined efforts of the College Board to expand the role of AP tests.

39. For a number of years Professor Michael Kirst at Stanford has also emphasized the importance of signaling and of aligning college admissions criteria with K–12 curricula. See, for example, Kirst and Venezia 2001.

40. Colleges and universities contemplating dropping requirements that applicants take the new SAT should carefully consider the benefit of the Writing component—and not just to them but, through these signaling effects, to the educational system in general. It is also worth recalling that the AP English Language test has a writing component.

41. The decision by the Board of Regents of the University of California to stop requiring SAT II tests (made at the time this book was in its near-final iteration) needs to be understood in the complex context of admissions policies at the University of California, where there is continuing concern about how to give more flexibility to local campuses. We are in no position to comment on the pros and cons of the overall set of new admissions policies recently announced (see Jaschik 2009; Keller and Hoover 2009). These important changes in admissions policies have to be understood in the light of the implications for

racial diversity of Proposition 209, which prohibited taking race into account in admissions to public institutions in California. Still, it would be unfortunate if this decision were interpreted nationally as a rejection of the value of content-based achievement tests. As the national data in this study show, such tests are valuable complements to high school grades.

REFERENCES

Agronow, S., and Studley, R. (2007). *Prediction of college GPA from new SAT test scores—A first look*. Paper presented at the annual meeting of the California Association for Institutional Research, Monterey, CA, November 16. Retrieved from http://www.cair .org/conferences/CAIR2007/pres/Agronow.pdf.

Allen, J., Robbins, S. B., Casillas, A., and Oh, I. (2008). Third-year college retention and transfer effects of academic performance, motivation, and social connectedness. *Research in Higher Education, 49*(7), 647–664.

Allen, J., and Sconing, J. (2005). *Using ACT assessment scores to set benchmarks for college readiness*. ACT Research Report 2005-3. Iowa City: ACT.

Atkinson, R. C. (2005). College admissions and the SAT: A personal perspective. *Journal of the Association for Psychological Science Observer, 18*(5), 15–22.

Atkinson, R. C., and Geiser, S. (2008). Beyond the SAT. *Forbes*, August 13, online edition.
———. (2009). *Reflections on a century of college admissions tests*. Research and Occasional Paper: CSHE.4.09. Berkeley: Center for Studies in Higher Education, University of California–Berkeley.

Bassiri, D., and Schulz, E. M. (2003). *Constructing a universal scale of high school course difficulty*. ACT Research Report 2003-4. Iowa City: ACT.

Burton, N. W., and Ramist, L. (2001). *Predicting success in college: SAT studies of classes graduating since 1980*. College Board Research Report 2001-2. New York: The College Board.

Bushong, S. (2009). Number of students doing well on AP tests is up, but racial gaps persist. *Chronicle of Higher Education*, February 5, online edition.

Camara, W. J. (2008). *Score trends, SAT validity, and subgroup differences*. Paper presented at the Harvard Summer Institute, Boston.

Camara, W. J., and Echternacht, G. (2000). *The SAT I and high school grades: Utility in predicting success in college*. College Board Research Notes RN-10. New York: The College Board.

Clark, M., Rothstein, J., and Schanzenbach, D. W. (2008). *Selection bias in college admissions test scores*. NBER Working Paper 14265. Cambridge, MA: National Bureau of Economic Research. Retrieved from http://www.nber.org/papers/w14265.pdf.

Conant, J. B. (1970). *My several lives: Memoirs of a social inventor*. New York: Harper and Row.

Cornwell, C. M., Mustard, D. B., and Van Parys, J. (2008). *How does the new SAT predict academic achievement in college?* Working paper. Athens: University of Georgia.

Coyle, T. R., and Pillow, D. R. (2008). SAT and ACT predict college GPA after removing *g*. *Intelligence, 36*, 719–729.

Dorans, N. J. (1999). *Correspondences between ACT and SAT I scores.* College Board Report 99-1, ETS RR 99-2. New York: College Entrance Examination Board.

Fitzsimmons, W. (2008). *Report of the commission on the use of standardized tests in undergraduate admission.* Alexandria, VA: National Association for College Admission Counseling.

Geiser, S. (2009). Back to the basics: In defense of achievement (and achievement tests) in college admissions. *Change* (January–February), 16–23. Retrieved from http://www.changemag.org/January-February%202009/full-back-to-basics.html.

Geiser, S., and Santelices, M. V. (2007). *Validity of high-school grades in predicting student success beyond the freshman year: High-school record vs. standardized tests as indicators of four-year college outcomes.* Research and Occasional Paper Series: CSHE.6.07. Berkeley: Center for Studies in Higher Education, University of California–Berkeley.

Geiser, S., and Studley, R. (2001). *UC and the SAT: Predictive validity and differential impact of the SAT I and SAT II at the University of California.* Oakland: Office of the President, University of California, Oakland.

Hoover, E. (2008). Admissions group urges colleges to "assume control" of debate on testing. *Chronicle of Higher Education,* September 22, online edition.

Jaschik, S. (2009). Unintentional whitening of U. of California? *Inside Higher Education,* February 5, online edition.

Just name, rank and SAT number. (2008). *New York Times,* November 24, A24.

Keller, J., and Hoover, E. (2009). U. of California to adopt sweeping changes in admissions policy. *Chronicle of Higher Education,* February 5, online edition.

Kirst, M., and Venezia, A. (2001). Bridging the great divide between secondary schools and postsecondary education. *Phi Delta Kappan, 83*(1), 92–97.

Kobrin, J. L., Patterson, B. F., Shaw, E. J., Mattern, K. D., and Barbuti, S. M. (2008). *Validity of the SAT for predicting first-year college grade point average.* Research Report 2008-5. New York: The College Board.

Kuncel, N. R., and Hezlett, S. A. (2007). Standardized tests predict graduate students' success. *Science, 315,* 1080–1081.

Lemann, N. (1999). *The big test: The secret history of the American meritocracy.* New York: Farrar, Straus and Giroux.

Lewin, T. (2009). A.P. program is growing, but black students lag. *New York Times,* February 5, A19.

Mattern, K. D., Patterson, B. F., Shaw, E. J., Kobrin, J. L., and Barbuti, S. M. (2008). *Differential validity and prediction of the SAT.* Research Report 2008-4. New York: The College Board.

Nairn, A., and Nader, R. (1980). *The reign of ETS: The corporation that makes up minds.* Washington, DC: Ralph Nader.

Roderick, M., Nagaoka, J., Allensworth, E., Coca, V., Correa, M., and Stoker, G. (2006). *From high school to the future: A first look at Chicago public school graduates' college enrollment, college preparation, and graduation from four-year colleges.* Chicago: Consortium on Chicago Research.

Rothstein, J. (2005). *SAT scores, high schools, and collegiate performance predictions.* Working paper. Princeton, NJ: Princeton University. Retrieved from https://eml.berkeley.edu/~jrothst/restingpapers/satpaper2_june2009.pdf.

Sackett, P. R., Kuncel, N. R., Arneson, J. J., Cooper, S. R., and Waters, S. D. (2009). Does socioeconomic status explain the relationship between admissions tests and post-secondary academic performance? *Psychological Bulletin, 135,* 1–22.

Salins, P. D. (2008). The test passes, colleges fail. *New York Times,* November 18, A27.

Sidhu, R. (2009). *Comparing the validity of ACT scores and high school grades as predictors of success in college.* Iowa City: ACT.

Woodruff, D. J., and Ziomek, R. L. (2004). *Differential grading standards among high schools.* ACT Research Report 2004-2. Iowa City: ACT.

Zwick, R., Brown, T., and Sklar, J. C. (2004). *California and the SAT: A reanalysis of University of California admissions data.* Research and Occasional Paper Series: CSHE 8-04. Berkeley: Center for Studies in Higher Education, University of California–Berkeley.

Zwick, R., and Green, J. G. (2007). New perspectives on the correlation of SAT scores, high school grades, and socioeconomic factors. *Journal of Educational Measurement, 44,* 23–45.

Comment

Michael Hurwitz and Meredith Welch

Bowen, Chingos, and McPherson (henceforth referred to as BCM) shed light on the complex relationships between high school grade point average (HSGPA), college entrance exam scores, and college completion using a rich set of administrative data from nearly 150,000 students beginning their studies at 68 public colleges in the fall of 1999.[1] While they maintain that high school grades and test scores are best used in combination, their statistical models reveal that high school grades tend to be stronger predictors of college completion than college entrance examinations.

The students in BCM's sample entered college nearly two decades ago, and since then, high school GPAs have steadily marched upward, particularly for higher-achieving, wealthier students. In chapter 3 of this volume, Hurwitz and Lee quantify these trends and document the increased bunching of grades in the A-range since the late 1990s. Such grade inflation and compression raises the question of whether the precisely estimated relationships between HSGPA, college entrance exam scores, and college completion in BCM's chapter stand the test of time. If grade inflation has decreased the reliability of HSGPA as a measure of academic preparation, we might expect the predictive power of high school grades to deteriorate relative to standardized assessment scores.

In this rejoinder, we present evidence consistent with this hypothesis. Replicating the work of BCM with data for students entering the same 68 colleges a decade later—in the fall of 2009—we offer evidence that the power of HSGPA to predict four- and six-year bachelor's degree completion has declined. By contrast, the incremental gains in college completion explained by SAT/ACT scores have simultaneously increased. In table 8a.1, we replicate the analyses of BCM, which appear in figure 8.1 (on page 198) and, in *Crossing the Finish Line*, appendix tables 6.1 and 6.2 using data from students entering the same 68 colleges one decade later.

Before delving into the similarities and differences between our results and those of BCM, we provide a quick refresher on how to interpret their (and our) model parameter estimates. Within each selectivity group of colleges, standardized test scores and HSGPA are transformed to have a mean of zero and a standard deviation of one, which allows for a meaningful comparison of the estimate sizes for test scores and high school grades.[2] Model parameter estimates are expressed as marginal, or incremental effects from probit models, holding the other predictor variables at their respective means. For example, the parameter estimate "0.037" in table 8a.1 (column 2, row 1) indicates that a one standard deviation–increase in SAT scores is associated with a 3.7 percentage point increase in the six-year bachelor's completion rate among students with mean HSGPAs at the 68 *Crossing the Finish Line* colleges. Conversely, the "0.069" parameter estimate in column 2, row 3 indicates that a one standard deviation–increase in HSGPA is associated with 6.9 percentage point increase in the six-year bachelor's completion rate among students with standardized assessment scores fixed at the mean across the sample of students entering these 68 colleges in 2009.

In their statistical models, BCM incorporate fixed effects for universities. The purpose of including these indicator variables is to ensure that the marginal effects are calculated from the variation in bachelor's completion *within* universities. On the one hand, this is sensible because including these fixed effects removes potentially confounding factors that are tied to student success, like institutional

Table 8a.1. Graduation rates by college entrance exam scores and HSGPA, 2009 entering cohorts

	68 Crossing the Finish Line colleges[a]		Flagship universities			State systems		
			SEL Is	SEL IIs	SEL IIIs	SEL As	SEL Bs	HBCUs
			Six-year graduation rates (2009)					
SAT (standardized)	0.065**	0.037**	0.017**	0.053**	0.013*	0.018**	0.022**	0.007
	(0.005)	(0.009)	(0.003)	(0.016)	(0.006)	(0.005)	(0.006)	(0.005)
HSGPA (standardized)	0.080**	0.069**	0.020**	0.061**	0.077**	0.045**	0.082**	0.096**
	(0.004)	(0.004)	(0.001)	(0.011)	(0.010)	(0.004)	(0.005)	(0.006)
Observations	146,165	146,165	22,056	38,977	16,629	18,821	41,348	8,334
			Four-year graduation rates (2009)					
SAT (standardized)	0.100**	0.061**	0.056**	0.075**	0.024**	0.026**	0.037**	0.020**
	(0.009)	(0.009)	(0.005)	(0.016)	(0.008)	(0.010)	(0.006)	(0.006)
HSGPA (standardized)	0.108**	0.099**	0.040**	0.082**	0.107**	0.074**	0.099**	0.078**
	(0.006)	(0.005)	(0.004)	(0.015)	(0.011)	(0.008)	(0.005)	(0.004)
Observations	146,165	146,165	22,056	38,977	16,629	18,821	41,348	8,334
University dummies?	No	Yes	Yes	Yes	Yes	Yes	Yes	Yes

Notes: HSGPA = high school grade point average; SEL = selectivity cluster; HBCU = historically black colleges and universities. Robust standard errors adjusted for clustering at the university level appear in parentheses. SAT scores and HSGPA are standardized to have a mean of zero and a standard deviation of one within each selectivity cluster, except for in the first two columns, where the mean and standard deviation are standardized across all 68 Crossing the Finish Line colleges. Reported coefficients are calculated from probit regressions as the predicted increase in graduation probability associated with increasing either SAT scores or HSGPA by one standard deviation, holding all control variables at their respective means. Sample includes students from the 2009 cohort who enrolled at sampled colleges on-time (within 180 days of HS graduation). For all 68 colleges, the standard deviation for SAT is 185.7 points and 0.51 for HSGPA. For each of the six categories of colleges, the standard deviations for HSGPA for SEL I, SEL II, SEL III, SEL A, SEL B, HBCUs are 0.34, 0.46, 0.46, 0.41, 0.51, 0.59, respectively. The standard deviations for SAT are 149.5, 179.2, 156.1, 139.8, 146.9, 120.4.

[a]Column 1 = Without university fixed effects; column 2 = With university fixed effects.

*p < 0.05, **p < 0.01.

resources. On the other hand, these fixed effects potentially contribute toward a downward bias in the marginal effects associated with SAT scores and HSGPA. If students were randomly sorted into universities, inclusion of university fixed effects would be an ideal methodological solution. This is obviously not the case; both HSGPA and SAT scores influence who is selected for admission, as well as who chooses to enroll, after gaining admission.

Our discussion emphasizes models with fixed effects for universities because this was the sensible choice of BCM, and consistent empirical choices allow for the comparison of parameter estimates over time. However, we dedicated the first column of table 8a.1 to presenting parameter estimates obtained from models without fixed effects. Compared to models that include university fixed effects (column 2 of table 8a.1), the marginal effects (column 1 of table 8a.1) of SAT scores without university fixed effects are 64% and 76% larger for the outcomes of four-year and six-year bachelor's completion, respectively. The differences in the HSGPA parameter estimates are much smaller—only 9% and 16%. As a result of selection by both universities and students, the fixed effects models likely understate the actual predictive validity of the SAT, and the models without fixed effects likely overstate the predictive validity, suggesting that the predictive validity lies somewhere between these estimates.

When we compare our more recent estimates to those of BCM, we find that, across most selectivity groupings, the predictive value of HSGPA has diminished over time while the predictive value of SAT scores has increased. In figures 8a.1 and 8a.2, we show graphically the difference in parameter estimates of SAT/ACT scores and HSGPA on completion rates between the 1999 cohort and the 2009 cohort. At the most selective (SEL I) flagship institutions (fig. 8a.1), the effect of a one standard deviation increase in SAT/ACT scores on four-year completion increased from 4.3 percentage points to 5.6 percentage points between the 1999 cohort and the 2009 cohort. This increase is expressed by the solid-shaded bar at the height of 0.013. At these same institutions, the marginal effects of HSGPA decreased by 3.4 percentage points per HSGPA standard deviation—from 7.4 percentage points to 4.0 percentage points between these two periods.

Our results from the 2009 cohort are largely consistent with BCM in the sense that both analyses show that both HSGPA and college entrance examination scores are stronger predictors of four-year bachelor's completion than six-year bachelor's completion. These results are unsurprising because extending the time frame for degree completion leads to reduced variation in this outcome measure.

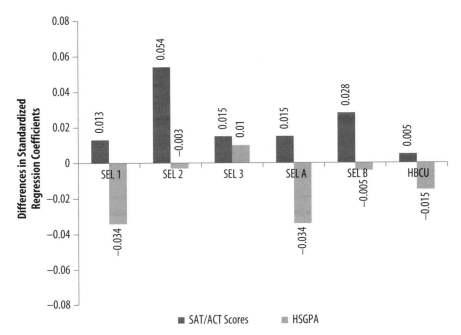

Fig. 8a.1. Differences in Standardized Regression Coefficients for Four-Year Bachelor's Completion between 1999 and 2009 Cohorts at the 68 *Crossing the Finish Line* Colleges. *Note*: SEL = selectivity cluster; HBCU = historically black colleges and universities; HSGPA = high school grade point average.

For example, only 16% of students at all SEL levels of the flagship sample failed to earn bachelor's degrees within six years, compared with the 39% noncompletion rate when the time frame is shortened to four years.

Table 8a.1, as well as the corresponding figures, expresses relationships between college entrance examination scores and college completion for students with the average HSGPA within each selectivity group. Presentation of data in this manner masks important differences in this relationship for students with different high school grades. We extend BCM's analyses by separately estimating the marginal effects of SAT scores on college completion at each point along the distribution of HSGPAs. In figure 8a.3, we show the incremental predictive value of test scores on college completion, along with 95% confidence bars, for all public flagships and other state colleges in BCM's original analyses.

For students with lower HSGPAs, SAT scores serve as modest predictors of both four-year and six-year bachelor's completion. The predictive power of the SAT tends to increase with HSGPA, particularly at the state colleges in BCM's sample.

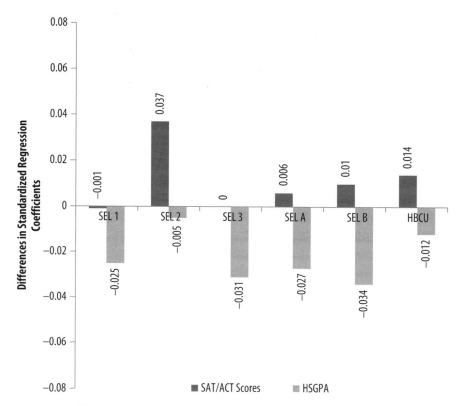

Fig. 8a.2. Differences in Standardized Regression Coefficients for Six-Year Bachelor's Completion between 1999 and 2009 Cohorts at the 68 *Crossing the Finish Line* Colleges. *Note*: SEL = selectivity cluster; HBCU = historically black colleges and universities; HSGPA = high school grade point average.

For example, at these 47 state colleges, the relationships between test scores and six-year completion are not statistically significant at conventional levels for students with HSGPAs in the B-range or lower. Among students with HSGPAs of A–, a one standard deviation–increase in SAT scores is associated with a 1.9 percentage point increase in six-year bachelor's completion. For students with grades of A and A+, estimates indicate that a one standard deviation increase in SAT scores is associated with a 4 to 4.2 percentage point increase in six-year bachelor's degree completion. At the 47 state colleges, an additional one standard deviation increase in SAT scores is associated with a 2.2 percentage point increase in four-year completion for students with B+ HSGPA averages, and a nearly 8 percentage point–increase for students with A+ HSGPA averages.

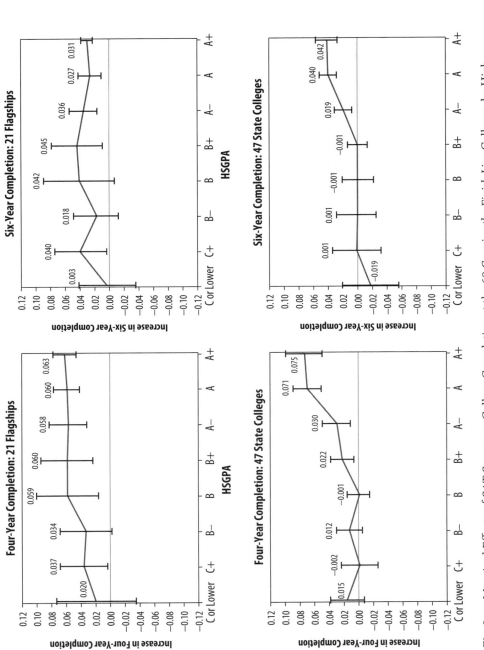

Fig. 8a.3. Marginal Effects of SAT Scores on College Completion at the 68 *Crossing the Finish Line* Colleges, by High School Grade Point Average (HSGPA) among Students from the 2009 Cohort

Why do test scores tend to have more predictive value for students with higher HSGPAs? One plausible explanation is that lower HSGPAs present a much more realistic depiction of student academic preparation than do higher HSGPAs. Stated bluntly, earning a low HSGPA, in spite of the documented culture of grade inflation, is likely a strong warning sign that the student lacks the academic preparation to succeed in college. By contrast, a higher GPA is a less reliable predictor of academic preparation for college because this group is a mishmash of students whose academic performance warrants high grades and less-stellar beneficiaries of grade inflation.

In the conclusion of chapter 6 in *Crossing the Finish Line*—reprinted just above— Bowen, Chingos, and McPherson conclude with a Shakespearean spin on the college entrance examination debate. They argue against framing the debate with the simple question, "To test or not to test?" We agree that such a simplification overlooks the many complexities of the relationships between postsecondary success and college entrance examination scores. College completion is one of many postsecondary success measures, and even if a college deems completion the most important outcome, our analyses caution against any paradigms in which the predictive value of standardized tests is assumed to be identical across all students. In this rejoinder, we have shown variation in the power of standardized tests and high school grades to predict bachelor's degree completion across different types of colleges and across different types of students within the same college. For *some* applicants at *some* colleges, poor high school grades alone may signify a risky admit. However, sustained grade inflation has made students bearing this scarlet letter increasingly rare. In an environment of continued high school grade inflation, especially for students attending wealthier high schools and at the high end of the HSGPA distribution, the "not to test" option leaves valuable insights into a student's probability of success on the table.

NOTES

1. Bowen, Chingos, and McPherson separate these colleges into flagship institutions and public non-flagship institutions. Each of these two groups is further divided based on selectivity or status as a historically black college or university (HBCU). The identities of these colleges are revealed in tables 1.1 and 1.2 in *Crossing the Finish Line*.

2. For the "overall sample" represented in the first two columns, we transform SAT scores and HSGPA so that these variables have a mean of zero and standard deviation of one across all 68 colleges.

REFERENCE

Bowen, W. G., Chingos, M. M., and McPherson, M. S. (2009). *Crossing the finish line: Completing college at America's public universities.* Princeton, NJ: Princeton University Press.

Reply

Matthew M. Chingos and Michael S. McPherson

We are grateful to Michael Hurwitz and Meredith Welch for using the rich set of administrative data available at the College Board to update our analysis of the ability of test scores and high school grade point average (HSGPA) to predict college graduation rates. Our work, on which we collaborated with our late colleague and friend William G. Bowen, drew on data on the entering class of 1999 at 68 public universities. Hurwitz and Welch conduct similar analyses using data on SAT takers in the entering class of 2009 at the same institutions.

The central conclusion of Hurwitz and Welch's analysis matches our own: high school grades are a stronger predictor of college graduation rates than are SAT scores. This is especially true at less-selective public universities, where the predictive power of grades is between 2.7 and 13.7 times that of test scores.

Hurwitz and Welch note that they tend to estimate a stronger predictive relationship for SAT scores, and a weaker relationship for high school grades, than we do. They attribute this shift to grade inflation, which Hurwitz and Lee document in chapter 3 of this volume. This explanation is plausible, but we believe it is incomplete, as there are at least two additional key differences between Hurwitz and Welch's analysis and our own that may lead to divergent results.

The first difference is that our analysis included both SAT and ACT takers, whereas Hurwitz and Welch only have access to data on SAT takers. Nationwide, ACT takers who also take the SAT score an average of 0.64 standard deviations higher (on the ACT) and have HSGPAs 0.44 standard deviations higher than ACT takers who do not take the SAT.[1] This suggests that excluding ACT takers at institutions where many or most students only take the ACT could bias upward the estimated predictive power of test scores, as Hurwitz and Welch show that the SAT is less predictive among students with lower high school grades.

The second difference is that Hurwitz and Welch's measure of HSGPA is based on students' responses to a single survey question about their cumulative GPA. Our analysis drew on a continuous prediction of GPA based on responses to the same question (on both the SAT and ACT surveys) as well as administrative data on the number of advanced placement (AP) exams taken and responses to additional survey questions about high school rank; average grades in each of six subject areas; enrollment in AP, accelerated, or honors courses in each of those subject areas; and number of years of coursework completed in each subject area.

Our prediction of GPA is based on the observed relationship between the factors listed above and actual HSGPAs among 41,371 students. The correlation between actual and predicted GPA is 0.80 for these students. We find that using predicted GPAs understates the relationship between high school grades and completion rates by 1–3 percentage points (per standard deviation increase in GPA) compared to using actual GPAs.[2] We suspect that the categorical self-reported GPA measure used by Hurwitz and Welch is more weakly correlated with actual high school GPAs, and thus causes them to understate the predictive power of grades (and potentially overstate the predictive power of test scores) by an even wider margin. We can only speculate about the magnitude of this bias, but it is plausible that it explains much or even all the differences between their results and ours.

We conclude by reiterating our gratitude to Hurwitz and Welch for updating our analysis using more recent data, and encourage researchers at the College Board to continue producing evidence on the predictive validity of different measures of college preparedness. We note that the College Board has the capacity to conduct such analyses not just for the 68 colleges in *Crossing the Finish Line*, but for all postsecondary institutions attended by students who take the SAT.

NOTES

1. Authors' calculations from the Education Longitudinal Study of 2002.
2. See appendix table 6.9c of *Crossing the Finish Line*.

PART III / Contemporary Challenges for College Admissions

9

How Do Percent Plans and Other Test-Optional Admissions Programs Affect the Academic Performance and Diversity of the Entering Class?

Rebecca Zwick

*T*he debate over the use of standardized tests in college admissions typically focuses on the group of mostly private institutions, notably small liberal arts colleges, that have jettisoned or minimized testing requirements in recent years. Far less
attention has been paid to the percent plans, based on high school class rank, that several large state universities adopted in the 1990s in response to growing restrictions on
the use of race in admissions. Rebecca Zwick takes on both forms of admissions practices
in this wide-ranging chapter. She forcefully argues that research findings often fail to
support advocates' claims that percent plans and test-optional admissions foster racial
and ethnic diversity and academic success.

Strictly speaking, the percent plans in Texas, California, and Florida are not test-
optional, because all three systems require applicants to take the ACT or SAT. But as a
practical matter, they function the same way. The only academic criteria that matter
under percent plans are high school grades, since students whose performance places
them at the top of their high school classes are automatically admitted. In addition to
presenting evidence that casts doubt on whether such plans have in fact achieved their
stated purposes of fostering racial diversity while remaining race-neutral, Zwick highlights transparency concerns: How can a student know what GPA he or she requires
for admission when that cutoff varies from school to school and changes every year?

As for test-optional plans, Zwick critiques the frequently cited research of William Hiss and Valerie Franks, in which the authors contend that there is little difference in collegiate outcomes between applicants who do and do not submit standardized test scores. Among other concerns, non-submitters were much less likely to major in rigorously graded STEM (science, technology, engineering, and math) fields, Zwick notes, citing an ACT study, and these students might well have earned worse grades had they done so. Moreover, although Hiss and Franks maintain that their 2014 study of 33 colleges and universities demonstrates that test-optional policies serve the purposes of affirmative action, Zwick argues that their results don't demonstrate whether minority enrollment rose or fell under test-optional admissions.

Zwick's analysis concludes with a warning about the potential unintended consequences of percent plans and test-optional policies. Testing critics may believe that emphasizing other factors will lessen the effects of socioeconomic disadvantage or the impact of race, but different measures of student performance, from grades to extracurricular activities, are just as liable to be influenced by socioeconomic status and race. She notes, too, that because of grade inflation, grades are likely to be increasingly less useful predictors of college achievement if tests are eliminated from the admissions process.

Following the clampdown on race-based affirmative action in the 1990s, American universities began to seek alternative ways to admit a diverse entering class that did not explicitly take race into consideration.[1] Among the ostensibly race-neutral admissions plans that emerged were percent plans, also called class rank plans. These plans, which are in effect in Texas, California, and Florida, provide for the automatic admission of students who are in the top tier of their high school class in terms of grades. All three state programs require applicants to complete certain high school courses and to take the SAT or ACT, but test scores are not considered in the admissions decisions. Because they draw top students from all high schools, including high-poverty schools and those with large percentages of students of color, these percent plans were expected to increase socioeconomic and racial diversity.

An overlapping development has been the adoption of "test-optional" admissions programs, which reduce or eliminate the use of standardized test scores as admissions criteria but may otherwise operate in fairly traditional ways. Because black, Latino, and low-SES (socioeconomic status) students perform more poorly, on average, on standardized admissions tests, the test-optional admissions policies have been promoted as a way to increase campus diversity (Long 2015; Zwick

1999). In the introduction to his recent book on this topic, Joseph Soares of Wake Forest University contends that at his institution, "as for many other colleges, there is an inverse relationship between the weight placed on high-stakes test scores and the diversity of an applicant pool and matriculating class" (Soares 2012, 3).

What are the pros and cons of the percent plans and test-optional admissions policies? Do these programs achieve their intended goals? Are they race-neutral? Are they fair?

The Percent Plans

The first of the class rank plans, the Texas Top 10% Plan, was a direct response to the 1996 *Hopwood* decision, which banned affirmative action admissions in Texas, Louisiana, and Mississippi. Under the Texas plan, as originally implemented, Texas students in the top 10% of their high school class were automatically admitted to any public Texas university they chose. The policy was enacted by the Texas legislature and signed into law by Governor George W. Bush in 1997. Not surprisingly, many eligible high school students chose one of the two flagship universities—Texas A&M and the University of Texas at Austin. UT Austin later obtained an exception to the policy that allowed it to reject some 10 percenters.[2] The original University of California percent plan, initiated in 1999, guaranteed that California students in the top 4% of their high schools would be admitted to UC, though not necessarily to the campus of their choice. The plan, formally called "eligibility in the local context" or ELC, was expanded from 4% to 9% in 2012. Florida's Talented 20 program was adopted in 2000 as part of Governor Jeb Bush's One Florida initiative, described in a press release as "an innovative plan to increase opportunity and diversity while ending racial preferences and set-asides in state contracting and university admissions."[3] Under the Talented 20 plan, students in the top 20% of each of the state's public high schools are guaranteed admission to one of the campuses of the state university system, "within space and fiscal limitations."[4] The Florida plan differs from its Texas and California counterparts in that recruitment, retention, and financial aid programs may still target underrepresented racial groups, even though race cannot be used in the admissions decision itself (Colavecchio 2009; Horn 2012; Marin and Lee 2003). Another difference among the plans is that whereas the California plan was enacted by the university, the Florida and Texas plans were imposed by the state.

Even before the first results were in, the percent plans met with criticism from both the right and the left. Conservatives feared that the plans would admit unqualified students, exclude talented students whose schools were "too good," and ultimately diminish the quality of top-notch state universities. Some in the civil rights community, including the US Civil Rights Commission itself, decried the fact that the plans depend for their success on the existence of racially segregated and underperforming schools. Critics from all sides argued that class rank plans could encourage students to attend inferior high schools and avoid challenging courses. Proponents, however, have continued to promote these plans as a race-neutral route to campus diversity.

Test-Optional Admissions

According to Robert Schaeffer, public education director of the National Center for Fair and Open Testing, better known as FairTest, "educators and policymakers . . . increasingly . . . identify standardized admissions tests as significant barriers to entry for thousands of academically qualified minority, first-generation, and low-income applicants. . . . By turning away from reliance on test scores, . . . institutions are promoting equity and excellence" (Schaeffer 2012, 153). FairTest maintains a list of roughly 850 "colleges and universities that do not use SAT/ACT scores to admit substantial numbers of students into bachelor degree programs." FairTest previously referred to this list as the "test-optional admissions list." The carefully reworded title reflects the fact that some of these institutions merely "deemphasize" tests rather than making them optional.[5]

The policies of the listed institutions vary widely. Two schools, Sarah Lawrence College and Hampshire College, recently enforced a "test-blind" policy—they announced that they would ignore standardized test scores even if students submitted them. However, Sarah Lawrence now has a conventional test-optional policy, meaning that scores will be considered if students wish to provide them (Espenshade and Chung 2012; Hoover 2014).[6] Other schools on the FairTest list require test scores, but not necessarily the ACT or SAT. For example, instead of submitting SAT or ACT scores, applicants to Hamilton College may submit any three exam scores from a menu of options, provided that a quantitative test and a verbal or writing test are among them.[7] The inclusion of certain schools on the FairTest list is a bit of a mystery. In 2014, I picked a school from my home state to examine further: San Jose State University. On the SJSU website, I found the following information for 2014 applicants: "Submit SAT or ACT test scores by Friday, December 20, 2013. . . . Freshman applicants are required to submit . . . scores from a test taken no later than November 2013. No exceptions! Submit your official scores by the deadline. Failure to do so will result in your application being withdrawn. . . . Your admission to SJSU is based on a combination of the grades you earned in the approved courses . . . and your official SAT/ACT scores." Similar information, without the dire warnings, appears on SJSU's site in 2016.[8]

But even if some schools may have landed on the list by mistake, it's clear that at least among liberal arts schools, there has been a slow but steady move to drop admissions test requirements. During the past decade, more than 50 highly selective liberal arts colleges have adopted test-optional policies (Belasco, Rosinger, and Hearn 2015). Here, I examine what is known about the impact of percent plans and test-optional admissions programs, beginning with diversity outcomes.

Diversity Outcomes of Percent Plans and Test-Optional Admissions

We can consider two types of data on the impact of these nominally race-neutral admissions programs on campus diversity: First, simulations that apply admissions rules mimicking these policies to data from actual applicants can offer some insight into the likely results of applying the policies in a systematic way. Second, data from schools that have actually implemented these programs can, of course, be analyzed. As we will see, both simulation data and findings from Texas, California, and Florida show the percent plans to be largely ineffective in increasing ethnic and socioeconomic diversity. In the case of test-optional programs, simulation data show some favorable impact on diversity, while research results from schools that have implemented the programs show mixed results.

PERCENT PLANS

Simulations of the effects of percent plans, based on applicants to elite colleges in the 1990s, were conducted by economists Anthony P. Carnevale and Stephen J. Rose. They concluded that 10% and 20% plans led to a substantial increase in the admission of "qualified" low-SES students in the entering class. (According to the authors' definition, qualified students are those with SAT scores of at least 1000 on a 200-to-1600 scale or equivalent ACT scores.) However, the percent plans had little impact on the percentage of qualified black and Hispanic students. In addition, Carnevale and Rose predicted low graduation rates under these plans. Modified class rank plans that required a minimum SAT score of 1000 (Verbal and Math scores combined) were found to produce lower percentages of black and Hispanic students than had actually enrolled in the schools in question (Carnevale and Rose 2003).

A more recent study by Carnevale, Rose, and Jeff Strohl led to different results. They used data from the Education Longitudinal Study of 2002 (ELS) to simulate

"10 percent models in which the criterion is relative performance in each of the nation's high schools" and concluded that these plans had a favorable impact on diversity. However, their results cannot be compared to the findings of other percent plan research. First, the students selected were those with the best admissions test scores in their high schools, rather than the best grades (Carnevale, Rose, and Strohl 2014). In addition, technical factors complicated the implementation: Because only a small number of students in any one high school participated in the ELS survey (an average of 20 per participating school), it is impossible to use the ELS database to determine if an ELS participant is in the top 10% of his or her senior class. The authors therefore had to use approximations in attempting to make these determinations.[9] Finally, two of the three percent plans they investigated also included socioeconomic or racial preferences.

For their book on admissions, Thomas Espenshade and Alexandra Walton Radford conducted a simulation study of two alternative versions of a top 10 percent plan, using applicant data from several selective public institutions. In one version, only in-state students were eligible for the percent plan; in the other, all applicants were allowed to benefit from the plan. In both cases, 10 percenters were admitted first; then typical admissions criteria (with no affirmative action) were applied to fill the remaining spaces. Both versions led to a reduction in the percentage of black students from 7.8% (the actual percentage of black students admitted to these schools) to 4.4%. The percentage of white students increased by 3.3%, and the percentages of Hispanic and Asian students were unaffected (Espenshade and Radford 2009). The likely reason for this pattern of results is that the actual admissions process included some form of affirmative action that benefited black students; the percent plan was not able to compensate for the elimination of that preference.

What can be learned from the three states that have percent plans in place? In a 2012 review of the impact on diversity of the percent plans in California, Florida, and Texas, researcher Catherine Horn concluded that "although varying in scope and rigor, the majority of findings related to racial/ethnic representation among admitted and enrolled students indicate that such policies did little to enhance diversity" (Horn 2012, 40). Here I consider the research on these three state plans.

Determining the success of percent plans in fostering diversity is not entirely straightforward. Often overlooked is the fact that percent plans constitute only one of several possible pathways to participating institutions and that some students admitted through a percent plan would have been accepted even in its absence.

At the University of California, for example, state residents can become eligible for admission not only through the ELC program, but through a "statewide path," which requires that candidates' admissions index values, based on their test scores and grades, be among the top students statewide, irrespective of which high school they attended.[10] There is likely to be a substantial overlap between this pool of applicants and the ELC pool. In fact, according to UC researchers William Kidder and Patricia Gándara, the 4% plan did not have a "discernible" effect on the diversity of UC's entering classes because most of the eligible students would have been eligible for UC anyway (Kidder and Gándara 2015). In short, simply looking at the ethnic-group composition of UC's entering classes tells us little about the effectiveness of the ELC program. Proper evaluation requires not only separate demographic data for the ELC admits, but information about which of these students would have been admitted through some alternative path—information that is not easily obtained.

A small analysis I conducted years ago illustrates the phenomenon of overlapping admissions paths. Out of 34,000 applicants to UC Santa Barbara in 2001, more than 3,300 were eligible for UC admission under the 4% plan, including more than 700 from underrepresented ethnic groups (American Indians, Alaskan Natives, African Americans, Chicanos, and Latinos). But of these 3,300, all but 77 (including 37 from underrepresented groups) would have been eligible for UC admission even without the 4% plan. Ultimately, none of the 77 were admitted to UCSB (Zwick 2002; 2007). And yet it could have been truthfully claimed that the ELC program yielded more than 3,000 eligible applicants, about 20% of whom were from underrepresented groups.

Beginning with the class entering in 2012, the University of California ELC plan was modified to accept the top 9% of each high school. According to Kidder and Gándara, the students applying through this program in 2012 were slightly less likely to be underrepresented minorities (URMs) than the overall pool of UC applicants. Why would this be the case? The researchers note that "many of the schools from which UC would hope to draw a more diverse pool of students neither prepare nor encourage their students to apply to the university, and most of these students have never known anyone who has attended UC" (Kidder and Gándara 2015, 24). At the flagship campuses, UC Berkeley and UC Los Angeles, the percentage of black students enrolled in 2013 was considerably lower than in 1995 (3.4% versus 5.7% for Berkeley; 3.9% versus 6% for UCLA) and the percentage of Chicano/Latino students was about the same as in 1995 (13% for Berkeley, 17% for UCLA) despite the statewide increase in the Chicano/Latino population.[11]

A 2003 study of Florida's Talented 20 plan by the Harvard Civil Rights Project pronounced the supposed successes of the program to be illusory. The researchers concluded that in 2000 and 2001, the program had influenced enrollment of URMs to only a trivial degree because "the overwhelming majority of students designated as Talented 20" would have been admitted even without the program (Marin and Lee 2003, 22–23). In addition, black and Hispanic students were found to be less likely to have completed the high school credits necessary to qualify for the Talented 20 program.

A later study by researchers from the University of Pennsylvania used data from 1995 through 2005 to examine whether Hispanics were well represented in Florida and Texas public universities relative to their inclusion among the state's high school graduates. These states were selected for study in part because of their implementation of percent plans. If the percentage of Hispanics was found to be the same among the enrolled college students as among the high school graduates, this would constitute "equity" according to the researchers. Not surprisingly, the study found that Hispanics were far above equity among first-time, full-time college enrollments at institutions designated as "Hispanic-serving" in both states, but results were much less favorable at other kinds of schools. At four-year public institutions (considered as a whole), they were somewhat above equity in Florida and somewhat below in Texas. Hispanics were found to be "substantially below equity" at four-year predominantly white institutions and public flagship universities in both Florida and Texas (Perna et al. 2010, 155, 162).

Findings on the impact of the Texas plan have been mixed. In 2010, the percentage of top 10%–eligible students enrolling in the state's elite institutions varied substantially among ethnic groups. Only 44% of eligible Hispanic students and 34% of black students enrolled, compared to 60% of white and 69% of Asian students (Flores and Horn 2015). Although the number of Hispanics in Texas higher education institutions has increased in recent years, their representation has actually decreased as a percentage of the Hispanic population in Texas, which has been growing substantially. At the state's most selective institutions, Texas A&M and UT Austin, Hispanic students constitute a smaller percentage of enrollments than during the affirmative action era (Flores and Horn 2015). This is particularly notable because UT Austin (but not A&M) reinstated racial preferences in admissions following the ruling in *Grutter v. Bollinger* (2003), in which the Supreme Court held that the University of Michigan Law School could continue to consider race in admissions as part of a holistic review of applications. It was UT's racial preferences, employed along with the 10 Percent Plan, that were challenged and ultimately upheld in *Fisher v. University of Texas at Austin* (2013; 2016). That these preferences survived four federal court decisions (two each by the Fifth Circuit Court and the US Supreme Court) could be seen as an acknowledgment by the courts that the 10 Percent Plan is not fully effective in achieving its diversity goals, at least at UT Austin.

Test-Optional Admissions

Does selecting students based on high school grades alone yield an entering class with a higher percentage of URMs and lower-income students than a selection procedure based solely on test scores? Simulation results appear to support this claim by proponents of test-optional admissions. I conducted some studies of ELS data that shed some light on this issue. Using data from roughly 2,200 applicants to 170 highly competitive colleges, I simulated 16 different admissions scenarios. I compared the resulting entering classes to each other and to the students who actually enrolled in the competitive schools in 2004. Because these enrollees constituted 41% of the applicants to the top schools, I used an admission rate of 41% for one set of scenarios. To mimic the admissions process at more selective schools, I also implemented a set of scenarios with a 10% admission rate. My analyses showed that selecting students based on high school grade point average (GPA) alone (with a 41% selection rate) resulted in a class with about 10% URMs (black, Hispanic, and American Indian students), compared to roughly 7% for selection based on admissions test scores alone. Among the actual enrollees, about 12% were URMs. The percentage of students from the bottom half of the socioeconomic distribution was about 19% for the GPA-based selection rule, 12% for the test-score-based rule, and 16% for the actual enrollees. The demographic differences between the class selected via the GPA rule and the one resulting from the test-score rule were even greater when only the top 10% of applicants were chosen. Overall, despite having considerably lower average admissions test scores, the two entering classes selected using GPA only tended to perform better in college than the two classes chosen using test scores only.[12]

In their more elaborate simulation, Thomas Espenshade and Chang Young Chung used as a starting point the prediction models of the admissions process that they had developed based on data from eight elite schools. Prediction was based on multiple factors, including academic characteristics, social class, and participation in extracurricular activities. Separate models were created for private and public colleges. To simulate the effects of a test-optional policy, they modified their models so that low SAT and ACT scores would be treated the same way as middling scores; high scores retained their original value. The goal was to represent a system in which low scores would not be a disadvantage, but high scores would remain advantageous. In addition, Espenshade and Chung increased the importance assigned to high school grades and other factors and attempted to simulate changes in the applicant pool resulting from the initiation of the test-optional policy. Results for private universities showed that under the assumption that black and Hispanic applications would increase by 30%, the percentages of black and Hispanic applicants selected would each increase from about 8% (the actual percentage admitted to these schools) to about 11%. The proportion of whites, and to a lesser degree Asians, would decrease. The socioeconomic distribution would shift somewhat toward lower income groups as well. Projected changes in the entering class were smaller for other types of applicant pools and for the public universities (Espenshade and Chung 2012).

But what have studies of actual test-optional schools shown? One of the first schools to go test-optional was Bates College in Maine, which dropped its SAT requirement in 1984 and eliminated all admissions test requirements in 1990. In 2014, Bates's former admissions director William Hiss and researcher Valerie Franks published a report on the results of test-optional admissions at 33 schools they selected from 120 institutions they originally contacted. The authors did not identify the schools or reveal how they were selected for inclusion, but noted that 20 private colleges and universities, 6 public state universities, 5 minority-serving institutions, and 2 art institutions participated in the study.

The researchers' conclusion about the impact of test-optional policies, in a nutshell: "non-submitters are out-performing their standardized testing" (Hiss and Franks 2014, 2). But what does this mean? Did non-submitters perform better than their test scores would have predicted? The study does not shed any light on that question. The authors did find, however, that for all the schools combined, submitters and non-submitters differed by only .05 points in terms of cumulative college GPA (2.88 versus 2.83) and by only 0.6% in graduation rates (64.5% versus 63.9%).[13] Overall, about 30% of students were non-submitters; these were "more likely [than submitters] to be first-generation-to-college enrollees, . . . minority students, women, Pell Grant recipients, and students with Learning Differences" (Hiss and Franks 2014, 3).[14]

The results of the Hiss and Franks study are not as straightforward as they might seem at first. For one thing, the college GPA findings need to be considered in light of the fact that non-submitters differed from submitters in terms of their chosen fields of study: Non-submitters were much less likely than submitters to major in science, technology, engineering, or math (STEM) fields, a pattern that held for the private, public, and minority-serving institutions. Results are further complicated by substantial differences among the participating schools in their populations and missions and in the specifics of the test-optional programs themselves. Even the definitions of submitters and non-submitters were less than straightforward. Some private schools never saw the test results of non-submitters; in other cases, "non-submitters" were asked to produce test scores to be used for research purposes. All six public universities in the study required all applicants to submit scores, but used percent plans to select a portion of their students. If an applicant's high school class rank qualified him for automatic admission, his test scores were not considered, and he was labeled a non-submitter for purposes of the Hiss and Franks study. However, some of these "non-submitters"—those who had above-average test scores—were excluded from certain analyses so as to avoid artificially boosting the performance data for non-submitters.

Further clouding the picture, the 33 participating schools submitted data from as many as eight entry years, though "institutions normally submitted two graduated class cohorts and two currently enrolled cohorts" (Hiss and Franks 2014, 5). The data were then combined across these varying numbers of entry years, obscuring any possible changes over time. Many of the reported results are combined across institutions as well, but fortunately some disaggregated results are reported. The results tell a subtly different story when they are examined separately by institution. For example, we can see that at 13 of the 15 private schools that provided graduation data, submitters were more likely to graduate than non-submitters, and at 15 of the 18 private schools providing relevant data, submitters had higher final college GPAs. Submitters had higher graduation rates at all five minority institutions participating in the study, though they had higher final GPAs at only two of these. Only a narrative description is given for the two participating art institutions; no formal statistics are included. At the single art institution that provided graduation data, submitters reportedly had a higher graduation rate. Cumulative GPAs are stated to be similar for submitters and non-submitters at one art institution and higher for non-submitters at the other.

It is at the six public institutions, all of which had percent plans, that the authors' claims about the academic advantages of test-optional policies are best supported. Here, "non-submitters" (those whose test scores were not used in admissions decisions) did have higher final GPAs at all six universities and higher graduation rates at the five schools for which results were available. Non-submitters also entered college with substantially better high school GPAs and SAT scores, but the superior outcomes for non-submitters held up even when those with high test scores were removed from the analysis.[15]

The impact of the test-optional policies on campus diversity is another story. Although the authors claimed that "optional testing seems to work as an affirmative action device" (Hiss and Franks 2014, 20, 30), their findings neither support nor contradict the claim that test-optional policies serve to increase minority enrollment: No information is provided as to the demographic composition of the admitted or enrolled students either before or after the implementation of test-optional admissions. The results do indicate that, if the results from all 33 schools are combined, non-submitters were more likely than submitters to be ethnic minorities, but this pattern did not hold true for the public universities, where non-submitters and submitters included identical percentages of URMs (15%); non-submitters also had a trivially higher average family income. At the public institutions, white students were slightly more likely to be non-submitters than Hispanic, black, or Asian students (only American Indians had a higher rate), whereas white students were least likely of all ethnic groups to be non-submitters at private schools.

In a study published after the Hiss and Franks report (but, surprisingly, making no mention of it), Andrew Belasco, Kelly Rosinger, and James Hearn of the University of Georgia examined the effects of test-optional admissions policies between 1992 and 2010.[16] They used data from 180 selective liberal arts colleges, 32 of which had adopted test-optional admissions. The researchers provide a harsh evaluation of these policies, claiming that they "have done little to meet their manifest goals of expanding educational opportunity for low-income and minority students" (Belasco, Rosinger, and Hearn 2015, 218). The proportions of Pell Grant recipients and URMs were found to be lower at test-optional than at test-requiring institutions, and these rates failed to increase following the introduction of test-optional policies. Test-optional schools did, however, receive larger numbers of applications than their test-requiring counterparts (net of other factors), and also reported higher SAT scores, allowing them to "enhance the appearance of selectivity." The gaps between test-optional and test-requiring institutions in terms of reported SAT scores and number of applications was found to increase over time, leading Belasco and his colleagues to argue that test-optional admissions "may serve to reproduce and maintain the current social structure—and its inequalities" (218).

Belasco's findings about institutional SAT scores are not surprising. It has long been observed that test-optional policies are likely to discourage those with low scores from submitting test results, thus raising an institution's average test score and possibly its ranking. Furthermore, if test-optional policies increase the number of applications, as has typically been found, the admission rate will drop, making the school appear more selective (Hoover and Supiano 2008; Yablon 2000; Zwick 2002). However, Belasco's determination that test-optional admissions fails to increase the percentage of URMs is at odds with simulation-based results. What could account for this discrepancy? One important difference is that Belasco and his colleagues studied the demographic makeup of students who actually enrolled in schools that had implemented test-optional admissions, while the simulations described here (mine included) examined only the impact of these selection rules on the makeup of the "admitted" students. It is possible that despite being admitted at higher rates under test-optional policies, students of color are less likely to actually enroll, perhaps for financial reasons. In addition, the Belasco results may be specific to liberal arts schools, which were the focus of the research.

Other Outcomes of Percent Plans and Test-Optional Admissions

Apart from their impact on diversity and college outcomes, what are the demonstrated effects of percent plans and test-optional admissions programs? In particular, how do they affect high school students' academic preparation, college aspirations, and application patterns?

A recent study of a large urban school district in Texas considered the question of whether the Texas 10 Percent Plan encouraged attendance at high-quality postsecondary institutions. The study, which found that the district's students in the top 10% were "more likely to be white and female and less likely to be low income than the typical student" (Daugherty, Martorelli, and McFarlin 2014, 65), focused on a comparison between students who barely exceeded the cutoff for the 10 Percent Plan to those who "just missed." The eligible students were much more likely than the ineligible students to enroll at one of the two Texas flagships, but this effect was concentrated in schools with high college-sending rates. There was little or no effect at the most disadvantaged schools, a finding that mirrors earlier research on the 10 Percent Plan (see Horn 2012). Furthermore, many of those who narrowly missed being in the top 10% enrolled in selective private schools outside Texas, leading the authors to conclude that the "increase in flagship enrollment . . . therefore has no effect on overall college enrollment or on the quality of college attended" (Daugherty, Martorelli, and McFarlin 2014, 64). On the plus side, they found no evidence that top 10% students were attending colleges that were too challenging for them. Being in the top 10% was not associated with dropping out of college or transferring to a less selective school, as some critics had feared.

Researchers have pointed out several other positive effects of percent plans, noting that they may increase student engagement and college aspirations, improve links between high schools and universities, and give high schools an incentive to improve the availability of college preparatory courses (Flores and Horn 2015; Horn 2012). Similarly, test-optional admissions might make the prospect of applying to college less daunting for some potential applicants, particularly students of color and those from lower socioeconomic brackets. Test-optional admissions have been found to increase the number of applications and, at least in some cases, the diversity of the applicant pool (Allman 2012; Belasco, Rosinger, and Hearn 2015; Espenshade and Chung 2012).

Are These Alternative Admissions Policies Fair?

Both percent plans and test-optional admissions have been touted as race-neutral alternatives to affirmative action. If indeed these policies increased the enrollment of underrepresented minorities and low-income students without using racial criteria, they might actually satisfy the fairness requirements of both sides of the political spectrum. Ironically, however, percent plans in particular have been criticized by both left and right: Even as their effectiveness in promoting diversity has been questioned, these policies have been challenged for failing to qualify as "race-neutral." Justice Ruth Bader Ginsburg has said that only an ostrich would describe percent plans in this way (*Fisher v. University of Texas at Austin*, 2013), and, demonstrating that politics does indeed make strange bedfellows, similar doubts have been expressed by Ward Connerly, one of the country's staunchest foes of affirmative action. Commenting on Florida's calculation, following preliminary studies, that 20% of students, not 15% or 10%, should be guaranteed admission under the state's plan, Connerly said, "If you're picking a number because you know that number is going to favor one group or another based on race, that's no different than a system of explicit preferences" (quoted in Selingo 2000).[17]

So what exactly does "race-neutral" mean? The answer is not always obvious. To start with a somewhat preposterous example, suppose a university asks applicants not for their own racial identity, but for their mothers' race. Suppose the university then grants admissions preferences to applicants whose mothers are members of underrepresented racial groups. Because the applicant's own racial status is never requested, can the school claim this is a race-neutral admissions policy? The answer is probably no. But what if the university instead uses information about the racial makeup of the applicant's high school or the community she lives in? Or what if the university tries to infer the applicant's race by combining the characteristics of her high school with her family's education, occupation, and income? How accurate would such an attempt be, and would it be legal in a state where affirmative action is banned? Would it be fair?

The accuracy side of this intriguing question was investigated by researcher Mark C. Long of the University of Washington. Using the ELS data for more than 15,000 tenth-graders, he was able to identify URMs (defined in his research as black, Hispanic, or Native American) with a fairly high degree of accuracy. To do this, he constructed prediction equations based on 195 pieces of data, including information about students' friends, high school, family situation, and test scores. Of the students tagged as URMs, 82% were, in fact, URMs; 18% of URM students were missed.[18] Remarkably, Long could identify URMs almost as well using just four pieces of information—whether each of the student's three best friends were URMs and whether the student was a native Spanish speaker.

Returning to the legal question, if race can be accurately "predicted," can this proxy be used in the admissions process without violating an affirmative action ban? Guidelines authored by experts in education law and published by the College Board note that intent may be relevant. A policy that is "facially race-neutral" may be considered "race-conscious" from a legal perspective if race-neutral criteria are deliberately used as a proxy for race: "If race is a motivation behind a facially race-neutral alternative, then it is *possible* that the alternative is not truly race-neutral" (Coleman, Palmer, and Winnick 2008, 5, 10). Universities attempting a covert form of racial affirmative action, it seems, are faced with a catch-22: If a particular factor—say, socioeconomic status—is a poor proxy for race, an admissions policy based on that factor will not have the desired result. However, if the proxy works too well or the intention is too obvious, the policy may be doomed from a legal point of view and would presumably be viewed as unfair by opponents of affirmative action.

Apart from the legalities, policies that use supposedly race-neutral methods for purposes of boosting racial diversity are violating the transparency principle of fairness: For example, although the percent plans' primary purpose is to promote racial and possibly socioeconomic diversity, they do not use explicit preferences that are comprehensible to applicants. A student who attends a poor black high school will face a less stringent eligibility criterion than a student attending a wealthy white high school, but neither student is likely to know what the applicable GPA cutoff is. More generally, because the GPA an applicant must attain to qualify for a percent plan varies across high schools, changes every year, and depends on the performance of other students, it is nearly impossible for a candidate to know how high his grades will need to be in order to make the cut.

Test-optional admissions programs present somewhat different transparency issues. Enrollment management experts Don Hossler and David Kalsbeek (2009) argue that "doing away with standardized tests may actually make the admissions system less transparent and fair and could negatively affect equality of access" (9). They predict that selective colleges that eliminate admissions test requirements will develop ever more sophisticated ways of evaluating the rigor of applicants' high schools. This method of calibrating the strength of applications would be entirely opaque to candidates.[19]

A separate transparency issue arising from test-optional policies is that applicants typically lack the information they need to decide whether it is to their advantage to submit their test scores. The schools' admissions websites provide little guidance. Bryn Mawr, a newcomer to test-optional admissions, says simply that "SAT I or ACT scores are optional for US citizens and US permanent residents." Wake Forest gives the following advice to candidates: "If you feel that your SAT or ACT with writing scores are a good indicator of your abilities, you may submit them and they will be considered in your admissions decision. If, however, you do not feel that your scores accurately represent your academic abilities, you do not need to submit them until after you have been accepted and choose to enroll." But how are applicants to know whether or not it's advantageous to submit their scores? It may be an easy decision for those with very high or very low scores, but it is likely to pose a challenge for the majority of applicants. From this perspective, the test-blind policy adopted by Hampshire College is a fairer one. Making the familiar claim that the SAT and ACT "more accurately reflect family economic status than potential for college success," the college stated in 2014 that it would "no longer consider SAT or ACT scores in any way as part of admissions and financial aid decisions."[20] This rule, at least provides a clear instruction to candidates.

In reality, however, test scores are not unique in their association with socioeconomic status or ethnicity. In explaining their finding that test-optional admissions policies did not improve diversity, Belasco and colleagues noted that academically rigorous high school programs, AP and honors courses, and extracurricular activities are more easily accessible in wealthier schools and that relying more heavily on these factors rather than on test scores may actually "perpetuate stratification within the postsecondary sector" (Belasco, Rosinger, and Hearn 2015, 218). I reported on some related findings in 1999, during a wave of strong opposition to the SAT at the University of California. According to popular wisdom, the SAT was responsible for excluding low-income and minority students from UC, but data analyses conducted by the California Postsecondary Education Commission and the UC Office of the President showed that the primary reason for ineligibility for UC admission was failure to complete the required high school coursework. Only 2.5% of California public high school students were ruled out solely because of inadequate test scores. Eliminating the SAT was expected to produce an increase of two percentage points in the eligibility rate for whites, from roughly 13% to 15%, and very little change for other ethnic groups (Zwick 1999).

One possible outcome of deemphasizing tests in the admissions process is that the value and meaning of high school grades may change. If tests play a role in "keeping grades honest," as some educators believe, their elimination may exacerbate grade inflation and decrease the usefulness of grades as predictors of college achievement. Under the percent plans, teachers can alter a borderline student's eligibility for college by boosting a single grade, which may contribute to an upward drift. In a recent opinion piece, Calvin Wolf, a high school teacher, made the further argument that eliminating admissions tests would lead to increased gaming of high school grades and would ultimately benefit the rich. As he put it, "wealthier parents have the time and money to spend all day 'networking' for their kids' GPA advantage. . . . The GPAs of rich kids applying to test-optional colleges and universities will inflate, but the GPAs of poor and minority kids . . . will not" (Wolf 2014).

In short, the socioeconomic disadvantages that depress test scores also affect other aspects of academic performance. This includes not only grades, but completion of required college preparatory courses, participation in extracurricular activities, and other résumé-enhancing pursuits. In addition, the achievements of Asian American and white students in these areas tend to exceed those of black, Latino, and Native American students. These patterns of academic accomplishment limit the degree to which percent plans or test-optional admissions programs can increase the admission rates of students from underrepresented groups or lower socioeconomic brackets. With regard to their potential role in increasing the enrollment of students of color, these programs are both less effective and less honest than racial preferences. They are a prime example of the attempts that educational institutions must now make to boost diversity while staying within the boundaries on the use of race in admissions that were established by the Supreme Court decisions in the *Grutter* (2003) and *Fisher* (2013, 2016) cases.

Perhaps the greatest contribution of percent plans and test-optional admissions is their apparent role in encouraging high school students who might be intimidated by test-score requirements to apply to college. Encouraging these less confident and often less prepared applicants to actually enroll and helping them to succeed may require much more.

NOTES

1. The opinions I have expressed in this chapter are my own and not necessarily those of Educational Testing Service. This chapter appeared in essentially the same form in *Who Gets In? Strategies for Fair and Effective College Admissions* (Cambridge, MA: Harvard University Press, 2017).

2. UT Austin was concerned that the automatic admission of a large number of 10 percenters left the university few additional seats to allocate. In 2009, the Texas legislature passed a law allowing UT Austin to reduce the number of 10 percenters it admits to 75% of its "available Texas resident spaces." For students applying in 2014, for example, this requirement implied that applicants needed to be in the top 7% of their high schools to be automatically admitted to UT Austin. See http://bealonghorn.utexas.edu/freshmen /decisions/automatic-admission.

3. See http://www.adversity.net/florida/jeb_bush_ends_quotas.htm#press_release.

4. See www.fldoe.org/Talented20.

5. A list dated 2009 is at http://www.fairtest.org/testoptional-admissions-list-tops-815; a list dated 2016 is at http://www.fairtest.org/university/optional.

6. See also https://www.hampshire.edu/admissions/faq-for-prospective-students and https://www.sarahlawrence.edu/admission/apply/first-year.html.

7. See https://www.hamilton.edu/admission/apply/requirements.

8. See http://info.sjsu.edu/web-dbgen/narr/admission/rec-7327.10786.10787.html; http://info.sjsu.edu/web-dbgen/narr/static/admission/freshman-req.html.

9. The ELS (base year) sample consists of 15,362 students from 752 high schools, an average of 20.4 ELS participants per participating high school. See Ingels et al. 2007, 50. According to e-mail messages from Jeff Strohl (June 20, 21, 22, and 27, 2016), the authors used the following procedure to label students as being in the top 10% of their high school classes: First, the authors discarded the data from high schools with very few ELS participants. Within each remaining school, they determined each ELS participant's rank *among the ELS participants at that school* and identified those whose admissions test scores were in the top 10%. Strohl noted that because high schools with too few students were excluded, this procedure resulted in a sample that was "not representative at the school level" (e-mail dated June 22, 2016). Overall, it is impossible to know whether this ranking method produced results similar to those that would have been obtained if data for the entire senior class in each school had been available.

10. See http://admission.universityofcalifornia.edu/freshman/california-residents /index.html.

11. See http://legacy-its.ucop.edu/uwnews/stat/statsum/fall2013/statsumm2013.pdf, http://legacy-its.ucop.edu/uwnews/stat/enrollment/enr1995/95sst7d.html.

12. The various entering classes attended different sets of colleges and differed somewhat in their choice of major as well. For further details, see chapter 2 in Zwick, *Who Gets In?*

13. No distinction was made among four-, five-, and six-year graduation rates.

14. Pell Grants are need-based grants provided by the federal government to low-income students.

15. The analysis in which those with high test scores were removed was for all six public universities combined; results of this analysis were not reported separately by institution; see Hiss and Franks 2014, 37.

16. Belasco is also the CEO of a college consulting firm, College Transitions LLC. A reprint of the article appears in this volume as chapter 10.

17. Florida's Talented 20 policy is clearly not race-neutral in any case because it permits race-conscious financial aid, recruiting, and retention programs.

18. Predictions made via probit regression were used to identify the N students most likely to be URMs, where N was equal to the actual number of URMs (Long 2015, 3–4). It follows that the percentage of URMs that were missed is equal to 100 minus the percentage of those tagged who were, in fact, URMs. Results were less impressive for two other data sets studied by Long.

19. These kinds of adjustments already take place at some colleges, at least informally. For an example of explicit adjustment of prior GPAs for law school applicants, see University of California Office of the Vice President 2008, 14.

20. See https://www.brynmawr.edu/admissions/first-year-students/standardized -testing-policy; http://admissions.wfu.edu/apply/sat.php; and https://www.hampshire.edu /news/2014/06/18/no-to-satsacts-not-even-optional-at-hampshire-college. The term "SAT I" in the Bryn Mawr quotation is an old name for the SAT.

REFERENCES

Allman, M. (2012). Going test-optional: A first year of challenges, surprises, and rewards. In J. A. Soares (Ed.), *SAT wars: The case for test-optional admissions* (pp. 169–176). New York: Teachers College Press.

Belasco, A. S., Rosinger, K. O., and Hearn, J. C. (2015). The test-optional movement at America's selective liberal arts colleges: A boon for equity or something else? *Educational Evaluation and Policy Analysis, 37*(2), 206–223.

Carnevale, A. P., and Rose, S. J. (2003). *Socioeconomic status, race/ethnicity, and selective college admissions.* New York: Century Foundation.

Carnevale, A. P., Rose, S. J., and Strohl, J. (2014). Achieving racial and economic diversity with race-blind admissions policy. In R. Kahlenberg (Ed.), *The future of affirmative action: New paths to higher education diversity after Fisher v. University of Texas* (pp. 187–202). Washington, DC: Century Foundation.

Colavecchio, S. (2009). A decade of Gov. Jeb Bush's One Florida has seen minority college enrollment rise. *Tampa Bay Times,* December 13. Retrieved from http://www

.tampabay.com/news/politics/legislature/a-decade-of-gov-jeb-bushs-one-florida-has
-seen-minority-college-enrollment/1058572.

Coleman, A. L., Palmer, S. R., and Winnick, S. Y. (2008). *Race-neutral policies in higher education: From theory to action.* New York: The College Board. Retrieved from http://diversitycollaborative.collegeboard.org/sites/default/files/document-library /race-neutral_policies_in_higher_education.pdf.

Daugherty, L., Martorelli, P., and McFarlin, I. (2014). The Texas ten percent plan's impact on college enrollment. *Education Next* (Summer), 63–69.

Espenshade, T. J., and Chung, C. Y. (2012). Diversity outcomes of test-optional policies. In J. A. Soares (Ed.), *SAT wars: The case for test-optional admissions* (pp. 177–200). New York: Teachers College Press.

Espenshade, T. J., and Radford, A. W. (2009). *No longer separate, not yet equal.* Princeton, NJ: Princeton University Press.

Fisher v. University of Texas at Austin. (2013). 570 U.S., Docket No. 11-345.

Fisher v. University of Texas at Austin. (2016). 579 U.S., Docket No. 14-981.

Flores, S. M., and Horn, C. L. (2015). *Texas top ten percent plan: How it works, what are its limits, and recommendations to consider.* Educational Testing Service issue brief. Retrieved from http://www.ets.org/Media/Research/pdf/flores_white_paper.pdf.

Grutter v. Bollinger. (2003). 539 U.S. 306., U.S. Docket No. 02-241.

Hiss, W. C., and Franks, V. W. (2014). *Defining promise: Optional standardized testing polices in American college and university admissions.* National Association of College Admission Counseling. Retrieved from http://www.nacacnet.org/research /research-data/nacac-research/Documents/DefiningPromise.pdf.

Hoover, E. (2014). Hampshire College will go "test blind." *Chronicle of Higher Education,* June 18. Retrieved from http://chronicle.com/blogs/headcount/hampshire-college -will-go-test-blind/38563.

Hoover, E., and Supiano, B. (2008). Wake Forest U. joins the ranks of test-optional colleges. *Chronicle of Higher Education,* May 27. Retrieved from http://chronicle .com/article/Wake-Forest-U-Joins-the-Ranks/834.

Horn, C. (2012). Percent plan admissions: Their strengths and challenges in furthering an equity agenda. *Pensamiento Educativo: Revista de Investigación Educacional Latinoamericana, 49*(2), 31–45.

Hossler, D., and Kalsbeek, D. (2009). Admissions testing and institutional admissions processes. *College and University, 84*(4), 2–11.

Ingels, S. J., Pratt, D. J., Wilson, D., Burns, L. J., Currivan, D., Rogers, J. E., and Hubbard-Bednasz, S. (2007). *Education Longitudinal Study of 2002: Base-Year to Second Follow-up Data File Documentation* (NCES 2008-347). Washington, DC: National Center for Education Statistics.

Kidder, W. C., and Gándara, P. (2015). *Two decades after the affirmative action ban: Evaluating the University of California's race-neutral efforts.* Educational Testing Service issue brief. Retrieved from http://www.ets.org/Media/Research/pdf/kidder _paper.pdf.

Long, M. C. (2015). *The promise and peril for universities using correlates of race in admissions in response to the Grutter and Fisher decisions.* Educational Testing Service issue brief. Retrieved from http://www.ets.org/Media/Research/pdf/long_white_paper.pdf.

Marin, P., and Lee, E. K. (2003). *Appearance and reality in the sunshine state: The Talented 20 program in Florida.* Cambridge, MA: Civil Rights Project at Harvard University.

Perna, L., Li, C., Walsh, E., and Raible, S. (2010). The status of equity for Hispanics in public higher education in Florida and Texas. *Journal of Hispanic Higher Education, 9*(2), 145–166.

Schaeffer, R. (2012). Test scores do not equal merit. In J. A. Soares (Ed.), *SAT wars: The case for test-optional admissions* (pp. 153–168). New York: Teachers College Press.

Schmitt, C. M. (2009). *Documentation for the restricted-use NCES-Barron's admissions competeness index data files.* NCES 2010-330. Washington, DC: National Center for Education Statistics.

Selingo, J. (2000). What states aren't saying about the "x-percent solution." *Chronicle of Higher Education,* June 2. Retrieved from http://chronicle.com/article/What-States-Arent-Saying/33201.

Soares, J. A. (2012). Introduction. In J. A. Soares (Ed.), *SAT wars: The case for test-optional admissions* (pp. 1–9). New York: Teachers College Press.

University of California Office of the Vice President–Student Affairs and Office of the General Counsel (2008). *Race, sex and disparate impact: Legal and policy considerations regarding University of California admissions and scholarships.* Briefing report for the Committee on Educational Policy. Retrieved from http://regents.universityof california.edu/regmeet/may08/e2attach.pdf.

Wolf, C. (2014). Op-ed: Rise of test-optional college admissions will backfire. *Digital Journal,* July 25. Retrieved from http://www.digitaljournal.com/news/politics/op-ed-rise-of-test-optional-college-admissions-will-backfire/article/392519.

Yablon, M. (2000). Test flight: The real reason colleges are abandoning the SAT. *New Republic,* October 30, 24–25.

Zwick, R. (1999). Eliminating standardized tests in college admissions: The new affirmative action? *Phi Delta Kappan,* (December), 320–324.

———. (2002). *Fair game? The use of standardized admissions tests in higher education.* New York: RoutledgeFalmer.

———. (2007). College admissions in twenty-first-century America: The role of grades, tests, and games of chance. *Harvard Educational Review, 77*(4), 419–428.

———. (2017). *Who gets in? Strategies for fair and effective college admissions.* Cambridge, MA: Harvard University Press.

10

The Test-Optional Movement at America's Selective Liberal Arts Colleges

A Boon for Equity or Something Else?

Andrew S. Belasco, Kelly O. Rosinger, and James C. Hearn

*T*est-optional supporters often claim that dropping SAT or ACT admissions testing requirements will increase the number of underrepresented minority and low-income students on campus. While much of the prior research on test-optional admissions is based on case studies that are of limited scope and generalizability, this chapter moves beyond those limitations to use time-series, cross-sectional (i.e., panel) data from 180 selective liberal arts colleges in the United States across nearly two decades (1992 to 2010). This chapter also lends an important contribution to the debate about standardized admissions tests through its sophisticated use of a difference-in-differences (DiD) approach, a statistical technique that attempts to replicate an experimental research design.

Belasco, Rosinger, and Hearn deftly examine whether test-optional admissions policies have increased low-income and minority student enrollment, and whether these policies have led to greater numbers of applications and higher test scores. To conceptualize their research, the authors draw on Robert Merton's manifest and latent functions of social action to examine the intended (manifest) and unintended (latent) functions of social policies, and how these functions serve to maintain and reinforce the current social structure and its existing inequalities.

Belasco and his colleagues find that on average, test-optional policies enhance the perceived selectivity, rather than the diversity, of participating institutions. They note that the adoption of test-optional admissions policies is not an adequate solution to *providing educational opportunity for low-income and minority students. Moreover, test-optional admission policies may, in fact, perpetuate stratification within the postsecondary sector by assigning greater importance to credentials that are more accessible to advantaged populations because test-optional colleges rely more heavily on school-specific measures, such as strength of curriculum or involvement outside the classroom, to draw comparisons between prospective students.*

The authors suggest that test-optional institutions should reexamine their recruitment strategies because many of these institutions largely ignore geographically remote areas and low-income schools in favor of more cost-effective or "fruitful" locales. Institutions that do not reach underrepresented students, through recruitment or other outreach initiatives, will face difficulty improving diversity in meaningful and significant ways on their campuses, regardless of their admissions policies.

When the first Scholastic Aptitude Test (SAT) was administered in 1926 (Gambino 2013), advocates promoted the test as a measure of intellect and a mechanism of educational and social opportunity. At a time when access to higher education was largely determined by status, the SAT aimed to distinguish academic aptitude from "accidents" of birth and fortune and to identify talented students who would otherwise have gone unnoticed (Lemann 1999). With the arrival of the SAT, a new meritocratic system emerged, one that promised to sort students into college on the basis of academic potential rather than social status (Jencks and Riesman 1968; Karabel 1984; Katz 1978). Over the next 30 years, use of the SAT at US colleges and universities increased dramatically, and by the late 1950s, the test was being administered to more than half a million high school students annually. In 2012, the number of students taking the SAT and/or American College Testing (ACT) exceeded 1.6 million, with many students taking both exams and taking the SAT and/or ACT more than once to increase scores (Lewin 2013). Currently, most four-year colleges and universities use standardized test scores as one factor in making admissions decisions.

Given their role in the college admissions process, standardized tests have been the subject of extensive research, and many studies have attempted to measure the predictive validity of these increasingly influential exams. Some research suggests that the SAT, coupled with high school grade point average (GPA), provides a better prediction of a student's future academic performance than high school GPA alone (Sackett et al. 2012; Shaw et al. 2012). However, other studies have challenged the SAT as a reliable predictor of future college success (Crouse and Trusheim 1988; Geiser and Studley 2002; Rothstein 2004) and have highlighted the persistent and positive relationship between standardized test performance and socioeconomic background as well as disparities in performance by race (Blau, Moller, and Jones 2004; Camara and Schmidt 1999; Fischer et al. 1996; Freedle 2003). This latter body of research has prompted some colleges to question whether reliance on standardized testing has reinforced the exact college-related barriers that initial proponents of the SAT intended to eradicate (Epstein 2009).

Consequently, support for the SAT, ACT, and similar standardized tests has waned at a small but growing number of institutions, and a "test-optional movement" has emerged, particularly among liberal arts colleges, many of which have sought to eliminate or de-emphasize the use of standardized tests in the admissions process. Today, more than 50 selective liberal arts colleges have adopted test-optional admissions policies, along with approximately 800 other institutions across the United States (FairTest 2013).

Despite public claims that test-optional policies have improved socioeconomic and racial diversity, some have questioned the motives of test-optional colleges and believe that test-optional admissions policies constitute yet another strategy to raise an institution's rank and admissions profile (Diver 2006; Ehrenberg 2002; Hoover 2010). In this article, we explore both the generally stated goals of test-optional policies—expanding college opportunity and diversity—and the criticism that these policies are implemented merely to promote greater institutional standing. More specifically, we employ a difference-in-differences (DiD) analytical approach to examine whether test-optional admissions policies have achieved a commonly stated objective of increasing low-income and minority student enrollment, and also whether such policies have led to increased institutional status in the form of greater application numbers and higher reported test scores. To that end, our study addresses four research questions:

Research Question 1: Do colleges enroll significantly more (or fewer) low-income students (measured by Pell Grant recipient enrollment) after adopting test-optional admissions policies?

Research Question 2: Do colleges enroll significantly more (or fewer) underrepresented minorities after adopting test-optional admissions policies?

Research Question 3: Do colleges experience a significant rise (or decline) in freshman-year applications after adopting test-optional admissions policies?

Research Question 4: Do colleges report significantly higher (or lower) average test scores after adopting test-optional admissions policies?

Literature Review

Although standardized tests assume a conspicuous role in the current college landscape, they were not widely used by postsecondary institutions until the mid-twentieth century, when the GI Bill of 1944 and subsequent growth in the 18- to 24-year-old population prompted an unprecedented rise in the demand for post-secondary education. Between 1950 and 1970—commonly referred to as the era of "college massification"—enrollment in US higher education grew nearly five-fold (Gumport et al. 1997). As college applications surged across the United States, selective colleges, in particular, were compelled to adopt new screening methods to sort through larger, more competitive, and increasingly heterogeneous applicant pools (Alon and Tienda 2007; Lemann 1999; Posselt et al. 2012); and many such institutions began to rely on standardized testing as one admissions screening mechanism.

Although the SAT and ACT originally were designed to promote college access—specifically, by identifying academically talented students, regardless of background—there has been much debate surrounding the predictive validity of these exams. Previous research has revealed a positive correlation between SAT scores and postsecondary GPA, and has also indicated that standardized test scores, in conjunction with high school GPA, serve as a better predictor of first-year academic performance than high school GPA alone (Kobrin et al. 2008; Sackett et al. 2012). However, other research contends that standardized tests have become proxies for privilege and have perpetuated class and race divisions within postsecondary education (see, e.g., Grodsky, Warren, and Felts 2008 for review of educational testing and social stratification). Several studies have cited a strong positive correlation between standardized test achievement and socioeconomic status (SES) (Blau, Moller, and Jones 2004; Camara and Schmidt 1999; Fischer et al. 1996; Freedle 2003; Rothstein 2004), and also between standardized test achievement and white racial status (Camara and Schmidt 1999; Rothstein 2004); while other research has suggested that standardized test scores lose much of their ability to predict postsecondary success (i.e., first-year GPA) when student SES (Geiser and Studley 2002) and high school racial and socioeconomic diversity (Rothstein 2004) are considered. These findings may be attributed, at least in part, to the fact that socioeconomically advantaged students are more likely to purchase test preparation materials, enroll in test preparation classes, hire a tutor, and engage in other activities that are likely to boost test scores (Buchmann, Condron, and Roscigno 2010; Park 2012). Finally, other critiques suggest that test scores—when compared with other measures of academic achievement, such as high school GPA or class rank—are insufficient gauges of motivation, inquisitiveness, and other qualities that contribute to learning and success (Atkinson and Geiser 2009; Hoffman and Lowitzki 2005).

Despite extensive research challenging the predictive validity of standardized tests, there are several recent studies indicating that the SAT and ACT continue to predict academic performance, even when background is considered (e.g., Bettinger, Evans, and Pope 2011; Sackett et al. 2009; Sackett et al. 2012). For example, Sackett and colleagues (2012) found in an analysis of three large-scale data sets that the association between SAT scores and first-year academic performance decreases only slightly when socioeconomic background is considered, suggesting that the SAT remains a useful predictor of future academic achievement. In addition, Bettinger et al. (2011) discovered that ACT subscores in English and mathematics are highly predictive of first-year and second-year college GPA, even after controlling for race, gender, and (college) campus fixed effects.

While education researchers debate the merits of standardized testing, the overwhelming majority of selective colleges and universities continue to hold firm to their standardized testing requirements and use standardized test scores, among other academic and extracurricular factors, in making admissions decisions. In fact, many selective institutions have become more reliant on standardized testing in recent decades. Alon and Tienda (2007), for example, used data from two nationally representative studies to discover that, on average, America's most selective schools ascribe more weight to test scores than grades when evaluating applicants. Alon and Tienda attribute increased dependence on test scores to the perceived need for a standardized metric that is able (or that claims to be able) to identify the "aristocracy of talent" among an ever-growing pool of qualified applicants; however, they and others (Ehrenberg 2002; Epstein 2009) also attribute increased reliance to the rising prominence of college rankings systems, such as those released by *U.S. News & World Report*. Although contributing a relatively small percentage to the magazine's ranking formula (7.5% to 8.125% in recent years), average institutional SAT/ACT score is the largest predictor of *U.S. News* rank (Webster 2001), and its influence may be subsumed within other measures that *U.S. News* uses to determine an institution's rank score, such as academic reputation (as reported by college administrators and high school counselors).

Indeed, enrollment managers and admissions officers face increasing pressure to enroll classes with stronger academic credentials each year. These institutional pressures have resulted in several recent cases of institutional test scores being misrepresented or deliberately manipulated for institutional purposes (e.g., Fuller 2012; Hoover 2012a; Supiano 2012). Consequently, given their influence and the "elasticity of admissions data" (Hoover 2012b), standardized test scores have been assigned considerable, and perhaps undue, emphasis in the admissions process, especially by institutions seeking to improve their standing in the rankings hierarchy.

While selective colleges, in general, have exhibited a stronger commitment to standardized testing over time, there is a growing minority of competitive institutions, primarily within the liberal arts sector, that has decided to de-emphasize or eliminate the use of standardized test scores in the admissions process. Interestingly, the test-optional "movement" among liberal arts colleges began in earnest after the speech of a university president, University of California's (UC) Richard Atkinson, who declared to the American Council on Education that overreliance on the SAT was "distorting educational priorities and practices" (Atkinson 2001). Although UC never implemented Atkinson's recommendation that the university system abandon its SAT I admission requirement, Atkinson's speech prompted the College Board to redesign the SAT, which featured a new writing section and de-emphasized assessing student aptitude in favor of testing student preparation (Epstein 2009). The speech also prompted scores of selective liberal arts colleges to abandon or de-emphasize standardized testing requirements in their admission processes (Epstein 2009). Over the past decade, and despite the release of a revised SAT, more than 50 liberal arts colleges identified by Barron's *Profile of American Colleges* as "very competitive," "highly competitive," or "most competitive" have adopted test-optional policies that allow applicants to choose, without penalty, whether or not to submit their SAT or ACT scores.

In addition to expressing concerns about the biases and validity of standardized assessments, test-optional colleges commonly report that test-optional policies enhance the ethnic and economic diversity of their respective campuses without compromising the academic quality or performance of their student bodies (Bates College 2004; Jaschik 2006; McDermott 2008). Espenshade and Chung's (2011) simulation study supports such claims, suggesting that test-optional policies would lead to an increase in the percentage of black, Hispanic, and low-SES students at adopting institutions; however, it relied on predicted probabilities of admission to make assertions about *yield*, even though acceptance does not necessarily result in enrollment, especially in the case of underrepresented populations (Smith, Pender, and Howell 2013).

To date, few studies have assessed the relationship between test-optional policies and campus diversity. Moreover, we know little about whether the implementation of test-optional policies leads to benefits that are less altruistic and more institution-specific. Several higher education leaders and reports have argued that colleges adopt test-optional policies to increase institutional status and selectivity (Ehrenberg 2002; Epstein 2009; Yablon 2001), specifically through higher application numbers and reported standardized test scores. Case studies examining individual institutions' test-optional policies provide some evidence that the adoption of these policies results in increased applications from students who might otherwise not have applied (e.g., Bates and Providence colleges; Epstein 2009). One such study of Mount Holyoke College revealed that students "underperforming" on the SAT were more likely to withhold their results from the test-optional college (Robinson and Monks 2005), leading to higher institution-reported SAT scores. However, there have been no broad studies (i.e., studies focusing on multiple colleges) examining the effects of test-optional adoption. Thus, we know little about how the test-optional movement as a whole has influenced the admissions and enrollment profiles of participating colleges.

Conceptual Framework

To conceptualize how test-optional policies might influence admissions and enrollment at liberal arts colleges, we consider the overt and less overt intentions of test-optional adoption. To do so, we draw on Merton's influential understanding of the manifest and latent functions of social action (e.g., Merton 1957). Merton's approach allows us to examine the intended (manifest) and unintended (latent) functions of social policies, and how these functions serve to maintain and reinforce the current social structure and its existing inequalities (Merton 1936, 1957).

Manifest functions refer to the intended and recognized purposes of test-optional policies. These manifest functions are institutions' commonly stated goals for adopting policies that de-emphasize or eliminate the use of test scores. Institutions that have adopted test-optional policies often cite efforts to improve diversity and to "level the playing field" for groups of students who, on average, tend to be disadvantaged by higher education's reliance on standardized testing (Cortes 2103; Epstein 2009; Espenshade and Chung 2011). By encouraging a more holistic review of applicants, test-optional admissions policies are intended to reduce the inequalities in college access that standardized test scores arguably promote. Analyzing the manifest functions of test-optional policies thus allows us to determine whether these policies have achieved a commonly stated goal of increasing postsecondary opportunity through enhancing campus economic and ethnic diversity—at liberal arts colleges specifically.

Although previous research often focuses on the recognized outcomes of test-optional policies, we extend our understanding of these policies by considering the unintended or unrecognized outcomes, or latent functions, that test-optional policies fulfill. As Merton (1957) suggested, the analysis of latent functions provides a particularly interesting area of sociological inquiry by considering how less overt outcomes enable institutions to maintain their current social position. Although test-optional admissions policies largely are hailed as efforts to expand access at selective institutions, it is also possible they serve a less noted purpose of increasing institutional status and perceived selectivity.

In a 2006 op-ed piece in the *New York Times*, former president of Reed College, Colin Diver, called attention to possible ulterior motives behind test-optional adoption. He suggested that under test-optional policies, low-scoring students would choose not to submit their test scores, and as a consequence, test-optional colleges would increase their average institutional test scores and standing in the *U.S. News* rankings. Diver and others (e.g., Ehrenberg 2002) also argued that institutions adopting policies that de-emphasize the use of standardized test scores encourage more applications from students who may otherwise have not applied on the basis of a test requirement or average test score.

Finally, and as Diver (2006) and Epstein (2009) noted, institutions may be aware of the implications that test-optional policies have for both enrollment and status. It is possible that college administrators may consciously adopt these policies with an eye toward increasing diversity *and* appearing more selective. If so, what may seem latent to others may actually be a manifest function and motivating factor that shapes the admissions policies administrators choose to adopt. That is, test-optional admissions policies may constitute a "double play" strategy (Bourdieu 1996, 271) that institutions use to promote social aims and subtly influence institutional standing. If this assessment proves accurate, test-optional policies may ultimately reaffirm the position of selective institutions, and their role in maintaining and reproducing stratification within higher education and society more broadly (Bourdieu 1993; Bourdieu and Wacquant 1992).

Hence, in this analysis, we examine the possibility that although test-optional policies overtly seek to expand educational opportunity, they may also result in better institutional position through increased numbers of applications and higher reported SAT/ACT scores for use in institutional rankings. Thus, in Merton's account, even if test-optional policies fail to achieve their manifest functions, institutions may still adopt or continue these policies because they fulfill a desirable latent function of increasing institutional standing.

Data and Sample

To assess how test-optional policies shape diversity and admissions profiles at liberal arts colleges, we collected time-series, cross-sectional (i.e., panel) data on 180 selective liberal arts colleges in the United States. Our panel spans nearly two decades, from 1992 to 2010, and includes annual institution-level data on several outcomes of interest, namely, the percentage of students receiving a Pell Grant (any dollar amount), the percentage of students identifying as an underrepresented minority (African American, Hispanic, or Native American), the number of freshman applications submitted to an institution, and an institution's average reported SAT score (twenty-fifth percentile, Critical Reading, and Math combined). Our primary independent variable is dichotomous and indicates whether colleges in the sample possess a test-optional admissions policy during a given year. We assign test-optional status only to those colleges that have made the submission of *all* test scores optional for *all* students, *and* that do not penalize applicants who wish to withhold their test scores. For example, several liberal arts colleges have adopted test-flexible admissions policies—that do not require SAT scores, but that still require applicant scores from one or several other standardized tests (e.g., ACT, Advanced Placement [AP], or SAT subject tests)—and/or have made the submission of test scores optional for only a small subset of high-achieving students. These colleges cannot be considered test-optional in a definitional sense and are designated as "test-requiring" for the purposes of this study.

In addition to our dependent and primary independent variables, we also include controls for several time-variant variables that are likely to influence the diversity and admission profile of a liberal arts college, specifically full-time enrollment (FTE), annual tuition and fees, institutional grant award per FTE, education and related expenditures per FTE, admission rate, and a dichotomous variable indicating whether an institution adopted a no-loan financial aid policy in a given year. Financial measures are adjusted for inflation using the consumer price index to reflect 2010 dollars and are logged to ease interpretation and provide a more normal distribution to the data.

Table 10.1.   Sample liberal arts colleges adopting test-optional policies

College (city, state)	Year of adoption
Wheaton College (Wheaton, MA)	1993
Dickinson College (Carlisle, PA)	1995
Hartwick College (Oneonta, NY)	1996
Muhlenberg College (Allentown, PA)	1997
Mount Holyoke College (South Hadley, MA)	2002
Pitzer College (Claremont, CA)	2004
Sarah Lawrence College (Bronxville, NY)	2005
Chatham University (Pittsburgh, PA)	2006
College of the Holy Cross (Worcester, MA)	2006
Knox College (Galesburg, IL)	2006
Lawrence University (Appleton, WI)	2006
St. Lawrence University (Canton, NY)	2006
Susquehanna University (Selinsgrove, PA)	2006
Bennington College (Bennington, VT)	2007
Drew University (Madison, NJ)	2007
Eckerd College (St. Petersburg, FL)	2007
Franklin & Marshall College (Lancaster, PA)	2007
Gettysburg College (Gettysburg, PA)	2007
Guilford College (Greensboro, NC)	2007
Gustavus Adolphus College (St. Peter, MN)	2007
Hobart and William Smith Colleges (Geneva, NY)	2007
Juniata College (Huntingdon, PA)	2007
Lake Forest College (Lake Forest, IL)	2007
Lycoming College (Williamsport, PA)	2007
Union College (Schenectady, NY)	2007
Augustana College (Rock Island, IL)	2008
Denison University (Granville, OH)	2008
Wittenberg University (Springfield, OH)	2008
Albright College (Reading, PA)	2009
Goucher College (Towson, MD)	2009
Marlboro College (Marlboro, VT)	2009
Smith College (Northampton, MA)	2009

Data incorporated into the panel come from multiple postsecondary data sources, including the US Department of Education, the Integrated Postsecondary Education Data System (IPEDS), the Delta Cost Project, and the College Board's (2011) *Annual Survey of Colleges*. The data encompass years before and after test-optional "treatment," thereby providing a suitable data space within which to employ DiD modeling.

A quasi-experimental technique, DiD, employs a fixed-effects strategy to isolate group- or aggregate-level changes resulting from a particular intervention or policy. Specifically, DiD exploits time-induced variation to control for potential observed and unobserved differences that exist across treated and control groups and that may obscure effects that are attributed to the treatment itself (Gelman and Hill 2006). In this study, DiD allows us to assess whether test-optional colleges experienced significant changes in the above-mentioned outcomes after adoption of their respective policies, controlling for potentially confounding time trends and preexisting differences between test-optional and test-requiring institutions.

To reduce bias and meet identifying assumptions of the DiD model (discussed further below), we limit our sample to liberal arts colleges that *Barron's* Admissions Competitive Index categorizes as "competitive," "very competitive," "highly competitive," or "most competitive." Institutions at which standardized tests are not likely to figure prominently in the admissions process are excluded from the analysis, specifically institutions that are classified by *Barron's* as "less competitive," "non-competitive," or "special"—all of which have relatively high acceptance rates (more than 85%), admit applicants with low standardized test scores, and/or admit applicants largely on the basis of nonacademic credentials. In addition, we focus our analysis on liberal arts colleges, in particular, because, during the period of our study, test-optional policies were adopted primarily by institutions in this sector.[1] Table 10.1 lists the test-optional liberal arts colleges within our panel and the academic year (ending) in which test-optional policies were adopted.

Analytic Technique

In cross-sectional evaluations of test-optional initiatives, estimated effects may confound policy-related gains in diversity and admissions profile with unobservable, institution-level attributes, which may also contribute to these outcomes, such as a college's culture or academic environment. Likewise, a pure time-series analysis may uncover a significant post-policy effect, but the effect may be spurious owing to time trends that move most or all colleges to experience a change in their Pell rates or reported SAT scores, for example. In contrast, DiD controls for enrollment trends *and* pretreatment differences between institutions, in effect, using both as baselines against which to compare the after-intervention outcomes of test-optional and test-requiring schools. This enables us to distinguish whether, and to what extent, postimplementation effects are attributable to the test-optional policy itself. The DiD model is formally expressed as

$$Y_{cy} = \beta_0 + \beta_1 T_c + \beta_2 A_{cy} + \gamma \mathbf{X}_{cy} + \delta_1 T_c A_{cy} + \varepsilon_{cy}, \tag{1}$$

where Y_{cy} is an outcome of interest; T_c is a dichotomous measure indicating whether a college, c, received the test-optional "treatment" during any year in the panel, y, and captures pretreatment differences between optional and non-optional schools; A_{cy} is a dichotomous measure equaling "1" in years during and after implementation of a test-optional policy and captures changes in our outcomes of interest that may have occurred in the absence of a test-optional policy; X_{cy} indicates a vector of relevant covariates described above; and δ_1, the coefficient of interest, interacts with the intervention and time indicators and represents the DiD estimate, where

$$\delta_1 = (Y_{Treat\ (after)} - Y_{Treat(before)}) - (Y_{Control\ (after)} - Y_{Control\ (before)}), \tag{2}$$

which represents the difference in outcomes between the pre- and post-policy time periods, while controlling for preexisting differences in outcomes between test-optional and test-requiring institutions.

Given the standard ordinary least squares (OLS) formulation of the above model, it is necessary to account for characteristics of our data and sample, which could lead to bias and/or inefficient estimates, even within the DiD framework. First, given that colleges instituted test-optional policies in different years, the simplified model in equation 1 may over- or underestimate the effect of test-optional intervention, as it assigns treatment to colleges that did not yet implement a test-optional policy. As a corrective measure, we incorporate institution– and year–fixed effects to specify the exact year in which a participating school received intervention and, in contrast to the simplified model in equation 1, to account for variation in the duration of "treatment" among test-optional colleges (Bertrand, Duflo, and Mullainathan 2004; Dynarksi 2004). In particular, we estimate the following revised model, which should provide more refined evidence of test-optional effects:

$$Y_{cy} = \alpha A_c + \beta B_y + \gamma X_{cy} + \delta_1 T_{cy} + \varepsilon_{cy}, \tag{3}$$

where A_c and B_y are fixed effects for colleges, c, and years, y, respectively; X_{cy} represents a vector of included covariates; ε_{cy} is an idiosyncratic error term; and δ_1 is our coefficient of interest and equal to "1" in any academic year when an institution's incoming class of students benefited from a test-optional admission policy. For example, if a college adopted a test-optional admissions policy during the 2004–2005 academic year for the incoming class of 2005–2006, the institution is first indicated as a test-optional college in the 2005–2006 academic year, as 2005–2006 is the first year in which test-optional policies may affect institutional indicators, such as Pell rates, minority rates, average test scores, and *reported* application numbers.[2]

In addition, given that our analysis encompasses multiple years before and after test-optional "intervention," we also conduct a series of Durbin-Watson tests, which yield evidence of serial correlation in the simple and revised models (equations 1 and 3, respectively) for all outcomes. To correct for possible Type 1 error, we incorporate cluster-robust standard errors into each of our models (White 1980), which adjust the estimated variance-covariance matrix to account for correlated residuals within clusters (i.e., colleges) and which should provide for efficient estimates of a test-optional effect, especially given that our sample has an N greater than 50 (Bertrand, Duflo, and Mullainathan 2004).

Finally, after estimating both models, we explore whether our DiD design meets the assumption of parallel trends. To yield unbiased estimates, DiD models must meet the strong assumption that treated and control groups would exhibit parallel trends in the absence of intervention (Angrist and Pischke 2009)—which, according to Abadie (2005), "may be implausible if pre-treatment characteristics that are thought to be associated with the dynamics of an outcome variable are unbalanced between the treated and untreated group" (2).

Potentially, there are differences between test-optional and test-requiring colleges not accounted for by equation 3, and which may influence selection into "treatment," as well as the direction and rate at which outcomes among the two groups change. While preintervention data and the aforementioned covariates control for at least some of these differences, there may be other influential variables omitted from our models, which could potentially preclude accurate estimation of a test-optional effect.

Causal inference via DiD requires that we construct an appropriate counterfactual scenario where treated units (i.e., test-optional colleges) are instead assigned to the control group (i.e., test-requiring colleges), and vice versa—because any unit can be observed under only one of two conditions. To infer a causal effect of test-optional intervention, we must adequately approximate the outcomes of a "treated" college under control conditions (i.e., if it did not participate in test-optional admissions). If we can construct this counterfactual condition or "what if" scenario for treated units in our sample, we can *estimate* the average treatment effect of the test-optional policy: $E[Y_{1c} - Y_{0c}]$. Doing so, however, requires that we compare test-optional schools with "control" schools, which, given their characteristics and context, would exhibit similar trends in the absence of test-optional "treatment." If treated and control colleges within our sample differ on particular unobservables that lead to diverging outcomes, regardless of intervention, we cannot determine whether or which portion of a potential test-optional effect is attributable to the policy itself or to another difference, policy change, or event that is not accounted for by our model and that may also influence selection into treatment or our outcomes.

Although the parallel trends assumption is not formally testable, we adopt three techniques to examine whether parallel trends criteria have been met. First, and as indicated previously, we estimate each model on a disaggregated sample of colleges that share similar institutional characteristics and that are most likely to adopt test-optional policies, namely, selective, liberal arts colleges. Restricting our sample to institutions of the same sector and similar selectivity levels should provide sufficient overlap (i.e., a range of common support) between test-optional and test-requiring schools, and consequently, allow us to extrapolate counterfactual outcomes via a DiD regression.

Second, we add an institution-specific trend to our set of covariates (Angrist and Pischke 2009), which controls for the possibility that test-optional and test-requiring schools may have experienced different admissions- and campus-related trends prior to policy implementation. Trend variables are created by regressing each dependent variable on year, for each institution, using data from 1992 to 1995, the period before all but one institution in our data set adopted a test-optional policy.[3] The trend variables incorporated into our models multiply the resulting coefficients by year and are unique for each institution-year, and as such, allow institutions to follow a different trend throughout the panel. If estimated effects are robust, the inclusion of institution-specific trends should not alter the magnitude or significance of the coefficients of our test-optional indicator.

Finally, after estimating our models, we conducted a series of placebo tests to confirm that effects are evident only after policy implementation and are not the result of some other factor unaccounted for by equation 3 (Bertrand, Duflo, and Mullainathan 2004). To carry out placebo testing, we estimate models for each outcome, including only panel data for years before test-optional intervention (1992–1995), and then assign test-optional "treatment" to colleges in all years after 1992. We anticipate that placebo models indicating treatment in 1993, 1994, and 1995 will yield insignificant effects of a test-optional policy, because policy implementation is synthetic and never actually occurs. However, if our test-optional indicator is significant, we must consider that effects attributed to the outcome being modeled are spurious (and possibly null), and that changes in the outcome, if any, are due to other unobservable measures.

Limitations

Despite the application of several bias-reducing techniques, this study is still limited in three important ways. First, there are several colleges for which we were unable to collect preadoption data. Five colleges, namely, Bard, Bates, Bowdoin, Hampshire, and Lewis and Clark, implemented test-optional policies before 1992 and as early as 1965. While efforts were made to collect data prior to 1992, inconsistencies in IPEDS reporting (for grant awards and minority enrollment) and missing College Board data (for SAT scores and freshman applications) prevented us from expanding our panel to earlier years. Although "early-adopting" colleges constitute a small percentage of all test-optional colleges, and adopted policies prior to, and irrespective of, the test-optional movement, their influence could shed light on the long-term influence of test-optional initiatives. With this in mind, additional research might explore other techniques to examine test-optional-related changes among this unique group of institutions.

Second, while our fixed-effects identification strategy controlled for time-invariant omitted variables that may confound the institution-related effects of test-optional policies, it did not control for variables that change over time, which were not incorporated into our models and that may ultimately confound our estimates. For example, given the inconsistencies in endowment reporting during the period of our study, we were unable to include a variable for each college's annual institutional endowment—a potentially important indicator of campus diversity and admissions competitiveness. Although we collected data on an adequate proxy, institutional grant award per student, there may still be other elements of endowment that contributed to our outcomes of interest, above and beyond what is used for financial aid. In addition, a measure indicating the percentage of students submitting test scores may have provided for finer distinctions between test-optional programs and a more nuanced discussion on the relationship between test-optional "participation" and our dependent variables; however, reliable data for this indicator were not available.

Finally, several variables have missing data, specifically those for Pell rate (0.85%), reported SAT score (1.81%), applications (2.31%), and acceptance rate (2.31%). As a robustness check, we imputed missing values using chained equations and compared the results of our models with imputed data against our original models (with missing data). Our results remained the same; however, our findings may still be susceptible to non-response bias, especially because the majority of missingness occurs within a particular time frame, namely, the first five years of our panel.

Results

The graphs in figure 10.1 illustrate changes in institutional diversity and admissions profile during the period of our study for both test-optional and test-requiring colleges. Graphs A and B show, respectively, that test-optional colleges enrolled a lower proportion of Pell recipients and underrepresented minorities, on average, than test-requiring institutions—during all years of the panel. Furthermore, and somewhat to our surprise, graphs A and B reveal that test-optional colleges did not make any progress in narrowing these diversity-related gaps after they adopted test-optional policies. In contrast, graphs C and D suggest that test-optional adopters did achieve relative gains on certain admissions-related indicators. For example, while test-optional institutions reported higher average SAT scores in initial years of the panel, their margins increased in later years, by approximately 25 points on average, as graph C shows.[4] Graph D also depicts steadily increasing margins in application totals between test-optional and test-requiring schools.

In the first year of our panel, (eventual) test-optional colleges received 150 more applications, on average, than their test-requiring counterparts; by the end of our panel, test-optional colleges were receiving approximately 550 more applications.[5]

While the graphs in figure 10.1 illuminate changes in our outcomes of interest, they cannot communicate the magnitude and significance of such changes, especially given that additional factors, besides test-optional policy implementation, may have contributed to differences in diversity and admissions-related trends between test-optional and test-requiring institutions. Indeed, the descriptive statistics in table 10.2 reveal substantial growth in other institution-level indicators, which may have contributed to diverging outcomes between the two groups. For example, table 10.2 shows that institutional grant dollars per FTE at test-optional colleges more than doubled in constant dollars over the course of our panel and averaged more than $13,000 per student by 2010, which may explain relative gains in the number of applications received at these schools. In addition, test-optional colleges experienced greater increases in tuition and fee prices in constant dollars during the period of our study, which may have prevented optimal numbers of low-income and/or minority students from applying, and consequently, may have suppressed the positive effects that test-optional policies might have otherwise had

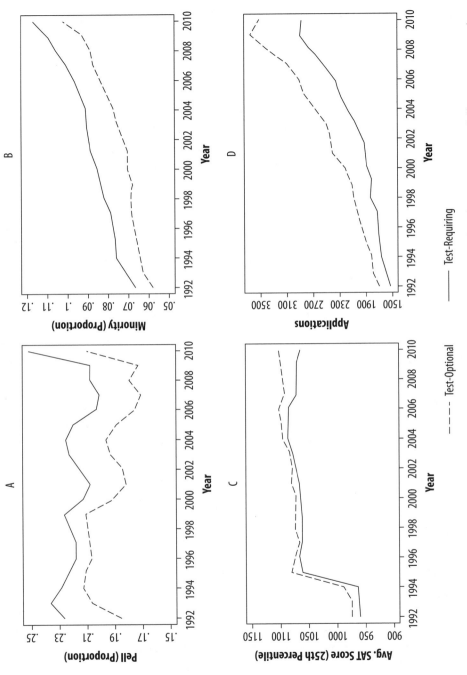

Fig. 10.1. Institutional Diversity and Admissions Profiles (Averages for Test-Optional and Test-Requiring Colleges, 1992–2010)

Table 10.2. Means (and standard deviations) of independent variables (test-optional vs. test-requiring colleges)

Variable	Minimum	Maximum	Test-optional (1992)	Test-optional (2010)	Test-requiring (1992)	Test-requiring (2010)
Independent						
No-loan policy	0.00	1.00	0.00	0.03	0.00	0.11
Undergraduate enrollment (FTE)	59.61	7,686.76	1,541.36	1,951.56	1,489.35	1,750.80
			(640.57)	(607.10)	(869.12)	(1,059.47)
E&R expenditures (per FTE)	6,744.15	97,196.20	22,861.79	29,151.73	19,753.82	27,946.33
			(5,226.24)	(7,712.33)	(6,870.28)	(11,922.24)
Tuition and fees	3,124.96	45,895.54	22,682.09	35,477.97	17,397.40	28,909.37
			(3,226.14)	(4,008.84)	(5,361.74)	(7,604.14)
Institutional grant award (per FTE)	3.26	21,933.67	6,308.39	13,358.18	4,592.59	11,494.75
			(1,667.48)	(3,079.46)	(2,214.47)	(4,588.02)
Admission rate	0.15	1.00	0.71	0.59	0.72	0.60
			(0.10)	(0.15)	(0.17)	(0.20)
Dependent						
Proportion Pell	0.03	0.82	0.19	0.21	0.23	0.25
			(0.08)	(0.08)	(0.12)	(0.12)
Proportion minority	0.00	0.56	0.06	0.10	0.07	0.12
			(0.03)	(0.05)	(0.05)	(0.07)
Applications	23	10,068	1,706.16	3,524.38	1,544.91	2,980.06
			(927.05)	(1,545.08)	(1,215.49)	(2,121.63)
Reported SAT score (25th percentile)	600	1,440	975.48	1,102.90	960.22	1,062.25
			(73.30)	(97.44)	(129.75)	(142.60)
Institutions (N)			32	32	148	148

Note: E&R expenditures = Education and related expenditures. FTE = full-time enrollment.

on the diversity of adopting institutions. If tuition remained constant, would test-optional policies have contributed to increases in low-income and minority enrollment—as many test-optional colleges have claimed, and despite what the graph in figure 10.1 indicates? Can diverging application totals be attributed to test-optional polices, increased grant aid, or both? Results from our DiD models address these and other such questions.

Table 10.3 displays our regression results, which appear to confirm what the graphs in figure 10.1 suggest—that test-optional admissions policies do not increase the diversity of policy-adopting liberal arts colleges, on average. In particular, when controlling for unobserved heterogeneity (via institution- and year-fixed effects) and other time-varying characteristics, test-optional policies failed to effect a positive change in the proportion of low-income and minority students enrolling at test-optional institutions. This finding contradicts simulated analyses of test-optional programs (Espenshade and Chung 2011) and is also counter to the reports of several test-optional colleges (Bates College 2004; Jaschik 2006; McDermott 2008). Yet, given the descriptive nature and narrow focus of these past studies—previous reports consisted mostly of case studies focusing on one or a small number of institutions—and the quasi-experimental nature of our own study, we are confident that results yielded from our models are robust and provide some evidence that test-optional policies overall have not been the catalysts of diversity that many have claimed them to be.

Despite their seemingly nonsignificant impact on racial and economic diversity, test-optional policies appear to benefit adopting colleges in other, more institution-promoting ways. As indicated in the third set of columns in table 10.3, implementing a test-optional admissions policy appears to exert a positive and significant influence on the number of applications a college receives. Specifically, after controlling for fixed effects, institution-specific trends, and other influential covariates, our results suggest that liberal arts colleges receive approximately 220 more applications annually, on average, after adopting a test-optional policy. This constitutes a substantial increase, especially given that colleges in our sample enroll only 400 first-year students annually, on average; however, the statistical significance of our finding may have more to do with our data than our test-optional indicator. Indeed, normality tests (Jarque and Bera 1987; Royston 1991) offered some evidence that our variable for applications was positively skewed. To partially correct for non-normality, we reestimated our model using the square-root transformation of our "applications" measure and found that effects for test-

Table 10.3. Estimating the effects of test-optional policies

Model	Proportion Pell			Proportion minority			Applications[a]			Reported SAT		
	(1)	(2)	(3)	(4)	(5)	(6)	(7)	(8)	(9)	(10)	(11)	(12)
Test-optional policy	−0.009	−0.006	−0.012	−0.003	−0.004	−0.003	300.643*	234.023*	221.331*	25.664**	27.184***	25.674**
	(0.010)	(0.009)	(0.009)	(0.004)	(0.005)	(0.005)	(134.250)	(112.853)	(107.781)	(7.903)	(7.974)	(7.792)
Non-loan policy		0.008	0.004		0.008	0.009		563.741***	610.153***		21.418***	23.257***
		(0.007)	(0.008)		(0.005)	(0.005)		(157.404)	(166.925)		(4.780)	(5.129)
Undergraduate FTE (ln)		−0.041	−0.041		0.026	0.026		789.916*	1,118.951**		34.410	35.541
		(0.041)	(0.043)		(0.019)	(0.017)		(405.044)	(364.396)		(20.379)	(21.243)
E&R expenditures (ln)		−0.025	−0.026		0.000	0.002		541.808*	693.587**		57.086**	59.039**
		(0.030)	(0.031)		(0.015)	(0.014)		(265.210)	(251.308)		(17.671)	(18.345)
Tuition & fees (ln)		0.002	0.008		−0.008	−0.007		291.776	220.377		22.082	15.015
		(0.020)	(0.018)		(0.008)	(0.007)		(201.747)	(179.190)		(18.054)	(18.426)
Grant/FTE (ln)		0.010	0.011		0.006	0.006		−37.337	−50.833		2.646	2.029
		(0.006)	(0.006)		(0.003)	(0.003)		(52.192)	(55.039)		(3.933)	(3.992)
Admission rate		0.020	0.026		0.003	−0.003		−2,611.427***	−2,578.454***		−63.437***	−69.176***
		(0.019)	(0.019)		(0.011)	(0.011)		(334.937)	(336.692)		(17.688)	(17.612)
Observations	3,389	3,269	3,262	3,418	3,292	3,292	3,339	3,292	3,269	3,356	3,243	3,182
R²	.893	.891	.898	.846	.851	.854	.908	.928	.932	.917	.920	.922
Year-fixed effects	Yes	Yes	Yes	Yes	Yes	Yes	Yes	Yes	Yes	Yes	Yes	Yes
Institution-fixed effects	Yes	Yes	Yes	Yes	Yes	Yes	Yes	Yes	Yes	Yes	Yes	Yes
Institution-specific trend	No	No	Yes	No	No	Yes	No	No	Yes	No	No	Yes
Placebo effect[b]	—	—	—	—	—	—	No	No	No	No	No	No

Note. Robust standard errors clustered at the institution level are reported in parentheses. FTE = full-time enrollment; E&R expenditures = educational and related expenditures; ln = natural logarithm.

[a] Models incorporating the square-root transformation of applications produce positive yet insignificant results.

[b] We test for placebo effects in models where the test-optional coefficient is significant.

*p<.05 **p<.01 ***p<.001.

optional adoption were still positive but no longer significant.[6] As such, our analysis provides interesting, yet inconclusive, results on the relationship between test-optional policies and application numbers.

Finally, test-optional policies also appear to be associated with an increase in reported test scores. Consistent with the claims of past reports (Ehrenberg 2002; Yablon 2001), liberal arts colleges that implement test-optional policies experience a subsequent rise in their reported SAT scores, by approximately 26 points, on average, all else equal. Furthermore, the magnitude and significance of these test-related effects remain consistent across models, even after controlling for trends, other potential confounders, and possible placebo effects—suggesting that results with respect to this outcome are quite robust. In sum, findings from our analyses indicate that test-optional policies enhance the appearance of selectivity, rather than the diversity, of adopting institutions.

Discussion

Our findings suggest that test-optional admissions policies, as a whole, have done little to meet their manifest goals of expanding educational opportunity for low-income and minority students. However, we find evidence that test-optional policies fulfill a latent function of increasing the perceived selectivity and status of these institutions. In doing so, these policies may serve to reproduce and maintain the current social structure—and its inequalities—within US higher education.

While this study provides evidence of how test-optional admissions policies shape diversity and admissions profiles, more broadly, it serves as a reminder of the values that are reflected in the process of selecting students into liberal arts colleges.

The SAT and other standardized tests were initially adopted to sort students according to academic ability rather than status and background. This sorting mechanism, however, favored wealthy students and reinforced their disproportionate presence at the nation's most selective institutions. In a way, the SAT became an adaptive mechanism that upper-class families used to secure their future social status (Alon 2009)—which, in part, may explain why the SAT continues to predominate the selective college admissions process. While selective institutions have become increasingly open to considering SAT alternatives, other standardized assessments—including the ACT, Advanced Placement, International Baccalaureate (IB), and SAT subject tests—are vulnerable to the same inequities. For example, affluent students and families can often "buy" their way to improved scores on any standardized test by hiring a private tutor, enrolling in a test preparation course, and/or registering for several administrations of the same exam (Lemann 1999; Lewin 2013; Vigdor and Clotfelter 2003). Previous research shows that one or more of these costly strategies usually results in improved standardized test scores and better admissions prospects at selective colleges and universities (Buchmann, Condron, and Roscigno 2010).

Despite the clear relationship between privilege and standardized test performance, the adoption of test-optional admissions policies does not seem to be an adequate solution to providing educational opportunity for low-income and minority students. In fact, test-optional admission policies may perpetuate stratification within the postsecondary sector, in particular, by assigning greater importance to credentials that are more accessible to advantaged populations. Without access to standardized test data for every applicant, test-optional colleges rely more heavily on school-specific measures, such as strength of curriculum or involvement outside the classroom, to draw comparisons between prospective students; however, several studies reveal that the availability of advanced (AP, IB, and honors) courses and extracurricular opportunities is unequally distributed across socioeconomic groups (Espenshade and Radford 2009; Iatarola, Conger, and Long 2011; Klugman 2013; Perna et al. 2013), and that low-SES students face greater obstacles to participating in the classes and activities that facilitate selective college enrollment (Klugman 2012). As a result, test-optional colleges may be inadvertently trading one inequitable policy for another—a troubling notion given that 11 additional selective liberal arts colleges have adopted test-optional polices in the past two years alone, advancing what Diver (2006) referred to as a "new front in the admissions arms race."[7]

Although implications for policy and practice are not entirely clear, our study reveals that eliminating or de-emphasizing standardized tests in the admissions process has not reduced educational inequalities, on average. These results indicate that the connection between social status and college admission is deeply embedded (Thacker 2005), and perhaps more than the test-optional movement could have predicted. Our study also indicates that selective institutions cannot be relied on, at least solely, to stem disparities in postsecondary access, which is not entirely surprising, given that most selective colleges and universities rely on a host of external resource providers that place significant emphasis on institutional position and rank (e.g., students, families, government, industry, etc.) (Bastedo and Bowman 2011; Meredith 2004).

Nevertheless, if test-optional and other selective colleges are sincere in their desires to increase access and enroll more underrepresented students, they might consider acknowledging the SAT and other similar tests as imperfect yet useful indicators of academic achievement, as Diver (2006) and Epstein (2009) suggested, while learning to more appropriately situate a student's test score within his or her particular context.

Test-optional and other selective institutions might also consider reexamining their recruitment strategies. A wave of recent research on postsecondary "undermatch" reveals that a majority of high-achieving, low-income students fail even to apply at selective colleges and are generally unaware of the admissions requirements and benefits associated with selective higher education (Belasco and Trivette 2015; Hoxby and Avery 2012; Smith, Pender, and Howell 2013). These findings are likely related to current recruitment practices at many selective colleges, which pay inadequate attention to the places where underrepresented students live and learn, largely ignoring geographically remote areas and/or low-income schools in favor of more cost-effective or "fruitful" locales (Hill and Winston 2010; Stevens 2007). Arguably, institutions that fail to reach a majority of underrepresented students, through recruitment or other outreach initiatives, will find it difficult to improve diversity in meaningful and significant ways, regardless of their admissions criteria. If test-optional and other selective colleges genuinely aim to become more inclusive, they must meet underrepresented students where they actually are, instead of where they "should be."

However, as intimated previously, achieving a more equitable approach to student recruitment and applicant evaluation will likely depend on the extent to which selective colleges can meet their market-related needs. To that end, it is important that selective institutions collaborate with other stakeholders to devise *and promote* new measures of excellence within higher education that could include the extent to which institutions enroll and graduate underrepresented students, the amount of resources institutions allocate to public service, average student debt load, and other indicators of postsecondary outcomes that demonstrate what colleges do, rather than whom they accept. Until US higher education learns to distinguish excellence from prestige, institutions across all sectors will remain prone to prioritizing status over equity—merely to survive, at least.

Finally, it is important that selective institutions be more transparent and forthcoming about the extent to which they can accommodate disadvantaged populations. Most undermatch studies examining the lack of high-achieving, low-income students at selective institutions fail to discuss how selective colleges would respond to an influx of low-income applicants, for example. In this scenario, would Amherst or Pomona adjust its enrollment strategy to accommodate a significantly greater number of financially needy students? Or, is it more likely that a greater number of needy students would be competing for (roughly) the same number of seats? How would a similar scenario play out at Dickinson or Denison? Although answers to these questions may prompt contempt among the general public or lead to politically unpopular proposals—such as those recommending significant increases to federal and/or state aid for low-income students—they would propel discussion on what is really required to improve diversity at America's most competitive colleges, compelling all parties to deal in reality rather than ideals.

NOTES

1. A review of the FairTest newsletter archives (www.fairtest.org) and various college websites revealed that 37 of 44 competitive institutions (as defined by *Barron's*) adopting test-optional policies before 2010 were liberal arts colleges.

2. The College Board commonly reports an institution's application numbers for the prior academic year. For example, application data in College Board's *Annual Survey of Colleges* labeled 2010 indicate the number of applications submitted in 2009.

3. Trend indicators for Wheaton College (Massachusetts), which adopted a test-optional admissions policy in 1993 (academic year ending), were created using data from 1992 and 1993 only, the two years before the institution could have experienced any "test-optional effects."

4. All colleges experienced sharp increases in their reported SAT scores after the College Board re-centered score scales in 1995 to provide easier performance comparisons among the contemporary test-taking population.

5. Growth in Pell rates and declines in application totals after 2009 are likely attributed to the Great Recession, and its negative influence on demand for liberal arts education.

6. Normality tests, along with descriptive statistics and histograms, show that a square-root transformation performs better than a log-transformation in allowing for more normal distribution. However, skewness and kurtosis tests still detect some non-normality within our transformed variable.

7. Including Agnes Scott College, Connecticut College, Earlham College, Furman College, Illinois College, Manhattanville College, Moravian College, St. Leo College, University of the South, Ursinus College, and Washington and Jefferson.

REFERENCES

Abadie, A. (2005). Semiparametric difference-indifferences estimators. *Review of Economic Studies, 72*, 1–19.

Alon, S. (2009). The evolution of class inequality in higher education: Competition, exclusion, and adaptation. *American Sociological Review, 74*, 731–755.

Alon, S., and Tienda, M. (2007). Diversity, opportunity, and the shifting meritocracy in higher education. *American Sociological Review, 72*, 487–511.

Angrist, J., and Pischke, J. (2009). *Mostly harmless econometrics*. Princeton, NJ: Princeton University Press.

Atkinson, R. C. (2001). *Standardized tests and access to American universities*. The 2001 Robert H. Atwell Distinguished Lecture, delivered at the 83rd annual meeting of the American Council on Education, February 18, Washington, DC.

Atkinson, R. C., and Geiser, S. (2009). Reflections on a century of college admissions tests. *Educational Researcher, 38*, 665–676.

Bastedo, M. N., and Bowman, N. A. (2011). College rankings as an interorganizational dependency: Establishing the foundation for strategic and institutional accounts. *Research in Higher Education, 52*, 3–23.

Bates College. (2004). PowerPoint analysis: SAT submitters and non-submitters, October 10. Retrieved from http://www.bates.edu/news/2004/10/10/powerpoint -analysis.

Belasco, A. S., and Trivette, M. J. (2015). Aiming low: Estimating the scope and predictors of postsecondary undermatch. *Journal of Higher Education, 86*(2), 233–263.

Bertrand, M., Duflo, E., and Mullainathan, S. (2004). How much should we trust differences-in-differences estimates? *Quarterly Journal of Economics, 119*, 249–275.

Bettinger, E. P., Evans, B. J., and Pope, D. G. (2011). *Improving college performance and retention the easy way: Unpacking the ACT exam,* No. w17119. Cambridge, MA: National Bureau of Economic Research.

Blau, J. R., Moller, S., and Jones, L. V. (2004). Why test? Talent loss and enrollment loss. *Social Science Research, 33*, 409–434.

Bourdieu, P. (1993). *The field of cultural production*. Cambridge: Polity Press.

———. (1996). *The state nobility: Elite schools in the field of power*. Stanford, CA: Stanford University Press.

Bourdieu, P., and Wacquant, L.J.D. (1992). *An invitation to reflexive sociology*. Cambridge: Polity Press.

Buchmann, C., Condron, D. J., and Roscigno, V. J. (2010). Shadow education, American style: Test preparation, the SAT and college enrollment. *Social Forces, 89*, 435–461.

Camara, W. J., and Schmidt, A. E. (1999). *Group differences in standardized testing and social stratification,* College Board Report No. 99-5. New York: College Entrance Examination Board.

College Board. (2011). *Annual survey of colleges 1990–2010*. New York: The College Board.

Cortes, C. M. (2013). Profile in action: Linking admission and retention. *New Directions for Higher Education, 2013*(161), 59–69.

Crouse, J., and Trusheim, D. (1988). *The case against the SAT*. Chicago: University of Chicago Press.

Diver, C. S. (2006). Skip the test, betray the cause. *New York Times*, September 18. Retrieved from http://www.nytimes.com/2006/09/18/opinion/18diver.html?_r=0.

Dynarksi, S. (2004). The new merit aid. In C. Hoxby (Ed.), *College choices: The economics of where to go, when to go, and how to pay for it* (pp. 63–100). Chicago: University of Chicago Press.

Ehrenberg, R. (2002). Reaching for the brass ring: The *U.S. News & World Report* rankings and competition. *Review of Higher Education, 26*, 145–162.

Epstein, J. (2009). Behind the SAT optional movement: Context and controversy. *Journal of College Admission*, (Summer), 9–19.

Espenshade, T. J., and Chung, C. Y. (2011). Diversity outcomes of test-optional policies. In J. A. Soares (Ed.), *SAT wars: The case for test-optional admissions* (pp. 177–200). New York: Teachers College Press.

Espenshade, T. J., and Radford, A. W. (2009). *No longer separate not yet equal: Race and class in elite college admission and campus life.* Princeton, NJ: Princeton University Press.

FairTest: The National Center for Fair and Open Testing. (2013). Test score optional list. Retrieved from http://www.fairtest.org/university/optional.

Fischer, C. S., Hout, M., Jankowski, M. S., Lucas, S. R., Swidler, A., and Voss, K. (1996). *Inequality by design.* Princeton, NJ: Princeton University Press.

Freedle, R. O. (2003). Correcting the SAT's ethnic and social-class bias: A method for reestimating SAT scores. *Harvard Educational Review, 73*, 1–43.

Fuller, A. (2012). Median SAT scores can get murky. *Chronicle of Higher Education*, September 12. Retrieved from http://chronicle.com/blogs/headcount/median-sat -scores-they-can-get-murky/31596.

Gambino, M. (2013). Document deep dive: What was on the first SAT? *Smithsonian Magazine*, April 12. Retrieved from http://www.smithsonianmag.com/ist/?next= /history/document-deep-dive-what-wason-the-first-sat-21720496.

Geiser, S., and Studley, W. R. (2002). UC and the SAT: Predictive validity and differential impact of the SAT I and SAT II at the University of California. *Educational Assessment, 8*, 1–26.

Gelman, A., and Hill, J. (2006). *Data analysis using regression and multilevel/hierarchical models.* New York: Cambridge University Press.

Grodsky, E., Warren, J. R., and Felts, E. (2008). Testing and social stratification in American education. *Annual Review of Sociology, 34*, 385–404.

Gumport, P. J., Iannozzi, M., Shaman, S., and Zemsky, R. (1997). *The United States country report: Trends in higher education from massification to post-massification.* Stanford, CA: National Center for Postsecondary Improvement.

Hill, C. B., and Winston, G. C. (2010). Low-income students and highly selective private colleges: Geography, searching, and recruiting. *Economics of Education Review, 29*, 495–503.

Hoffman, J. L., and Lowitzki, K. E. (2005). Predicting college success with high school grades and test scores: Limitations for minority students. *Review of Higher Education, 28*, 455–474.

Hoover, E. (2010). Colleges explore shades of gray in making entrance tests optional. *Chronicle of Higher Education*, March 21. Retrieved from http://chronicle.com /article/Colleges-Explore-Shades-of/64758.

———. (2012a). Claremont McKenna official resigns after falsely reporting SAT scores. *Chronicle of Higher Education*, January 31. Retrieved from http://chronicle.com/blogs /headcount/claremontmckenna-official-resigns-after-falsely-reportingsat-scores /29556.

———. (2012b). Inflated SAT scores reveal "elasticity of admissions data." *Chronicle of Higher Education*, February 1. Retrieved from http://chronicle.com/blogs /headcount/inflated-sat-scores-revealelasticity-of-admissions-data/29575.

Hoxby, C. M., and Avery, C. (2012). *The missing "one-offs": The hidden supply of high-achieving, low income students*, No. w18586. Cambridge, MA: National Bureau of Economic Research.

Iatarola, P., Conger, D., and Long, M. C. (2011). Determinants of high schools' advanced course offerings. *Educational Evaluation and Policy Analysis, 33*, 340–359.

Jarque, C. M., and Bera, A. K. (1987). A test for normality of observations and regression residuals. *International Statistical Review, 55*, 163–172.

Jaschik, S. (2006). Momentum for going SAT optional. *Insider Higher Ed*, May 26. Retrieved from http://www.insidehighered.com/news/2006/05/26/sat.

Jencks, C., and Riesman, D. (1968). *The academic revolution*. Garden City, NJ: Doubleday.

Karabel, J. (1984). Status group struggle, organizational interests, and limits of institutional autonomy. *Theory and Society, 13*, 1–40.

Katz, J. (1978). Epilogue: The admissions process—Society's stake and the individual's interest. In H. S. Sacks (Ed.), *Hurdles: The admission dilemma in American higher education* (pp. 318–347). New York: Atheneum.

Klugman, J. (2012). How resource inequalities among high schools reproduce class advantages in college destinations. *Research in Higher Education, 53*, 803–830.

———. (2013). The advanced placement arms race and the reproduction of educational inequality. *Teachers College Record, 115*, 1–34.

Kobrin, J. L., Patterson, B. F., Barbuti, S. M., Mattern, K. D., and Shaw, E. J. (2008). *Validity of the SAT for predicting first-year college grade point average*. New York: The College Board.

Lemann, N. (1999). *The big test: The secret history of the American meritocracy*. New York: Farrar, Straus and Giroux.

Lewin, T. (2013). Testing, testing: Most students are taking both the ACT and SAT. *The New York Times*, August 2. Retrieved from http://www.nytimes.com/2013/08/04 /education/edlife/more-studentsare-taking-both-the-act-and-sat.html.

McDermott, A. (2008). Surviving without the SAT. *Chronicle of Higher Education*, September 25. Retrieved from http://chronicle.com/article/Surviving-Without-the -SAT/18874.

Meredith, M. (2004). Why do universities compete in the rankings game? An empirical analysis of the effects of the *U.S. News & World Report* college rankings. *Research in Higher Education, 45*, 443–461.

Merton, R. K. (1936). The unanticipated consequences of purposive social action. *American Sociological Review, 1*, 894–904.

———. (1957). *Social theory and social structure*. New York: Free Press.

Park, J. J. (2012). It takes a village (or an ethnic economy): The varying roles of socioeconomic status, religion, and social capital in SAT preparation for Chinese and Korean American students. *American Educational Research Journal, 49*, 624–650.

Perna, L. W., May, H., Yee, A., Ransom, T., Rodriguez, A., and Fester, R. (2013). Unequal access to rigorous high school curricula: An exploration of the opportunity to benefit from the International Baccalaureate Diploma Programme (IBDP). *Educational Policy*, June 20. doi:10.1177/0895904813492383.

Posselt, J. R., Jaquette, O., Bielby, R., and Bastedo, M. N. (2012). Access without equity: Longitudinal analyses of institutional stratification by race and ethnicity, 1972–2004. *American Educational Research Journal, 49*, 1074–1111.

Robinson, M., and Monks, J. (2005). Making SAT scores optional in selective college admissions: A case study. *Economics of Education Review, 24*, 393–405.

Rothstein, J. M. (2004). College performance predictions and the SAT. *Journal of Econometrics, 121*, 297–317.

Royston, P. (1991). Estimating departure from normality. *Statistics in Medicine, 10*, 1283–1293.

Sackett, P. R., Kuncel, N. R., Arneson, J. J., and Waters, S. D. (2009). Does socioeconomic status explain the relationship between admissions tests and postsecondary academic performance? *Psychological Bulletin, 135*, 1–22.

Sackett, P. R., Kuncel, N. R., Beatty, A. S., Rigdon, J. L., Shen, W., and Kiger, T. B. (2012). The role of socioeconomic status in SAT-grade relationships and in college admissions decisions. *Psychological Science, 23*, 1000–1007.

Shaw, E. J., Kobrin, J. L., Patterson, B. F., and Mattern, K. D. (2012). *The validity of the SAT for predicting cumulative grade point average by college major.* New York: The College Board.

Smith, J., Pender, M., and Howell, J. (2013). The full extent of student-college academic undermatch. *Economics of Education Review, 32*, 247–261.

Stevens, M. L. (2007). *Creating a class: College admissions and the education of elites.* Cambridge, MA: Harvard University Press.

Supiano, B. (2012). Emory U. intentionally misreported admissions data, investigation finds. *Chronicle of Higher Education*, August 17. Retrieved from http://chronicle.com/blogs/headcount/emoryu-intentionally-misreported-admissions-datainvestigation-finds/31215.

Thacker, L. (Ed.). (2005). *College unranked: Ending the college admissions frenzy.* Cambridge, MA: Harvard University Press.

Vigdor, J. L., and Clotfelter, C. T. (2003). Retaking the SAT. *Journal of Human Resources, 38*, 1–33.

Webster, T. J. (2001). A principle component analysis of the *U.S. News & World Report* tier rankings of colleges and universities. *Economics of Education Review, 20*, 235–244.

White, H. (1980). Using least squares to approximate unknown regression functions. *International Economic Review, 21*, 149–170.

Yablon, M. (2001). Test flight: The scam behind SAT bashing. *New Republic, 30*, 24–25.

11

The Effect of Going Test-Optional on Diversity and Admissions

A Propensity Score Matching Analysis

Kyle Sweitzer, A. Emiko Blalock, Dhruv B. Sharma

*I*n this chapter, Sweitzer, Blalock, and Sharma use institutional theory to better understand a postsecondary institution's decision to adopt a test-optional admissions policy. They then empirically examine the impact of these decisions on a range of objectives and outcomes. Specifically, they focus on whether going test-optional, on average, can be expected to increase an institution's average SAT scores, increase the number of applicants, decrease the acceptance rate, and increase the proportion of disadvantaged minority students—all stated or unstated objectives of colleges and universities considering test-optional policies.

In order to estimate the impact of test-optional policy on these factors, the authors use data from over 100 institutions measured between 1999 and 2014. Although they are not able, of course, to randomly assign colleges to adopt a test-optional policy, they estimate the impact using a quasi-experimental, panel data, and propensity score matching approach that simulates the results of such a hypothetical experiment.

The authors find that going test-optional, on average, predicts higher reported SAT scores, but has no statistically significant effect on the number of applications, overall acceptance rates, or the proportion of underrepresented students of color enrolling in the institution. In other words, while a shift to a test-optional admissions policy appears to "do no harm" with respect to most institutions' objectives, neither should such a policy *change be expected to deliver real change in application rates or diversity on campus. Although contrary to many anecdotal and single-case studies of test-optional policy shifts, these findings echo those observed in the small but growing systematic, empirical test-optional literature such as the Belasco et al. study reproduced in chapter 10.*

Over the past decade, an increasing number of colleges and universities have decided to go "test-optional" in undergraduate admissions, letting applicants decide whether or not to submit standardized test scores (SAT/ACT). While a handful of institutions made such a move many years ago, there appears to have been an increase in recent years. Hundreds of four-year institutions do not require prospective undergraduates to submit a standardized admissions test, and hundreds of others have reduced the degree to which standardized test scores play a role in admissions decisions (National Center for Fair and Open Testing 2016). There have been many accounts of the growing trend to remove standardized tests for college admissions in the media (Edmonds 2015; Gray 2015; Groux 2012; O'Shaughnessy 2014), but surprisingly few analytical studies on the outcomes of this trend. Moreover, studies that do account for the effect of going test-optional often are single-institution studies that do not provide a larger comprehensive picture of the trend. We contribute to research in this arena by taking a different statistical approach from any existing test-optional study. We also discuss what test-optional policies may mean for admissions practices, as the trend does not appear to be slowing.

Understanding the Decision to Go Test-Optional

We examine the test-optional phenomenon using elements of institutional theory and examine why colleges adopt seemingly risky admissions policies in a risk-averse environment such as higher education (e.g., going test-optional versus the established practice of requiring test scores). Institutional theory describes structural interactions within an organization and also the connecting systems and relationships between organizations in the same organizational field (Scott and Davis 2007). In the context of our study, colleges and universities reside in the organizational field of higher education. Thus, the structural interactions and connecting relationships are the policies, practices, and norms of each institution on one another. The lineage of institutional theory is derived first from examining the distinctive nature of organizations, and more recently from observing their homogeneity (DiMaggio and Powell 1983; Selznick 1996). Institutional theories, in essence, examine the organization and its policies, practices, and norms, and the relationship of those elements to other organizations.

In the field of higher education, status and prestige play an important role in determining institutional behavior. Conrad and Eagan (1989) suggest the pursuit of prestige is a "game" institutions play to increase status within the field. Colleges and universities may alter specific policies, practices, or norms, such as recruiting high-performing faculty, raising tuition, and changing admissions requirements in order to gain or increase prestige. Altering admissions requirements may be one motivation for why colleges and universities adopt a test-optional policy, which is to increase institutional prestige. The prevalence of embracing test-optional policies explains the "adoption of structures, practices, and beliefs that conform to normative expectations for legitimacy" (Wilkins and Huisman 2012, 629). As such, the more institutions adopt test-optional policies, the more normative and legitimate this behavior becomes, reducing risks for less-prestigious institutions seeking to improve their standing.

An example of institutions following policies deemed legitimate may be observed in the changing attitudes of admissions officials toward college entrance exams. Admissions officials have historically relied on SAT/ACT scores to distinguish between the widely varying levels of rigor among high schools. The popularity of using standardized tests in admissions has varied over time (Haney 1981). More recently, many institutions seem to favor high school grade point average (GPA) or other admissions methods over SAT/ACT scores (Hiss and Franks 2014; Rothstein 2004; Shahani, Dipboye, and Gehrlein 1991). Such "holistic" practices—favoring high school GPA, interviewing potential candidates, and considering how other academic or extracurricular activities relate to college success—are now the preferred narrative. Thus, not only can colleges and universities market more "holistic" admissions practices by adopting test-optional policies; there is very little risk in doing so.

Finally, institutional theory suggests certain practices become embedded within the established system of the organization (Scott 2013), and such practices pervade the institution's values and culture (Selznick 1996). Thus, for institutions seeking to enroll a more diverse student body, going test-optional may be seen as a way to culturally shift practices within the institution. Shifting practices within an organization takes time, however, and the rationality for making such shifts may not always align with the intended organizational aim for making specific changes. Referring specifically to studies from institutional theorist Philip Selznick, Scott (2013) explains: "Selznick's institutional school tends to produce an 'expose' view of organizations. Organizations are not the rational creatures they pretend to be but vehicles for embodying (sometimes surreptitious) values" (23). The original intent for colleges and universities to go test-optional may be to help them achieve their goals of increasing diversity or advancing more holistic admissions practices.

The Test-Optional Movement

Increased use of the SAT paralleled the expansion of higher education enrollment during the middle of the twentieth century (Syverson 2007). Primarily used as a measure of talent, the SAT aimed to increase access through meritocratic methods for those wanting to pursue a higher education. In 1968, the University of California system universally adopted the SAT, securing the exam's place as a stepping stone to higher education (Epstein 2009). In more recent years, however, increased criticism has been aimed at the SAT for being a barrier to college access and a poor indicator of student success (Camara and Echternacht 2000; Espenshade and Chung 2010; Haney 1981; Sedlacek and Adams-Gaston 1992).

In response to criticisms of overreliance on standardized tests and the suggestion that they are a barrier to increased access, many colleges and universities have adopted "test-optional" policies. Such policies relax or remove test requirements and emphasize other scholastic achievements for college admissions. A handful of institutions began giving prospective undergraduate students the choice of whether or not to submit their scores on standardized admissions tests beginning in the 1960s. However, the majority of institutions that are now test-optional adopted this policy since 2000 (Epstein 2009; National Center for Fair and Open Testing 2016).

Institutions that decide to go test-optional in freshman admissions primarily cite the desire to implement more "holistic" application review as their rationale (Jaschik 2007). A holistic admissions process typically includes reviewing an applicant's entire portfolio and taking all material into consideration without eliminating candidates based on specific admission requirements or minimums (Rigol 2004). In doing so, institutions typically claim they increase access, providing an opportunity for students to enroll who may be successful in college but perform poorly on standardized tests. A complementary motivation for going test-optional often cited by institutions is increasing the diversity of the institution's student body. That is, removing the SAT/ACT requirement may invite more applicants from diverse backgrounds (Espenshade and Chung 2012; Hiss and Franks 2014).

Bowdoin College instituted a test-optional policy in 1970, and Shaffner (1985) analyzed the impact of the policy on the college. This single-institution study found that in the few years immediately after Bowdoin went test-optional, the number of students applying to the college increased dramatically. Four years after implementing the test-optional policy, Bowdoin required students who did not submit SAT scores in the admissions process to submit their scores after gaining acceptance. As such, Shaffner's analysis offers an opportunity to examine the differences between students who submitted test scores compared with those who did not. Shaffner provides statistical evidence that prospective students who chose not to submit standardized test scores did not score as highly as those who chose to submit. However, since the study examined just one highly selective, highly ranked institution, the results may not be generalizable.

In 1984, Bates College, an institution very similar to Bowdoin College in its size, mission, academic selectivity, and location, adopted a test-optional policy. The institution conducted an analysis of the results of this policy 20 years after implementation (Bates College 2005). The college found no difference between those who submitted test scores and those who did not in academic performance and graduation rates. The policy also resulted in Bates nearly doubling the number of applications it received and increasing the number of enrolled students-of-color. An increase in students-of-color was also reported at College of the Holy Cross, a liberal arts institution that adopted a test-optional policy in 2006. Ultimately, Holy Cross experienced positive results, with each incoming class representing a more geographically and ethnically diverse population after the college implemented the policy (McDermott 2008).

In a related and more recent study, Hiss and Franks (2014) analyzed 33 institutions across various institutional types (Carnegie classifications) and claimed to find an effect of test-optional policies on institutional outcomes. They found that "non-submitting" students, or those who chose not to submit test scores, were likely to be from underrepresented and under-served populations, specifically first-generation to attend college and students with learning differences. They also found that non-submitters performed equally well once admitted, and their graduation rates were almost identical to students who typically submit with above-average test scores. The Hiss and Franks report echoes Shaffner's (1985) findings, suggesting students who choose to submit test scores are those who, on average, have higher scores across institutional types. Nonetheless, although Hiss and Franks examined a larger pool of institutions beyond the previous single-institution analyses, there are limitations to their study. Their analysis is not generalizable, as the majority of the non-submitter data came from just two public institutions. Also, Hiss and Franks compared non-submitters who met certain criteria with students who did not.

Another recent study sought to identify motivators beyond holistic admissions to understand why institutions choose to adopt a test-optional policy. Belasco, Rosinger, and Hearn (2014) analyzed 32 liberal arts colleges to examine the effect on admissions statistics and student diversity after the adoption of a test-optional admissions policy (see chapter 10, where this study is reproduced). Their findings reveal that colleges choosing a test-optional approach did not improve their goals of increasing diversity as measured by change in the proportion of Pell Grant recipients or minority student enrollment. However, these institutions saw an improvement in their average SAT score. The study by Belasco et al. (2014) employs a superior methodology compared with the prior test-optional analyses by drawing comparisons between institutions through a difference-in-differences statistical approach. Additionally, the study applies a theoretical lens to help explain latent effects on the institution when test-optional policies are adopted. The Belasco study highlights a possible reason that some colleges and universities adopt a test-optional admissions policy. That is, adopting such policies may provide other, latent benefits beyond the stated goals of increasing access and diversity, a claim counter to the common narrative regarding holistic admissions.

Despite the increasing number of institutions moving to a test-optional policy, relatively few analytical studies have examined the issue. The handful of existing studies on test-optional policies outlined above do not necessarily come to the same conclusions regarding the impact on student diversity and admissions. Additionally, the findings from most of these studies are limited. Reports from small, liberal arts colleges such as Bowdoin, Bates, and Holy Cross were conducted by internal researchers, and their findings are often for institutional evaluation purposes rather than empirical research on the subject of adopting test-optional policies. Additionally, the larger study from Hiss and Franks (2014) uses a nonrepresentative sample of self-selected institutions and does not control for other latent variables, such as institutional motivation for adopting test-optional policies. Finally, few studies apart from Belasco, Rosinger, and Hearn incorporate a theoretical or conceptual lens to better understand and explain the effect of test-optional policies.

While each of these studies adds to the narrative of going test-optional, generalizability is not necessarily their aim. Thus, we extend research in this area by taking a different analytical approach from that employed in any existing study on such policies in order to better understand the growing trend in test-optional admissions. In addition, we frame our study within organizational theories to provide better grounding for our analysis. Our discussion of what test-optional policies may mean for the field of higher education and admissions practices contributes more depth to this subject, as the trend does not appear to be slowing.

A Different Analytical Approach

Our study's primary purpose is to compare the effects on admissions statistics and student diversity of institutions going test-optional with those that remain test-requiring. The gold standard for comparative studies is a randomized controlled design, in which units (colleges) are assigned to a treatment (test-optional) or control (test-requiring) group based on a random draw. This process of randomization enables unbiased estimation of the treatment effect, in which an institution's characteristics do not systematically affect choice of treatment assignment and resultant effect. The primary limitation of observational studies that do not assign schools to treatments based on random assignment is that institutional characteristics can lead to biased estimates of the intervention's (switching to test-optional) effect. Institutions, even in the same Carnegie Classification, can differ considerably in a number of ways, leading to biased estimates of the effect of going test-optional. Simply comparing outcomes of the group of colleges that adopted a test-optional policy against the group of those that did not may mask differences between the two groups that would account for different outcomes between the two sets of institutions. Furthermore, since test-optional institutions did not all adopt the policy at the same time, a comparison with non-test-optional institutions after the year of implementation is difficult (since non-test-optional institutions have no year of implementation). In the extant literature, no consensus exists regarding which year to use to compare the outcomes of test-optional schools to non-test-optional schools after policy implementation. For instance, Belasco et al. (2014) employs a time series, cross-sectional, difference-in-differences analytical approach that uses all available information of colleges before and after they switch. A limitation to this approach is that data from schools that do not switch to test-optional admissions may not be comparable with those that switch, partly owing to not knowing when a test-requiring school might have switched. The Belasco study acknowledges the possibility of bias or confounding as a result of time-varying covariates. In addition, there could be efficiency issues attributable to the use of fixed-effects for colleges and study years, as against repeated measures within colleges and study years.

Rather than choosing an arbitrary year for comparison purposes, a more defensible approach to define "switch year" is as follows: if two schools are similar to each other on a given set of observed characteristics, and only one of the schools switched to test-optional admissions, then define the year of switch for both schools as the year the test-optional school made the switch. This approach can be implemented through a process of matching based on propensity scores (Rosenbaum and Rubin 1983) and is an example of a "counterfactual/ potential outcomes" causal inference model. A propensity score represents the probability of a school being assigned to the treatment conditional on the observed characteristics. A test-optional school and a test-requiring school with the same propensity score are comparable on their observed characteristics and can therefore be matched. If all characteristics that influence whether or not a school switches to test-optional admissions are used to estimate the propensity scores, matching schools based on their propensity scores can mimic the process of random assignment of a randomized design, enabling unbiased estimation of a treatment effect. We assert that a focused comparison with matched colleges gives better estimation of the causal effects of switching to test-optional admissions.

Our study differs from the existing test-optional analyses in that we calculated propensity scores to match test-optional institutions with non-test-optional (test-requiring) institutions. We seek to examine if adopting a test-optional admissions policy has any effect on certain admissions metrics and student racial/ethnic diversity. By matching test-optional institutions with test-requiring institutions across several characteristics, our statistical approach allows us to mimic how a test-optional institution would differ across several metrics if it had not switched admissions policies. Institutional theory guides our research by identifying the reasons colleges and universities choose to adopt test-optional policies (low-risk, increase in student diversity) and the covert values associated with the switch. Our analysis specifically addresses the four research questions below.

Research Questions

RESEARCH QUESTION 1

Applicants to test-optional colleges have the choice of whether or not to submit their scores on standardized admissions tests. Thus, it is likely that applicants who submit their scores will have performed better compared with applicants who do not submit scores. As such, we ask: Do colleges that adopted a test-optional policy observe higher average SAT scores in the years after the switch than they otherwise would have observed had they not made the policy shift, ceteris paribus?

RESEARCH QUESTION 2

Since applicants with low test scores may be discouraged from applying to college, we ask: Do colleges switching to a test-optional policy receive more undergraduate applications in the years after the transition than they otherwise would have received had they not made the policy shift, ceteris paribus?

RESEARCH QUESTION 3

Since we hypothesize that test-optional colleges saw an increase in their applicant count after adopting a test-optional policy, we ask: Do test-optional colleges admit a lower percentage of their applicants after switching to a test-optional policy, thus improving their admissions acceptance rate, than they otherwise would have admitted had they not made the policy shift, ceteris paribus?

RESEARCH QUESTION 4

Since students-of-color tend to perform less favorably on standardized admissions tests than white students, it is likely that more students-of-color will be encouraged to apply to, and ultimately enroll in, test-optional colleges. Thus, we ask: Do test-optional colleges experience an increase in the percentage of first-year students-of-color in the years after the switch above what they otherwise would have experienced had they not made the policy shift, ceteris paribus? Note that the US Department of Education's Integrated Postsecondary Education Data System (IPEDS) does not capture race/ethnicity for applicants; this information is gathered only for enrolled students. As such, we were not able to examine if test-optional colleges experienced an increase in applicants-of-color.

Data and Methodology

The National Center for Fair and Open Testing's website (http://www.fairtest .org) identifies institutions with a test-optional policy in undergraduate admissions. Such institutions have different levels of test-optional guidelines (i.e., test-optional only for students falling within a certain percentile of their high school class, have a certain GPA, etc.). It is important to note that this study includes only institutions that are explicitly test-optional, regardless of any other stipulations. We did not want to allow for the possibility that an institution's decision to go test-optional was based on any intervening variables that could affect the outcome. We checked IPEDS to ensure each institution remained categorized as test-optional. We also checked the Carnegie Classification of Institutions of Higher Education

(2016) website to identify each institution's Carnegie classification, selecting only those categorized as liberal arts colleges for this analysis. Although the test-optional movement has spread across various types of institutions, the trend appears to be most popular among liberal arts colleges. Also, limiting the study to liberal arts colleges ensures that only those institutions with the same general mission and focus on undergraduate education are considered in the comparative analyses.

We identified the date that institutions implemented the test-optional policy either from the FairTest website or by contacting the school directly. We removed institutions for which we could not find a date of implementation as well as those with an open admissions policy. We did not include online-only institutions, as well as those with specialized missions. Finally, we did not include historically black colleges and universities, and minority-serving institutions, since part of the study examines if going test-optional has any impact on the percentage of students-of-color enrolling in these institutions.

We collected institution-specific, cross-sectional data from 1999 through 2014. This time frame covers the years before and after each test-optional institution implemented the policy. For most institutions, we typically had at least four years of data prior to, and four years after, their switch to test-optional status (although fewer years of data were available for the institutions that adopted a test-optional policy more recently). Admissions data include counts of applications and admits, acceptance rates, and the SAT/ACT interquartile range, all obtained via IPEDS. We obtained high school class rank from *U.S. News & World Report*'s annual editions of *America's Best Colleges*. ACT scores were converted into SAT scores using concordance tables available from the College Board (2016). The average of the SAT interquartile range (IQR) was computed for each college for each year and was used as the measure of central tendency for SAT scores. A limitation to this approach is that the IQR may not be symmetrical about the mean for every institution. However, both IPEDS and *U.S. News* only provide admissions test IQR scores, and not mean test scores. Enrollment data include total and first-time student counts by race/ethnicity. We also collected graduation rates (six-year); total expenditures-per-student; cost of tuition, room, and board; and average institutional grant of financial aid per student. Counts for the various racial/ethnic student populations in IPEDS were combined to get each institution's count of students-of-color for the total enrolled; total degree-seeking; and total degree-seeking, first-time student categories. Table 11.1 provides descriptive statistics on the dependent variables included in the analysis.

Table 11.1.   Means of dependent variables

Dependent variables	Test-optional schools ($N=35$)		Test-requiring schools ($N=80$)	
	Avg. 4 years before switch	Avg. 4 years after switch	Avg. 4 years before switch	Avg. 4 years after switch
Average SAT score	1195	1202	1212	1211
Number of applicants	3,265	3,811	2,979	3,552
Acceptance rate	61.1%	58.6%	59.8%	56.1%
Freshmen of color	13.0%	17.9%	15.5%	19.8%

In this study, if a test-optional school and a test-requiring school had similar propensity scores, we matched them and assigned the test-requiring school the same "switch year" as that of the test-optional school. In order to find test-optional and test-requiring schools that were similar to each other by matching using propensity scores, we used the following six institutional characteristics: average six-year graduation rate; high school class rank of freshmen (top 10%); total undergraduate enrollment; expenditures-per-student; cost of tuition, room, and board; and average institutional grant of financial aid. We used a logistic regression model to estimate the probability of a school switching (a binary choice) based on the six institutional characteristics. We then found the propensity score for each school in the study, and if a test-optional school had a propensity score within a small distance/caliper of a test-requiring school, we did a one-to-many match, matching the test-optional school with the test-requiring schools within that caliper. Once we had these matched institutions, we assigned the switch year of the test-optional school to be the "switch" year of the test-requiring school.

Since some of this information was not available for all schools for all years, a single mean imputation approach was used to approximate missing yearly data before an average was calculated (Little and Rubin 2002). Because of the need to account for the missing patterns, the following logistic regression model was used to calculate the propensity scores,

$$logit[Prob(Y_i = 1 | X_i = x_i)] = \beta_0 + \beta x_i, i = 1, 2, \ldots, n$$

where n is the total number of schools in the study, Y_i is a binary variable that takes value 1 if school i is a test-optional school (0 otherwise), x_i is the observed value of X_i, the matching covariates (plus, an indicator for whether or not the school has missing data) for school i, $\beta_0 \& \beta$ are the coefficient values, while *logit* stands for log-odds, and *Prob* stands for probability.

After matching each test-optional institution to its nearest non-test-optional neighbor on the propensity score metric, covariate balance (for the matching covariates) was assessed via t-tests to confirm that the matching covariates were similar for the matched test-optional and test-requiring schools. Tables 11.2a and 11.2b provide descriptive statistics on the variables used in the propensity score matching analysis, as well as this assessment of balance.

Table 11.2a.   Means (standard deviations) of variables prior to propensity score matching and t-test results from balance tests

	Test-optional schools ($N = 39$)	Non-test-optional ($N = 135$)	t-test p-value
Average six-year graduation rate	73.0% (10.0%)	67.1% (16.1%)	.006
Freshmen in top 10% of their high school class	39.2% (13.1%)	37.6% (20.6%)	.577
Undergraduate enrollment	1,773 (633)	1,708 (965)	.621
Expenditures per student	$22,213 ($6,669)	$19,560 ($9,106)	.048
Tuition, room, board	$30,735 ($3,947)	$23,672 ($8,864)	.0000
Average institutional grant aid	$16,414 ($3,955)	$12,983 ($6,608)	.0001

Table 11.2b.   Means (standard deviations) of variables after propensity score matching and t-test results from balance tests

	Test-optional schools ($N = 35$)	Non-test optional ($N = 80$)	t-test p-value
Average six-year graduation rate	73.2% (10.4%)	73.7% (12.2%)	.811
Freshmen in top 10% of their high school class	39.6% (13.8%)	42.8% (21.0%)	.343
Undergraduate enrollment	1,798 (628)	1,769 (723)	.829
Expenditures per student	$21,804 ($6,879)	$22,533 ($8,742)	.633
Tuition, room, board	$30,155 ($3,734)	$28,539 ($5,096)	.061
Average institutional grant aid	$15,996 ($3,929)	$15,946 ($5,666)	.956

While we may not have captured all of the variables that could impact a college's decision to switch to test-optional admissions, these variables cover a wide range of distinguishing characteristics across institutions. We also note that these six metrics tend to be consistent over time, changing little during the four years that precede and follow the year of implementation (switch year) for test-optional institutions. Specifically, all usable information we collected across the 16 years were used in calculating these average values for the six variables. That is, we excluded years that were missing information owing to lack of collection and imputed years that were missing some information.

There were a total of 39 test-optional schools and 135 test-requiring schools with a full set of data available. After conducting propensity score matching, we analyzed 35 test-optional schools and 80 test-requiring schools. See appendix table 11.1, which lists the names of these test-optional liberal arts colleges and the year they adopted the test-optional policy. Appendix table 11.2 lists the test-requiring liberal arts colleges used in the matching propensity score analysis, along with the year used for comparison purposes (see appendix). Data for the four years preceding the switch and four years after the switch were collected for a total of eight years of outcomes data for each institution.

Since we collected information on eight years for each institution, we implemented hierarchical linear models to examine our research questions (Littell et al. 2006; Singer and Willett 2003). Specifically, for each outcome, we regressed two independent variables: a standardized year variable and a binary variable for switch year (0 for a school that did not switch or for a switch school before switching, and 1 for after switching). We accounted for the institution-specific repeated measurements by introducing a random intercept for each school. If this switch year variable is significant, it implies that there is an effect of switching to test-optional admissions on the given dependent variable. We assume that the effect of switching causes a bump (up or down) in the outcome variable, and that the effect of switching does not necessarily follow an increasing or decreasing trend over time. Table 11.3 displays a summary of the results.

Results

RESEARCH QUESTION 1

Results from the hierarchical model reveal that there is a significant effect of switching to a test-optional policy regarding standardized admissions tests. Average SAT scores of test-optional schools were higher than test-requiring schools over the same time period by an average of 10.4 points ($p < .0001$). We observed

Table 11.3.   Summary of results

	Coefficient	Standard error	Degrees of freedom	*t*-value	*p*-value
Average SAT score					
Intercept	1207	10.58	770	114.0	<0.001
Switch year	10.4	2.71	770	3.9	0.001
Year	−0.14	0.32	770	−0.4	0.659
Number of applicants					
Intercept	2711	180	777	15.1	<0.001
Switch year	100	73.7	777	1.4	0.177
Year	146	8.8	777	16.6	<0.001
Acceptance rate					
Intercept	61.6%	0.018	776	34.2	<0.001
Switch year	0.004%	0.009	776	0.5	0.650
Year	−0.007%	0.001	776	−6.4	<0.001
% freshmen of color					
Intercept	12%	0.010	781	12.2	<0.001
Switch year	0.005%	0.004	781	1.3	0.202
Year	0.011%	0.001	781	21.7	<0.001

that SAT scores of test-optional liberal arts colleges increased by an average of approximately 7 points (on a 1600-point scale) in the years after the switch, while the SAT score of the comparison group of liberal arts colleges dropped by an average of 1 point over the same time period.

RESEARCH QUESTION 2

Results from the hierarchical model reveal that after test-optional liberal arts colleges made the transition to test-optional policies, they averaged 100 more applications per year compared with the increase among similar test-requiring institutions over the same time frame, although these results were not statistically significant ($p = 0.177$). We observed that total applications of test-optional liberal arts colleges grew by 546 in the years after the switch, while the total applicants of the comparison group of liberal arts colleges grew by 573 over the same time period. We note that missing data was deleted in the outcome analysis, and this can account for the discrepancy between the raw numbers and the model results.

RESEARCH QUESTION 3

Results from the hierarchical model show that after test-optional liberal arts colleges made the transition to test-optional policies, their acceptance rates remained about the same (0.004% change). The effect was not statistically significant ($p = 0.65$). We observed that acceptance rates of test-optional liberal arts colleges dropped by 0.03% in the years after the switch, while the acceptance rates of the comparison group of liberal arts colleges dropped by 0.04% over the same time period.

RESEARCH QUESTION 4

Results from the hierarchical model reveal that after test-optional liberal arts colleges made the transition to test-optional policies, the percentage of freshmen, degree-seeking students-of-color remained about the same (0.005% change) in comparison with non-test-optional schools, and this effect was not statistically significant (p-value = 0.202). We observed that test-optional liberal arts colleges increased the percentage of freshman, degree-seeking students-of-color by 0.05% in the years after the switch, while the percentage change among schools in the comparison group of liberal arts colleges was an increase of 0.04% over the same time period.

Summary and Implications of Findings

The variables in our analysis examine whether adopting a test-optional admissions policy has an effect on freshmen admissions and student racial diversity. The admissions statistics were either changed in the positive direction, or not affected at all. After switching to a test-optional policy, liberal arts colleges saw a slightly greater increase in their average SAT score compared with what they would have experienced had they not gone test-optional. Test-optional institutions did not experience an effect on the number of applications or in the acceptance rate compared with what they would have experienced had they not switched to a test-optional policy. Although there are additional admissions metrics that we did not capture (high school GPA, high school class percentile), our analysis suggests that switching to a test-optional admissions policy appears to have had no negative impact regarding admissions statistics, and perhaps results in a net positive in this regard.

However, in terms of racial diversity, the percentage of freshmen students-of-color did not change in either direction for liberal arts colleges after making the switch to test-optional admissions. In fact, we find that test-requiring institutions increased student diversity to the same degree as that of test-optional institutions. This result contradicts one of the often-stated justifications institutions provide for implementing a test-optional policy, which is to diversify the student body. Our analysis suggests that institutions should not rely on a test-optional approach to admissions as a means to increasing the racial diversity of the student body. This finding supports that of Belasco, Rosinger, and Hearn (2014) who found that test-optional liberal arts colleges did not increase student diversity after making the switch to test-optional admissions. Furthermore, this result suggests that the motivation for adopting a test-optional policy is not to diversify the student body, since student diversification appears to be related more to an institution's desire to do so. Rather, institutions adopt a test-optional policy to improve their admissions statistics. Indeed, since so many institutions have adopted such policies, the potential reward outweighs the potential risk.

The institutions in our analysis cover only a portion of the test-optional institutions. Plenty of other colleges and universities that were beyond the scope of this study have also transitioned to a test-optional admissions policy (although many of these are not traditional four-year institutions). Thus, further analyses are needed to examine if these findings hold true for these institutions as well. It appears that despite the often-stated goals of increasing access and student diversity by adopting a holistic admissions policy, the only real changes test-optional institutions experience is an improvement in some of their admissions credentials. The fact that test-requiring colleges were able to increase the percentage of nonwhite incoming freshmen, without implementing a test-optional policy, suggests such increases may be more a matter of institutional commitment than a shift in admissions requirements.

The movement toward test-optional admissions does not appear to be slowing. Institutions considering such policies should be cautious, however, of possible unintended consequences. Going test-optional almost guarantees extra work on the part of the admissions staff (Allman 2012; McDermott 2008). Indeed, a "holistic" admissions process typically involves more careful analysis of applicants' essays, extracurricular activities, backgrounds, and interviews. Institutions may need to hire more admissions officers to handle the additional analysis and review (regardless of whether or not the number of applications increases).

Another consequence of going test-optional is the likely criticism that comes after announcing the switch, such as the notion that the institution is lowering its standards (McDermott 2008). Colleges and universities considering a transition to test-optional admissions must be prepared to address such concerns, which often come from alumni and other constituents. As a whole, the impact of going test-optional in admissions varies across institutions. Adopting such policies may provide other, latent effects beyond the stated goals of increasing access and diversity—and that run counter to the common narrative regarding holistic admissions.

Appendix table 11.1. Test-optional liberal arts colleges
and year of switch to test-optional policy

Agnes Scott College	2010
Albright College	2009
Augustana College	2008
Bard College	2013
College of the Holy Cross	2006
Connecticut College	2009
Denison University	2008
Drew University	2007
Earlham College	2012
Franklin & Marshall College	2007
Furman University	2012
Gettysburg College	2007
Goucher College	2009
Green Mountain College	2007
Guilford College	2007
Gustavus Adolphus College	2007
Illinois College	2008
Juniata College	2007
Knox College	2006
Lake Forest College	2007
Lawrence University	2006
Marlboro College	2009
Mount Holyoke College	2002
Pitzer College	2004
Saint Anselm College	2011
Saint Michael's College	2011
Sewanee–University of the South	2010
Smith College	2009
Stonehill College	2010
Susquehanna University	2006
Union College	2007
Ursinus College	2011
Washington & Jefferson College	2007
Washington College (MD)	2013
Wittenberg University	2008

REFERENCES

Allman, M. (2012). Going test-optional: A first year of challenges, surprises, and rewards. In J. A. Soares (Ed.), *SAT wars: The case for test-optional college admissions* (pp. 169–176). New York: Teachers College Press.

Bates College. (2005). 20-year Bates College study of optional SATs finds no differences. Bates News. Retrieved from http://www.bates.edu/news/2005/10/01/sat-study.

Belasco, A. S., Rosinger, K. O., and Hearn, J. C. (2014). "The test-optional movement at America's selective liberal arts colleges: A boon for equity or something else?" *Educational Evaluation and Policy Analysis, 37*(2), 206–223.

Camara, W. J., and Echternacht, G. (2000). The SAT I and high school grades: Utility in predicting success in college. Research Notes, RN-10, July. Retrieved from https://research.collegeboard.org/sites/default/files/publications/2012/7/researchnote-2000-10-sat-high-school-grades-predicting-success.pdf.

Carnegie Classification of Institutions of Higher Education. 2016. Institution lookup. Retrieved from http://carnegieclassifications.iu.edu.

College Board. (2016). SAT-ACT concordance tables. Retrieved from https://research.collegeboard.org/programs/sat/data/concordance.

Conrad, C. F., and Eagan, D. J. (1989). The prestige game in American higher education. *Thought and Action, 5*(1), 5–16.

DiMaggio, P. J., and Powell, W. W. (1983). The iron cage revisited: Institutional isomorphism and collective rationality in organizational fields. *American Sociological Review, 48*(2), 147–160.

Edmonds, D. (2015). "When colleges go test-optional, who benefits?" *Forbes,* July 30. Retrieved from http://www.forbes.com/sites/noodleeducation/2015/07/30/when-colleges-go-test-optional-who-benefits.

Epstein, J. P. (2009). Behind the SAT-optional movement: Context and controversy. *Journal of College Admission, 204,* 8–19.

Espenshade, T. J., and Chung, C. Y. (2010). Standardized admission tests, college performance, and campus diversity. Office of Population Research, Princeton University. Retrieved from https://www.princeton.edu/~tje/files/Standardized%20AdmissionTests.pdf.

———. (2012). Diversity outcomes of test-optional policies." In J. A. Soares (Ed.), *SAT wars: The case for test-optional college admissions* (pp. 177–200). New York: Teacher's College Press.

Gray, E. (2015). Bubble trouble for standardized testing: Why the SAT and the ACT are competing for students long before college. *Time,* October 12.

Groux, C. (2012). More colleges to test-optional for admissions. *U.S. News & World Report.* Retrieved from http://www.usnewsuniversitydirectory.com/articles/more-colleges-go-test-optional-for-admissions_12816.aspx#.VgAFa5doOSp.

Haney, W. (1981). Validity, vaudeville, and values: A short history of social concerns over standardized testing. *American Psychologist, 36*(10), 1021–1034.

Hiss, W. C., and Franks, V. W. (2014). Defining promise: Optional standardized testing policies in American college and university admissions. National Association for

College Admission Counseling. Retrieved from https://www.luminafoundation.org /files/resources/definingpromise.pdf.

Jaschik, S. (2007). Making holistic admissions work. *Inside Higher Ed*, March 2. Retrieved from https://www.insidehighered.com/news/2007/03/02/holistic.

Littell, R. C., Milliken, G. A., Stroup, W. W., Wolfinger, R. D., and Schabenberger, O. (2006). *SAS for Mixed Models* (2nd ed.). Cary, NC: SAS Institute.

Little, R.J.A., and Rubin, D. B. (2002). *Statistical analysis with missing data* (2nd ed.). New York: Wiley and Sons.

McDermott, A. (2008). Surviving without the SAT. *Chronicle of Higher Education*, September 25. Retrieved from http://chronicle.com/article/Surviving-Without-the -SAT/18874.

National Center for Fair and Open Testing (FairTest). (2016). 925+ accredited colleges and universities that do not use ACT/SAT scores to admit substantial numbers of students into bachelor-degree programs." Retrieved from http://www.fairtest.org /university/optional.

O'Shaughnessy, L. (2014). Who's benefiting from test-optional colleges? CBS News, July 25. Retrieved from http://www.cbsnews.com/news/whos-benefiting-from-test -optional-colleges.

Rigol, G. W. (2004). *Selection through individualized review: A report on phase IV of the admissions models project*. New York: College Entrance Examination Board.

Rosenbaum, P. R., and Rubin, D. B. (1983). The central role of the propensity score in observational studies for causal effects. *Biometrika, 70*(1), 41–55.

Rothstein, J. M. (2004). College performance predictions and the SAT. *Journal of Econometrics, 121*(1), 297–317.

Scott, W. R. (2013). *Institutions and organizations: Ideas, interests, and identities.* Thousand Oaks, CA: Sage Publications.

Scott, W. R., and Davis, G. F. (2007). *Organizations and organizing: Rational, natural, and open system perspectives.* Upper Saddle River, NJ: Pearson Prentice Hall.

Sedlacek, W. E., and Adams-Gaston, J. (1992). "Predicting the academic success of student-athletes using SAT and noncognitive variables." *Journal of Counseling and Development, 70*(6), 724–727.

Selznick, P. (1996). Institutionalism "old" and "new." *Administrative Science Quarterly, 41*(2), 270–277.

Shaffner, P. E. (1985). "Competitive admission practices when the SAT is optional." *Journal of Higher Education, 56*, 55–72.

Shahani, C., Dipboye, R. L., and Gehrlein, T. M. (1991). The incremental contribution of an interview to college admissions. *Educational and Psychological Measurement, 51*(4), 1049–1061.

Singer, J. D., and Willett, J. B. (2003). *Applied longitudinal data analysis: Modeling change and event occurrence.* New York: Oxford University Press.

Syverson, S. (2007). The role of standardized tests in college admissions: Test-optional admissions. *New Directions for Student Services, 118*(Summer), 55–70.

U.S. News & World Report. (1998–2014). *America's Best Colleges* (1999–2015 eds.).

Wilkins, S., and Huisman, J. (2012). The international branch campus as transnational strategy in higher education. *Higher Education, 64*(5), 627–645.

The Future of College Admissions

Jack Buckley, Lynn Letukas, and Ben Wildavsky

When we conceived this project, our central goal was to assemble an authoritative collection of some newer research on admissions testing, with an emphasis on methodological rigor that has too often been lacking from the testing debate. Beyond pure research, we also wanted to devote some attention to the on-the-ground perspective of college enrollment officers who have joined the test-optional movement or have considered changing their policies concerning testing. The chapters that resulted underscore the paradox that now characterizes the central debate over the role of standardized testing in admissions: Despite considerable evidence in favor of their value as an element of the admissions process, assessments once viewed as instruments of opportunity are now seen by critics, including some enrollment managers, as potentially thwarting student success or exacerbating inequality.

On the one hand, we hear from contributors like Sackett and Kuncel; Zwick; Shaw; and Belasco, Rosinger, and Hearn that standardized tests like the SAT and ACT have significant predictive validity, not only for first-year grades but for other college outcomes. We learn that admissions tests predict future academic performance well (especially when combined with grades) for all students, regardless of race, gender, or socioeconomic status. We read that research used to justify the claim that test-optional admissions boosts minority enrollment has significant flaws.

At the same time, the chapters by Maguire and Lucido make it clear that some admissions officers continue to view standardized testing warily at best. One of Lucido's interviewees at a test-optional college frets that conventional tests don't capture applicants' "multiple intelligences." Some admissions leaders believe testing requirements are particularly likely to intimidate and discourage potential minority applicants. Maguire himself accepts that tests provide useful predictive validity but argues that there is a worthwhile trade-off in increasing racial and economic diversity via test-optional policies in exchange for what he calls a modest decline in schoolwide GPA performance.

One more rationale cited by test-optional proponents is particularly striking: the claim that the only way to prevent misuse use of testing is in effect to tie the hands of admissions officers. Making admissions tests voluntary, the argument goes, forces enrollment managers to match their practice with their long-standing rhetoric about keeping the use of tests in perspective. But this invites a question: what prevents admissions officers from doing so without going test-optional? Given the well-documented evidence for the usefulness of tests as an admissions tool—along with well-established guidance that tests should be used together with grades and other criteria—couldn't enrollment managers continue to require the SAT or ACT but ensure that their staff are trained to use the tests appropriately? After all, colleges trust themselves to administer challenging policies such as need-blind admissions without taking important information off the table. Conversely, if tests aren't useful enough to be required of all students, why would admissions officers want *any* students to submit them? One answer, of course, lies in the reputation-management functions of test-optional admissions—notably their tendency to increase institutional test-score averages given that students with lower scores are less likely to submit SAT or ACT results.

Perhaps the biggest reason for continued interest in test-optional admissions is simply that colleges see little downside—and a number of upsides—from implementing the policy. Colleges' announcements about opening up access and bringing greater racial diversity to campus tend to garner positive publicity. Rigorous research doesn't generally support such claims, as several chapters in this volume show, but nor does it indicate that test-optional policies harm racial or socioeconomic diversity. More complex questions about whether making tests optional reduces optimal matches between student and college, with negative consequences for academic performance and other outcomes, still need better long-term research.

College admissions certainly isn't the only field in which research doesn't fully inform policy. But the findings of Hurwitz and Lee on grade inflation should give pause even to those who are not fully persuaded by the evidence about the value of testing presented in other chapters. High school grade point averages continue to rise, with significant compression at the high end, making it particularly hard to distinguish applicants from one another. With these trends especially pronounced among students at affluent, white high schools, the notion that relying more heavily on grades will reduce inequities in the admissions process seems implausible.

The debate over the appropriate weighting of tests versus high school grades will inevitably continue, but it would be fortunate for students and colleges alike if admissions officers and test makers could return to first principles and seek approaches that would be more productive for all parties. In this vein, perhaps the time has come for a twenty-first-century version of the 1899 meeting that laid the groundwork for more uniform and transparent admissions requirements.

At such a convening, admissions officers, high schools, and test makers could collaborate on building an opportunity-driven admissions process that functions equitably for all students. Their deliberations probably wouldn't lead to the use of mechanistic grade-and-test-score indices for all students, but neither would they give admissions officers license to make entirely subjective decisions. The admissions world needs to be clear about exactly what student characteristics it wants and needs to know about, then work with measurement experts to find ways of systematically, accurately, and reliably gathering that information.

This kind of approach would be in keeping the emerging view that holistic review of undergraduate applications must be undertaken rigorously and systematically for its multidimensional approach to fulfill its promise. The College Board, for example, has launched a pilot project on the future of admissions that includes the creation of a numerical index that measures assorted dimensions of student disadvantage. This allows more rigorous assessment of the context in which student achievement occurs, helping admissions officers make sound decisions without abandoning the useful information that testing provides.

Building more effective admissions practice will take a lot of work, of course, starting with creating a common knowledge base. Even popular practices like holistic review, as researcher Michael Bastedo of the University of Michigan has shown, have no clear definition: his survey of more than 300 admissions officers found that half thought holistic review meant looking at an applicant's entire file, 20% thought it meant looking at the "whole person," and 30% defined it as considering an applicant's "whole context."

As the admissions discussion moves forward, it has become clear that developing more useful, fine-tuned data for decision making will require more attention to rigorous research, not less. Test scores certainly need not be the only item in the admissions toolkit, but enrollment managers have ample reason to take them seriously as an important gauge of academic potential. Maximizing opportunity for students means considering high-quality information about their accomplishments and potential. There is surely plenty of room for creating better assessments and processes that are responsive to the needs of students, schools, and colleges. But as the research in this volume shows, there is no reason to believe that eliminating the information provided by tests provide will open doors for more aspiring students.

Contributors

Editors

Sean P. "Jack" Buckley is senior vice president at American Institutes for Research (AIR). He leads AIR's research and evaluation area, where he oversees projects across their entire range of subject areas, including education, health, and the workforce both in the United States and internationally, always with the goal expanding our knowledge about how best to improve people's lives, particularly the disadvantaged. Buckley has a deep background in applied statistics and education research. Before joining AIR, he helped lead the redesign of the SAT at the College Board, where he served as senior vice president of research and was responsible for all research and psychometrics across their entire range of products and services. Before that, he served as commissioner of the US Department of Education's National Center for Education Statistics (NCES). In that role he was responsible for the measurement of all aspects of US education, including conducting the National Assessment of Educational Progress and coordinating US participation in international assessments. While at NCES he also acted as a senior technical adviser to Department of Education Leadership and co-chair of its data strategy team. Additionally, he served as deputy commissioner of NCES earlier in his career. Buckley is known for his research on school choice—particularly charter schools—and on statistical methods for public policy and education. He has researched and taught applied statistics as a tenured associate professor at New York University and as an assistant professor of education research, measurement, and evaluation at Boston College. A former US Navy surface warfare officer and nuclear reactor engineer, he holds doctoral and master's degrees in political science from SUNY Stony Brook and a bachelor's degree in government from Harvard.

Lynn Letukas is an associate research scientist at the College Board, where she conducts content validity studies and program evaluations. Currently, her research focuses on preparing students for success in rigorous courses and increasing student access to postsecondary education. Prior to joining the College Board, Letukas was an assistant professor of sociology at the University of Wisconsin–La Crosse. She received her PhD in sociology from the University of Delaware.

Ben Wildavsky is senior fellow and executive director of the College Board Policy Center in Washington, DC. He was previously director of higher education studies at the Rockefeller Institute of Government and policy professor at SUNY–Albany, where he maintains a faculty affiliation. A former senior scholar at the Kauffman Foundation and guest scholar at the Brookings Institution, he is the author of *The Great Brain Race: How Global Universities Are Reshaping the World* (Princeton University Press) and coeditor of *Reinventing Higher Education: The Promise of Innovation* (Harvard Education Press). His articles have appeared in the *Atlantic*, the *Washington Post*, the *Wall Street Journal*, *Foreign Policy*, the *New Republic*, and many other publications. Wildavsky, a former education editor of *U.S. News & World Report*, has written numerous policy reports, including the final report of the Secretary of Education's Commission on the Future of Higher Education. He received a bachelor's degree in comparative literature from Yale University.

CONTRIBUTORS

Andrew S. Belasco is a higher education researcher, counselor, and CEO of College Transitions, an education consulting firm. His work has been published in the nation's top higher education journals and featured in dozens of media outlets, including the *New York Times, Washington Post*, NPR, and others.

A. Emiko Blalock is a graduate assistant and PhD candidate at Michigan State University in higher, adult, and lifelong education. Previous to her position at Michigan State University, she was at Seattle University as an instructor and member of the advisory committee for the nonprofit management and leadership program, and a practitioner in the nonprofit sector. Her research interests include faculty issues in US higher education, curriculum development for emerging and professional fields of study, and organizational change in higher education.

William G. Bowen (1933–2016) was the president of Princeton University and president emeritus of the Andrew W. Mellon Foundation.

Jim Brooks is the assistant vice president for student services and enrollment management and director of student financial aid and scholarships at the University of Oregon (UO). Before joining the UO six years ago, Brooks worked in financial aid offices at flagship research 1 institutions in Missouri and Indiana. He has served in various roles and committees on the national, regional, and state levels, and has presented addresses at conferences on all of these levels. His presentations have covered topics of strategic enrollment management, program creation, and financial aid management.

Matthew M. Chingos is a senior fellow at the Urban Institute, where he studies education-related topics at both the K–12 and postsecondary levels. Chingos's areas of expertise include class-size reduction, standardized testing, teacher quality, student loan debt, and college graduation rates. His current research examines the long-term effects of school choice policies, student transportation, and college living costs. Before joining Urban, Chingos was a senior fellow at the Brookings Institution. He is the coauthor of *Crossing the Finish Line: Completing College at America's Public Universities* and *Game of Loans: The Rhetoric and Reality of Student Debt*. His work has also been published in academic journals, including the *Journal of Public Economics*, *Journal of Policy Analysis and Management*, *Educational Evaluation and Policy Analysis*, and *Education Finance and Policy*. He has received support from the US government and several philanthropic foundations. Chingos received a BA in government and economics and a PhD in government from Harvard University.

James C. Hearn is professor and associate director in the Institute of Higher Education at the University of Georgia. His recent research has examined organizational change in independent colleges and universities and trends toward marketization and performance accountability in public postsecondary systems.

Michael Hurwitz is a senior director at the College Board. His current research focuses on issues of college access, enrollment, and completion. He received his bachelor's degree in chemistry from Williams College, a master's degree in meteorology from Penn State, and a doctorate in quantitative policy analysis from the Harvard Graduate School of Education.

Jonathan Jacobs is the director of student services and enrollment management research at the University of Oregon. In addition, his research analyzes the impact of various academic and financial factors on choosing a university, performing successfully once there, and graduating on time. Prior to arriving at the University of Oregon in 2011, Jacobs worked at the Oregon University System, where he analyzed Oregon University data for state legislators and Oregon's higher education board. He earned a bachelor's degree in film from San Francisco State University and an MBA from Portland State University.

Nathan R. Kuncel is the Marvin D. Dunnette distinguished professor of industrial-organizational psychology and a McKnight Presidential Fellow at the University of Minnesota, where he also earned his doctorate. Prior to returning to the University of Minnesota, he was a member of the faculty at the University of Illinois. Kuncel's research generally focuses on how individual characteristics (intelligence, personality, interests) influence subsequent work, academic, and life success as well as efforts to model and measure success. Recently, his research has examined the meaning and measurement of critical thinking, effective measurement of inter- and intrapersonal characteristics, and the effects of judgment and decision making on the utility of admissions and hiring decisions. His research has appeared in *Science, Harvard Business Review, Psychological Bulletin, Review of Educational Research, Psychological Science,* and *Perspectives on Psychological Science,* among others. He edited the Industrial and Organizational section of the three-volume APA *Handbook of Testing and Assessment in Psychology.* Kuncel is a fellow of the Association for Psychological Science and the Society for Industrial and Organizational Psychology. He received the Anne Anastasi Award from the American Psychological Association—Division 5, the Cattell Research Award from the Society of Multivariate Experimental Psychology, and the Jeanneret Award from the Society for Industrial and Organizational Psychology. Kuncel is an enthusiastic, but not terribly fast, triathlete, which barely lets him keep up with his kids.

Jason Lee is the lottery scholarship and financial aid research director for the Tennessee Higher Education Commission. Previously, he worked as a policy and research intern at the College Board and as a research and teaching assistant within the Institute of Higher Education at the University of Georgia, where he is a current doctoral candidate. Before pursuing his PhD, Lee worked as a college administrator in a number of departments and roles and as a high school English teacher in both Pennsylvania and Nevada. Lee's primary research interests include higher education finance and policy, especially the rigorous analysis of the effects of policies and programs on student decision making.

Jerome A. Lucido is professor of research and associate dean of strategic enrollment services for the University of Southern California's Rossier School of Education. He is also executive director of the USC Center for Enrollment Research, Policy, and Practice. He served from August 2006 to July 2010 as USC's vice provost for enrollment policy and management. While vice provost, Lucido also served as a trustee of the College Board, as chair of the College Board's Task Force on Admissions in the 21st Century, and as vice chair of the Commission on Access,

Admission, and Success in Higher Education. He has played a leading role at the national level in initiatives to improve access for low-income and underrepresented students and to design and execute effective and principled college admission and enrollment management practices. Lucido came to USC from the University of North Carolina at Chapel Hill, where he guided enrollment planning and management, and oversaw the Offices of Undergraduate Admissions, Scholarships and Student Aid, and the University Registrar. Prior to his work at UNC, he served as assistant vice president for enrollment services and academic support at the University of Arizona. His career in higher education began at Kent State University, where he served as associate director of admissions prior to assuming the director of admissions position at the University of Arizona. Lucido holds a PhD degree in higher education from the University of Arizona, a master of education degree from Kent State University, and a bachelor of science degree in business administration from Miami University in Oxford, Ohio.

Eric Maguire joined the Franklin & Marshall community in the summer of 2015 as vice president and dean of admission and financial aid. Although new to this role, Maguire is familiar with the college, having served from 2000 to 2009 in various admission capacities. During his previous tenure, he contributed to important gains in the college's profile and selectivity. A first-generation student himself, Maguire was excited to rejoin Franklin & Marshall in order to help advance the college's access and talent recruitment initiatives. Most recently, he served as vice president for enrollment and communication at Ithaca College (2009–2015) where he is credited with leading a dramatic increase in applications and significant improvements to student quality, diversity, and retention. Maguire holds a bachelor's degree from Muhlenberg College and an MS in higher education administration from Indiana University.

Krista Mattern is a director of ACT's Statistical and Applied Research Department. Her research focuses on evaluating the validity and fairness of both cognitive and noncognitive measures for predicting student success. She is also interested in higher education issues such as college choice, major selection, and college completion. Her work has been published in journals such as the *Journal of Applied Psychology, Educational Measurement: Issues and Practice, Educational and Psychological Measurement,* and the *Journal of College Student Development.* Mattern received her PhD in industrial and organizational psychology with a minor in quantitative psychology from the University of Illinois, Urbana-Champaign.

Michael S. McPherson is president emeritus of the Spencer Foundation, where
he served as president for fourteen years before retiring in 2017. Previously, he
served as president of Macalester College in St. Paul, Minnesota for seven years.
He is a nationally known economist whose expertise focuses on the interplay
between education and economics. McPherson, who is coauthor and editor of
several books, including *Lesson Plan: An Agenda for Change in American Higher
Education, Crossing the Finish Line: Completing College at America's Public Universities; College Access: Opportunity or Privilege?; Keeping College Affordable;* and
Economic Analysis, Moral Philosophy, and Public Policy; was founding coeditor of
the journal *Economics and Philosophy.*

Kelly O. Rosinger is an assistant professor in the Department of Education Policy
Studies and a research associate in the Center for the Study of Higher Education
at the Pennsylvania State University. Her research focuses on the behavioral and
informational barriers that students face during the college-going process and
the impact of policies and interventions aimed at mitigating inequalities in
college enrollment, choice, and completion. Her publications include articles
in *Educational Evaluation and Policy Analysis, Journal of Higher Education,*
and *Review of Higher Education,* and her work has been cited by the *New York
Times, Washington Post,* NPR, and *Forbes,* among other national and local media
outlets. Rosinger earned a PhD in higher education and master's degree in
public administration and policy, both from the University of Georgia (UGA),
and a bachelor's degree in journalism from the University of North Carolina–
Chapel Hill. After completing her doctorate, she was an Institute of Education
Sciences' postdoctoral research fellow in EdPolicyWorks at the University of
Virginia. She worked in college admissions at UGA prior to beginning her
doctoral work.

Paul R. Sackett is the Beverly and Richard Fink distinguished professor of psychology and liberal arts at the University of Minnesota. He received his PhD in
industrial and organizational psychology at the Ohio State University in 1979.
His research interests revolve around various aspects of testing and assessment
in workplace, educational, and military settings. Sackett has served as editor of
two journals: *Industrial and Organizational Psychology: Perspectives on Science and
Practice* and *Personnel Psychology.* He has also served as president of the Society
for Industrial and Organizational Psychology, as co-chair of the committee
producing the Standards for Educational and Psychological Testing, as a
member of the National Research Council's Board on Testing and Assessment,

as chair of the American Psychological Association's Committee on Psychological Tests and Assessments, and as chair of the APA's Board of Scientific Affairs.

Edgar Sanchez is a senior research scientist at ACT, Inc., studying issues of postsecondary admissions, national testing programs, test preparation efficacy, and intervention effectiveness. He has published research in this area and presented at both regional and national conferences. Sanchez received his doctorate and master's degrees in educational psychology from the University of Texas at Austin.

Dhruv B. Sharma is a senior statistician at the Center for Statistical Training and Consulting at Michigan State University, where he collaborates with researchers on a variety of different subject areas. He earned a PhD in statistics from North Carolina State University in 2010, followed by a postdoctoral research fellowship in biostatistics from the Harvard School of Public Health and Dana-Farber Cancer Institute in 2012.

Emily J. Shaw serves as senior director of validity research and services at the College Board, where she is responsible for leading a team of researchers and database statisticians to produce test validity and college readiness and success research. Her team partners with four- and two-year institutions to conduct local and national validity studies and builds a longitudinal database of college outcomes that began in 2007 and serves as the backbone of much of the College Board's higher education research agenda. Shaw's primary areas of interest include test validity, applied admissions, and college success research. She has a PhD in educational psychology and a master of education degree in counseling and personnel services from Fordham University, and a bachelor of science degree in human development from Cornell University. She has chaired various committees for Division D (Measurement and Research Methodology) of the American Educational Research Association and Division 5 (Quantitative and Qualitative Methods) of the American Psychological Association.

Kyle Sweitzer is a data resource analyst in the Office of Planning and Budgets at Michigan State University. He primarily analyzes university rankings and ratings, conducting institutional peer comparisons, and informing academic administrators in making strategic decisions. He earned his PhD in higher education administration from Pennsylvania State University in 2008.

Roger J. Thompson is the vice president for student services and enrollment management for the University of Oregon. He is responsible for services that contribute to enhancing the student experience, recruitment, retention, and graduation.

Thompson earned a BA in broadcasting from California State University, Long Beach; an MS from the University of Central Missouri; and a doctorate in higher education policy and administration from the University of Southern California.

Meredith Welch is a policy research analyst at the College Board, where her work focuses on issues of college access, financing, and completion. Previously, she spent several years as an analyst on the higher education team at The Education Trust. She holds a bachelor's degree in economics and Spanish from the University of Michigan.

Rebecca Zwick is a distinguished presidential appointee in the statistical analysis, data analysis, and psychometrics research area at Educational Testing Service and professor emerita at the Gevirtz Graduate School of Education at the University of California, Santa Barbara (UCSB). Currently, she is conducting research on college admissions, which is the topic of her book, *Who Gets In? Strategies for Fair and Effective College Admissions*. She received her doctorate in quantitative methods in education at the University of California, Berkeley, completed a postdoctoral year at the L. L. Thurstone Psychometric Laboratory at the University of North Carolina at Chapel Hill, and obtained an MS in statistics at Rutgers University. She spent 12 years as a researcher at ETS in Princeton, New Jersey, followed by 13 years as a professor at UCSB.

Index

Numbers in *italics* indicate figures or tables

Sackett, Paul R., 26–30, 33–34, 148–49, 218n6, 264

Salins, Peter D., 218n8

Sanchez, E. I., 126, 128, 130, 132, 133, 136

San Jose State University, 242–43

Sarah Lawrence College, 242

SAT: administered at age 13, 25; as barrier to college access, 291; coaching and, 33; curriculum's focus on, 2; equity and, 67; initial intent of, 261; as measurement of academic skills, 193; net predictive power of, 202–3; non-public schools and, 77–79; opposition to, at University of California, 255; participation in, and grade inflation, 77; performance on, by ACT takers, 234–35; predictive validity of, 44, 148–49, 263–64, 291; predictive value of, 7, 43, 52–53, 194, 229; pretesting of items on, 52; prevalence of, 261, 291; redesign of, 148, 149, 190–91, 222n31, 265; sorting mechanism of, 280; test-taking population, selection into, 77; validity studies of, 43. *See also* SAT scores

SAT discrepant students, 129; FYGPA and, 134; underprediction for, 138

SAT scores: added value of, above HSGPA, 43–46; college GPA and, *17*, 40, 44, 52–53, 210; college outcomes, and, 40, 45–47; course placement and, 47–48; decline in, 64, 69; family income and, *177*, 209; FYGPA and, 43–44, 49–51, 54–55, 56, 176–77; grade compression and, 82; graduation rates and, 45–47, 196–200, 229, 230–31; highly selective colleges and, 194; HSGPA and, 41, 74–75; in math, and college majors, *19*; institutional, 250–51; overreliance on, 148; parental education and, 176, 209; and performance in specific college courses, 47–48; predictive power of, 41; race/ethnicity and, 79, *80*, 208–9; retention and, 40, 45, 53; SAT II tests and, 213; SES and, 25–29, 53, 208–9, 280; in verbal reasoning, and college majors, *19*

SAT test takers, HSGPAs of, 69

SAT Total score discrepant, 121, 128

SAT II (subject tests), 29, 212–13, 223n33, 223n36, 280

SAT writing test (SATW): predictive value of, 211–12; signaling effect of, 215, 223n40

Schaeffer, Robert, 242

scholarly citations, graduate admissions test scores and, 20

Schwab, Bill, 181

Scott, W. R., 290–91

selection bias, 220n17

selective institutions: benefits to, of test-optional admissions, 278–80; DiD analysis of, 270–78; marketplace needs of, 282; position of, test-optional policies reaffirming, 267–68; reassessing use of standardized tests, 281–82; recruitment strategies at, reassessment of, 282; SAT's predominance in, 280; standardized testing requirements at, 264, 265; test-optional policies at, 265; undermatch at, 282–83

Selznick, Philip, 290–91

SES. *See* socioeconomic status

Shaffner, P. E., 291–92

Shaw, E., 138

Shen, W., 30

signaling effects, 214–16, 223n40

situational judgment tests, predictive value of, 21

six-year graduation rates: AP tests and, 213; HSGPA and, 197, 199–202, 204–5; SAT II and, 213; test scores and, 197

small-scale samples, value of, 14–15

Smith College, 147, 155–56

Soares, Joseph, 241

social policies, functions of, 260, 266–67

social sciences, correlation coefficients in, 41

socioeconomic status, 3, 5, 14; affecting alternative measures of student performance, 240; class rank and, 84; coaching and, 33, 35; educational measures related to, 53; grade inflation and, 77–79; HSGPA and, 67, 209–10; SAT scores and, 25–29, 208–9, 280; standardized test scores and, 13, 176, 262, 263; test-optional admissions policies and, 154, 186–87, 262, 265

standardization, importance of, 42

standardized admissions tests: abandonment of, 4–5; academic success and, 177; admissions officials' reliance on, 290; alternatives to, 20–22; bias and, 3, 13, 14, 30–32; coaching and, 32–35 (*see also* coaching); college outcomes and, 43–49; curriculum's focus on, 1–2; debates about, 13, 14, 7–8, 173; demographic variables and, 178 (*see also* socioeconomic status); discouraging minority applicants, 162–63; diversity and, 8; enlightened practice of, 166; era of, 1; fairness of, 6, 51–52; field-specific, 20; FYGPA and, 40–41; GPA and, 25;